Trade Remedy Laws

Global Trade Law Series

VOLUME 59

Series Editors

Introduction and Contents/Subjects

The *Global Trade Law Series* addresses key issues in international trade law. It covers a broad range of topics, including WTO dispute settlement, free trade agreements, investment law and arbitration, export control, and compliance with international trade obligations.

Objective & Readership

The volumes published in this series are aimed at offering high-quality analytical information and practical solutions, for practitioners, policy makers and academics.

Frequency of Publication

2-3 new volumes published each year.

The titles published in this series are listed at the end of this volume.

Trade Remedy Laws

The Trojan Horse in the Multilateral Trading System

María Moreno Sancho

Wolters Kluwer

Published by:
Kluwer Law International B.V.
PO Box 316
2400 AH Alphen aan den Rijn
The Netherlands
E-mail: lrs-sales@wolterskluwer.com
Website: www.wolterskluwer.com/en/solutions/kluwerlawinternational

Sold and distributed by:
Wolters Kluwer Legal & Regulatory U.S.
920 Links Avenue
Landisville, PA 17538
United States of America
E-mail: customer.service@wolterskluwer.com

ISBN 978-94-035-3929-4

e-Book: ISBN 978-94-035-3939-3
web-PDF: ISBN 978-94-035-3949-2

Summary of Contents

Table of Contents

List of Abbreviations

AD	Anti-dumping
ADA	Anti-dumping Agreement
ASCM	Agreement on Subsidies and Countervailing Measures
ASG	Agreement on Safeguards
COVID-19	Coronavirus Disease 2019
CSPV	Crystalline Silicon Photovoltaic
CVD	Countervailing Duty
DSB	Dispute Settlement Body
DSU	Dispute Settlement Understanding
EC	European Communities
EEC	European Economic Community
EU	European Union
GATT	General Agreement on Tariffs and Trade
ICITO	Interim Commission for the International Trade Organization
ILO	International Labour Organization
IMF	International Monetary Fund
ITO	International Trade Organization
LRWs	Large Residential Washing Machines
MFN	Most-Favoured-Nation
MOF of China	Ministry of Finance of the People's Republic of China
MOFCOM	Ministry of Commerce of China
NAFTA	North American Free Trade Agreement
NME	Non-market Economy

OECD	Organisation for Economic Co-operation and Development
OJEU	Official Journal of the European Union
SCM	Subsidies and Countervailing Measures
UK	United Kingdom
UN	United Nations
UNCTAD	United Nations Conference on Trade and Development
UNTS	United Nations Treaty Series
US	United States
USCBP	United States Customs and Border Protection
USDOC	United States Department of Commerce
USITA	United States International Trade Administration
USITC	United States International Trade Commission
USMCA	Unites States-Mexico-Canada Agreement
USTR	United States Trade Representative
VER	Voluntary Export Restraint
WTO	World Trade Organization

Preface

This book is based on the PhD thesis, *Trade Remedy Laws: A Problem in the History of the Multilateral Trading System*, which questions the need for trade remedy laws, i.e., anti-dumping, countervailing and safeguard measures, in the multilateral trading system, following the highest rise in protectionism in its history and the dysfunction of the Appellate Body of the World Trade Organization. The book is divided into three parts: The first offers a taxonomy of trade-restrictive measures imposed at the outbreak of the US–China trade war, where trade remedy laws have proved not to be the escape clause of protectionism, but to undermine the multilateral trading system. The second explores the origins and evolution of multilateral trade remedy laws (*lege lata*). The third suggests their abolition, along with a revision of multilateral rules on subsidies as well as the incorporation of an agreement on competition, and environmental and labour standards in the multilateral trading system (*lege ferenda*). All of the above is aimed at enhancing trade, competition and global welfare.

Introduction

I OBJECT AND OBJECTIVES

This book has arisen at a critical moment, the highest rise in protectionism in the history of the multilateral trading system. An unprecedented succession of trade-restrictive measures, referred to as the US–China trade war, was accompanied by the obstruction of the appointment of members of the World Trade Organization Appellate Body, the ultimate guarantor of the multilateral trading system. Consequently, while the legal framework was breached, the judicial mechanism to adjudicate disputes ceased functioning. This collapse of the multilateral trading system has affected international trade relations and global value chains by creating legal uncertainty and increasing costs to exporters, importers, and ultimately consumers.

Trade tensions emerged among WTO Members in 2017, following the expiration of Section 15 of the Protocol of Accession of China to the WTO, whereby the burden of proof was shifted in anti-dumping and countervailing duty proceedings conducted against imports from China. For its part, China requested compliance with its Protocol of Accession, while some WTO Members decided on the continuation of this 'non-market economy' treatment to imports from China. Particularly, the US imposed a variety of trade-restrictive measures on imports from China through the invocation of different legal instruments, including trade remedy laws, against which China imposed retaliatory measures. The prevailing unilateralism has raised several questions that this research project attempts to answer in order to strengthen the multilateral trading system.

The object of this book is to question the need for trade remedy laws (anti-dumping and countervailing duties, and safeguard measures) in the multilateral trading system. The first objective to be attained is to determine whether trade remedy laws are the escape valve of protectionism that facilitates trade liberalization or, on the contrary, undermine the multilateral trading system. The taxonomy of trade-restrictive measures at the outbreak of the trade war intends to address this question. Having inferred the problem that trade remedy laws currently entail for the multilateral trading system, the second objective is to search their raîson d'être. Historical research of the origins and evolution of multilateral trade remedy laws to the current legal framework (*lege lata*) has been conducted to elucidate it. Based on lessons drawn from the historical research, the third objective is to propose a normative amendment aimed at guaranteeing that multilateral trade laws contribute to the strengthening of the multilateral trading system (*lege ferenda*).

II RESEARCH METHODOLOGY AND SOURCES

The interdisciplinary nature of the materials analysed involves Law, Economics and Politics; therefore, this book combines empirical, historical and exegetic research methods.

To address the first objective, a taxonomy has been elaborated, departing from the empirical observation of the unilateral measures and issues that originated the trade war between the US and China. Unilateral measures that were imposed at the beginning of the trade war have been classified on the basis of the legal instrument invoked. Notwithstanding measures have been extended for a period longer than the years covered in this research, the initial measures have sufficed to attain the first objective. The taxonomy covers a critical moment in international trade relations, the 'brazen unilateralism' that began in 2018, when the trade war escalated with the imposition of tit-for-tat tariff measures between the US and China, the multilateral legal framework was abandoned and the WTO Appellate Body ceased functioning. The escalation in the US-China trade ceased when the Phase One trade deal between both countries entered into force at the beginning of 2020. Therefore, it has been selected as the end of the observation period, of the unilateral measures imposed at the beginning of the trade war, necessary to achieve the first objective.

Coincidentally, at that precise moment, the COVID-19 pandemic surprised the world. Unilateral trade measures proliferated, encompassing not only import restrictions, but also export restrictions on medical and health supplies; governments engaged in massive subsidies; and confinement resulted in delays in the production and transportation of goods. The observation during this period (2017-2020) was reflected in an Excel table, which permitted the classification of the measures into three categories, according to the legal instrument invoked: first, trade remedy measures by the US; second, national security measures by the US, and retaliatory and safeguard measures by other WTO Members; and third, rise in tariffs by the US and retaliatory measures by China (tit-for-tat measures). Since the onset of the trade war, a spillover effect was created and protectionist measures proliferated, comprising a variety of disciplines within the multilateral trading system (import and export restrictions, subsidies, environmental and labour standards, etc.), which have also been considered later in this research.

Once the empirical observation was sufficient to deduce that trade remedy laws played an essential role in the revival of protectionism, the next objective was to seek the raîson d'être of multilateral trade remedy laws in order to understand the reasons why they were incorporated and their role in the multilateral trading system. This historical research is the basis on which the proposal presented in the third part has been built. To this end, historical and exegetic methods, a chronological study was conducted to research the origins of each of the three trade remedy laws, in their corresponding historical context, and their normative evolution in the multilateral trading system until the current legal framework.

Where possible, primary source has been the basis of this historical research, notwithstanding secondary sources have been used to present the historical background of the origins of trade remedy laws aimed at understanding the raîson d'être of the first worldwide provisions (e.g., Adam Smith's *The Wealth of Nations* and Viner's *Dumping: A Problem in International Trade*). Thereafter, primary sources have been used to analyse the first worldwide provisions on trade remedies, their incorporation into the multilateral trading system and their evolution within it. This has included national legislation, documents of multilateral conferences and trade negotiations held by the League of Nations and United Nations, and the resulting trade agreements, beginning with the GATT, ITO Charter and the specific agreements resulting from the GATT rounds of multilateral trade negotiations, finalizing with the (currently in force) WTO Agreements on Subsidies and Countervailing Measures, Anti-dumping and Safeguards.

For the analysis of the provisions on trade remedies and subsidies in the main multilateral legal texts, an exegetic method has been used. Besides the provisions set out in the aforementioned legal documents, a study of the GATT dispute settlement reports (from 1948 to 1994) has been included in order to carry out a more exhaustive analysis and better understand the evolution of the multilateral trade remedy laws to the current WTO Agreements. For this reason, this study does not include all WTO disputes on trade remedies and subsidies. Nonetheless, when addressing the third objective, some WTO dispute settlement reports have been used in order to better understand the complexities of current issues relating to trade remedy laws and their application by WTO Members.

The third objective has been achieved through a combination of the historical, exegetic and inductive methods. The historical research has been used to focus on the main substantive issues with respect to trade remedy laws aimed at elaborating a propositional argumentation. Likewise, the third objective connects with the results obtained through the empirical observation, reinforcing the need to seek a solution, which is presented as a unity, notwithstanding each of the three trade remedy laws has been analysed separately. Given the intrinsic relationship of trade remedy laws with subsidies and competition, chapters on these two disciplines have been included, as well as a final chapter has been devoted to environmental and labour standards due to the recent trends to enact trade remedy legislation in order to protect these standards in the countries of origin. To attain this third objective, the work of a selection of experts, including – but not restricted to – J.J. Barceló III, R. De Grey, M. Finger, B. Hoekman, G. Horlick, J. Jackson, A. Smith, F. Snyder, E. Vermulst, J. Viner, in the field has been used to support the proposed solution. Particular gratitude is addressed to Professors J.J. Barceló III, M. Bronckers, M. Finger, B. Hoekman, G.N. Horlick and F. Snyder for their courtesy, time and interest in discussing (online) the ideas hereby suggested.

III STRUCTURE OF THE BOOK

Based on the objectives and research methodology, the book is structured in three parts, which describe the current trade tensions, analyse the origins of the problem and provide a solution for the future. The first part consists of a taxonomy of the unilateral measures imposed at the beginning of the trade war. The second part presents a historical overview of multilateral trade remedy laws. The third part offers a proposal to strengthen the multilateral trading system.

The first part consists of three chapters, the division of which corresponds to the classification of unilateral measures imposed at the beginning of the trade war. The first part is introduced by the non-market economy treatment to China, permitted by its Protocol of Accession to the WTO until 2017. Chapter 1 deals with trade remedy laws imposed by the US and its obstruction to the appointment of members of the WTO Appellate Body. Chapter 2 explores the US invocation of the national security exception, retaliation by other WTO Members, and related disputes brought to the WTO. Chapter 3 describes the tit-for-tat tariff measures imposed by the US and China.

The second part is divided into three chapters, and introduced by Adam Smith's ideas on trade, production and consumption. Chapter 4 retraces the origins of each of the three trade remedy laws. Chapter 5 explores the incorporation of trade remedy laws and subsidy disciplines into the multilateral trading system through the conferences held by the League of Nations and United Nations, and their evolution in GATT Articles VI, XVI and XIX. Chapter 6 offers the normative evolution of trade remedy laws and subsidies during the GATT rounds of multilateral trade negotiations until the WTO Agreements on Subsidies and Countervailing Measures, Anti-dumping, and Safeguards.

The third part aims to present a coherent proposal comprising several multilateral disciplines, addressed separately in six chapters. Chapter 7 proposes an amendment to the multilateral disciplines on subsidies. Chapters 8, 9 and 10 advocate the abolition of each of the trade remedy laws, i.e., countervailing duties, anti-dumping and safeguards, respectively. Chapter 11 addresses the incorporation of a multilateral agreement on competition and trade-restrictive measures into the WTO framework. Chapter 12 calls for the inclusion of environmental and labour standards in the multilateral trading system.

Part I The Outbreak of the US–China Trade War: Trade Remedy Laws, National Security and Tit-for-Tat Tariff Measures

Introduction: Protocol of Accession of China to the WTO: Amendments to US and EU Anti-dumping and Countervailing Duty Laws

The Fourth Ministerial Conference of the World Trade Organization (WTO), held in Doha in November 2001, approved – by consensus – the accession of the People's Republic of China (China) to the Marrakesh Agreement Establishing the WTO.[1] In December 2001,[2] China became a member of the WTO on the terms and conditions established in its Protocol of Accession to the WTO. With respect to trade remedy laws, its Sections 15 and 16 set out specific rules for anti-dumping, countervailing duty and safeguards proceedings involving imports of Chinese origin.[3]

Section 16 established a specific safeguard mechanism, whereby other WTO Members were permitted to apply safeguards on imports of Chinese origin on a discriminatory basis for twelve years from the date of accession, i.e., until December 2013. Section 15 concerned price comparability in anti-dumping and countervailing duty proceedings. The latter constitutes the legal basis of what has commonly been known as the 'non-market economy' (NME) treatment to China.[4] When determining dumping, Section 15(a)(ii) allowed WTO members to use a methodology that is not

1. Pursuant to the Decision-Making Procedures under Articles IX and XII of the Marrakesh Agreement Establishing the World Trade Organization agreed by the General Council. WTO document L/93, 24 November 1995.
2. China was one of the twenty-three signatories of the General Agreement on Tariffs and Trade (GATT) in 1947. Nevertheless, following the 1949 revolution, the Chinese government in Taiwan announced its withdrawal from the GATT system. In 1986, China notified the GATT of its decision to seek resumption of its status as a GATT Contracting Party. UNTS, Vol. 55, pp. 187-316 at 188. GATT document L/6017, 14 July 1986. WTO website information, viewed at: https://www.wto.org/english/news_e/pres01_e/pr243_e.htm.
3. WTO document L/432, 23 November 2001, pp. 8-10.
4. For a detailed analysis of the concept of 'non-market economy', *see* F. Snyder, The Origins of the Nonmarket Economy: Ideas, Pluralism and Power in EC Anti-dumping Law about China, *European Law Journal*, Vol. 7, No. 4, 2001, pp. 369-424 https://doi.org/10.1111/1468-0386.00135.

based on a strict comparison with Chinese prices or costs, provided producers could not clearly show that market economy conditions prevailed in their industry.[5] This provision whereby the burden of proof is shifted, i.e., a presumption of non-market economy conditions prevails unless otherwise proved, was due to expire fifteen years after the accession, i.e., in December 2016.[6]

The expiry of the provision has been the subject of both academic literature[7] and policy debate. China submitted two complaints to the WTO (DS515 and DS516),[8] challenging certain US and EU provisions on the determination of the normal value in anti-dumping proceedings involving imports of Chinese origin contained in the US Tariff Act of 1930 and the EU Basic Anti-dumping Regulation,[9] respectively. According to China, following the expiry of Section 15(a)(ii), the methodologies used by the EU and the US in anti-dumping proceedings were inconsistent with the General Agreement on Tariffs and Trade 1994 (GATT),[10] and the Agreement on Implementation of Article VI of the GATT 1994, i.e., Anti-dumping Agreement (ADA).[11] On its side, the EU and

---

5. Section 15(a) of the Protocol on the Accession of the People's Republic of China to the WTO reads: '*In determining price comparability under Article VI of the GATT 1994 and the Anti-Dumping Agreement, the importing WTO Member shall use either Chinese prices or costs for the industry under investigation or a methodology that is not based on a strict comparison with domestic prices or costs in China based on the following rules:*

   (i) If the producers under investigation can clearly show that market economy conditions prevail in the industry producing the like product with regard to the manufacture, production and sale of that product, the importing WTO Member shall use Chinese prices or costs for the industry under investigation in determining price comparability;
   (ii) The importing WTO Member may use a methodology that is not based on a strict comparison with domestic prices or costs in China if the producers under investigation cannot clearly show that market economy conditions prevail in the industry producing the like product with regard to manufacture, production and sale of that product.' WTO document L/432, 23 November 2001, p. 9.

6. Section 15(d) of the Protocol on the Accession of China to the WTO establishes '*In any event, the provisions of subparagraph (a)(ii) shall expire 15 years after the date of accession.*' WTO document L/432, 23 November 2001, p. 9.
7. *See*, for example, J. Miranda, Interpreting Paragraph 15 of China's Protocol of Accession, *Global Trade and Customs Journal*, Vol. 9, No. 3, 2014, pp. 94-103 https://doi.org/10.54648/gtcj2014013; T.R. Posner, A Comment on Interpreting Paragraph 15 of China's Protocol of Accession by Jorge Miranda, *Global Trade & Customs Journal*, Vol. 9, No. 4, 2014, pp. 146-153 https://doi.org/10.54648/gtcj2014017; J. Miranda, More on Why Granting China Market Economy Status after December 2016 Is Contingent upon Whether China Has in Fact Transitioned into a Market Economy, *Global Trade and Customs Journal*, Vol. 11, No. 5, 2016, pp. 244-250 https://doi.org/10.54648/gtcj2016033; E.A. Vermulst, J.D. Sud, S.J. Evenett, Normal Value in Anti-dumping Proceedings Against China Post-2016: Are Some Animals Less Equal Than Others?, *Global Trade and Customs Journal*, Vol. 11, No. 5, 2016, pp. 212-228 https://doi.org/10.54648/gtcj2016030.
8. *US – Measures Related to Price Comparison Methodologies* (DS515), Complainant: China; *EU – Measures Related to Price Comparison Methodologies* (DS516), Complainant: China. WTO documents DS515/1, 15 December 2016; DS516/1, 15 December 2016.
9. Regulation (EU) 2016/1036 of the European Parliament and of the Council of 8 June 2016 on Protection Against Dumped Imports from Countries Not Members of the European Union (codification). OJEU, L.176, 30 June 2016.
10. General Agreement on Tariffs and Trade (GATT). UNTS, Vol. 55, pp. 187-316. UNTS, Vol. 1867, p. 187, 15 April 1994.
11. Agreement on the Implementation of Article VI of GATT 1994, Marrakesh Agreement Establishing the World Trade Organization, Annex 1A. UNTS, Vol. 1868, p. 201, 15 April 1994.

the US argued that GATT Article VI, further reflected in its Note 2 *Ad* paragraph 1 as well as ADA Article 2 allow them to continue using a methodology that is not based on a strict comparison with Chinese prices or costs in anti-dumping proceedings.[12] China requested the establishment of a panel only in the dispute with the EU (not with the US), which was composed in July 2017, but lapsed in 2020 following China's request to suspend the Panel's work.[13]

On account of the expiration date of Section 15(a)(ii), the US and the EU have amended their respective anti-dumping and countervailing duty laws, in order to continue disregarding prices or costs in China in anti-dumping and countervailing duty proceedings involving imports of Chinese origin. The US has subsequently modified its Tariff Act of 1930, through the enactment of the American Trade Enforcement Effectiveness Act, and the Enforce and Protect Act of 2015; and amendments of its regulations on anti-dumping and countervailing duty proceedings under Part 351 of the Title 19 of the Code of Federal Regulations.[14] On its part, the EU has amended its Basic Anti-dumping Regulation and Anti-subsidy Regulation several times after the expiration date of Section 15(a)(ii), i.e., December 2016.

The United States

The American Trade Enforcement Effectiveness Act amended, in 2015, the US Tariff Act of 1930 provisions regarding material injury, particular market situation and distortion of market prices or costs in anti-dumping and countervailing duty proceedings. First, it impedes the US International Trade Commission (USITC) from dismissing material injury '*merely because that industry is profitable or because the performance of that industry has recently improved*'. Second, the Act permits the use of another methodology to determine the normal value (i.e., construct the normal value by disregarding prices in the exporting country) when the US investigating authority determines (pursuant to ADA Article 2.2)[15] that the particular market situation in the exporting country prevents a proper comparison between the normal value and the export price. Third, in cases where the investigating authority determines that a subsidization exists, the Act grants it the discretion to disregard some of the exporters' sales, i.e., price or cost values supplied by an interested party.[16]

12. *European Union – Measures Related to Price Comparison Methodologies* (DS516). First Written Submission by the European Union, pp. 9-17, 25, 54, 94-97, 14 November 2017. Third Party Submission of the United States of America, pp. 58-59, 21 November 2017, viewed at: https://ustr.gov/sites/default/files/enforcement/DS/US.3d.Pty.Su.pdf.
13. WTO documents DS516/9, 10 March 2017; DS516/10, 11 July 2017; DS516/14, 15 June 2020.
14. Notwithstanding in the US, 'antidumping' is written together, for the homogeneity of this book, it will be written according to the WTO terminology, i.e., 'anti-dumping'.
15. ADA Article 2.2 reads as follows: '*When there are no sales of the like product in the ordinary course of trade in the domestic market of the exporting country or when, because of the particular market situation or the low volume of the sales in the domestic market of the exporting country, such sales do not permit a proper comparison, the margin of dumping shall be determined by comparison with a comparable price of the like product when exported to an appropriate third country, provided that this price is representative, or with the cost of production in the country of origin plus a reasonable amount for administrative, selling and general costs and for profit.*'
16. American Trade Enforcement Effectiveness Act. Title V, Improvements to Antidumping and Countervailing Duty Laws, Sections 501-507 of the Trade Preferences Extension Act of 2015. Public Law No. 114-27, 29 June 2015, WTO document G/ADP/N/1/USA/1/Suppl.20, 16 July 2015.

The Trade Facilitation and Enforcement Act, amending the US Tariff Act of 1930, contains the Enforce and Protect Act of 2015, whereby the Trade Remedy Law Enforcement Directorate has been established at the US Customs and Border Protection (USCBP) to prevent and counter the evasion of anti-dumping and countervailing duty orders, and procedures to investigate claims of such evasion have been set out.[17] Accordingly, the US has created a new section in the Tariff Act of 1930, '*Procedures for Investigating Claims of Evasion of Antidumping and Countervailing Duty Orders*', and incorporated Part 165 under Title 19 of the Code of Federal Regulations, '*Investigation of Claims of Evasion of Antidumping and Countervailing Duties*', which has been amended in 2024.[18]

Furthermore, between 2016 and 2024, the US Department of Commerce (USDOC) has subsequently amended Part 351 of Title 19 of the Code of Federal Regulations.[19] In 2016, the USDOC modified regulations concerning price adjustments in anti-dumping duty proceedings, applying to proceedings starting on or after 1 September 2016. When calculating (constructed) export price, and normal value, the US Department (Secretary) will not accept a price adjustment '*that is made after the time of sale unless the interested party demonstrates, to the satisfaction of the US Department, its entitlement to such an adjustment*'.[20] In 2020, it amended two regulations concerning benefit and specificity in countervailing duty proceedings, thereby clarifying that state-owned enterprises can constitute a 'group' of enterprises and setting out rules for determining the benefit of subsidies resulting from the exchange of an undervalued currency.[21]

---

17. Enforce and Protect Act of 2015 of the Trade Facilitation and Trade Enforcement Act of 2015. Title IV, Prevention of Evasion of Antidumping and Countervailing Duty Orders. US Public Law 114-125, Trade Preferences Extension Act of 2015, 24 February 2016, as amended through Public Law 117-286, 27 December 2022. WTO document G/ADP/N/1/USA/1/Suppl.23, 1 April 2016.
18. Investigation of Claims of Evasion of Antidumping and Countervailing Duties, Title 19, Part 165 of the Code of Federal Regulations. US Federal Register, Vol. 81, No. 162, 22 August 2016, pp. 56477-56490. US Federal Register, Vol. 89, No. 53, 18 March 2024, pp. 19239-19262.
19. Part 351 of Title 19 of the Code of Federal Regulations Contains Rules and Procedures Concerning Antidumping and Countervailing Duty Proceedings Under Title VII of the US Tariff Act of 1930.
20. Modification of Regulations Regarding Price Adjustments in Antidumping Duty Proceedings. Title 19, Section 351.102.b. and 351.401 of the Code of Federal Regulations. US Federal Register, Vol. 81, No. 57, 24 March 2016, pp. 15641-15646. Correction to Applicability Date for Modification of Regulations Regarding Price Adjustments in Antidumping Duty Proceedings. US Federal Register, Vol. 81, No. 148, 2 August 2016, pp. 50617-50618.
21. Modification of Regulations Regarding Benefit and Specificity in Countervailing Duty Proceedings. Section 351.502, Specificity of domestic subsidies, clarifies that when determining whether a subsidy is specific, the term 'group' of enterprises or industries includes 'enterprises that buy or sell goods internationally to comprise such a group'. Notably, the 2010 US Commerce's Policy Bulletin 10.1 clarified that state-owned enterprises can constitute a 'group' of enterprises.

    Section 351.528, Exchanges of undervalued currencies, sets out rules on USDOC's determination of undervaluation and benefit in cases of subsidies resulting from the exchange of an undervalued currency. To determine a currency undervaluation, the equilibrium real effective exchange rate will be considered, i.e., the gap between the country's real effective exchange rate and that achieved by an external balance over the medium term that reflects appropriate policies. The USDOC will normally not include the monetary and related credit policy of an independent central bank or monetary authority. In case of currency undervaluation, the amount of the benefit will normally be based on the difference in the amount of currency between what the firm received in exchange for US dollars and what it would have received. The Department of the Treasury will be requested to provide its evaluation and

In 2021, the USDOC modified regulations concerning the time for submission of comments regarding industry's support; new shipper reviews; scope matters, importer reimbursement certifications filed with USCBP; and service lists, entries of appearance, and importer filing requirements for access to business proprietary information. In addition, it promulgated new regulations concerning circumvention, covered merchandise referrals received from USCBP, and USDOC requests for certifications from interested parties to establish whether merchandise is subject to an anti-dumping or countervailing duty order.[22] In 2023, some of these regulations were amended, particularly, procedures governing the filing and service of documents, and those regarding updates to the scope ruling, circumvention, and covered merchandise referral; and two provisions were deleted after having been invalidated by the US Court of Appeals for the Federal Circuit.[23]

More recently, in 2024, the USDOC revised and codified some regulations with respect to, *inter alia*, circumvention; scope rulings; covered merchandise referrals; filing requirements; the use of new factual information; calculation of normal value; particular market situation; countervailable subsidies; facts available hierarchy, surrogate value and benchmark in countervailing duty proceedings. Notably, the protections of the environment, labour and human rights, and intellectual property in foreign countries are included in anti-dumping and countervailing duty proceedings. More specifically, the foreign government's inaction in providing such protections is considered a countervailable subsidy; permits disregarding prices in exporting countries in anti-dumping and countervailing duty proceedings; and is taken into account to determine the existence of a particular market situation ('*which may distort or contribute to the distortion of the cost of production*') in the exporting country, permitting the construction of the normal value in the determination of dumping, thereby disregarding prices in the exporting country.[24]

European Union

In 2016,[25] the EU replaced its Basic Anti-dumping Regulation 1225/2009 with Regulation (EU) 2016/1036 and its Basic Anti-subsidies Regulation 597/2009 with Regulation

conclusion regarding these issues during a countervailing duty proceeding. US Federal Register, Vol. 85, No. 23, 4 February 2020, pp. 6031-6044.

22. Regulations to Improve Administration and Enforcement of Antidumping and Countervailing Duty Laws, US Federal Register, Vol. 86, No. 179, 20 September 2021, pp. 52300-52384.
23. Administrative Protective Order, Service, and other Procedures in Antidumping and Countervailing Duty Proceedings, US Federal Register Vol. 88, No. 188, 29 September 2023, pp. 67069-67081.
24. Regulations Improving and Strengthening the Enforcement of Trade Remedies Through the Administration of the Antidumping and Countervailing Duty Laws, US Federal Register, Vol. 89, No. 58, 25 March 2024, pp. 20766-20841. *See* Ch. 12.
25. Previously, in 2014, the competence for the imposition of duties was transferred from the Council to the Commission. Sections 18 and 22 of Regulation 37/2014 of the European Parliament and of the Council of 15 January 2014 amending certain regulations relating to the common commercial policy as regards the procedures for the adoption of certain measures. OJEU, L.18, 21 January 2014. WTO document G/ADP/N/1/EU/1/Rev.1/Suppl.4, 10 April 2014. It was later incorporated under Article 9.4 of Regulation (EU) 1036/2016 and Article 15.1 of Regulation (EU) 1037/2017.

(EU) 2016/1037.[26] Since then, both have been amended three times by Regulation 2017/23, Regulation 2018/825, and Delegated Regulation 2020/1173.[27] Through these amendments, the EU has modified its methodology to determine dumping and injury. Additionally, the EU Commission is now granted the discretion to self-initiate investigations also in case of threat of retaliation by third countries; and interim reviews, which could result in the withdrawal from a previously agreed undertaking, in cases where environmental and labour circumstances change in exporting countries. Anti-circumvention rules have been amended, distinguishing between EU importers, having the right to show they are not engaged in circumvention practices, and producers in a third country, whose engagement in such practices is determined by the Commission.

With respect to dumping determination, notwithstanding it has abandoned the 'non-market economies' terminology, the EU Commission is allowed to continue using a methodology that is not based on a strict comparison with prices or costs in the exporting country.[28] Under the current regime, the normal value can be constructed, thereby prices or costs in the exporting country disregarded, in cases where the Commission determines the existence of '*significant distortions*', i.e., imports' prices or costs '*are not the result of free market forces because they are affected by substantial government intervention*', based on whether an '*adequate level of social and environmental protection*' is provided by exporting countries, including compliance with core conventions of the International Labour Organization and multilateral environmental agreements.[29]

When determining injury to EU industries in anti-dumping and countervailing duty proceedings, the EU is now permitted to add actual or future costs derived from compliance with the mentioned labour and environmental standards.[30] When the

26. Regulation (EU) 2016/1036 of the European Parliament and of the Council of 8 June 2016 on Protection Against Dumped Imports From Countries Not Members of the EU–Codified Version. OJEU, L.176, 30 June 2016, p. 21. Regulation (EU) 2016/1037 of the European Parliament and of the Council of 8 June 2016 on Protection Against Subsidized Imports From Countries Not Members of the EU – Codified Version. OJEU, L.176, 30 June 2016, p. 33. European Commission online information.
27. Regulation (EU) 2016/1036 and Regulation (EU) 2016/1037 have been amended by Regulation (EU) 2017/2321, of 12 December 2017, OJEU, L.338, 19 December 2017, pp. 1-7; Regulation (EU) 2018/825 of 30 May 2018, OJEU, L.143, 7 June 2018, pp. 1-18; and Delegated Regulation (EU) 2020/1173 of 4 June 2020. The latter merely establishes a pre-disclosure of four weeks, whereby the EU Commission announces the eventual imposition of provisional anti-dumping and countervailing duties. OJEU, L.259, 10 August 2020, pp. 1-4.
28. Albania, Armenia, Azerbaijan, Belarus, China, Georgia, the Kyrgyz Republic, Moldova, Mongolia, North Korea, Tajikistan, Turkmenistan, Uzbekistan and Vietnam. OJEU, L.176, 30 June 2016, p. 26.
29. EU Regulation 2017/2321 of the European Parliament and of the Council, of 12 December 2017, amending Regulation (EU) 2016/1036 on Protection Against Dumped Imports From Countries Not Members of the European Union and Regulation (EU) 2016/1037 on Protection Against Subsidised Imports From Countries Not Members of the European Union. OJEU, L.338, 19 December 2017. WTO document G/ADP/N/1/EU/3/Suppl.2, 23 January 2018.
30. Regulation (EU) 825/2018 of the European Parliament and the Council of 30 May 2018, amending Regulation 2016/1036 on Protection Against Dumped Imports From Countries Not Members of the European Union and Regulation (EU) 2016/1037 on Protection Against Subsidised Imports From Countries Not Members of the European Union. OJEU, L.143, 7 June 2018. WTO documents G/ADP/N/1/EU/3/Suppl.3, 2 July 2018.

injury is calculated on a target price basis, which should reflect the actual cost of production of the EU industry, a minimum profit margin of 6% is established. In addition, when determining anti-dumping duties, distortions on raw materials (accounting for at least 17% of the cost of production) should be taken into account to apply the lesser duty rule, i.e., injury can be removed with duties lesser than the margin of dumping.[31] Notably, the lesser duty rule may not be applied when determining countervailing duties.[32]

Furthermore, the EU has enacted Regulation 2022/2560 to deal with foreign subsidies that distort the EU market regarding any economic activity, including concentrations and public procurement procedures. The EU Commission is entrusted to investigate and redress financial contributions provided by third countries that confer a benefit to an undertaking engaging in an economic activity in the EU market, thereby enabling it to improve its competitive position and adversely affecting competition in the EU market.[33]

This first part consists of a taxonomy of the most relevant trade-restrictive measures imposed during the US–China trade war. Based on the classification of these measures, this first part is divided into three chapters: The first covers trade remedies and the obstruction of the appointment of the WTO Appellate Body members; the second presents US national security measures, the different responses by other WTO Members, and related disputes; and the third chapter describes the escalation of the tit-for-tat tariff measures, initiated in 2018, between the US and China.

31. *Ibid.*, p. 6. Article 7(b).2.a clarifies that '*distortions on raw materials consist of the following measures: dual pricing schemes, export taxes, export surtax, export quota, export prohibition, fiscal tax on exports, licensing requirements, minimum export price, value added tax (VAT) refund reduction or withdrawal, restriction on customs clearance point for exporters, qualified exporters list, domestic market obligation, captive mining if the price of a raw material is significantly lower as compared to prices in the representative international markets*'.
32. *Ibid.*, p. 14. *See* Ch. 12.
33. Regulation (EU) 2022/2560 of the European Parliament and of the Council of 14 December 2022 on Foreign Subsidies Distorting the Internal Market, OJEU, L.330, 23 December 2022.

CHAPTER 1
Trade Remedies by the United States

Since 2017, the US has increased the imposition of trade remedies, some of which are intended to counter the alleged circumvention of previous anti-dumping and countervailing duties, such as the safeguards on solar products and washing machines that marked the outbreak of the trade war between the US and China in 2018. This chapter explores, first, some relevant US anti-dumping and countervailing proceedings since 2017; second, the subsequent imposition of safeguards to prevent the circumvention of the previously imposed duties and related WTO disputes; and, third, the US obstruction of the appointment of members of the WTO Appellate Body since 2017, alleging overreach in their interpretations of WTO Agreements, particularly on Anti-dumping, Subsidies and Countervailing Measures, and Safeguards.

I US ANTI-DUMPING AND COUNTERVAILING DUTIES IN 2017

The US Administration under President Trump exponentially increased the number of anti-dumping and countervailing duty investigations, accounting for more than 250 (more than 200% increase compared to the previous administration).[34] The US imposition of anti-dumping and countervailing measures since 2017 has also

34. USITA, US Department of Commerce Issues Affirmative Preliminary Determination in the Countervailing Duty Investigation of Imports of Vertical Shaft Engines From China, 16 June 2020: '*Since the beginning of the current administration, Commerce has initiated 257 new antidumping (AD) and CVD investigations – this is a 238 percent increase from the comparable period in the previous administration (...) Commerce currently maintains 526 AD and CVD orders which provide relief to American companies and industries impacted by unfair trade*', viewed at: https://www.trade.gov/press-release/us-department-commerce-issues-affirmative-preliminary-determination-countervailing-2. '*Between 1995 and 2017, the United States initiated 659 AD investigations*'. WTO document TPR/S/382/Rev.1, 27 March 2019, p. 65, para. 3.74. Between 2015 and 2021, the US initiated more than 300 anti-dumping investigations and more than 140 countervailing duty investigations. WTO document TPR/S/434, 9 November 2022, pp. 93, 97.

increased, reaching the highest number since 1995,[35] some of which were the subject of disputes brought to the WTO, e.g., anti-dumping and countervailing duties imposed on ripe olives from Spain,[36] and related WTO dispute *US – Ripe Olives from Spain*.[37]

As of June 2022, the USITC reported 671 anti-dumping (497) and countervailing (174) measures in place.[38] Among the anti-dumping and countervailing duties in force as of June 2022, almost half (46%) have been applied to iron and steel products. The other half is distributed among chemicals and pharmaceuticals (14%); agricultural products (9%); metals and minerals (more than 9%); plastics and rubber (more than 5%); miscellaneous manufactured products (more than 4%); textiles and apparel (4%); and machinery and equipment (more than 3%). The countries most affected by the measures are China, Korea, India, Taiwan and Japan.[39] The distribution of US anti-dumping and countervailing measures among targeted countries since 2017 continues to reflect the US tendency since 1995.[40] Chinese imports have remained the main target, accounting for around 30% of US anti-dumping duties and almost 50% of US countervailing duties in force.[41]

US anti-dumping and countervailing duty proceedings are conducted by the USDOC's International Trade Administration (USITA), responsible for dumping and subsidy determinations, as well as the enforcement of the duties; and by the US International Trade Commission (USITC), entrusted to determine injury (or threat thereof) to the domestic industry. Notwithstanding that an investigation may be self-initiated by the USDOC, as well as initiated at the request of petitioners, before 2017, there had only been three self-initiated investigations since 1980,[42] the most recent one in 1991.[43] Notably, in November 2017, the USDOC self-initiated anti-dumping and countervailing duty investigations on common alloy aluminium sheet from China.[44]

35. WTO online information, viewed at: https://www.wto.org/english/tratop_e/adp_e/AD_MeasuresByRepMem.pdf and https://www.wto.org/english/tratop_e/scm_e/CV_MeasuresByRepMem.pdf.
36. Ripe Olives From Spain: Final Results of the Expedited First Sunset Review of the Antidumping and Countervailing Duty Orders. US Federal Register, Vol. 88, No. 212, 2023, pp. 75554-75560.
37. *United States – Anti-dumping and Countervailing Duties on Ripe Olives From Spain* (DS755). The Panel found US measures to be inconsistent with GATT Article VI, the ADA and the ASCM. WTO document DS577/R, 19 November 2021.
38. On 30 June 2016, there were 269 anti-dumping and 69 countervailing measures in place. WTO document TPR/S/350, 14 November 2016, pp. 59, 60.
39. USITC, Anti-dumping and Countervailing Duty Orders in place as of 13 June 2022, viewed at: https://usitc.gov/trade_remedy/documents/historical_orders_data.xls.
40. WTO online information, viewed at https://www.wto.org/english/tratop_e/adp_e/AD_MeasuresRepMemVsExpCty.pdf, https://www.wto.org/english/tratop_e/scm_e/CV_MeasuresRepMemVsExpCty.pdf.
41. The following most targeted countries do not account for 10% each (except India, accounting for almost 15% of countervailing duties). USITC, Anti-dumping and Countervailing Duty Orders in place as of 13 June 2022, viewed at: https://usitc.gov/trade_remedy/documents/historical_orders_data.xls.
42. In 1980, the competence was transferred from the US Treasury to the USDOC.
43. WTO document TPR/S/382, 12 November 2018, p. 62, para. 3.66.
44. USITC, Common Alloy Aluminum Sheet from China, Investigation Nos 701-TA-591 and 731-TA-1399 (Final). Publication 4861, January 2019, viewed at: https://www.usitc.gov/publications/701_731/pub4861.pdf.

Negative injury determinations by the USITC terminate investigations,[45] as it occurred in the case '*Bombardier*', a Canadian aircraft manufacturer. In 2017, following a petition by Boeing, the USDOC initiated an investigation and recommended imposing anti-dumping and countervailing duties on imports of large civil aircraft from Canada.[46] In October 2017, Bombardier's newest aircraft C series was subject to provisional measures totalling nearly 300%.[47] In order to avoid the anti-dumping and countervailing duties, Bombardier had sold the majority stake (50.01%) of its newest project to Airbus and moved some of the production to its plant in Alabama.[48] Afterwards, in 2018, the USITC unanimously determined that '*the C Series did not harm Boeing and discarded a US Commerce Department recommendation*',[49] and the provisional measures were terminated.[50]

Furthermore, pursuant to the Enforce and Protect Act of 2015, the US imposed anti-circumvention measures on imports originating in China and Vietnam following the alleged evasion of anti-dumping duties by transhipping products through Thailand, Malaysia, the Philippines or the Subic Bay.[51] In March 2017, a Presidential Executive Order established the enhanced collection and enforcement of anti-dumping and countervailing duties, as well as violations of trade and customs laws. Based on risk assessments conducted by USCBP, the Order provided for the imposition of bonds and other legal measures to ensure the liability of anti-dumping and countervailing duties.[52] Allegations of evasion of anti-dumping and countervailing duties on crystalline silicon photovoltaic (CSPV) cells and large residential washing machines (LRWs) prompted, in 2017, the USITC to initiate, upon request, two safeguard investigations on these products.

The US has imposed anti-dumping and countervailing duties on imports of CSPV cells from China since 2012 (*Solar I*).[53] China submitted a complaint to the WTO

45. Title 19, Part 351 of the US Code of Federal regulations.
46. '*The decision could also put at risk some of Bombardier's 28,000 aerospace jobs, including those at its Belfast operations. The Northern Ireland facility makes wings for several of the company's aircraft including the C Series, and employs 4,500 people. About 1,000 work on the C Series.*' P. Hollinger, P. Waldmeir, US to Bombardier Puts Jobs in Canada and U.K. at Risk, *Financial Times*, 27 September 2017.
47. WTO documents G/ADP/N/314/USA, 18 September 2018; G/SCM/N/334/USA, 27 September 2018.
48. The FT View editorial board, Bombardier's Deal with Airbus Is Bad For Business, *Financial Times*, 17 October 2017.
49. A. Lampert, L. Wroughton, USITC Details Why It Rejected Cseries Duties, Says Boeing Not Hurt, *Reuters*, 14 February 2018.
50. WTO documents G/ADP/N/314/USA, 18 September 2018; G/SCM/N/334/USA, 27 September 2018.
51. USCBP, Notices of Final Determination, viewed at: https://www.cbp.gov/trade/trade-enforcement/tftea/enforce-and-protect-act-eapa/notices-final-determination#.
52. US Whitehouse, A Presidential Executive Order on Establishing Enhanced Collection and Enforcement of Anti-dumping and Countervailing Duties and Violations of Trade and Customs Laws, 31 March 2017, viewed at: https://trumpwhitehouse.archives.gov/presidential-actions/presidential-executive-order-establishing-enhanced-collection-enforcement-antidumping-countervailing-duties-violations-trade-customs-laws/.
53. Crystalline Silicon Photovoltaic Cells, Whether or Not Assembled Into Modules, From the People's Republic of China: Countervailing Duty Order, and Amended Final Determination of Sales at Less Than Fair Value, and Antidumping Duty Order. US Federal Register, Vol. 77,

against *US – Countervailing Measures* on certain products from China, following which the Dispute Settlement Body (DSB) Panel and Appellate Body (AB) found, in 2014, that the USDOC had acted inconsistently with the Agreement on Subsidies and Countervailing Measures (ASCM).[54] Furthermore, petitions against charges of circumvention of the duties on CSPV cells by Chinese producers[55] led the USDOC to impose further measures in 2015: Anti-dumping duties on CSPV products (solar cells, modules, laminates and panels) from Taiwan (*Solar II Taiwan*),[56] as well as anti-dumping and countervailing duties on CSPV products assembled in China with cells from a third country (*Solar II China*).[57] Following the corresponding sunset reviews, both measures (*Solar I* and *Solar II*) have been extended and remain in force.[58]

Moreover, in 2021, anti-dumping and countervailing duties on CSPV cells from China (*Solar I*) were extended to imports from Vietnam, and anti-dumping duties on solar products from China and Taiwan (*Solar II*) were extended to imports from Korea, without having conducted an anti-circumvention investigation.[59] In addition, anti-dumping and countervailing duties on CSPV cells and modules from China (*Solar I*) were extended to imports from Cambodia, Malaysia, Thailand and Vietnam, following an affirmative anti-circumvention investigation.[60] US President Biden issued a proclamation declaring a situation of emergency, whereby solar cells from these four

No. 236, 7 December 2012, pp. 73017-73021. For more details, *see* J.A. García López, M. Moreno Sancho, The US and EU Solar Trade Remedies Saga: The Globalization of Mercantilism, *Journal of World Trade*, Vol. 56, No. 4, 2022, pp. 615-632 https://doi.org/10.54648/trad2022025.

54. WTO dispute *United States – Countervailing Duty Measures on Certain Products from China* (DS437). Following the Compliance Panel and Appellate Body Reports (DSU Article 21.5), the matter was referred to arbitration (DSU Article 22.6). In January 2022, the Arbitrator determined that, as a result of the WTO-inconsistent methodologies in these US countervailing duty proceedings, China may request authorization from the DSB to suspend concessions or other obligations up to the accorded level of nullification or impairment accruing to it, which was fixed at USD 645,121 million per annum. WTO documents DS437/R, 14 July 2014; DS437/AB/R, 18 December 2014; DS437/AB/ARB, 26 January 2022.
55. WTO document G/SG/N/10/USA/7, 26 January 2018.
56. Certain Crystalline Silicon Photovoltaic Products from Taiwan: Antidumping Duty Order. US Federal Register, Vol. 80, No. 32, 18 February 2015, pp. 8596-8597.
57. Certain Crystalline Silicon Photovoltaic Products From the People's Republic of China: Antidumping Duty Order; and Amended Final Affirmative Countervailing Duty Determination and Countervailing Duty Order US Federal Register, Vol. 80, No. 32, 18 February 2015, pp. 8592-8596.
58. Crystalline Silicon Photovoltaic Cells, Whether or Not Assembled Into Modules, From the People's Republic of China: Final Results of the Expedited First Sunset Review of the Antidumping Duty Order. US Federal Register, Vol. 83, No. 48, 12 March 2018, p. 10663. Crystalline Silicon Photovoltaic Products From the People's Republic of China and Taiwan: Final Results of the Expedited First Sunset Reviews of the Antidumping Duty Orders. US Federal Register, Vol. 85, No. 88, 6 May 2020, p. 26938; Certain Crystalline Silicon Photovoltaic Products From the People's Republic of China: Final Results of the Expedited Sunset Review of the Countervailing Duty Order. US Federal Register, Vol. 85, No. 88, 6 May 2020, p. 26929.
59. Notice of Scope Rulings. US Federal Register Vol. 86, No. 162, 25 August 2021, pp. 47476-47478.
60. Antidumping and Countervailing Duty Orders on Crystalline Silicon Photovoltaic Cells, Whether Or Not Assembled Into Modules, From the People's Republic of China: Final Scope Determination and Final Affirmative Determinations of Circumvention With Respect to Cambodia, Malaysia, Thailand, and Vietnam. US Federal Register, Vol. 88, No. 162, 23 August 2023, pp. 57419-57433.

countries would be exempted from the duties until June 2024 or until the emergency terminates, whichever occurs first.[61]

In parallel, prior to the 2017 USITC safeguard investigation on LRWs,[62] washing machines from Korea had been subject to US anti-dumping duties and countervailing duties since 2012. As a result, Korea brought the case *US – Washing Machines* to the WTO.[63] The Appellate Body concluded that US measures were inconsistent with GATT Articles VI, ADA Articles 2.4 and 9.3, and ASCM Article 19.4.[64] Remarkably, the Appellate Body in the *US – Washing Machine* dispute found that applying zeroing under the weighted average-transaction methodology was inconsistent with ADA Article 2.4.2.[65] This interpretation was confirmed by the Appellate Body in the case *US – Anti-dumping Methodologies (China)*,[66] which also concluded that ADA Article 2.4.2 does not permit the combining of comparison methodologies,[67] and that the application of the weighted average-transaction methodology is only allowed to '*pattern transactions*'.[68] Soon after the Appellate Body released its report on *US – Anti-dumping Methodologies (China)*, in June 2017, the US blocked the appointment of the Appellate Body.

Moreover, allegations of circumvention of anti-dumping and countervailing duties, through the shift in production to China, prompted the USDOC to impose anti-dumping duties on LRWs from China in 2017.[69] In May 2019, the USDOC announced the revocation of the anti-dumping and countervailing duties on imports of LRWs from Korea,[70] unlike the anti-dumping duties on LRWs from China, which were

61. Declaration of Emergency and Authorization for Temporary Extensions of Time and Duty-Free Importation of Solar Cells and Modules From Southeast Asia. US Federal Register, Vol. 87, No. 111, 9 June 2022, pp. 35067-35069.
62. WTO document G/SG/N/6/USA/12, 12 June 2017.
63. *United States – Anti-dumping and Countervailing Measures on Large Residential Washers from Korea* (DS464). WTO document DS464/1, 3 September 2013.
64. Following the US failure to comply in 2017 with the AB's recommendations and rulings within the period awarded by the Arbitrator (DSU Article 21.3), and its objection to the level of suspension of concessions proposed by Korea, the matter was referred to arbitration (DSU Article 22.6). The Arbitrator determined that the level of nullification or impairment caused by the anti-dumping duties was USD 74.40 million, and USD 10.41 million in the case of countervailing duties. WTO documents DS464/AB/R, 7 September 2016; DS464/RPT, 13 April 2017; DS464/19, 23 January 2018; DS464/ARB, 8 February 2019.
65. WTO document DS464/AB/R, 7 September 2016, para. 6.10.
66. *United States – Certain Methodologies and Their Application to Anti-dumping Proceedings Involving China* (DS471).
67. '*While the Panel and Appellate Body found certain parts of the USDOC's methodology inconsistent – most notably applying W-T to all transactions and the use of zeroing – they refrained from finding the use of average prices in the Nails test inconsistent. While the US has moved away from the Nails test, the Appellate Body seems to have opened the door for future implementation of the pattern test to be based on average prices rather than actual transaction prices.*'. T.J. Prusa, E.A. Vermulst, United States: Certain Methodologies and Their Application to Anti-dumping Proceedings Involving China – Nails in the Coffin of Unfair Dumping Margin Calculation Methodologies, *World Trade Review*, Vol. 18, No. 2, 2019, pp. 287-307 https://doi.org/10.1017/s1474745619000053.
68. WTO document DS471/AB/R 11 May 2017, para. 5.107.
69. Large Residential Washers From the People's Republic of China: Amended Final Affirmative Antidumping Duty Determination and Antidumping Duty Order. US Federal Register, Vol. 82, No. 23, 6 February 2017, pp. 9371-9373.
70. WTO document DS464/17/Add.26, 18 February 2020.

extended in 2022 following the sunset review.[71] *'The scope of the antidumping duty order on LRWs from China is identical to the scope of the safeguard measure on LRWs.'*[72]

II US SAFEGUARDS IN 2017

Pursuant to procedures set under Section 201 of the Trade Act 1974, which implements GATT Article XIX, the US initiated, in 2017, safeguards investigations on CSPV cells[73] and LRWs.[74] Notably, the US had not initiated any safeguard investigation since 2002,[75] when safeguard measures were imposed on (carbon and) steel products, and found to be inconsistent with GATT Article XIX and the Agreement on Safeguards (ASG) by the Panel and AB.[76] In 2017, following the USITC determination of material injury in the domestic industry, the US President ordered the imposition of safeguards, in the form of tariff quotas, on CSPV cells and LRWs in order to counter the alleged evasion of anti-dumping and countervailing duties through transhipment to third countries.

A Safeguards on Crystalline Silicon Photovoltaic Cells

A safeguard investigation on CSPV cells was initiated, in May 2017, by the USITC pursuant to a petition from Suniva, Inc., which was '*controlled by Shungeng International Clean Energy, a Chinese company listed on the Hong Kong Stock Exchange*'.[77] The petitioner alleged an increase in import quantities (of more than 50%) and serious injury in the domestic industry (whose market share fell from 21% in 2012 to 11% in 2016, loss of 1,200 manufacturing jobs, and a fall in wages by 27% during the 2012-2016 period), and claimed that the evasion of anti-dumping and countervailing duties had constituted unforeseen developments for the domestic industry.[78]

In February 2018, following the recommendation by the USITC, the US President mandated the imposition of safeguard measures on imports of CSPV products in the form of a tariff quota on solar cells and an increase in duties on imports of modules for four years.[79] Additional tariffs were imposed, above an annual quota of 2.5 gigawatts, as follows: 30% in the first year, 25% in the second year, 20% in the third year, and

71. Large Residential Washers From the People's Republic of China: Continuation of the Antidumping Duty Order. US Federal Register, Vol. 87, No. 167, 30 August 2022, pp. 52904-52905.
72. USITC, Large Residential Washers: Evaluation of the Effectiveness of Import Relief. Investigation No. TA-201-076 (Evaluation), Publication 5453, August 2023, pp. 6, 11.
73. WTO document G/SG/N/6/USA/11, 29 May 2017.
74. WTO document G/SG/N/6/USA/12, 12 June 2017.
75. WTO online information, viewed at: https://www.wto.org/english/tratop_e/safeg_e/SG-MeasuresByRepMember.pdf.
76. WTO document DS248/AB/R, DS249/AB/R, DS251/AB/R, DS252/AB/R, DS253/AB/R, DS254/AB/R, DS258/AB/R, DS259/AB/R, 10 November 2003.
77. T. Mitchell, Trump's Simple Cure For Solar Panel Ills Ignores Complexities, *Financial Times*, 30 January 2018.
78. WTO document G/SG/N/6/USA/11, 29 May 2017.
79. WTO document G/SG/N/10/USA/7, 26 January 2018.

15% in the fourth year.[80] Major exporting countries of CSPV products to the US during the investigation were Canada, China, Germany, Japan, Korea, Malaysia, Mexico, the Philippines, Singapore, Taiwan, Thailand and Vietnam.[81]

In response to the US imposition of safeguards, certain WTO Members announced retaliatory measures. Pursuant to ASG Article 8.2, China, Japan and Korea announced the eventual suspension of tariff concessions and other obligations towards the US.[82] In addition, Korea and China brought complaints to the WTO against the *US – Safeguard Measure on PV Products*.[83] A Panel report was only issued in the dispute initiated by China, where the US was found to have acted inconsistently with the '*unforeseen developments*' requirement (GATT Article XIX.1.a), as well as the causal link between the increased imports and the serious injury, and the non-attribution of injury caused by other factors (ASG Articles 2.1, 3.1, 3.2 and 4.2.b).[84] Following the issuance of the Panel report, China notified its intention to appeal to the (since 2017) blocked Appellate Body.[85]

Notably, the one-year effects of the US imposition of safeguards on the solar sector were reported by the US Solar Energy Industries Association. In 2019, the US solar industry suffered '*devastating harm*', including the loss of 62,000 jobs, an increase in US prices of solar panels (50% higher than the global average) and higher carbon dioxide emissions (26 million metric tons for 10.5 gigawatts of lost solar deployment).[86] While safeguard measures on CSPV cells were due to expire in February 2022, some companies established in the US (Auxin Solar Inc.,[87] Suniva Inc.,[88] Hanwha Q CELLS USA Inc.,[89] LG Electronics USA, Inc.,[90] and Mission Solar Energy)[91] requested the continuation of safeguard measures to the USITC.[92] In

80. WTO document G/SG/N/6/USA/11, 29 May 2017; WTO document G/SG/N/10/USA/7, 26 January 2018; US Federal Register Vol. 83, No. 17, 25 January 2021, pp. 3541-3551.
81. WTO document G/SG/N/10/USA/7, 26 January 2018.
82. These countries announced that the retaliatory safeguard measure would take the form of an increase in duty on selected products originating in the US and would be imposed on the earliest date between 7 February 2021 and the date in which the US safeguard measure is found to be inconsistent with the ASG by the DSB. WTO documents G/SG/N/12/CHN/2, 5 April 2018; G/SG/N/12/KOR/3, 6 April 2018; G/SG/N/12/JPN/3, 6 April 2018.
83. WTO disputes *United States – Safeguard Measure On Imports Of Crystalline Silicon Photovoltaic Products*. Complainants: Republic of Korea (DS545) and China (DS562).
84. WTO document DS562/R, 2 September 2021.
85. WTO document DS562/12, 20 September 2021.
86. The Solar Energy Industries Association, *The Section 201 Tariffs On Imported Solar Cells And Modules Have Caused Great Harm to the US Solar Industry and the Broader Economy,* December 2019, viewed at: https://www.seia.org/research-resources/adverse-impact-section-201-tariffs.
87. 100% US-owned company. http://www.auxinsolar.com/.
88. Suniva was founded in 2008, out of the Georgia Institute of Technology's University Center for Excellence in Photovoltaics, sponsored by the US Department of Energy. In 2015, it was acquired by a Chinese conglomerate, Shunfeng International Clean Energy. In 2017, it filed for bankruptcy, from where it exited in 2019. It is now US-owned by Lion Point Capital. https://suniva.com/.
89. After the Great Recession of 2008, Q Cells, German-owned and based, ceased to be one of the world's largest solar cell manufacturers and was acquired, in 2012, by Hanwha Group, a large South Korean business conglomerate. https://www.hanwha.com/en.html.
90. Subsidiary of LG Electronics, Korean-owned.
91. Operated by OCI Enterprises Inc, Korean-owned.
92. WTO document G/SG/N/6/USA/11/Suppl.2, 10 August 2021.

February 2022, the safeguards on CSPV cells were extended, with the exclusion of bifacial panels.[93]

B Safeguards on Large Residential Washing Machines

Allegations of evasion of anti-dumping and countervailing duties against the Korean producers LG and Samsung, the largest exporters of LRWs to the US, had prompted the USDOC to impose, in 2017, anti-dumping duties on LRWs from China.[94] A US producer of LRWs, Whirlpool Corporation, petitioned the USITC for a safeguard investigation on LRWs, alleging imports of LRWs had doubled from 2012 to 2016 (increasing from 1.60 million units in 2012 to 3.21 million units in 2016), serious injury in the domestic industry, and evasion of anti-dumping duties by moving production to third countries as unforeseen developments.[95] During the period of investigation, major exporting countries of LRWs were China, Korea, Mexico, Thailand and Vietnam.[96] The USITC claimed that, in 2012, LG and Samsung had shifted production from Korea to China and, after the anti-dumping order on LRWs from China in 2017, to Vietnam and Thailand. As a result of the initiation of the safeguard investigation in 2017, both Samsung and LG announced plans to open production facilities in the US.[97]

After the USITC's affirmative determination of serious injury to the domestic industry, the US President approved the imposition of safeguards on LRWs in the form of tariff quota for the period of three years, starting on 7 February 2018. The imposition of additional tariffs within the quota of 1.2 million units was applied as follows: 20% in the first year, 18% in the second year, and 16% in the third year. Out of the quota, applied additional tariffs were 50% in the first year, 45% in the second year, and 40% in the third year. These additional tariffs also applied to covered parts exceeding 50,000 units in the first year; 70,000 units in the second year; and 90,000 units in the third year.[98] The US measure on LRWs affected USD 303,566 million of annual imports from Korea as of the year 2017, resulting in USD 151,783 million of duty to be collected by the US.[99] Canada was excluded from the measure. In 2019, Turkey and India were removed from the list exempting developing country WTO Members from the safeguards.[100] The US Trade Representative (USTR) announced that the tariff rate quota of

93. WTO documents G/SG/N/10/USA/7/Suppl.13, 8 February 2022; G/SG/N/10/USA/7/Suppl.14, 10 February 2022.
94. USITC, Large Residential Washers: Evaluation of the Effectiveness of Import Relief. Investigation No. TA-201-076 (Evaluation), Publication 5453, August 2023, p. 6.
95. WTO document G/SG/N/6/USA/12, 12 June 2017.
96. WTO document G/SG/N/10/USA/8, 26 January 2018.
97. USITC, Large Residential Washers: Evaluation of the Effectiveness of Import Relief. Investigation No. TA-201-076 (Evaluation), Publication 5453, August 2023, p. 9.
98. WTO document G/SG/N/10/USA/8, 26 January 2018.
99. WTO document G/SG/N/12/KOR/2, 6 April 2018.
100. WTO document G/SG/N/10/USA/8/Suppl.2, 22 May 2019; G/SG/N/10/USA/8/Suppl.3, 7 June 2019.

1.2 million washer machines would be allocated quarterly instead of annually (300,000 units per quarter), beginning in February 2020.[101]

Following the petition by Whirlpool on the extension of the safeguard measure to the USITC, which concluded that the continuation of safeguards was '*necessary to prevent or remedy the serious injury to the domestic industry and that there was evidence that the domestic industry was making a positive adjustment to import competition*', the US President ordered, in 2020, the extension of safeguards for another period of three years, and the measure was terminated in February 2023.[102]

In response to the US imposition of safeguards on LRWs in 2018, China and Korea announced an eventual retaliation, suspending tariff concessions and other obligations towards the US, pursuant to ASG Article 8.2.[103] In addition, Korea submitted a complaint to the WTO against the *US – Safeguard Measure on Washers*.[104] In 2022, the Panel report concluded that US safeguards were inconsistent with GATT Article XIX.1(a), as well as ASG Articles 2.1, 3.1, 4.2(b), 4.2(c), 8.1 and 12.3.[105] In 2023, the US and Korea reached a mutually agreed solution.[106]

III BLOCK OF THE WTO APPELLATE BODY

The US has blocked the appointment of the members of the Appellate Body since June 2017. The term of six of the seven members of the Appellate Body expired at the end of 2019;[107] hence, the Appellate Body remained ineffective. Afterwards, the US appealed the Compliance Panel report of the *US – Carbon Steel (India)* dispute,[108] announcing

101. USTR, Additional Action Taken to Provide Relief to US Washing Machine Manufacturers, 20 December 2019, viewed at: https://ustr.gov/about-us/policy-offices/press-office/press-releases/2019/december/additional-action-taken-provide-relief-us-washing-machine-manufacturers.
102. USITC, Large Residential Washers: Evaluation of the Effectiveness of Import Relief. Investigation No. TA-201-076 (Evaluation), Publication 5453, August 2023, p. 5.
103. China and Korea announced that the retaliatory safeguard measure would take the form of an increase in duty on selected products originating in the US and would be imposed on the earliest date between 7 February 2021 and the date in which the US safeguard measure is found to be inconsistent with the ASG by the DSB. WTO documents G/SG/N/12/CHN/3, 5 April 2018; G/SG/N/12/KOR/2, 6 April 2018.
104. *United States – Safeguard Measure on Imports of Large Residential Washers* (DS546). WTO document DS546/4, 16 August 2018.
105. WTO document DS546/R, 8 February 2022.
106. WTO document DS546/13, 1 May 2023.
107. A. Beattie, The Unappealing Fate of the WTO's Appellate Body, *Financial Times*, 9 December 2019. The term of the remaining Appellate Body member expired at the end of 2020. WTO website information, viewed at: https://www.wto.org/english/tratop_e/dispu_e/appellate_body_e.htm#:~:text=Currently%2C%20the%20Appellate%20Body%20is,expired%20on%2030%20November%202020.
108. In 2019, the Compliance Panel report (DSU Article 21.5) had concluded that US countervailing measures on imports of certain hot-rolled carbon steel flat products from India were inconsistent with the GATT and the ASCM, and that the US had failed to comply with the DSB's recommendations and rulings – as modified by the Appellate Body report – in the original dispute *United States – Countervailing Measures on Certain HotRolled Carbon Steel Flat Products from India* (DS436). WTO documents DS436/AB/R, 8 December 2014; DS436/RW, 15 November 2019.

that it would confer with India on the way forward, including resolving the dispute at that stage or considering alternatives to the appellate process.[109]

When the Appellate Body ceased functioning in 2019, the US National Foreign Trade Council presented 'Proposals on Overreach', addressing the US concerns with the WTO AB, which mainly included expanding or narrowing the reach of WTO provisions, providing advisory opinions, exceeding the ninety-day timeframe for appeals, and interpreting the ADA in a way that narrows the discretion of WTO Members' administering authorities on implementing its provisions.[110] In spite of its rejection of the proposal to reform the Appellate Body prepared by New Zealand's Ambassador Walker, the US concluded that WTO Members should resolve the Appellate Body crisis by elaborating on that report '*by deciding upon agreed interpretations of dispute settlement rules, or by amending those rules*'.

A year later, the USTR published a report '*to provide a thorough examination of the Appellate Body's failure to comply with the WTO Agreements*' and to complain against its interpretations, particularly concerning the WTO Agreements on Technical Barriers to Trade, Safeguards, Antidumping, and Subsidies and Countervailing Measures. The USTR complained against the AB's interpretations for rendering trade remedy laws ineffective, thereby diminishing WTO Members' rights and obligations. More specifically, the US alleged that several of those interpretations had '*directly harmed the ability of the United States to counteract economic distortions caused by non-market practices of countries like China*'.[111]

With respect to safeguards, the USTR accused the Appellate Body of creating a high threshold for serious injury and inventing the requirement to demonstrate '*unforeseen developments*' for imposing safeguard measures. Concerning subsidies and countervailing duties, the USTR claimed that the AB's interpretation of 'public body', provided by the Appellate Body in the *US – Anti-dumping and Countervailing Duties (China)* dispute, i.e., '*an entity that possesses, exercises or is vested with governmental authority*', favours non-market economies.[112] In addition, it criticized the Appellate Body for imposing the obligation on WTO Members to show the existence of 'non-market prices' in order to disregard prices in the subsidizing country when calculating a subsidy. Regarding anti-dumping, the USTR complained against the AB's prohibition of the use of 'zeroing' to determine dumping margins, '*imposing an obligation on Members to calculate margins of dumping by offsetting the calculation of dumping by non-dumped transactions (i.e., transactions where the export price exceeds normal value)*'. Furthermore, the USTR claimed that the Appellate Body had limited the simultaneous imposition of anti-dumping and countervailing duties when using

109. WTO documents DS436/21, 19 December 2019; DS436/23, 18 July 2023 (mutually agreed solution).
110. '*If the language of an Antidumping Agreement provision provides scope for administering authorities to exercise discretion in how the provision is implemented, WTO adjudicators may not narrow that discretion.*' B. Hirsh, *Resolving the WTO Appellate Body Crisis: Proposals on Overreach*, Commissioned by the National Foreign Trade Council, December 2019.
111. USTR, Report on the Appellate Body of the World Trade Organization, 2020.
112. WTO document DS379/AB/R, 11 March 2011, para. 317.

a non-market economy (NME) methodology, by requiring WTO Members that the concurrent application does not result in '*double remedies*'.[113]

113. USTR, Report on the Appellate Body of the World Trade Organization, 2020, pp. 82, 88, 95, 105, 110, 114, 115.

CHAPTER 2

National Security

This chapter covers the US national security investigations on steel and aluminium, and the subsequent imposition of additional ad valorem duties on imports of these products. It also explores several WTO Members' reactions, namely the imposition of safeguards on imports of steel; submission of complaints to the WTO against US measures; and retaliation, against which the US submitted complaints to the WTO.

I US SECTION 232 TARIFFS ON STEEL AND ALUMINIUM

Section 232 of the US Trade Act of 1962 (Section 232)[114] implemented the national security clause enshrined under GATT Article XXI, '*Security Exceptions*'.[115] Section 232 investigations were conducted by the US Department of the Treasury until 1980, when the competence was transferred to the USDOC,[116] which conducted twenty-two investigations prior to 2025. Between 2017 and 2024, the USDOC conducted eight Section 232 investigations on steel, aluminium, automobiles, uranium, titanium

114. Safeguarding national security, Section 232 of the Trade Expansion Act of 1962, codified as Section 1862 of Title 19 of the US Code (USC). US Public Law 87-794, 11 October 1962.

115. GATT Article XXI, *Security Exceptions*, reads as follows: '*Nothing in this Agreement shall be construed*

(a) to require any contracting party to furnish any information the disclosure of which it considers contrary to its essential security interests; or

(b) to prevent any contracting party from taking any action which it considers necessary for the protection of its essential security interests

(i) relating to fissionable materials or the materials from which they are derived;

(ii) relating to the traffic in arms, ammunition and implements of war and to such traffic in other goods and materials as is carried on directly or indirectly for the purpose of supplying a military establishment;

(iii) taken in time of war or other emergency in international relations; or

(c) to prevent any contracting party from taking any action in pursuance of its obligations under the United Nations Charter for the maintenance of international peace and security.'

116. The authority to conduct trade remedies investigations was also transferred from the US Department of the Treasury to the Department of Commerce, effective from January 1980.

sponge, transformers, vanadium and neodymium iron-boron permanent magnets. The latter was conducted under US President Biden's Administration.[117] The first US Administration under President Trump reached affirmative determinations in the seven investigations. Only with respect to steel and aluminium, import restrictions in the form of additional ad valorem duties were imposed. In the rest of the cases, other actions were taken, such as negotiations (e.g., automobiles),[118] the creation of working groups to revive the US industry (e.g., uranium)[119] or ensure supply (e.g., titanium sponge),[120] or creating a monitoring regime (e.g., transformers).[121,122]

117. The other fourteen investigations were conducted before 2001. Bureau of Industry and Commerce of the US Department of Commerce, Section 232 Investigations: The Effect of Imports on the National Security. The second US Administration under President Trump has initiated more Section 232 investigations, including on copper, timber and lumber, semiconductors, pharmaceuticals, trucks, critical minerals, commercial aircrafts and jet engines, viewed at: https://www.bis.doc.gov/232.
118. On 23 May 2018, the USDOC initiated a Section 232 investigation on imports of automobiles. On 17 February, the Secretary of Commerce's report was submitted to the President, who instructed the USTR to negotiate with the EU and Japan, among others. US Proclamation 9888 of 17 May 2019, Adjusting Imports of Automobiles and Automobile Parts Into the United States. US Federal Register, Vol. 84, No. 98, 21 May 2019, pp. 23433-23435.
119. On 18 July 2018, the US initiated an investigation under Section 232 on imports of uranium. Although the US Secretary of Commerce found imports of uranium threatened and impaired national, the US President decided not to impose measures, but issues the Memorandum on the Effect of Uranium Imports on the National Security and Establishment of the United States Nuclear Fuel Working Group on 12 July 2019, aimed at conducting an analysis of national security to revive and expand domestic nuclear fuel production. Publication of a Report on the Effect of Imports of Uranium on the National Security: An Investigation Conducted Under Section 232 of the Trade Expansion Act of 1962, as Amended. US Federal Register, Vol. 86, No. 145, 2 August 2021.
120. On 4 March 2019, the USDOC initiated an investigation into titanium sponge imports. The US Secretary of Commerce reported that imports on titanium sponge, of which 94.4% in 2018 were from Japan, threatened to impair the national security. Accordingly, the US President ordered the establishment of a working group with Japan in order to '*to ensure access to titanium sponge in the US for use for national defense and critical industries in an emergency*'. US Presidential Memorandum on the Effect of Titanium Sponge Imports on the National Security, 27 February 2020.
121. In May 2019, the US signed a Joint Statement with Mexico, whereby Mexico committed to strictly monitor exports of electrical transformer laminations and cores made of non-North American grain-oriented electrical steel (GOES). USTR, USTR Statement on Successful Conclusion of Steel Negotiations with Mexico, 5 November 2020.
122. The US also introduced export controls invoking national security, particularly adding Huawei to the Entity List. Following the US Congress' enactment of the Export Control Reform Act of 2018, as part of the National Defense Authorization Act for Fiscal Year 2019, Public Law Nos: 115-232, the US Department of Commerce's Bureau of Industry and Security (BIS) published an advance notice of proposed rule-making for identifying emerging technologies essential to US national security. The BIS controls the export of dual-use and less sensitive military items through the Export Administration Regulations (EAR). Section 744 of the US EAR contains the 'Entity List' (first published in 1997, for weapons of mass destruction programmes), with the persons subject to specific licensing requirements on exports, reexports and transfers. In May 2019, the BIS determined that Huawei had been involved in activities contrary to the national security or foreign policy interests. Therefore, Huawei and sixty-eight non-US affiliates of Huawei located in twenty-six countries were added to the Entity List by a rule that created a temporary general licence. In the following months, more than fifty non-US affiliates of Huawei, located in twenty-five different destinations, were added to the Entity List. US Federal

In Memorandum for the US Secretary of Commerce on '*Steel Imports and Threats to National Security*', US President Trump, recognizing the close relation of the US economic welfare to US national security and considering the impact of foreign competition in the steel industry on the economic welfare of US industries, pursuant to Section 232,[123] stated that the US had imposed '*more than 150 antidumping and countervailing duty orders on steel products, but they have not substantially alleviated the negative effects that unfairly traded imports have had on the United States steel industry*'.[124]

Following Section 232 investigations on imports of steel and aluminium,[125] the US Secretary of Commerce submitted reports on the effect of steel and aluminium on national security[126] and provided recommendations to the US President.[127] On 8 March 2018, US President Trump issued two Presidential Proclamations announcing the imposition of additional tariff of 25% on steel[128] and 10% on aluminium,[129] effective on 23 March 2018. Initially, steel imports from Canada and Mexico were exempted from the additional 25% tariff; as well as aluminium imports from Canada, Mexico, the EU, Australia, Argentina, Korea and Brazil were exempted from the 10% additional tariff.

Register, Vol. 83, No. 223, 19 November 2018, pp. 58201-58202; Vol. 84, No. 99, 22 May 2019, pp. 23468-23471; Vol. 84, No. 121, 24 June 2019, pp. 29371-29374; Vol. 84, No. 162, 21 August 2019, pp. 43487-43501.

123. Section 232.c of the Trade Expansion Act of 1962.
124. US Presidential Memorandum on Steel Imports and Threats to National Security, 20 April 2017.
125. Before Section 232 investigations on steel and aluminium were initiated, in January 2017, the US brought a case to the WTO, *China – Subsidies to Producers of Primary Aluminium*, claiming imports of aluminium had been subsidized in a manner inconsistent with GATT Article XVI.1 and ASCM Articles 5 and 6. Nevertheless, the US did not request the establishment of a panel. WTO document DS519/3, 31 January 2017.
126. USDOC Bureau of Industry and Security Office of Technology Evaluation reports: The Effect of Imports of Steel on the National Security, 11 January 2018; The Effect of Imports of Aluminum on the National Security, 11 January 2018.
127. Recommendations on imports of steel: '*1. A global tariff of at least 24% on all steel imports from all countries, or 2. A tariff of at least 53% on all steel imports from 12 countries (Brazil, China, Costa Rica, Egypt, India, Malaysia, Republic of Korea, Russia, South Africa, Thailand, Turkey and Vietnam) with a quota by product on steel imports from all other countries equal to 100% of their 2017 exports to the United States, or 3. A quota on all steel products from all countries equal to 63% of each country's 2017 exports to the United States*'. Recommendations on aluminium: '*A tariff of at least 7.7% on all aluminum exports from all countries, or A tariff of 23.6% on all products from China, Hong Kong, Russia, Venezuela and Vietnam. All the other countries would be subject to quotas equal to 100% of their 2017 exports to the United States, or A quota on all imports from all countries equal to a maximum of 86.7% of their 2017 exports to the United States*'. USDOC, Secretary Ross Releases Steel and Aluminum 232 Reports in Coordination with White House, 16 February 2018.
128. '*For the purposes of this proclamation, "steel articles" are defined at the Harmonized Tariff Schedule (HTS) 6digit level as: 7206.10 through 7216.50, 7216.99 through 7301.10, 7302.10, 7302.40 through 7302.90, and 7304.10 through 7306.90, including any subsequent revisions to these HTS classifications.*' US Presidential Proclamation 9705 of 8 March 2018, Adjusting Imports of Steel into the United States. US Federal Register, Vol. 83, No. 51, 15 March 2018, pp. 11625-11630 at 11627.
129. US Presidential Proclamation 9704 of 8 March 2018, Adjusting Imports of Aluminum into the United States, 15 March 2018, pp. 11619-11624; US Presidential Proclamation 9705 of 8 March 2018, Adjusting Imports of Steel into the United States. US Federal Register, Vol. 83, No. 51, 15 March 2018, pp. 11625-11630.

In the absence of an '*alternative satisfactory solution*', the US announced the imposition of tariffs from different dates depending on the country of origin of imports: 1 May (Korea), 1 June (Canada, Mexico and EU), and 1 July (Argentina, Australia and Brazil).

Accordingly, quantitative restrictions on steel imports were agreed with Korea,[130] Brazil, and Argentina,[131] and on aluminium imports with Argentina.[132] Korea and Brazil did not agree on quotas for aluminium; therefore, the US imposed an additional tariff of 10% on imports of aluminium from these countries. Australia was exempted from the Section 232 tariffs, without fixing quantitative restrictions, after reaching an agreement with the US.[133] On their part, Canada and Mexico opted to retaliate by increasing their tariffs on imports from the US, against which the US submitted complaints to the WTO, alleging that the measures by Canada and Mexico violated GATT Articles I and II.[134] After reaching a mutually agreed solution with Canada and Mexico, the US exempted these countries from the additional 25% tariff on steel and 10% tariff on aluminium. As a result, Argentina, Australia, Canada and Mexico were permanently exempted from the Section 232 steel and aluminium tariffs, and Brazil and Korea solely from the additional 25% tariff on steel. Imports of steel from Turkey were exempted for a couple of months from the 25% additional tariff; yet, in August 2018, the US doubled the tariff on imports of steel from Turkey, i.e., an additional 50% tariff.[135] Imports of steel and aluminium from the EU were subject to these tariffs from June 2018 to January 2022.[136]

130. US Presidential Proclamation 9740 of 30 April 2018, Adjusting Imports of Steel Into the United States. US Federal Register, Vol. 83, No. 88, 7 May 2018, pp. 20683-20705.
131. US Presidential Proclamation 9759 of 31 May 2018, Adjusting Imports of Steel into the United States. US Federal Register, Vol. 83, No. 108, 5 June 2018 pp. 25857-25877.
132. US Presidential Proclamation 9758 of 31 May 2018, Adjusting Imports of Aluminum into the United States. US Federal Register, Vol. 83, No. 108, 5 June 2018, pp. 25849-25855.
133. Congressional Research Service, Section 232 Investigations: Overview and Issues for Congress, 18 May 2021, p. 9; US Presidential Proclamation 9758 of 31 May 2018, Adjusting Imports of Aluminum Into the United States. US Federal Register, Vol. 83, No. 108, 5 June 2018, pp. 25849-25855; Proclamation 9759 of 31 May 2018, Adjusting Imports of Steel Into the United States. US Federal Register, Vol. 83, No. 108, 5 June 2018 pp. 25857-25877.
134. *Canada – Additional Duties on Certain Products from the United States* (DS557), *Mexico – Additional Duties on Certain Products from the United States* (DS560). WTO documents DS557/4, 27 May 2019; DS560/4, 3 June 2019; DS557/1, 19 July 2018; DS560/1, 19 July 2018.
135. US Presidential Proclamation 9893 of 19 May 2019, Adjusting Imports of Aluminum Into the United States. US Federal Register, Vol. 84, No. 100, 23 May 2019, pp. 23983-23985; US Presidential Proclamation 9894 of 19 May 2019, Adjusting Imports of Steel Into the United States, US Federal Register, Vol. 84, No. 100, 23 May 2019, pp. 23987-23989. US Presidential Proclamation 9980 of 24 January 2020, on Adjusting Imports of Derivative Aluminum Articles and Derivative Steel Articles into the United States, 29 January 2020. US Federal Register, Vol. 85, No. 19, 29 January 2020, pp. 5281-5293.
136. US Presidential Proclamation 9710 of 22 March 2018, Adjusting Imports of Aluminum Into the United States; US Presidential Proclamation 9739 of 30 April 2018, Adjusting Imports of Aluminum Into the United States. US Federal Register, Vol. 83, No. 88, 7 May 2018, pp. 20677-20682.

II RETALIATION AND WTO DISPUTES

A Safeguards: *Additional Duties on Certain Products from the United States*

The US imposition of Section 232 tariffs created a spillover effect on the imposition of safeguards on imports of steel by several WTO Members, including Costa Rica,[137] South Africa,[138] Turkey,[139] the Arab States of the Gulf,[140] Thailand,[141] Russia, the Kyrgyz Republic, Kazakhstan, Armenia,[142] and the EU.[143]

Additionally, retaliatory measures were imposed by some WTO Members (besides Canada and Mexico), namely China, the EU, India, Mexico, Russia and Turkey, as well as merely announced by Japan. Alleging US measures to be safeguards, rather than national security measures, these countries complained against the US absence of notification of the alleged 'safeguards'; hence, they invoked the right to retaliate pursuant to GATT Article XIX.3 and ASG Article 8.2., thereby notifying the suspension of substantially equivalent concessions and other obligations to the US trade.

---

137. On 19 March 2018, Costa Rica initiated an investigation on imports of bars and rods of steel for concrete reinforcement. WTO document G/SG/N/6/CRI/4, 26 March 2018.
138. Before Section 232 tariffs, in March 2018, South Africa initiated a safeguard investigation into the surge of imports of threaded fasteners of iron or steel and imposed ad valorem duties. On 20 April 2018, South Africa initiated a safeguard investigation on import of other screws fully threaded with hexagon heads made of steel and imposed ad valorem duties. WTO documents G/SG/N/6/ZAF/6, 24 April 2018; G/SG/N/7/ZAF/3, 1 August 2018; G/SG/N/7/ZAF/3/Suppl.1, 7 August 2018; G/SG/N/6/ZAF/7, 4 March 2019; G/SG/N/7/ZAF/4, 11 July 2019; G/SG/N/7/ZAF/5, 16 September 2020; G/SG/N/6/ZAF/7/Suppl.1, 3 April 2023.
139. Turkey initiated, in April 2018, an investigation on imports of iron and steel products, imposed provisional tariff quotas, but terminated the investigation in 2019 without imposing a definitive measure. WTO documents G/SG/N/6/TUR/24, 3 May 2018; G/SG/N/7/TUR/13, 5 October 2018; G/SG/N/7/TUR/13, 13 May 2019.
140. The Cooperation Council for the Arab States of the Gulf imposed, in May 2018, a definitive safeguard measures in the form of tariff increase on flat-rolled products of iron or non-alloy steel. WTO document G/SG/N/10/ARE/1/Suppl.2, 30 April 2018; G/SG/N/8/ARE/3/Suppl.1, 12 May 2021.
141. Thailand excluded, in June 2018, Egypt and China from the list of exempted countries of certain safeguard measures that were in force concerning imports of hot-rolled steel flat products. WTO documents G/SG/N/10/THA/2/Suppl.4, 26 June 2018; G/SG/N/10/THA/3/Suppl.3, 26 June 2018.
142. Russia, the Kyrgyz Republic, Kazakhstan and Armenia initiated, in August 2018, a safeguard investigation on imports of certain flat-rolled steel products imported into the customs territory of the Eurasian Economic Union and imposed a tariff quota for a year. WTO documents G/SG/N/6/RUS/5, 20 September 2018; G/SG/N/8/RUS/4/Suppl.1, 26 August 2019.
143. On 26 March 2018, the EU initiated, in March 2018, an ex officio safeguard investigation on certain steel imports and imposed a tariff quota, imposing an additional duty of 25% on imports out of quota, extended until 2024. Notably, the Panel in *European Union – Safeguard measures on certain steel products* found that the EU safeguards were inconsistent with GATT Article XIX.1(a) and ASG Article 4.1(b). WTO documents G/SG/N/6/EU/1, 27 March 2018; G/SG/N/6/EU/1/Suppl.1, 29 June 2018; G/SG/N/7/EU/1, 18 July 2018; G/SG/N/8/EU/1, 4 January 2019; G/SG/N/8/EU/1/Suppl.1, 7 February 2019; G/SG/N/8/EU/1/Suppl.3, 2 June 2023; DS595/R, 29 April 2022; EU Commission Implementing Regulation 2021/1029 of 24 June 2021 amending Commission Implementing Regulation (EU) 2019/159 to prolong the safeguard measure on imports of certain steel products, OJEU, L.225, 25 June 2021.

More specifically, in April 2018, China suspended concessions and other obligations on selected US imports, including fresh fruits, dried fruits and nuts (15%); grape wine (15%); denatured ethyl alcohol (15%); ginseng roots (15%); seamless tubes, pipes and hollow profiles, of iron or steel (15%); meat and edible meat offal of swine (25%); aluminium waste (25%).[144] India imposed, in June 2018, additional duties ranging from 10% to 50% on US imports, including certain fruits (10-25%), vegetables (10%), imports of steel and iron (15%), and motorcycles (50%).[145] Russia retaliated in August 2018, by increasing tariffs from 25% to 40% on certain imports from the US.[146] Turkey increased, in June 2018, tariffs between 5% to 40% on selected products originating in the US, including fruits, cereals, food preparations, beverages, tobacco, coal, plastics, wood, paper, iron and steel products, mechanical appliances and motor vehicles.[147] The EU notified retaliatory measures in the form of an additional 25% tariff on a wide range of US imports (and exceptionally 10% on playing cards), effective from June 2018.[148] Moreover, both the EU and Japan reserved their right to increase tariffs on certain US products on the earliest date between three years from the US measure and the DSB's ruling concerning the inconsistency of US measures with WTO Agreements.[149]

In response to these retaliatory measures, the US submitted complaints to the WTO, *Additional duties on certain products from the United States*, against Canada, China, the EU, Mexico, Turkey, Russia and India, claiming that their measures appeared to be inconsistent with GATT Article I, for being discriminatory, and GATT Article II, for exceeding the WTO Schedules of concessions.[150] While a mutually agreed solution was reached with Canada and Mexico in May 2018,[151] a panel was composed with respect to the other five disputes. The US agreed on a mutual solution with the EU in 2022,[152] and India in 2023.[153] In the disputes against China and Turkey, the Panel report found that neither GATT Article XIX.3 nor ASG Article 8.2 applied and that Chinese and Turkish measures against US imports were inconsistent with GATT

144. WTO document G/SG/N/12/CHN/1, 3 April 2018.
145. WTO document G/SG/N/12/IND/1, 18 May 2018; G/SG/N/12/IND/1/Rev.1, 14 June 2018.
146. WTO document G/SG/N/12/RUS/2, 22 May 2018.
147. WTO document G/SG/N/12/TUR/6, 22 May 2018; G/SG/N/12/TUR/6/Suppl.1, 15 August 2018.
148. Article 2 of EU Commission Implementing Regulation 2018/724 of 16 May 2018 on certain commercial policy measures concerning certain products originating in the United States of America. OJEU, L.122, 17 May 2018, p. 16.
149. WTO documents G/SG/N/12/EU/1, 18 May 2018; G/SG/N/12/JPN/4, 22 May 2018; G/SG/N/12/JPN/4/Suppl.1, 20 June 2018; G/SG/N/12/JPN/4/Suppl.2, 7 April 2020.
150. *Additional Duties on Certain Products from the United States*, complainants: Canada (DS557), China (DS558), the EU (DS559), Mexico (DS560), Turkey (DS561), Russia (DS566) and India (DS585). WTO documents DS557/1, 19 July 2018; DS558/3, 28 January 2019; DS559/3, 28 January 2019; DS560/1, 19 July 2018; DS561/3, 1 March 2019; DS566/3, 28 January 2019; and DS585/3, 10 January 2020.
151. WTO documents DS557/4, 27 May 2019; DS560/4, 3 June 2019; DS557/1, 19 July 2018; DS560/1, 19 July 2018.
152. WTO document DS559/7, 21 January 2022.
153. WTO document DS585/7, 17 July 2023.

Articles I and II.[154] As of June 2025, the Panel report on the dispute with Russia was still pending.[155]

B United States – Certain Measures on Steel and Aluminium Products

Besides imposing retaliatory measures, Canada, China, India, the EU, Mexico, Norway, Russia, Switzerland and Turkey submitted complaints to the WTO against US measures, *US – Steel and Aluminium Products*, alleging inconsistency with GATT Article XIX, on safeguards.[156] The US reached a mutually agreed solution with Canada and Mexico in 2019; the EU in 2022; and India in 2023.[157] The Panel reports on the disputes with China, Norway, Switzerland, and Turkey found that the US. additional tariffs on steel and aluminium were imposed pursuant to GATT Article XXI, on security exceptions,[158] and not GATT Article XIX, on safeguards,[159] in a manner inconsistent with GATT Articles I.1, II.1, XI.1, and XXI(b)(iii).[160] In the dispute with Russia, the work of the panel was suspended, at the request of Russia, in June 2023.[161]

154. WTO documents DS558/R, 16 August 2023; DS561/R, 19 December 2023.
155. WTO documents DS566/8, 22 January 2024; DS566/9, 2 December 2024.
156. *United States – Certain Measures on Steel and Aluminium Products*; complainants: China (DS544), India (DS547), the EU (DS548), Canada (DS550), Mexico (DS551), Norway (DS552), Russia (DS554), Switzerland (DS556) and Turkey (DS564).
157. WTO documents DS550, 27 May 2019; DS551/13, 3 June 2019; DS548/19, 21 January 2022; DS547/15, 18 July 2023.
158. During the GATT (1948-1994), CONTRACTING PARTIES considered measures justified under Article XXI(b) in nine cases. One case relates to subpara. (b)(ii), a Czechoslovak complaint in 1949 against US national security export control (licences). The other eight cases involve subpara. (b)(iii): US suspension obligations with Czechoslovakia, in 1951; prohibition of Czechoslovak imports by Peru, in 1954; Ghana ban on imports of Portuguese goods, in 1961; US embargo on trade with Cuba, in 1962; Egypt boycott against Israel and secondary boycott, in 1970; EC, Australia and Canada trade measures against Argentina, in 1982; US imports of sugar from Nicaragua, in 1982; and US embargo on trade with Nicaragua, in 1985. WTO document MTN.GNG/NG7/W/16, 18 August 1987, paras 14-23. During the existence of the WTO, the DSB has only resolved a dispute concerning GATT Article XXI, *Russia – Measures Concerning Traffic in Transit* (DS512), in which the Panel rejected that Article XXI (b) was '*self-judging*' or '*non-justiciable*' and found that while it allows a member to '*take any action which it considers necessary for the protection of its essential security interests*', the action '*must objectively be found to meet the requirements in one of the enumerated subparagraphs of that provision*'. WTO document DS512/R, 5 April 2019, paras 7.101, 7.103.
159. The first WTO disputes concerning US safeguard measures on steel, *United States – Definitive Safeguard Measures on Imports of Certain Steel Products*, were brought by the EU (DS248), Japan (DS249), Korea (DS251), China (DS252), Switzerland (DS253), Norway (DS254), New Zealand (DS258), Brazil (DS259) and Chinese Taipei against the US imposition of tariff quotas in 2002. The Appellate Body report upheld the Panel's finding on the inconsistency of US safeguard measures with GATT Article XIX GATT, arguing that the US had failed to provide a 'reasoned conclusion' in relation to 'unforeseen developments' for each specific safeguard measure. Accordingly, the US terminated the safeguard measures on 3 December 2003. WTO documents G/SG/D20/1, 13 March 2002; DS248/R, DS249/R, DS251/R, DS252/R, DS253/R, DS254/R, DS258/R, DS259/R, 11 July 2003; DS248/AB/R, DS249/AB/R, DS251/AB/R, DS252/AB/R, DS253/AB/R, DS254/AB/R, DS258/AB/R, DS259/AB/R, 10 November 2003.
160. WTO documents DS544/R, 9 December 2022; DS552/R, 9 December 2022; DS556/R, 9 December 2022; DS564/R, 9 December 2022.
161. WTO document DS554/24, 26 June 2023; DS554/25, 25 June 2024.

In addition to the suspension of Section 232 tariffs and retaliatory tariffs on US products and related WTO disputes, the mutually agreed solution between the US and the EU included negotiations on a bilateral agreement, the EU–US Global Arrangement on Sustainable Steel and Aluminium (GSA), '*to restore market-oriented conditions and reduce carbon emissions in the steel and aluminium sectors*'.[162] In February 2022, the US and Japan agreed to address non-market excess capacity in the global steel and aluminium sectors, implementing, *inter alia*, anti-dumping and countervailing duties and safeguard measures.[163]

162. EU Commission, Joint EU-US Statement on a Global Arrangement on Sustainable Steel and Aluminium, 31 October 2021. USTR, Steel & Aluminum US-EU Joint Statement, 31 October 2021.
163. USDOC, United States-Japan Joint Statement, 7 February 2022.

Chapter 3
US–China Tit-for-Tat Tariff Measures

This chapter offers the escalation of additional tariff measures imposed by the US and China on each other's products since 2018. GATT Article II provides that WTO Members' products shall '*be exempt from ordinary customs duties in excess of those set forth and provided*' in the (WTO) Schedule of concessions of the WTO Member in which they are imported.[164] The escalation took place through four rounds of tariff measures until the first deal was reached: first, in July and August 2018; second, in September 2018; third, in June 2019; and fourth, in September 2019. Another increase in tariffs was scheduled for December 2019, but the US and China agreed to suspend it and signed the Phase One trade deal on 15 January 2020, which, together with the outbreak of the COVID-19 pandemic, ceased the tariff escalation between the US and China (Figure 3.1).

164. GATT Article II.2 permits the imposition of, *inter alia*, anti-dumping and countervailing duties and charges equivalent to internal taxes.

Figure 3.1 Tit-for-Tat Tariff Measures

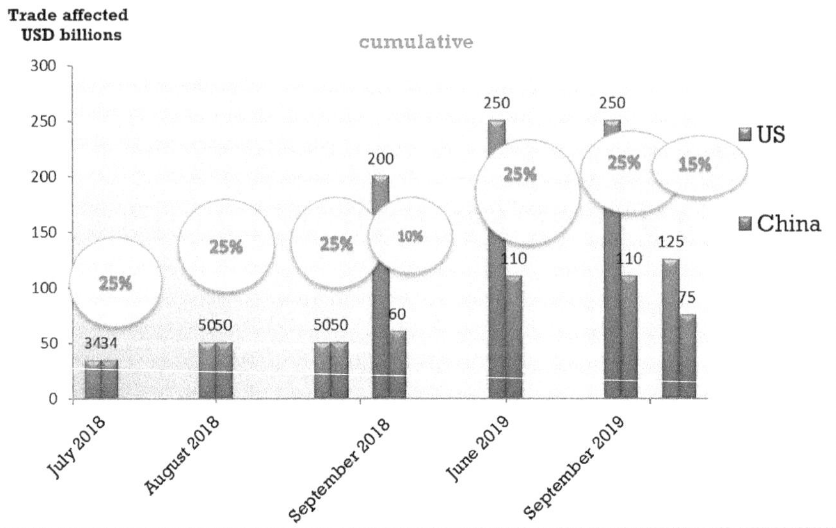

Source: Created by the author.

I WTO DISPUTES AND FIRST ROUND

In March 2018, the US submitted a complaint to the WTO, *China – Intellectual Property Rights II*, alleging that China's measures appeared to be inconsistent with Articles 3 and 28 of the Agreement on Trade-Related Aspects of Intellectual Property Rights,[165] claiming an estimated USD 50 billion in annual harm to the US.[166] Previously, in August 2017, the USTR was instructed to conduct an investigation,[167] to determine whether

165. *China – Certain Measures Concerning the Protection of Intellectual Property Rights* (DS542). WTO document DS542/1, 26 March 2018. The EU also requested consultations with China, claiming China's measures to be inconsistent with the Agreement on Trade-Related Aspects of Intellectual Property Rights (Articles 3, 28, 33 and 39); GATT Article X:3(a); and the Protocol of Accession of China to the WTO (para. 2(A)(2) of Part I). The EU did not request the establishment of a panel on *China – Certain Measures on the Transfer of Technology* (DS549). WTO document DS549/1, 6 June 2018.
166. WTO online information: https://www.wto.org/english/news_e/news18_e/dsb_19nov18_e.htm.
167. Section 302(b)(1)(A) of the Trade Act of 1974 authorizes the USTR to investigate whether the conduct of a US trading partner is actionable under Section 301 of the Trade Act of 1974, which includes three categories of potentially actionable acts, policies, or practices of a US trading partner. Section 301 sets out three categories of acts, policies, or practices of a foreign country that are potentially actionable: (i) trade agreement violations; (ii) acts, policies or practices that are unjustifiable (defined as those that are inconsistent with US international legal rights) and that burden or restrict US Commerce; and (iii) acts, policies or practices that are unreasonable or discriminatory and that burden or restrict US Commerce. US Presidential Memorandum for the United States Trade Representative, 14 August 2017.

China's '*acts, policies, and practices related to technology transfer, intellectual property, and innovation*' were actionable under Section 301 of the Trade Act of 1974 (Section 301).[168] In April 2018, the USTR announced that China's policies were found unreasonable or discriminatory and had burdened or restricted US commerce; hence, the USTR determined China's conduct to be actionable under Section 301.[169] In view of the tariff measures that the US would eventually impose, China submitted a complaint to the WTO, *US – Tariff Measures (China)*.[170]

A US Lists 1 and 2 (25% on USD 50 Billion)

Along with the findings of the Section 301 investigation, the USTR published a list of products originating in China, with an estimated annual value of USD 50 billion,[171] on which an additional duty of 25% was to be imposed, subject to a request for exclusion.[172] The list of 1,333 tariff subheadings covered chemical products (including pharmaceutical products); rubber and articles thereof; iron, steel, aluminium and articles thereof; machinery and mechanical appliances; vehicles, aircraft, vessels and associated transport equipment; as well as optical, photographic, cinematographic, measuring, precision, checking, medical or surgical instruments or apparatus.[173] In June 2018, the USTR announced an amendment to the list,[174] and the imposition of the 25% additional tariff on USD 50 billion of Chinese imports in two sets:[175] From 6 July 2018, on USD 34 billion per year (List 1, consisting of 818 tariff subheadings);[176] and from 23 August 2018, on the remaining USD 16 billion (List 2, covering 279 tariff subheadings).[177]

---

168. Initiation of Section 301 Investigation; Hearing; and Request for Public Comments: China's Acts, Policies, and Practices Related to Technology Transfer, Intellectual Property, and Innovation. US Federal Register, Vol. 82, No. 163, 24 August 2017, pp. 40213-40215.
169. USTR, Findings of the Investigation Into China's Acts, Policies, and Practices Related to Technology Transfer, Intellectual Property, and Innovation under Section 301 of the Trade Act of 1974, 22 March 2018, p. 3.
170. *United States – Tariff Measures on Certain Goods from China* (DS543).
171. USTR, Section 301 Product List Fact Sheet, 29 June 2018, viewed at: https://ustr.gov/about-us/policy-offices/press-office/fact-sheets/2018/june/section-301-product-list-fact-sheet.
172. Notice of Product Exclusions: China's Acts, Policies, and Practices Related to Technology Transfer, Intellectual Property, and Innovation. US Federal Register, Vol. 84, No. 131, 9 July 2019, pp. 32821-32826.
173. Notice of Determination and Request for Public Comment Concerning Proposed Determination of Action Pursuant to Section 301: China's Acts, Policies, and Practices Related to Technology Transfer, Intellectual Property, and Innovation. US Federal Register Vol. 83, No. 67, 6 April 2018, pp. 14906, 14910-14954.
174. In June 2018, 818 tariff subheadings from the original list were maintained, and 515 tariff subheadings were removed; 284 new tariff subheadings were proposed to be added after further review. USTR, Section 301 Product List Fact Sheet, 29 June 2018, viewed at: https://ustr.gov/about-us/policy-offices/press-office/fact-sheets/2018/june/section-301-product-list-fact-sheet.
175. USTR Issues Tariffs on Chinese Products in Response to Unfair Trade Practices, 15 June 2018.
176. USTR, Statement By US Trade Representative Robert Lighthizer on Section 301 Action, 10 July 2018.
177. USTR, USTR Finalizes Second Tranche of Tariffs on Chinese Products in Response to China's Unfair Trade Practices, 7 August 2018.

B China's Retaliation (25% on USD 50 Billion)

In response to US measures, China announced the imposition of an equivalent additional 25% ad valorem duty on US imports valued at USD 50 billion.[178] Replicating the US action, on 16 June 2018, China revised the list of US products and divided the measure into two sets: The first, effective on 6 July 2018, targeted USD 34 billion (545 tariff subheadings)[179] and the second, imposed on 23 August 2018, USD 16 billion (333 tariff subheadings).[180]

Besides retaliating, China brought another case to the WTO, *US – Tariff Measures on Certain Goods from China II*, alleging that the US additional 25% tariffs on USD 16 billion of Chinese products exceeded the WTO Schedule of concessions.[181] On its part, the US requested the establishment of a panel in the dispute *China – Intellectual Property Rights II*. Nevertheless, in June 2019, the US and China agreed to suspend the proceedings until 2020.[182]

II SECOND AND THIRD ROUNDS

A US List 3 (10%-25% on USD 200 Billion)

US President Trump directed the USTR to take further action and identify USD 200 billion worth of Chinese imports to be subject to an additional 10% tariff.[183] The US list with imports from China included almost all products (6,031 tariff subheadings), namely meat; fish; dairy products; vegetable products; prepared food, beverages, tobacco; mineral products; chemical products; plastics and rubber; wood; textiles; footwear; articles of stone, glass, ceramic; base metals; machinery; vehicles, aircraft, ships; furniture; and works of art.[184] On 24 September 2018, an additional 10% duty was imposed on 5,745 tariff subheadings of Chinese imports.[185] The level of the additional tariff was increased from 10% to 25%,[186] effective on 24 September 2018.[187]

---

178. MOFCOM of China, Ministry of Commerce Announcement No. 34 of 2018 on the Imposition of Tariffs on Certain Imported Goods Originating in the United States, 4 April 2018, viewed at: http://www.mofcom.gov.cn/article/b/e/201804/20180402728516.shtml.
179. MOFCOM, Announcement on Imposing Tariffs on Some Goods Originating in the United States, 17 June 2018.
180. MOFCOM of China, Announcement No. 64 on the imposition of additional tariffs on some goods originating in the United States, 8 August 2018, viewed at: http://www.mofcom.gov.cn/article/ae/ai/201808/20180802773926.shtml.
181. *United States – Tariff Measures on Certain Goods from China II* (DS565). WTO document DS565/1, 27 August 2018.
182. *China – Certain Measures Concerning the Protection of Intellectual Property Rights* (DS542). WTO documents DS542/10, 14 June 2019; DS542/12, 5 March 2020.
183. US White House, Statement from the President Regarding Trade with China, 18 June 2018.
184. Request for Comments Concerning Proposed Modification of Action Pursuant to Section 301: China's Acts, Policies, and Practices Related to Technology Transfer, Intellectual Property, and Innovation. US Federal Register, Vol. 83, No. 137, 17 July 2018, pp. 33608-33728.
185. USTR, USTR Finalizes Tariffs on USD 200 Billion of Chinese Imports in Response to China's Unfair Trade Practices, 18 August 2018.
186. USTR, Statement by US Trade Representative Robert Lighthizer on Section 301 Action, 10 May 2019.

B China's Retaliation (5%-25% on USD 60 Billion)

Against the US second round of ad valorem duties, China retaliated by imposing 5%, 10%, 20% or 25% additional tariffs on US imports valued at USD 60 billion, affecting products of 5,207 tariff subheadings, which were included in four lists. List 1 was subject to an additional 25% duty and covered 2,493 products (including agricultural, textiles, chemicals, metal and machinery);[188] List 2 was hit with an additional 20% duty and consisted of 1,078 products (such as foods, paperboard, chemicals and works of art);[189] List 3 was targeted with an additional 10% duty and covered 974 products (agricultural, chemicals, glassware products);[190] and List 4 was subject to an additional 5% duty and consisted of 662 products (including chemicals, machinery, medical equipment).[191] Mirroring the US, on 24 September 2018, China increased tariffs on these 5,207 tariff subheadings, valued at USD 60 billion: 5% on products included in Lists 3 and 4, and 10% on products covered in Lists 1 and 2.[192]

C 'Truce', December 2018-May 2019

In December 2018, the US and China signed a truce on the escalation of some of the additional tariffs for ninety days, whereby the US committed to refrain from increasing to 25% the additional 10% tariff on USD 200 billion of Chinese imports (in force since September 2018).[193] On its part, China suspended, from 1 January to 15 December 2019, retaliatory additional tariffs of 5% and 25% imposed on US imports (211 tariff subheadings) of auto parts (67 subheadings) and auto products (144 tariff subheadings), respectively.[194] The truce was extended until May 2019.[195]

187. Notice of Modification of Section 301 Action: China's Acts, Policies, and Practices Related to Technology Transfer, Intellectual Property, and Innovation. US Federal Register, Vol. 83, No. 184, 21 September 2018, pp. 47974-48192.
188. MOFCOM of China, 25% additional tariffs on US products, List 1, viewed at: http://images.mofcom.gov.cn/www/201808/20180803202819697.pdf.
189. MOFCOM of China, 20% additional tariffs on US products, List 2, viewed at: http://images.mofcom.gov.cn/www/201808/20180803202835549.pdf.
190. MOFCOM of China, 10% additional tariffs on US products, List 3, viewed at: http://images.mofcom.gov.cn/www/201808/20180803202856881.pdf.
191. MOFCOM of China, 5% additional tariffs on US products, List 4, viewed at: http://images.mofcom.gov.cn/www/201808/20180803202917053.pdf.
192. MOFCOM of China, Ministry of Commerce Announcement No. 69 of 2018 on the imposition of additional tariffs on some goods originating in the United States, 18 September 2018, viewed at: http://www.mofcom.gov.cn/article/ae/ai/201809/20180902788241.shtml.
193. US White House, Statement from the Press Secretary Regarding the President's Working Dinner with China, 1 December 2018.
194. MOFCOM of China, Regular Press Conference of the Ministry of Commerce, 20 December 2018.
195. L. Hornby, Donald Trump's extension of China trade talks suits both sides, *Financial Times*, 25 February 2019.

D Third Round, Resumption of Tariff Increase

1 *US List 3 (Increase to 25% on USD 200 Billion)*

After the truce between December 2018 and May 2019, the US resumed the increase of the additional tariffs from 10% to 25% on around USD 200 billion of Chinese imports. The measure, which had previously been in force from 24 September to December 2018, was effective on 1 June 2019,[196] subject to a request for exclusion.[197]

2 *China's Increase in Tariffs (to 10%-35% on USD 60 Billion)*

China also resumed the increase in tariffs of 5 or 10% on USD 60 billion of US products (affecting 5,207 tariff subheadings) that had already been subject to additional tariffs of 10%, 15%, 30% or 35% from September to December 2018. The measure was also effective from 1 June 2019, for which a tariff exclusion system was launched by the State Council Customs Tariff Committee of China.[198]

III FOURTH ROUND AND WTO DISPUTE

A US List 4 (15% on USD 125 Billion)

The USTR was instructed to raise tariffs on '*essentially all remaining imports*' originating in China,[199] valued at approximately USD 300 billion (List 4, covering 3,805 tariff subheadings).[200] Based on health, safety and national security reasons, certain products were removed from the list. From 1 September 2019, an additional 15% duty was imposed on certain Chinese products valued at USD 125 billion (List 4A), subject to exclusions upon request.[201] The measure was delayed until 15 December 2019 for other articles (List 4B), including '*cell phones, laptop computers, video game consoles, certain toys, computer monitors, and certain items of footwear and clothing*'.[202] The imposition

196. USTR, Notice Regarding Application of Section 301 Action, 31 May 2019.
197. USTR, China Section 301-Tariff Actions and Exclusion Process, USD 200 Billion Product Exclusion Process, viewed at: https://ustr.gov/issue-areas/enforcement/section-301-investigations/section-301-china/200-billion-trade-action.
198. MoF of China website, State Council Customs Tariff Committee Exclusion System on goods subject to tariffs from the United States, June 2019, viewed at: https://gszx.mof.gov.cn/.
199. USTR, Statement By US Trade Representative Robert Lighthizer on Section 301 Action, 10 May 2019.
200. Notice of Modification of Section 301 Action: China's Acts, Policies, and Practices Related to Technology Transfer, Intellectual Property, and Innovation. US Federal Register, Vol. 84, No. 161, 20 August 2019, pp. 43304-43471.
201. Procedures for Requests to Exclude Particular Products from the August 2019 Action Pursuant to Section 301: China's Acts, Policies, and Practices Related to Technology Transfer, Intellectual Property, and Innovation. US Federal Register, Vol. 84, No. 206, 24 October 2019, pp. 57144-57152.
202. USTR, USTR Announces Next Steps on Proposed 10 Percent Tariff on Imports from China, 13 August 2019.

of tariffs scheduled to be imposed in December 2019 was suspended due to the announcement of the One Phase trade deal.[203]

B China's Retaliation (5%-10% Tariffs on USD 75 Billion)

In response, China announced the imposition of additional tariffs of 5% or 10% on certain US imports, with an estimated value of USD 75 billion, also divided into two sets, scheduled for September (affecting 801 tariff subheadings) and December 2019 (covering 916 tariff subheadings). In addition, China submitted a complaint to the WTO, *US – Tariff measures on certain goods from China III*, alleging that the US additional 15% tariff on USD 300 billion of Chinese products exceeded the WTO Schedule of concessions.[204] In September 2020, the Panel in *US – Tariff Measures* (China) concluded that US additional ad valorem duties of 25%, imposed from 6 July 2018 on Chinese products with an annual trade value of USD 34 billion (affecting 818 tariff subheadings), and of 15%, imposed from 21 September 2018 on Chinese products with an annual trade value of USD 200 billion (covering 5,745 tariff subheadings), were inconsistent with GATT Articles I and II.[205]

IV PHASE ONE TRADE DEAL AND COVID-19 PANDEMIC

In December 2019, the Phase One trade deal between the US and China was announced to be signed on 15 January 2020. Meanwhile, the US and China suspended the additional tariffs scheduled to take effect on 15 December 2019.[206] The Phase One trade deal between China and the US entered into force on 14 February 2020, covering eight chapters: intellectual property, technology transfer, trade in food and agricultural products, financial services, macroeconomic policies and exchange rate matters, expanding trade, bilateral evaluation and dispute resolution, and transparency.[207] China and the US agreed to refrain from competitive currency devaluation and the targeting of exchange rates for competitive purposes. Moreover, the parties affirmed to disclose publicly '*foreign exchange reserves data and forward positions according to the*

203. Notice of Modification of Section 301 Action: China's Acts, Policies, and Practices Related to Technology Transfer, Intellectual Property, and Innovation. US Federal Register, Vol. 84, No. 243, 18 December 2019, p. 69447.
204. *United States – Tariff measures on certain goods from China III* (DS587). WTO document DS587/1, 4 September 2019.
205. WTO document DS543/R, 15 September 2020.
206. Notice of Modification of Section 301 Action: China's Acts, Policies, and Practices Related to Technology Transfer, Intellectual Property, and Innovation. US Federal Register, Vol. 84, No. 243, 18 December 2019, p. 69447. MoF of China, 19 December 2019, viewed at: http://www.mof.gov.cn/zhengwuxinxi/zhengcefabu/201912/P020191219362467972158.pdf. MoF of China, Announcement of the Tariff Commission of the State Council on the second exclusion list for the first batch of goods subject to tariffs on the United States and Canada, 19 December 2019, viewed at: http://www.mof.gov.cn/zhengwuxinxi/zhengcefabu/201912/t20191219_3444518.htm.
207. USTR, Economic and Trade Agreement Between the United States of America and the People's Republic of China, 15 January 2020.

IMF's Data Template on International Reserves and Foreign Currency Liquidity every month'.[208]

As part of the Phase One trade deal, China committed to exceeding, during the following two years, i.e., until December 2021, the 2017 baseline on US imports by USD 200 billion, including USD 78 billion in additional manufactured goods, USD 54 billion in additional energy purchases, USD 32 billion in additional farm products purchases, and USD 38 billion worth of services.[209] Seeking to fulfil its commitments, in February 2020, China reduced the additional tariffs on USD 75 billion of imports from the US that had been subject to additional tariffs from 1 September 2019:[210] From 10% to 5%, on 916 tariff subheadings; and from 5% to 2.5%, on 801 tariff subheadings.[211] Moreover, China granted tariff exemptions for one year to US products that had been subject to retaliatory measures,[212] including wood, books, machinery, mechanical appliances, electrical equipment (covering 55 tariff subheadings)[213] and medical instruments (affecting 10 tariff subheadings),[214] as well as 696 other tariff subheadings.[215]

Furthermore, in February 2020, in order to prevent and control the COVID-19 pandemic,[216] China suspended additional tariffs that had been imposed in response to US Section 301 and resumed its tariff concession obligations that had been suspended in response to US Section 232 measures.[217] For its part, the US reduced the additional

208. *Ibid.*, Article 5.1.4 and 5.3.1.a.
209. *Ibid.*, p. 6.
210. MoF of China, The Tariff Commission of the State Council issued an announcement adjusting the additional tariff measures on some imported goods originating in the United States, 6 February 2020, viewed at: http://gss.mof.gov.cn/gzdt/zhengcejiedu/202002/t20200206_3466538.htm.
211. MoF of China, Announcement of the Tariff Commission of the State Council on Adjusting Tariff Measures on Certain Imported Goods Originating in the United States Taxation Commission Announcement No. 1 of 2020, 6 February 2020, viewed at: http://gss.mof.gov.cn/gzdt/zhengcefabu/202002/t20200206_3466540.htm.
212. MoF of China, Announcement of the Tariff Commission of the State Council on the first exclusion list for the second batch of goods subject to tariffs on the United States and Canada, 21 February 2020, viewed at: http://gss.mof.gov.cn/gzdt/zhengcefabu/202002/t20200221_3472600.htm; http://gss.mof.gov.cn/gzdt/zhengcefabu/202002/P020200221548080947968.pdf.
213. MoF of China, http://gss.mof.gov.cn/gzdt/zhengcefabu/201908/P020190823604938915640.pdf.
214. MoF of China, http://gss.mof.gov.cn/gzdt/zhengcefabu/202002/P020200221548081402304.pdf.
215. MoF of China, Announcement of the Tariff Commission of the State Council on Excluding Market-Based Procurement of Products Subject to Tariffs from the United States and Canada Tariff, 17 February 2020, viewed at: http://www.gov.cn/zhengce/zhengceku/2020-02/18/content_5480381.htm; http://www.gov.cn/zhengce/zhengceku/2020-02/18/5480381/files/8bf2639310d24dda96dda90e590100b8.pdf.
216. The COVID-19 pandemic prompted several WTO Members to, initially, impose export restrictions on medical devices and products, and afterwards, increase subsidization. S.J. Evenett, Sicken Thy Neighbour: The Initial Trade Policy Response to COVID-19, *The World Economy*, Vol. 43, No. 4, 2020, pp. 828-839 https://doi.org/10.1111/twec.12954. B. Hoekman, P.C. Mavroidis, WTO Reform: Back to the Past to Build for the Future, *Global Policy*, Vol. 12, No. 3, 2021, pp. 5-12 https://doi.org/10.1111/1758-5899.12924.
217. MoF of China, Notice of the Customs Tariff Commission of the State Council on Not Implementing Tariff Measures against the United States and Canada on Imported Materials for the Prevention and Control of the Pneumonia Epidemic of New Coronavirus Infection, 1 February 2020, viewed at: http://www.gov.cn/zhengce/zhengceku/2020-02/01/content_5473754.htm.

tariffs from 15% to 7.5% on USD 125 billion of Chinese imports (List 4A);[218] some of which were exempted from tariffs, in March 2020, due to the Coronavirus pandemic, particularly medical devices and products such as masks, medical gloves, surgical gowns, sanitary wipes and soap.[219]

218. Notice of Modification of Section 301 Action: China's Acts, Policies, and Practices Related to Technology Transfer, Intellectual Property, and Innovation. US Federal Register, Vol. 85, No. 14, 22 January 2020, p. 3741.
219. Notice of Product Exclusions: China's Acts, Policies, and Practices Related to Technology Transfer, Intellectual Property, and Innovation. US Federal Register, Vol. 85, No. 47, 10 March 2020, pp. 13970-13972.

PART II History of Multilateral Trade Remedy Laws

Introduction: The Wealth of Nations and the Balance of Trade

> Consumption is the sole end and purpose of all production; and the interest of the producer ought to be attended to only so far as it may be necessary for promoting that of the consumer. The maxim is so perfectly self evident that it would be absurd to attempt to prove it. But in the mercantile system the interest of the consumer is almost constantly sacrificed to that of the producer; and it seems to consider production, and not consumption, as the ultimate end and object of all industry and commerce.[220]

The mercantilist system, criticized by Adam Smith in *The Wealth of Nations*, centred its political economy on the balance of trade, i.e., exceed of exportation over importation. Accordingly, a country's aim was to increase its quantity of gold and silver by turning the balance of trade in its favour. This commercial system arose from merchants, '*those who were supposed to understand trade*', who addressed their arguments to '*parliaments and to the councils of princes, to nobles and to country gentlemen,* (...) *who were conscious to themselves that they knew nothing about the matter*'. Since exportation might '*frequently be advantageous to the country*', prohibitions on exportation were recognized to be '*hurtful to trade*'. Along with the promotion of exportation, merchants advocated the restraint of import competition, whereby they could raise the price of their products domestically, as well as increase their production to sell more abroad. '*Merchants knew perfectly in what manner* [foreign trade] *enriched themselves* (...) *But to know in what manner it enriched the country was no part of their business.*'[221]

This is how the '*two great engines for enriching the country*' became, on the one hand, restraints upon importation, and on the other hand, encouragements to exportation. The only end and purpose of production was turning the balance of trade into a more advantageous one for the domestic country than for foreign countries. Identifying the wealth of a country with its balance of trade was an erroneous conception. Experience had demonstrated that '*foreign trade enriched the country*', and

220. A. Smith, *The Wealth of Nations*, [1776], 2000, p. 877.
221. As Adam Smith relates, export prohibition (of gold and silver) had 'anciently' been part of the policy of most of European nations. *Ibid.*, pp. 560-564, 587, 588.

the real wealth of a country would depend upon the abundance of consumable goods. '*It may take place in the whole globe of the earth, of which the wealth, population, and improvement may be either gradually increasing or gradually decaying.*' Therefore, the balance that reflects the prosperity of every country is, as Adam Smith elucidated, the balance of produce and consumption, which is '*entirely different*' from the balance of trade. '*If the exchangeable value of the annual produce, it has already been observed, exceeds that of the annual consumption, the capital of the society must annually increase in proportion to this excess.*' '*The balance of produce and consumption may be constantly in favour of a nation, though what is called the balance of trade be generally against it.*'[222]

The misconception of centring the political economy on the balance of trade prompted some European nations to enact regulations aimed at restraining imports – by either imposing high duties or absolute prohibition – as well as encouraging exports – through '*drawbacks*', '*bounties*', '*advantageous treaties of commerce*' and '*establishing colonies*'. These were the principal instruments whereby the mercantilist system attained a positive balance of trade. Rather than improving their business on their own, domestic manufacturers were the sole beneficiaries of these regulations, aimed at restraining import competition. Meanwhile, the liberty of the subject was '*plainly sacrificed to the futile interests of our merchants and manufacturers*, [who] *think it reasonable that they themselves should have the monopoly of the ingenuity of all their countrymen*'.[223]

For centuries, countries continued to enact regulations aimed at encouraging exportation and restricting importation by, *inter alia*, granting subsidies and refunding excise and taxes on exportation, as well as imposing tariffs and non-tariff barriers, such as anti-dumping and countervailing duties. In the late XIX century and at the beginning of the XX century, some attempts were made to change the view that economic policy should focus on the balance of trade. Nevertheless, it was not until after World War II that a general multilateral trade agreement was concluded.

The GATT was signed in 1947 by twenty-three countries (governing most of the world) to reciprocally reduce tariffs and obliged themselves to general clauses to refrain from a variety of trade-restrictive measures. GATT Contracting Parties shared the view that '*mistakes concerning economic policy were a major cause of the disasters that led to World War II*'. The first five GATT negotiation rounds exclusively focused on tariff reductions. To minimize the competition from imports, without the protection of tariffs, '*many domestic producer interests began turning to a variety (more than a thousand) of non-tariff barriers*'.[224] Consequently, while the progressive reduction of

222. *Ibid.*, pp. 560, 564, 587, 652, 653.
223. '*The laudable motive of all these regulations is to extend our own manufactures, not by their own improvement, but by the depression of those of all our neighbours, and by putting an end, as much as possible, to the troublesome competition of such odious and disagreeable rivals. Our master manufacturers think it reasonable that they themselves should have the monopoly of the ingenuity of all their countrymen.*' *Ibid.*, pp. 587, 588, 876.
224. The first five GATT negotiation rounds took place in Geneva, 1947; Annecy, 1949; Torquay, 1950; Geneva, 1956; and Dillon, 1961-1962. J.H. Jackson, *Restructuring the GATT System*, 1990, pp. 9, 10, 36, 37.

tariffs took place, GATT Contracting Parties significantly increased non-tariff barriers, particularly, anti-dumping and countervailing duties.

In the subsequent GATT negotiations rounds, the Kennedy Round (1962-1967) and Tokyo Round (1973-1979), special attention was given to anti-dumping and countervailing duties.[225] As a result of the Kennedy Round, (some) GATT Contracting Parties enacted the Agreement on Implementation of Article VI of the General Agreement on Tariffs and Trade, known as the 1967 Anti-dumping Code. The Tokyo Round (1973-1979) concluded with the enactment of the 1979 Anti-dumping Code and the first Agreement on Subsidies and Countervailing Measures, the Agreement on Interpretation and Application of Articles VI, XVI and XXIII of the General Agreement on Tariffs and Trade, hereinafter 'the SCM Code'.

The inclusion of trade remedy laws, whose purpose and end are to restrain imports, is inconsistent with the intention of GATT Contracting Parties in 1947, which was to reciprocally reduce tariffs and refrain from imposing trade-restrictive measures. The regression to buckle under the strain of domestic producers' interests (enhanced by the enactment of Codes and Agreements on trade remedies) reminds of Adam Smith's description of the mercantile system, where the interest of the consumer is '*constantly sacrificed to that of the producer*'.[226]

For a better understanding of the purpose and interaction of trade remedies, this second part offers a historical review of trade remedy laws from their origin until the last and current multilateral trade remedy laws. Since this book presents a multilateral perspective, the immeasurable subject of trade remedy laws in each of the different countries is not offered. Nonetheless, multilateral trade remedy laws were influenced by national legislation as well as trade remedy laws incorporated in bilateral or plurilateral trade agreements (and vice versa at a later stage); hence, the influence will be highlighted where necessary for the purpose of this book. Although this book mainly focuses on trade remedies, i.e., anti-dumping and countervailing duties, and safeguard measures, it cannot be pursued without an overview of the other side of the balance, i.e., subsidies, which encourage exports. Indeed, countervailing duties are precisely aimed at counteracting subsidies; thus, the latter are a 'sine qua non' element for the existence of former and are established under the same WTO Agreement.

This second part consists of three chronological chapters: First, the origins and evolution of trade remedy laws before the GATT; second, trade remedy laws during the preparatory work of the GATT and the ITO Charter; and third, their evolution through the history of the GATT until their latest (and current) version in the WTO Agreements on Subsidies and Countervailing Measures, Anti-dumping, and Safeguards.

225. J.H. Jackson, *Restructuring the GATT System*, 1990, p. 37.
226. A. Smith, *The Wealth of Nations*, [1776], 2000, p. 877.

Chapter 4

Origins of Trade Remedy Laws

This fourth chapter provides an overview of the history of trade remedy laws from the earliest provisions until their treatment in the preparatory work of the GATT and the ITO Charter in 1945. Section I focuses on the origin of countervailing duties, initially included in bilateral treaties (as an 'anti-bounty clause'), enacted in domestic legislation, and incorporated in the first multilateral trade agreement and institution, the Brussels Sugar Conventions of 1902, whereby prior authorization by a permanent commission was required. Section II presents the first anti-dumping law, enacted by Canada in 1904, as well as the expansion of anti-dumping and countervailing duty laws in the 1920s, which would later inspire the foundations of GATT Article VI. Section III offers an overview of the League of Nations Economic Conferences (whose works influenced the creation of the multilateral trading system), where subsidies, anti-dumping, and countervailing duties were part of the discussions, and the first safeguard provision was proposed.

I ORIGINS OF COUNTERVAILING DUTY LAWS

The origin of countervailing duty laws stems from two of the four means of the mercantilist system aimed at encouraging exportation: bounties and drawbacks. Bounties were given to beginning manufacturers or industries '*as supposed to deserve a particular favour*', with the intention that they sold their goods '*as cheap, or cheaper than their rivals in the foreign market*'.[227] During the XVII and XVIII centuries, export bounties were a prominent feature of the mercantilist system.[228] Drawbacks, whereby the excise or import duty was (partially or totally) reimbursed to the merchant upon exportation, seemed to be the most reasonable of the encouragements to exportation. By overturning the duty, drawbacks tend to preserve, as Adam Smith observed, the '*natural division and distribution of labor in the society*'. At their first institution in

---

227. A. Smith, *The Wealth of Nations*, [1776], 2000, pp. 588, 662.
228. J. Viner, *Dumping: A Problem in International Trade*, 1923, p. 163.

England in the XVII century, drawbacks were established by an English Act of Parliament, which imposed the then-only existing duties upon the importation of foreign goods, later called the '*Old Subsidy*'. This Act permitted merchants, '*English or alien*', to draw back half of the duty upon exportation. Since the imposition of the '*Old Subsidy*', when the importation of certain foreign goods exceeded what was necessary for home consumption, the entire duties were refunded upon exportation.[229]

Drawbacks were the most prominent means of exportation encouragement from the beginning of the XIX century. Nevertheless, they were then referred to as indirect export bounties, distinguishing between refunds of internal excise taxes and drawbacks of import duties. Indirect export bounties were very important for the European industries of sugar, flour-milling and spirits. Legislation of indirect export bounties was complex, and it was '*extremely difficult for outsiders to detect the existence and to ascertain the amount of a bounty*'. In particular, the case of sugar reflected the difficulty and the need to constantly amend drawbacks and refunds of excises to balance the system. If very strictly administered, the system may be too burdensome for the government and industry, while it may otherwise result in excessive refunds for producers.[230]

A First Countervailing Duty Provisions

Before a countervailing duty provision was created, the bilateral commercial treaty between France and the German Zollverein included an 'anti-bounty clause', whereby France committed not to refund excise duties. Subsequent European bilateral treaties in the 1860s incorporated it as a reciprocal commitment between the parties. In 1864, the Sugar Convention enshrined an 'anti-bounty clause', whereby parties committed not to grant excessive bounties. Its failure in the 1870s prompted some European countries to include a retaliatory measure to offset bounties under the 'anti-bounty clause' of their commercial treaties. In 1890, the world's first countervailing duty provision was enacted in domestic legislation. In 1902, it was incorporated in the first multilateral trade agreement, the Brussels Sugar Convention, requiring prior verification of the existence and estimation of the amount of the bounty by a supranational permanent commission.

229. This occurred with the English monopolies of the tobacco trade of the colonies of Virginia and Maryland. England consumed less than 15% of the tobacco it imported from the colonies. Therefore, in order to encourage exportation, the 'Old Subsidy' (importing duties) was totally drawn back if the exportation occurred within three years. Similar treatment was provided, by the time Adam Smith reported, to the sugar from the English monopolies of the West Indian Islands. To promote its exportation, all the importing duties were drawn back upon exportation within a year, while (only) half of the Old Subsidy was retained (or refunded) if exported within three years. A. Smith, *The Wealth of Nations*, [1776], 2000, pp. 654-656.

230. J. Viner, *Dumping: A Problem in International Trade*, 1923, pp. 163-165.

1 'Anti-bounty Clause' in Bilateral Treaties and the Sugar Convention of 1864

The earliest 'anti-bounty clause' was included in European bilateral commercial treaties, whereby countries committed not to refund excise duties or grant drawbacks in excess of the amount of internal taxes on products that were exported.[231] The first 'anti-bounty clause' was a unilateral commitment by France[232] in the bilateral treaty with the German Zollverein, signed in 1862.[233] France committed not to grant refunds on exportation above the (but the exact) amount of the excise taxes that had been imposed. This unilateral commitment did not apply to drawbacks, i.e., refunds of import duties, but only to refunds of excise taxes. The 'anti-bounty clause' became reciprocal in the treaty of 1865 between Austria and the German Zollverein, and applied to direct export bounties,[234] excessive refunds of excise taxes and drawbacks of import duties.[235]

Concerns about export bounties had spread in European countries. Britain was particularly eager to end the export bounties. For British colonies,[236] which exported sugar to Great Britain under a free trade regime, the competition of foreign-subsidized sugar in the British market represented a threat. In France, exporters of refined sugar were granted high (excessive) drawbacks from import duties on raw sugar, in order to compete with other European sugar-producing countries. This was at the expense of maintaining high prices on the domestic sugar market and '*draining the French treasury*

231. *Ibid.*, p. 166.
232. French Ministers of Commerce, Finance and Foreign Affair recommended in 1855 the abolition of sixteen prohibitions on imports and practically all those on exports, the reduction of duty on nineteen imports, and the admission of 241 articles duty-free. A.A. Iliasu, The Cobden-Chevalier Commercial Treaty of 1860, *The Historical Journal*, Vol. 14, No. 1, 1971, pp. 67-98 at 79 https://doi.org/10.1017/s0018246x00007408. Following the signature of the commercial treaty with Britain in 1860, France concluded commercial treaties '*with Belgium in 1861, the Zollverein in 1862 (effective in 1865), Italy in 1863, Switzerland in 1864, Sweden, Norway, Spain, and the Netherlands in 1865, and Austria in 1866*'. As in the Anglo-French Cobden-Chevalier Treaty, these agreements entailed significant new tariff reductions and included the most-favoured-nation clause, which '*proved to be a remarkably efficient instrument that encouraged other countries to join and also receive MFN treatment*'. D.A. Irwin, Multilateral and Bilateral Trade Policies in the World Trading System: An Historical Perspective, in J. De Melo, A. Panagariya, *New Dimensions in Regional Integration*, 1993, pp. 90-119 at 97.
233. Treaty of Commerce between France and Zollverein. British and Foreign State Papers, Vol. LV, 1864-1865, pp. 299-344.
234. Viner explains the distinction of a direct and an indirect official export bounty: '*In connection with official export bounties, the term direct is generally applied to open and acknowledged bounties and the term indirect to bounties which result from excessive refunds of excise taxes or excessive drawbacks upon import duties which had been collected on the exported commodities or the materials from which they were made.*' J. Viner, *Dumping: A Problem in International Trade*, 1923, p. 163, footnote 1.
235. *Ibid.*, p. 167.
236. '*In the mid-1840s and 1850s, Britain eliminated all tariff preferences for colonial supplies of timber, sugar, and other raw materials and also granted tariff autonomy to its self-governing colonies, allowing them to abolish preferences that favoured British manufactures.*' D.A. Irwin, Multilateral and Bilateral Trade Policies in the World Trading System: An Historical Perspective, in J. De Melo, A. Panagariya, *New Dimensions in Regional Integration*, 1993, pp. 90-119 at 98.

needlessly'.[237] Hence, French consumers were subsidizing the exportation of refined sugar.

Due to the ruinous subsidy competition between major sugar-growing countries in Europe, Great Britain, Belgium, the Netherlands and France signed, in 1864, the Sugar Convention, whereby they agreed on the elimination of excessive refunds of excises and drawbacks on sugar exports,[238] notwithstanding the abolition of bounties on the exportation of refined sugar was proposed.[239] '*This type of sugar regime permitted countries to protect their newly developing domestic beet sugar production without weakening or inhibiting the export potential of their domestic sugar-refining industry.*'[240]

The full duty on raw sugar was reimbursed on the exportation of refined sugar. Export bounties (drawbacks and refunds of excise taxes) were often excessive since they were based on an estimated yield of refined sugar, which exceeded the actual amount of raw sugar. As a result, drawbacks on the exportation of refined sugar exceeded the duty that had been paid on imported raw sugar. '*The method of estimating the yield was imperfect and incorrect, and also gave opportunity for fraud or deception*', particularly in France, where refiners exploited this method to obtain an export bounty.[241] Consequently, due to some members' failure to comply and the technical difficulty of determining the normal yield of refined from raw sugar, the Sugar Convention became inoperative; notwithstanding, it remained in effect until 1875.[242]

2 Countervailing Duty Provision in National Legislation

After the failure of the Sugar Convention, it became a common practice among some European countries to insert in their commercial treaties an 'anti-bounty clause' providing for the imposition of retaliatory measures, which proved to be ineffective and inadequate in the absence of an enforcement mechanism, i.e., a '*higher authority to convict them of the practice*'.[243] Meanwhile, in Great Britain, the House of Commons debated whether to countervail a bounty was consistent with free trade. Following a

237. G.A. Pigman, Hegemony and Trade Liberalization Policy: Britain and the Brussels Sugar Convention of 1902, *Review of International Studies*, Vol. 23, No. 2, 1997, pp. 185-210 at 194 https://doi.org/10.1017/s026021059700185x.
238. J. Viner, *Dumping: A Problem in International Trade*, 1923, pp. 178, 179.
239. G. Martineau, The Brussels Sugar Convention, *The Economic Journal*, Vol. 14, No. 53, 1 March 1904, pp. 34-46 at 34 https://doi.org/10.2307/2220737.
240. Sir Louis Mallet, Minutes of the International Sugar Conferences on Drawbacks of Refined Sugars established by the Convention of 8 November 1864, Vol. 27, LXV, 1973, p. 597. Cited in G.A. Pigman, Hegemony and Trade Liberalization Policy: Britain and the Brussels Sugar Convention of 1902, *Review of International Studies*, Vol. 23, No. 2, 1997, pp. 185-210 at 195 https://doi.org/10.1017/s026021059700185x.
241. *Ibid.* The practice of obtaining a bounty out of the drawback of sugar exportation spread to Germany and Austria. In these countries, the duty was not based on the weight of the roots, but on a very low estimate of their yields. G. Martineau, The Brussels Sugar Convention, *The Economic Journal*, Vol. 14, No. 53, 1 March 1904, pp. 34-46 at 35-38 https://doi.org/10.2307/2220737.
242. J. Viner, *Dumping: A Problem in International Trade*, 1923, p. 179.
243. *Ibid.*, p. 168.

declaration by the Foreign Office,[244] the Crown ruled that imposing countervailing duties against imports of subsidized sugar would violate the most-favoured-nation clause of its commercial treaties.[245]

The inefficiency of the 'anti-bounty clause' in commercial treaties prompted several countries to enact legislation on countervailing duties. The world's first countervailing duty provision was established in the US to offset export subsidies on imported refined sugar. After extensive debate regarding the protection of the US sugar industry '*from highly subsidized European competitors*',[246] the US Congress enacted the countervailing duty provision on sugar imports under the US Tariff Act of 1890.[247] On the other side of the Atlantic,[248] Belgium enacted, in 1892, the first countervailing duty provision affecting all imports having received export subsidies. Similarly, the US countervailing duty provision was extended to all products under the US Tariff Act of 1897,[249] as well as by other countries, such as India in 1899, Serbia in 1904, Spain in 1906, France and Japan in 1910, and Portugal in 1921.[250]

B Brussels Sugar Convention, 1902

After the failure of the Sugar Convention of 1864, export bounties and drawbacks on sugar increased in European beet sugar-producing countries to the point of creating a

244. G. Martineau, The Brussels Sugar Convention, *The Economic Journal*, Vol. 14, No. 53, 1 March 1904, pp. 34-46 at 37 https://doi.org/10.2307/2220737.
245. D.A. Irwin, Multilateral and Bilateral Trade Policies in the World Trading System: An Historical Perspective, in J. De Melo, A. Panagariya, *New Dimensions in Regional Integration*, 1993, pp. 90-119, footnote 15.
246. K.A. O'Brien, The Applicability of the United States Countervailing Duty Law to Imports from Nonmarket Economy Countries, *Fordham International Law Journal*, Vol. 9, No. 3, 1985, Article 4, pp. 596-633 at 601, footnote 15 (citing H. Kaye, P. Plaia, M. Hertzberg, *International Trade Practice*, 1981, § 13.04).
247. US Tariff Act of 1890 (McKinley Tariff Act), 26 Stat., 51st Congress, 1st Session, Ch. 1244, 1890, pp. 567, 584. On 5 July 1890, the International Union for the Publication of Customs Tariffs was signed by the Argentine Republic, Austria-Hungary, Belgium, Bolivia, Chili, the Independent State of the Congo, the Republic of Costa Rica, Denmark and her colonies, France and her colonies, Great Britain and sundry British colonies, British India, the Dominion of Canada, the colonies of West Australia, the Cape of Good Hope, Natal, New South Wales, New Zealand, Queensland, Tasmania, Newfoundland and Victoria, Greece, Guatemala, the Republic of Hayti, Italy and her colonies, Mexico, the Netherlands and their colonies, Nicaragua, Paraguay, Peru, Portugal and her colonies, Roumania, Russia, Salvador, the Kingdom of Siam, Spain and her colonies, Switzerland, Turkey, the US, Uruguay and Venezuela. US library of Congress, Digital Collection, United States Treaties and Other International Agreements, United States Treaty Series (1795-1945), compiled by Charles I. Bevans, viewed at: https://www.loc.gov/law/help/us-treaties/bevans/m-ust000001-0172.pdf.
248. After 1879, the European trade policy clime deteriorated: The Bismark tariff of 1879 increased protection (particularly, to agricultural products), which was followed by other countries, such as France, Belgium, Switzerland, and Sweden, which increased tariffs. '*Germany returned to a more liberal policy in the 1890s and, under Chancellor Caprivi, signed several treaties that again reduced tariffs on agricultural goods and textiles.*' D.A. Irwin, Multilateral and Bilateral Trade Policies in the World Trading System: An Historical Perspective, in J. De Melo, A. Panagariya, *New Dimensions in Regional Integration*, 1993, pp. 90-119 at 101-102.
249. This provision was maintained in the US Tariff Acts of 1909 and 1913. US Tariff Act of 1897, Ch. 11, § 5, 30 Stat. 151, 205, 1897. J. Viner, *Dumping: A Problem in International Trade*, 1923, p. 169.
250. *Ibid.*, p. 171.

race to the bottom between Germany and Austria, on the one hand, and France, on the other hand. In order to protect their revenues, Austria and Germany had substituted indirect bounties (drawbacks) with direct bounties on the exportation of raw and refined sugar. Since France had adopted the former German system and was granting 'overpowering' drawbacks on the exportation of refined sugar, both Germany and Austria doubled their direct bounties in 1896. In reply, France granted a direct bounty to export sugar while maintaining the excessive drawback.[251]

Direct bounties were also granted in Russia to export surplus stocks. Moreover, Russia protected its sugar industry with a high protective import duty. This system allowed manufacturers to maintain a high price for sugar consumption, exporting below cost price *'and yet make an abnormal profit on their total production'*. This *'modus operandi'*, which caused over-production, entering world markets below cost price and the *'destruction of the natural sources of supply'*, was called 'dumping'.[252]

In response to the Russian system, Austria and Germany increased their 'surtax' on (refined) sugar, i.e., *'excess of import duty over the consumption'*. Unlike the Russian system, consisting of combinations organized by the State, German and Austrian 'cartels' were formed by *'private combinations of sugar manufacturers and refiners'*. Nevertheless, their advantage was also considered a 'State bounty' since it depended on the imposition of *'an excessively high import duty'*. The surtax imposed by Germany and Austria was increased *'in excess of what was necessary for the mere purpose of protecting the industry in its own market against outside competition'*. This excessive 'surtax' allowed them to increase prices for domestic consumers enabling them to fund export bounties. This was also considered the *'art of dumping'*.[253]

In summary, countries increased their consumption taxes on sugar in order to fund export bounties. As a result, the stimulus that export bounties caused on production was offset. Bounties were losing their effectiveness even as a stimulus for exportation due to their widespread prevalence.[254] Concerned about this situation,[255] sugar-producing countries, except Russia, signed the Brussels Sugar Convention in 1902. Germany, Austria, Hungary, Belgium, Spain, France, Great Britain, Italy, the

251. G. Martineau, The Brussels Sugar Convention, *The Economic Journal*, Vol. 14, No. 53, 1 March 1904, pp. 34-46 at 38 https://doi.org/10.2307/2220737.
252. *Ibid.*, p. 39.
253. Cartel bounties could accurately be calculated by adding the surtax to the actual price obtained by cartels and deducting from the sum 'the normal price for home consumption' (consumption duty plus export price *'–the world's price-'*). In 1902, it was found that the Austrian cartel bounty on sugar was 21.45 crowns per 100 kg, obtained from a normal price for home consumption of 61.55 and an actual price of 83 crowns per 100kg: giving an annual cartel fund of GBP 2,957,868. The German cartel bounty was estimated at 7.9 crowns per 100kg, obtained from an actual price of 27.95 and a normal price for home consumption of 20.05 marks per 50 kg; granting an annual cartel fund of GBP 5,558,495. *Ibid.*, pp. 39, 40.
254. J. Viner, *Dumping: A Problem in International Trade*, 1923, pp. 180-181.
255. *'The peculiarly acute circumstances which were characteristic of the sugar industry at the time that the Convention, after fifty years of almost continuous controversy, was finally negotiated and ratified, are not likely to be duplicated in the same degree in any other industry, especially if there is no recrudescence of the bounty system.'* *Ibid.*, p. 186.

Netherlands and Sweden (which included Norway),[256] desiring to equalize the conditions of competition between beet and cane sugars from different sources, agreed to abolish bounties and limit the surtax on sugar.[257] '*There is no recorded instance, prior to the Brussels Sugar Convention of 1902, of a country abolishing an export bounty in order to carry out its treaty obligations.*'[258]

The Brussels Sugar Convention, consisting of twelve articles, provided for the elimination of direct and indirect bounties on production and exportation (Article I);[259] the limitation of the '*surtax*',[260] i.e., '*difference between the rate of duty or taxation to*

256. Concluding protocol of the Convention, included in B. Taylor, The Brussels Sugar Convention, *The North American Review*, Vol. 190, No. 646, 1909, pp. 347-358 at 352.
257. Brussels Sugar Convention, signed on 5 March 1902, effective from 1 September 1903 (Article X). US Department of State, Office of the Historian, Papers Relating to the Foreign Relations of the United States, with the Annual Message of the President Transmitted to Congress on 2 December 1902, pp. 80-84: viewed at: https://history.state.gov/historicaldocuments/frus1902/pg_80; https://history.state.gov/historicaldocuments/frus1902/d70.
258. J. Viner, *Dumping: A Problem in International Trade*, 1923, p. 168.
259. Article I of the Brussels Sugar Convention, specified the instances in which domestic legislation may result in such advantages:

    (a) Direct bounties granted to exports;
    (b) Direct bounties granted to production.
    (c) Total or partial exemptions from taxation granted for a part of the manufactured output;
    (d) Profits derived from surplusages of output;
    (e) Profits derived from the exaggeration of the drawback;
    (f) Advantages derived from any surtax in excess of the rate fixed by article 3.

    Bounties under (c), (d), and (e) 'are practically interdependent' since a combination of the three might create a bounty: by estimating the yield ('output') under the actually obtained would result in excess of yield ('surplusages of output') (d), which would create a 'total or partial exemption from taxation granted for a part of the manufactured output' (c). Nevertheless, only a drawback of the total amount of the duty would create a bounty. For this reason, under Article II of the Brussels Sugar Convention, contracting parties bound themselves to submit to 'bond regime', i.e., without paying any duty. This prohibited the payment of a duty based on the 'estimated yield', which would prevent granting drawbacks on exportation of sugar. The bounty defined under paragraph (f) was the result of a compromise after '*a critical state of the negotiations*'. Great Britain was in favour of defining a cartel as '*advantages derived from any surtax*'. Nevertheless, only a limitation of the surtax, established under Article III, was accepted. Allowing a fixed rate in excess of the limitation of the surtax consisted of an exception to the abolition of all bounties on production and exportation. It permitted any bounty obtained with the surtax established (under Article III). G. Martineau, The Brussels Sugar Convention, *The Economic Journal*, Vol. 14, No. 53, 1 March 1904, pp. 34-46 at 41, 42 https://doi.org/10.2307/2220737.
260. Article III fixed the surtax at a maximum of 6 francs per 100kg on refined sugar, and 5.5 francs per 100kg on other sugars. This provision on the limitation of the surtax might be viewed as a tariff binding, consisting of a fixed rate, common to all countries, above the domestic tax on sugar. The provision on the limitation of the 'surtax' seems to be the first multilateral step towards national treatment (GATT Article III). The intention of limiting the amount of 'surtax' and defining a bounty based on the excess of 'surtax' stemmed from the idea that 'dumping' was encouraged by high tariff protection in the domestic market, '*especially in cases where the public authorities impose, provoke, or encourage coalitions among producers of sugar*'. '*As explained in the text of the unratified Convention of 1898, from which the surtax provision in the 1902 Convention was taken. Cf. Great Britain, Miscellaneous Papers No.5, 1902 (Cd. 1013) p. 19. Cf. also, C. S. Griffin, The Sugar Industry and Legislation in Europe, Quarterly Journal of Economics, XVII, 24.*' J. Viner, *Dumping: A Problem in International Trade*, 1923, pp. 181-183.

which foreign sugars are subjected and that imposed on the home product' (Article III);[261] and the imposition of a '*special duty*' (countervailing duty) on, or the total prohibition of, imported sugar to offset the effect of bounties (Article IV). A bounty was considered to be half of the amount exceeding the 'surtax'.[262] To offset the bounty, direct or indirect, countries committed themselves to impose a 'special duty' (countervailing duty) that '*shall not be less than the amount of the bounties* (...) *granted in the country of origin*' (Article IV). Countries incorporated the most-favoured-nation clause, by which they committed to reciprocally bind their lowest import tariff (rate) on sugar (Article V). Importantly, prior verification of the existence and estimation of the amount of bounties was required by a supranational permanent commission, whose decisions were binding on the members of the Convention.

The Brussels Sugar Convention was not only the first multilateral trade agreement, but also established the framework for the first supranational trade institution. The permanent commission, composed of delegates of 'high contracting parties', was entrusted with the compliance and enforcement of the Convention, and exercised as an advisory body in case disputes arose. Its decisions were taken by a vote of the majority, each member disposing of one vote, and shall come into effect within two months.[263] An appeal process from the commission's decision could be promoted within eight days; the final decision by the commission, delivered within a month from the date of the appeal, shall be 'executory' within two months. Attached to it, a permanent bureau was responsible for compiling, translating and publishing legislation and statistics regarding sugar worldwide (Article VII).

The Brussels Sugar Convention was 'successful in attaining its objectives, and was a distinct achievement in the difficult task of establishing international control of an economic problem essentially international in character'. Its members had to decide on its termination or extension in 1908 and 1912. In the first deliberation, Great Britain agreed on the renewal on the condition of being 'relieved of the obligation of imposing countervailing duties or prohibition on bounty-fed sugar', but committed not to

---

261. The 'surtax' provision of the Brussels Sugar Convention served as a model and was incorporated in the Indian national legislation and the British South Africa Customs Union. In 1902, India enacted a 'special duty' (countervailing duty) on imports of sugar imported from countries which had exceeded the 'surtax' established in the Brussels Sugar Convention (on refined sugar, 6 francs, and on other sugars, 5.5 francs per 100kg). The countervailing duty was established not to exceed the bounty (which was defined as half of the amount of the excess of the 'surtax'). In 1903, the British South Africa Customs Union provided for the application of the Brussels Sugar Convention countervailing duty provision to non-members, i.e., the imposition of a 'special duty' on imported sugar, equal to the amount of the subsidy received, from a country that was not member of the Brussels Sugar Convention. *Ibid.*, pp. 170, 171.
262. As an illustration, if the difference between foreign and domestic taxes on refined sugar, i.e., the 'surtax', is 11 francs per 100kg; then the excess over the limited amount established under the Brussels Sugar Convention (6 francs per 100kg on refined sugar) will be 5 francs per 100kg. According to the Convention, half of the excess, 2.5 francs per 100kg, was considered a bounty (this concept of half of the duty may come from the English Act establishing the Old Subsidy, which allowed for the drawback of half of the duties). *See* A. Smith, *The Wealth of Nations*, [1776], 2000, p. 655. Therefore, according to the Brussels Sugar Convention, a bounty was considered to be any of the instances as well as half of the (excess of) 'surtax' above the binding fixed rate.
263. J. Viner, *Dumping: A Problem in International Trade*, 1923, p. 182.

re-export products made by subsidized sugar to other members of the Convention. In the second debate in 1912, alleging to be injurious to its sugar-using industries and consumers, Great Britain withdrew from all the obligations under the Convention, yet committed to respect the fundamental provisions.[264]

Willing to grant higher tariff protection to their sugar industries, Italy and France withdrew from the Brussels Sugar Convention in 1915 and 1918, respectively. In 1918, Great Britain granted preferential treatment to imports of colonial sugar, as part of its imperial preference policy, but contrary to its former commitments under the Convention. In 1920, the Netherlands also withdrew from the Convention, which became ineffective in the wake of World War I due to, *inter alia*, changes in the sovereignty of some sugar-growing regions, and the expulsion of Germany from the Convention in 1919, provided for in the Treaty of Versailles, which established the League of Nations.

II ORIGINS OF ANTI-DUMPING LAWS

The origin of dumping comes from the practice of granting export bounties. Adam Smith observed that entrepreneurs privately agreed to grant export bounties, so-called unofficial bounties.[265] British manufacturers were first charged with this practice during the Industrial Revolution, although it was not yet referred to as 'dumping'. Initially, these practices were counteracted with countervailing duties; anti-dumping laws were later enacted.[266] At the beginning of the XX century, as 'dumping' became worldwide viewed as a problem in international trade, the first anti-dumping law was developed by Canada in 1904.

A Canada's 'Dumping Clause', 1904

The enactment of the anti-dumping law by Canada has been attributed to charges of dumping against the US Steel Corporation into the Canadian market.[267] By the end of the 1890s,[268] the US had overtaken the UK as the largest producer of iron and steel in

264. *Ibid.*, pp. 183-186.
265. '*A bounty upon exportation, by enabling* ["*merchants and manufacturers*"] *to send abroad the surplus part, and to keep up the price of what remains in the home market, effectually prevents* ["*that the home market should be overstocked with their goods, an event which a bounty upon production might sometimes occasion*"].' A. Smith, *The Wealth of Nations*, [1776], 2000, p. 678.
266. J. Viner, *Dumping: A Problem in International Trade*, 1923, pp. 36, 192.
267. *Ibid.*, p. 85.
268. '*The United States, which had lagged in oceangoing steamship development, was given a jump forward by the new steel navy of the 1880s, and a parallel improvement of specialized steel production. Varied manufacturers continued to be aided by tariffs.*' B. Hindle, S. Lubar, *Engines of Change, The American Industrial Revolution, 1790-1860*, 1986, p. 275. '*In contrast to Britain, both the United States and Germany were avowedly protectionist; by 1880 both national markets were surrounded by high tariff walls. In addition, in both of these countries, highly organized and sophisticated anticompetitive industrial combinations were formed for the purpose of reducing competition and exploiting their partial or complete monopoly power. In the United States, so-called "trusts" regulated output and prices in many major manufacturing industries, and in Germany, manufacturing was dominated by kartells (cartels) in which price and output restrictions were maintained through legally enforceable contractual commitments. It was the*

the world. In 1901, the US Steel Corporation was 'enormously profitable',[269] and became the first US '*billion-dollar corporation*',[270] controlling 60% of the US steel capacity.[271] The general policy among worldwide manufacturers of the time was exporting at prices lower than domestic prices.[272] In the case of the US Steel Corporation, one of its founders and chairman maintained that the company '*never delivered products abroad for less than the cost to the domestic customer at mill*'. Importantly, the export prices used were '*f.o.b. the mill*'.[273] Therefore, transportation costs were not taken into account in the comparison between export and domestic prices.

Canadian steel manufacturers, who already received bounties,[274] requested further import protection.[275] The Minister of Finance proposed the enactment of a 'dumping clause', the Canadian Bill No. 172, amending the Customs Tariff of 1897, which was first debated by the Committee on Ways and Means, approved by the

standard practice of both the American trusts and the German kartells to engage in large-scale dumping as a deliberate export strategy'. T. Howell, D. Ballantine, Dumping: Still a Problem in International Trade in National Research Council, in C. Wessner (ed.), *International Friction and Cooperation in High-Technology Development and Trade: Papers and Proceedings*, 1997, pp. 325-377 at 332.

269. '*In 1902, the first full year of operation, US Steel produced two-thirds of all US semi-finished steel, similar percentages of all rails and tin plate, virtually all wire, and typically lower percentages of other fabricated products. (...) The financial effects of the consolidation suggest it was enormously profitable*'. J.C. Carr, W. Taplin, *History of the British Steel Industry*, 1962, p. 164. Cited in D.O. Parsons, J.R. Edward, The United States Steel Consolidation: The Creation of Market Control, *Journal of Law and Economics*, Vol. 18, No. 1, 1975, pp. 181-220 at 1 https://doi.org/10.1086/466810.
270. The US Steel Corporation '*represented the culmination of the first great merger wave and the height of J.P. Morgan's influence over the American economy*'. C. Reback, Merger for Monopoly: The Formation of US Steel, *Essays in Economic and Business History*, Vol. 25, 2007, pp. 105-117 at 105.
271. D.O. Parsons, J.R. Edward, The United States Steel Consolidation: The Creation of Market Control, *Journal of Law and Economics*, Vol. 18, No. 1, 1975, pp. 181-220 at 181 https://doi.org/10.1086/466810.
272. '*An investigator for the British Board of Trade reported in 1903 that British manufacturers using steel as their raw material had greatly profited from the avail ability of German and American steel at dumping prices, and at some times were able to operate successfully only because of purchases of dumped materials. A curious case of this sort was that of the Welsh tin-plate industry (...) was able to hold other markets and to strengthen its position in its domestic market because of the availability at low prices of its important raw material, steel, which the United States Steel Corporation also produced, and which it dumped in South Wales.*' J. Viner, *Dumping: A Problem in International Trade*, 1923, p. 135.
273. W.L.C., Domestic and Export Prices of Steel. Testimony of Chairman Gary of the United States Steel Corporation, *The Iron Age*, Vol. 77, No. 16, 19 April 1906, pp. 1324-1328, viewed at Internet Archive: https://archive.org/details/sim_chiltons-iron-age_1906-04-19_77_16/page/1324/mode/2up?view=theater.
274. Official Report of the Debates of the House of Commons of the Dominion of Canada, Forth Session-Ninth Parliament, 4 Edward VII, Vol. LXVIII, Ottawa 1-10 August 1904, col. 8871.
275. In the previous decade, according to Richard Blain, one of the members of the House of Commons (from Peel), the Canadian Customs Tariff Act of 1897 had lowered tariffs for certain products, while increased tariffs of others. It introduced a preference tariff of 12.5% for imports from England, which was raised to 25% in 1898, and to 33.33% in 1900, and few years later, provided for a special surtax against German imports. *Ibid.*, cols. 8861, 8867.

Parliament, agreed by the Senate and assented by the Crown.[276] At the debate of the 'dumping clause' in the House of Commons, only the representative of Cape Breton, a federal district where two steel industries sat, argued in favour of the new provision, claiming that '*while there were tariffs on everything else there was no tariff on steel rails*'.[277] Since the 'dumping clause' was '*impossible for anyone* [else] *to understand*', it did not encounter opposition in the House of Commons.[278]

The 'dumping clause' established the imposition of a 'special duty' on imported like products,[279] of a class or kind also produced in Canada, at an export price (i.e., selling price) less than the fair market value. The 'special duty' was imposed over the established ordinary customs duty. It could neither exceed the difference between the selling price and fair market value (i.e., the margin of dumping) nor 50% of the ordinary customs duty established for that article.[280] In 1907, Canada amended the dumping clause to establish a maximum of 15% anti-dumping duty for all products, and excluded certain products from the measure.[281]

276. Canadian Bill (No. 172) was read, amended and passed on 9 August 1904; agreed, without amendment, by the Senate, and received royal assent on 10 August 1904. Votes and Proceedings of the House of Commons of the Dominion of Canada, Fourth session of the Ninth Parliament, from the 10 March to 10 August 1904, pp. 820, 918, 923, viewed at: https://parl.canadiana.ca/browse/eng/c/cproc/09-4.
277. Statement by Alexander Johnston, who represented Cape Breton. Official Report of the Debates of the House of Commons of the Dominion of Canada, Forth Session-Ninth Parliament, 4 Edward VII, Vol. LXVIII, Ottawa 1-10 August 1904, col. 8835.
278. Mr. Blain's critique of the decision of the Minister of Finance to pass the 'dumping clause': '*My hon. friend is evidently not satisfied because he wants a special legislation for steel industry. I make the statement the principle of stability of tariff has gone to the winds with all the other principles of hon. gentlemen opposite. Surely the hon. the Finance Minister will never plume himself again on the stability of tariff. I am positive he will not after he gets a proper understanding of this dumping clause.*' *Ibid.*, cols. 8861, 8867, 8868.
279. The 'dumping clause' was applied on '*imported round rolled wire rods not over three-eighths of an inch in diameter*'. Votes and Proceedings of the House of Commons of the Dominion of Canada, Fourth session of the Ninth Parliament, from the 10 March to 10 August 1904, p. 534.
280. Exceptionally, for certain products, the duty could not exceed 15% ad valorem. The provision was amended on 8 August 1904 to establish a temporary exemption for products that were not produced in Canada '*in substantial quantities and offered for sale to all purchasers on equal terms*'. Official Report of the Debates of the House of Commons of the Dominion of Canada, Forth Session-Ninth Parliament, 4 Edward VII, Vol. LXVIII, Ottawa 1-10 August 1904, cols. 8844-8845.
281. '*In the case of articles exported to Canada of a class or kind made or produced in Canada, if the export or actual selling price to an importer in Canada is less than the fair market value of the same article when sold for home consumption in the usual and ordinary course in the country whence exported to Canada at the time of its exportation to Canada, there shall, in addition to the duties otherwise established, be levied, collected, and paid on such article, on its importation into Canada, a special duty (or dumping duty) equal to the difference between the said selling price of the article for export and the said fair market value thereof for home consumption; and such special duty (or dumping duty) shall be levied, collected, and paid on such article, although it is not otherwise dutiable. Provided that the said special duty shall not exceed 15 per cent ad valorem in any case; Provided also that the following goods shall be exempt from such special duty, viz: (a) Goods whereon the duties otherwise established are equal to 50 per cent ad valorem; (b) Goods of a class subject to excise duty in Canada; (c) Sugar refined in the United Kingdom; (d) Binder twine or twine for harvest binders manufactured from New Zealand hemp, istle, or tampico fiber, sisal grass, or sunn, or a mixture of any two or more of them, of single ply*

The 'special duty' (anti-dumping duty) differed from an ordinary customs duty (tariff) in several aspects. First, it was left at the discretion of the '*satisfaction of the Minister of Customs*';[282] therefore, while tariffs had to be approved by the Parliament, agreed by the Senate and required royal assent, the 'special duty' was imposed at the discretion of the Minister of Customs. Second, the 'special duty' was imposed over tariffs, thus increasing the import duty above what had previously been agreed in Parliament. Third, it allowed discrimination among imports of the same kind, hence, the possibility to please certain domestic industries or companies at the government's discretion. Fourth, and not less relevant, it was a flexible mechanism to increase revenue at the expense of domestic consumers, which was already a concern in the Canadian Parliament.[283]

Notably, some Canadian steel-using industries complained about the anti-dumping duties when importing steel from the US. In practice, Customs officials were charged for often imposing anti-dumping duties that were too high by using inaccurate or obsolete foreign market price lists, as well as for occasionally imposing anti-dumping duties on Canadian importers although they demonstrated '*by affidavits from the foreign manufacturers and letters from dealers in the export market that the invoice price was the fair market value in the country of export*'. The repeal of the dumping clause was requested by the Toronto Board of Trade, which represented the interests of importers, alleging it was impossible to equitably administer, an encouragement for fraud, '*unwarranted restriction upon the freedom of purchase at the best price obtainable*', and '*injustice to the honest importer*'. Furthermore, Canadian consumers complained about it for depriving them of the benefit of foreign bargains.[284]

This historical overview of the enactment of the first anti-dumping law in Canada illustrates that the raison d'être of anti-dumping laws is no other than politically motivated protectionism.[285] The 'dumping clause' allowed the Canadian government to escape from raising tariffs while succumbing to manufacturers' pressure and increasing the requested protection for their industries. In essence, it was a political manoeuvre to disguise an increase in import duties (over the established tariff) through a methodology not easily understood, which additionally dissipated opposition in the Parliament.

---

and measuring not exceeding 600 feet to the pound.' Statutes of Canada, 1907, 6-7 Edward VII, Vols I-II, p. 134. Cited in J. Viner, *Dumping: A Problem in International Trade*, 1923, pp. 193-195.

282. Official Report of the Debates of the House of Commons of the Dominion of Canada, Forth Session-Ninth Parliament, 4 Edward VII, Vol. LXVIII, Ottawa 1-10 August 1904, col. 8844.
283. *Ibid.*, col. 8869.
284. Edward Porritt, Sixty Years of Protection in Canada, p. 409; W.J.A. Donald, *The Canadian Iron and Steel Industry*, p. 185; US Tariff Commission, Information concerning Dumping and Unfair Competition, p. 30; *Canadian Annual Review*, 1906, p. 584. T. Globe, *Why Houses Are Dear*, 23 May 1910. Cited in J. Viner, *Dumping: A Problem in International Trade*, 1923, pp. 203, 204.
285. '*There is little in that history to suggest that anti-dumping ever had a scope more particular than protecting home producers from import competition, and there is much to suggest that such protection was its intended scope.*' M. Finger, The Origins and Evolution of Antidumping Regulation, Policy Research Working Paper Series 783, *The World Bank*, 1991, p. 1.

B Anti-dumping Laws in Other Countries

Following the Canadian enactment of the first worldwide 'dumping clause', other countries enacted anti-dumping provisions: New Zealand, in 1905; Australia, in 1906; the Union of South Africa and Newfoundland, in 1914.[286] Main elements of the Canadian 'dumping clause' were included in the US, the Antidumping Act of 1921, which would later be incorporated in the GATT; notwithstanding, prior attempts to legislate against foreign dumping occurred, notably in 1913 and 1916.

In 1913, an anti-dumping provision similar to the Canadian 'dumping clause' was proposed to be included in the US Tariff Bill of 1913, which significantly lowered tariffs. Nevertheless, the US Senate Committee on Finance rejected it on the grounds that it would allow an '*unfriendly administration*' to raise by 15% the duties.[287] Therefore, the US Tariff Bill of 1913 did not include the anti-dumping provision, but maintained the countervailing duty provision against all subsidized imports from the US Tariff Act of 1897.

In 1916, following allegations against likely dumping after World War I by German chemical cartels, US industries increased their demands for protection against '*unfair foreign competition*'. In order to avoid opening tariffs for revision, the US administration under the Presidency of W. Wilson enacted an anti-dumping provision, which was included in the Revenue Act of 1916. The provision made unlawful the importation of products at a substantially lower price than the actual market value in the country of production, or of another country where they were commonly exported after adding import costs, provided it was intended to prevent injury, destruction, or the establishment of an industry in the US.[288] Despite the fact that the anti-dumping provision in the Revenue Act of 1916 remained in force until 2004,[289] it was only

286. The Australian anti-dumping law was mainly directed to protect Australian industries from US trusts' export practices. '*When the measure was introduced in the Australian Parliament critics pointed out that under so comprehensive a definition of unfair competition the penalties could be applied to almost any imports on the ground that they would lead to a diminution or cessation of Australian production of similar goods, or to Australian goods.*' J. Viner, *Dumping: A Problem in International Trade*, 1923, pp. 90, 204-207.
287. US 63 Congress, 1st Session, Senate Report 80, p. 3.
288. According to Viner, the anti-dumping provision did not add anything to the Sherman Antitrust Act of 1890, except making unlawful the importer's act and intent in predatory dumping, and making unnecessary to prove conspiracy. Previously, there had been an attempt to extend anti-trust rules under the Sherman Antitrust Act of 1890 to US imports throughout the enactment of Section 73 of the Wilson Tariff Act of 1894. Nevertheless, in 1909, in the case *American Banana Co. v. United Fruit Co. 213 US 347*, the US Supreme Court rejected the extraterritorial application of the Sherman Act of 1890 by ruling that a '*conspiracy in this country to do acts in another jurisdiction does not draw to itself those acts and make them unlawful if they are permitted by the local law*'. Since Section 73 of the Wilson Tariff Act of 1894 was not invoked in the case, Viner described the provision to be ineffective, as well as the anti-dumping provision in the Revenue Act of 1916. J. Viner, *Dumping: A Problem in International Trade*, 1923, pp. 240-244, 248.
289. In 2004, the US repealed it, following the recommendations of the WTO Appellate Body report on disputes *US – Anti-dumping Act of 1916* (DS136 and DS162, complainants: the European Communities and Japan, respectively). WTO document DS136/AB/R and DS162/AB/R, 28 August 2000.

invoked in one lawsuit, *Matsushita Electrical Industry Company v. Zenith Radio Corporation*, which was finally dismissed in 1970.[290]

In the years following World War I, various countries increased tariffs and granted subsidies to assist domestic industries and promote exports. Protectionist pressures led to the failure of the Brussels Sugar Convention and spread of anti-dumping and countervailing duty laws. In 1921, Canada, Australia, New Zealand, the Union of South Africa and Newfoundland amended their anti-dumping provisions. In the same year, Great Britain and the US enacted 'new and comprehensive' anti-dumping laws.[291]

Canada amended the methodology for determining the 'fair market value', by including that '*such value in no case to be lower than the wholesale price thereof at such time or place*'. The 'fair market value' would, in no case, be lower than the cost of production plus a reasonable profit, which would be decided by the Minister of Customs. In this amendment, products imported below the cost of production were subject to anti-dumping duties even in the absence of price discrimination, i.e., margin of dumping.[292] A further amendment in 1921 eliminated the requirement for imports to be below the cost of production,[293] granting the Minister of Customs the discretion to value products '*imported under such conditions as prejudicially to affect the interest of the Canadian producers*'.[294]

Following the US elections in 1920,[295] further demands for protection by US industries prompted the US to enact a new anti-dumping law. Inspired by the Canadian anti-dumping law, the US Congress approved the Antidumping Act of 1921 under Title II of the US Emergency Tariff Act of 1921.[296] The Chairman of the Ways and Means Committee advocated for its needs on the grounds of the '*ineffectiveness and the inadequacy of the antidumping provision in the Revenue Act of 1916*'. A report of a minority of the Senate Committee on Finance recommended against the adoption of the Antidumping Act of 1921, alleging it '*would entail serious administrative difficulty and expense, that it might serve completely or partially to destroy the free list in the ordinary tariff, and that by raising the prices of imported goods, it would perpetuate the high cost of living*'.[297]

290. *Matsushita Electrical Industry Co., Ltd. v. Zenith Radio Corp.*, 475 US574, 1986.
291. J. Viner, *Dumping: A Problem in International Trade*, 1923, p. 192.
292. Revised Statutes of Canada, 1906, Section 40, p. 48, as amended on 4 June 1921.
293. The modification was included in the Customs Act instead of the anti-dumping clause. J. Viner, *Dumping: A Problem in International Trade*, 1923, p. 200.
294. The Minister of Customs was permitted to value products without regarding other provisions of the Customs Act. J. Viner, *Dumping: A Problem in International Trade*, 1923, pp. 237, 238.
295. In 1921, the US Congress passed the temporary Emergency Tariff Act, and a year later the Fordney-McCumber Tariff Act of 1922. The latter raised tariffs above the level established in 1913 as well as '*authorized the president to raise or lower a given tariff rate by 50% in order to even out foreign and domestic production costs*'. US Department of State Office of the Historian, Protectionism in the Interwar Period, viewed at: https://history.state.gov/milestones/1921-1936/protectionism.
296. US 67th Congress, 1st Session, Ch. 14, pp. 11-15, viewed at: https://www.loc.gov/law/help/statutes-at-large/67th-congress/c67.pdf; J. Viner, *Dumping: A Problem in International Trade*, 1923, p. 258.
297. US 66th Congress, 2nd Session, House Representatives, p. 510.

After some modifications by the Senate Committee on Finance, the Antidumping Act of 1921 entrusted the Secretary of Treasury to conduct investigations to determine whether a domestic industry was being – or likely to be – injured or was prevented from being established due to the importation of products at less than its 'fair value', and publish the findings. Otherwise, the 'appraiser' was entrusted to report any suspicious case of dumping (i.e., whether the exporter's sales price was less than the foreign market value or, in its absence, than the cost of production), notify the Secretary of Treasury and '*withhold his appraisement report to the collector as to such merchandise*' until further order by the Secretary of Treasury, or until the publication of the finding.[298] If the appraiser had not reported to the collector before the finding was public, an anti-dumping duty was collected in addition to import duties imposed by law. The anti-dumping duty had to be equal to the difference between the foreign market value (or, in the absence of that value, its cost of production) and the exporter's sale price.[299]

The Antidumping Act of 1921 provided for the right of appeal and protest relating to anti-dumping duties, in particular to '*the purchase price, the exporter's sales price, and the action of the collector in assessing the special dumping*', as well as to those established for customs duties. In such appeals, the Act maintained the jurisdiction, powers and duties of '*the general appraisers, the Board of General Appraisers, and the Court of Customs Appeals*'.[300] The US Antidumping Act of 1921 inspired the anti-dumping provision of the US Suggested Charter of 1946, which was negotiated and redrafted during the preparatory work of the GATT and the ITO Charter, and would become the anti-dumping provision under GATT Article VI.

While most countries included countervailing duties in their anti-dumping legislation, the US maintained its countervailing duty provision in the statute regarding subsidies, as regulated in the US Tariff Act.[301] In the case of British South Africa, in 1914, and New Zealand, in 1921, their anti-dumping laws included a provision for the imposition of discretionary countervailing duties against official direct and indirect subsidies on production and exportation. In these countries, the tendency in the 1920s was to broaden the scope of anti-dumping laws in order to cover both official and unofficial bounties.[302]

The US Tariff Act of 1922 enlarged the scope of countervailing duty provision in order to cover both production and export subsidies as well as affect both official and

298. Section 201 'Dumping investigation' of the US Antidumping Act of 1921, Title II of the Emergency Tariff Bill, at US 67th Congress, 1st Session, Ch. 14, p. 11, viewed at: https://www.loc.gov/law/help/statutes-at-large/67th-congress/c67.pdf.
299. Section 202 'Special dumping duty' and Section 209 'Duties of appraisers' of the US Antidumping Act of 1921, Title II of the Emergency Tariff Bill, at US 67th Congress, 1st Session, Ch. 14, pp. 12 and 15, viewed at: https://www.loc.gov/law/help/statutes-at-large/67th-congress/c67.pdf.
300. Section 210 'Appeals and protests' of the US Antidumping Act of 1921, Title II of the Emergency Tariff Bill, at US 67th Congress, 1st Session, Ch. 14, p. 15, viewed at: https://www.loc.gov/law/help/statutes-at-large/67th-congress/c67.pdf.
301. J.H. Jackson, *World Trade and the Law of GATT (A Legal Analysis of the General Agreement on Tariffs and Trade)*, 1969, p. 404.
302. J. Viner, *Dumping: A Problem in International Trade*, 1923, pp. 171, 187.

unofficial subsidies (i.e., government and non-governmental sources).[303] It did not include injury to the domestic industry as a (previous) requirement to impose countervailing duties,[304] and as amended by the Tariff Act of 1930, laid the foundations of the GATT countervailing duty provision, except for the injury requirement.

The US countervailing duty provision under the Tariff Act of 1930 and the US Antidumping Act of 1921 inspired Article 11 of the US Suggested Charter of 1946, governing anti-dumping and countervailing duties, which served as a framework for GATT Article VI in 1947. The expansion of anti-dumping and countervailing duty laws at the beginning of the 1920s influenced the international economic conferences that were held by the League of Nations.

III LEAGUE OF NATIONS ECONOMIC CONFERENCES

The work of the League of Nations was fundamental for the development of the multilateral trading system after World War II. During the 1920s, the League of Nations held conferences in Brussels, 1920; Genoa, 1922; on the Simplification of Customs Formalities, 1923; Geneva, 1927; and three conferences on the Abolition of Import and Export Prohibitions and Restrictions, 1927-1929. The Economic Conference held in London in 1933 included a US proposal for a multilateral agreement, which incorporated a 'safeguarding provision' that can be considered the origin of the safeguard measure. The studies produced by the League of Nations would later influence the creation of the multilateral trading system.

A Conferences in the 1920s

1 Brussels, 1920; Genoa, 1922; Simplification of Customs Formalities, 1923

In 1920, the League of Nations organized the Brussels Economic and Financial Conference,[305] whose '*Committee on Trade was a failure*'. One of the '*six impeccable resolutions*' that it produced reaffirmed the objections against '*artificial trade barriers and price discrimination*'.[306] An International Economic Conference was held in Genoa in 1922 to establish the principles on which the multilateral trading system should be based. One of the three commissions was appointed to deal with economic and

303. *Ibid.*, p. 169.
304. US Tariff Act of 1922, Ch. 356, § 303, 42 Stat. 858, 935-936, 1922.
305. After its creation by the Peace Treaty of Versailles in 1919, the League of Nations held two conferences before the Genoa Conference in 1922: The Conference on International Co-operation in Statistics in London in 1919 and the International Financial Conference in Brussels in 1920. H. Aufricht, *Guide to League of Nations Publications. A Bibliographical Survey of the Work of the League, 1920-1947*, 1951, pp. 217-218.
306. H.A. Siepmann, The International Financial Conference at Brussels, *The Economic Journal*, Vol. 30, No. 120, December 1920, pp. 436-459, p. 449 https://doi.org/10.2307/2222869.

commercial matters.[307] Based on the report by the 'London Experts', the economic commission adopted some recommendations and submitted them to the Conference for adoption, including the establishment of the non-discrimination principle, i.e., most-favoured nation (Article 9) and national treatment (Articles 5 and 15). On the matter of dumping (Article 11), the commission recommended *'that the League of Nations should undertake at an early date an enquiry on the subject'*.[308]

In 1923, sponsored by the League of Nations, the International Conference on Customs Formalities reached the International Convention Relating to the Simplification of Customs Formalities, which covered many of the subjects included later in the GATT.[309] *'Recognising that the maintenance of world peace depends largely upon the principles on which the economic policies of nations are framed and executed'*, the League of Nations initiated in 1925 the preparatory work for the World Economic Conference of 1927 with the urgent mandate of reaching an economic agreement.

2 World Economic Conference, Geneva, 1927

The League of Nations World Economic Conference, held in Geneva in 1927, established three Commissions on commerce, industry and agriculture. Enhancing free international trade was considered a condition for world prosperity;[310] therefore, the Conference was aimed at eliminating or lowering barriers to international trade, taking into account the interests of producers, workers as well as consumers. To this end, the Commission on Commerce suggested the simplification of customs formalities, adoption of laws on bills of exchange, suppression of unfair commercial practices, and international development of commercial arbitration.[311]

---

307. *Inter alia, 'facilities and guarantees for the import and export of commercial products; legal guarantees for the re-establishment of commerce; protection of industrial property and copyrights; status of consuls; admission and position of foreigners in regard to the conduct of business; and technical assistance to industrial reconstruction'*. Papers relating to International Economic Conference, Genoa, April-May 1922, Presented to Parliament by Command of His Majesty, London, 1922, pp. 3, 17.
308. *'The economic and financial experts of the Powers responsible for the summoning of the conference at their meeting for the exchange of views, after examining together a number of suggestions and schemes, have prepared draft resolutions embodying the ideas and proposals which met with general acceptance.' Ibid.*, pp. 69-80.
309. H. Aufricht, *Guide to League of Nations Publications. A Bibliographical Survey of the Work of the League, 1920-1947*, 1951, pp. 217, 218. J.H. Jackson, *The World Trading System: Law and Policy of International Economic Relations*, 2nd ed., 2000, p. 35.
310. *'The experience of the years since the war proves that import and export prohibitions, and the arbitrary practices and disguised discriminations which result therefrom, together with the obstacles of all kinds placed on the circulation of goods and capital, have had deplorable results by hampering the normal play of competition, by imperilling both the essential supplies of some nations and the not less indispensable markets of others, and by bringing about an artificial organisation of production, distribution and consumption. Experience has shown, moreover, that the grave drawbacks of these measures have not been counterbalanced by the financial advantages or social benefits which were anticipated.'* League of Nations document C.E.I. 44 (1), 3 June 1927, pp. 5, 20.
311. The Commission on Commerce was divided in three Sub-Committees and covered liberty of trading, customs tariffs and commercial treaties, indirect methods of protecting national

The free circulation of raw materials and articles of consumption was highlighted as one of the essential conditions for creating a healthy industrial and commercial development of the world. In this line, the Conference emphasized the urgency to stabilize customs tariffs in order to increase '*commercial certainty for traders and investors*'. It recommended the removal or reduction of tariffs, including the abandonment of the common practice of increasing them before the negotiations to gain negotiating leverage. The establishment of a systematic customs nomenclature was included in the recommendations.[312]

Export duties were criticized for having the effect of 'increasing the cost of production or the cost of living in foreign countries [which] tends thereby to aggravate the natural inequalities arising from the geographical distribution of world wealth'. Therefore, the Conference recommended resorting to export duties only under very exceptional circumstances, i.e., 'to meet the essential needs of revenue or some exceptional economic situation or to safeguard the vital interests of the country'. In addition, the Conference considered that they 'should never discriminate between different foreign destinations'.[313]

In the aftermath of World War I, along with the increase in tariffs, domestic industries and their export trade had been particularly assisted by indirect subsidies, e.g., granting credits or guarantees. The Conference stressed the '*hidden dangers inherent in this means of encouraging production and exportation*'. It considered direct and indirect subsidies as a mere '*palliative*', an obstacle '*to the attempt to restore foreign trade to normal conditions*'; hence, the Conference recommended to refrain from having recourse to them. Furthermore, the Conference condemned the privileges and special immunities granted to State enterprises, recommending '*a more liberal policy in respect of foreign nationals and companies in the exercise of their commercial activities*'.[314]

Based on Viner's Memorandum on Dumping, prepared for the Conference,[315] dumping was considered a problem in international trade for which a twofold solution

---

commerce and shipping, and repercussion upon international commerce of reduced purchasing power. Section on liberty of trading included import and export prohibitions and restrictions; limitations, regulation or monopolization of trade; and economic and fiscal treatment of nationals and companies of one country admitted to settle in the country of another. Customs tariffs and commercial treaties consisted of obstacles to international trade arising from both: forms, level and instability of import and export tariffs; and customs nomenclature and classification. Indirect methods of protecting national commerce and shipping included subsidies, direct or indirect; dumping and anti-dumping legislation; discrimination arising from the conditions of transport; and fiscal measures discriminating against foreign imported goods. *Ibid.*, pp. 30, 51.

312. *Ibid.*, pp. 23, 31.
313. *Ibid.*, p. 31.
314. *Ibid.*, pp. 20, 33.
315. J. Viner, *Memorandum on Dumping*, League of Nations Document C.E.C.P. 36(1), 1926. Later, in 1933, Viner was requested to work at the economic committee of the League of Nations, where he acted under instructions, without involving his viewed with respect to free trade, as he noted later in an interview: '*I got a request from the State Department to act as deputy for James Harvey Rogers, who was the American representative at the economic committee of the League of Nations, in order to present certain views of Cordell Hull's. There had been a World Economic Conference at London, which the President had blown up. (...) I went to this meeting*

was recommended: on the one hand, the establishment of '*universally stable conditions of production*'; and, on the other hand, the avoidance of '*excessive, indirect of vexatious measures*' in case importing countries '*find themselves compelled to take defensive measures against dumping*'.[316]

To ensure the attainment of the aims of the Conference, countries were suggested to reach commercial treaties, which should contain the most-favoured-nation clause. Concerned about the enforcement of the agreed commitments, the Conference stated: '*While recognizing that, in the main, confidence must be reposed in the good faith of the contracting parties to fulfil their engagements, it is also clear that the possibility of recourse to a suitable arbitral or judicial procedure may often furnish the means of avoiding or settling difficulties whether of interpretation or of application.*' Accordingly, it recommended the inclusion of a provision to refer the interpretation or enforcement of commercial treaties '*to arbitration or preferably to the Permanent Court of International Justice*', which was suggested to be entrusted with special competence on commercial questions.[317]

3 *Abolition of Import and Export Prohibitions and Restrictions, 1927-1929*

The World Economic Conference, held in Geneva in 1927, '*condemned the system of import and export prohibitions*'. A draft for an International Convention for the Abolition of Import and Export Prohibitions and Restrictions had been prepared by the Economic Committee, and the Conference suggested its utilization '*to lead to a prompt general agreement*'. The Conference emphasized that the principles and provisions laid down in the draft International Convention '*should not be indirectly defeated by such means as export duties, the fixing of quotas, health regulations or any other measures not justified by exceptional or imperative circumstances*'.[318]

During 1927 and 1929, three International Conferences for the Abolition of Import and Export Prohibitions and Restrictions were held to enact an International Convention.[319] The Convention for the Abolition of Import and Export Prohibitions and Restrictions was opened for signature in November 1927 and entered into force in

---

in Geneva. The economic committee was hostile to this, largely on free trade grounds, anti-cartel grounds. It was a little funny that Hull's should have been pressing them in that direction and they should have been resisting him on the other direction. While I participated in other matters in which I could follow my free trade prejudices freely, without feeling that I was going to counter to American policy, on these matters I made it perfectly clear that I was acting under instructions and that my views were not involved.' Interview with Dr Jacob Viner by Mr Wendell H. Link on Wednesday, 11 February 1953 at Western Way, Princeton in L. Fiorito, S. Nerozzi, Jacob Viner's Reminiscences from the New Deal (11 February 1953), 2008, pp. 14-44 at 20, 21.

316. League of Nations document C.E.I. 44 (1), 3 June 1927, p. 34.
317. *Ibid.*, pp. 23, 27, 33.
318. *Ibid.*, pp. 20, 21.
319. First, in Geneva from 17 October to 8 November 1927; second, from 3 to 19 July 1928; and third, from 5 to 20 December 1929. H. Aufricht, *Guide to League of Nations Publications. A Bibliographical Survey of the Work of the League, 1920-1947*, 1951, pp. 225-226.

January 1930.[320] During that period, the 'High Contracting Parties' committed to adopt all appropriate measures to reduce the then-existing prohibitions and restrictions to a minimum and refrain from imposing any new prohibitions or restrictions.[321] The Convention on the Abolition of Import and Export Prohibitions and Restrictions was '*the most ambitious trade initiative of the League of Nations, but* [did] *not achieve the requisite 18 ratifications*'.[322]

Before the Monetary and Economic Conference, held in London in 1933, Great Britain argued in favour of the withdrawal from the Convention, claiming this action was taken to freely enter into agreements, '*bearing upon the question of prohibitions, quotas and similar restrictions*' which may result from the coming conference.[323] Following its example, other members, including the US,[324] withdrew from the Convention for the Abolition of Import and Export Prohibitions and Restrictions.[325]

B Conferences in the 1930s and the Origin of Safeguards

Following the 1929 stock market crash, with a view to concerted economic action, several League of Nations international conferences took place in Geneva during 1930 and 1931.[326] International trade had drastically contracted (around 66%) during 1929-1934,[327] due to countries' policies to combat the Great Depression, including

320. The Convention was signed on 8 November 1927 by '*Germany, Austria, Belgium, Great Britain, etc., Egypt, France, Hungary, Italy, Japan, Luxemburg, Roumania and Czechoslovakia*'. Convention on the Abolition of Import and Export Prohibitions and Restrictions, US Department of State Publication 8441, Treaties and other International Agreements of the United States of America, 1776-1949, Vol. 2: Multilateral Agreements 1918-1930, May 1969, pp. 651-682 at 662. US Library of Congress, Digital Collection, United States Treaties and Other International Agreements, United States Treaty Series (1795-1945), compiled by Charles I. Bevans, viewed at: https://www.loc.gov/law/help/us-treaties/bevans/m-ust000002-0651.pdf.
321. Article 2 of the Convention for the Abolition of Import and Export Prohibitions and Restrictions. *Ibid.*, p. 665.
322. C. VanGrasstek, *The History and Future of the World Trade Organization*, 2013, p. 42.
323. Telegram from the US Acting Secretary of State to the Chairman of the American Delegation to the Monetary and Economic Conference (Hull), 19 June 1933, viewed at the US Department of State Office of the Historian, historical documents of Foreign Relations of the United States, Diplomatic Papers 1933, General, Vol. I, viewed at: https://history.state.gov/historicaldocuments/frus1933v01/d588.
324. Convention on the Abolition of Import and Export Prohibitions and Restrictions, US Department of State Publication 8441, Treaties and other International Agreements of the United States of America, 1776-1949, Vol. 2: Multilateral Agreements 1918-1930, May 1969, pp. 651-682. US Library of Congress, Digital Collection, United States Treaties and Other International Agreements, United States Treaty Series (1795-1945), compiled by Charles I. Bevans, viewed at: https://www.loc.gov/law/help/us-treaties/bevans/m-ust000002-0651.pdf.
325. Washington Quits Trade Convention; Follows Example of Britain on Pact for Abolition of Import and Export Restrictions. Reservations to Blame Lacking Ratification by Requisite 18 Nations, 1927 Accord Was Put in Effect by Seven. The New York Times, 6 July 1933.
326. H. Aufricht, *Guide to League of Nations Publications. A Bibliographical Survey of the Work of the League, 1920-1947*, 1951, p. 228.
327. As an illustration, trade between the US and Europe drastically decreased from 1929 to 1932: US imports from Europe declined from USD 1,334 million to USD 390 million; while US exports to Europe fell from USD 2,341 million to USD 784 million. Protectionism in the Interwar Period, The Smoot-Hawley Tariff Act. US Department of State Office of the Historian, viewed at: https://history.state.gov/milestones/1921-1936/protectionism.

'*high tariffs, competitive currency devaluations,* [and] *discriminatory trading blocs*'.[328] The US had enacted a bill meant to provide relief for farmers by increasing tariffs on agricultural products. In turn, the industrial sector called for protection as well. The result was a tariff review and enactment of the Tariff Act of 1930, commonly known as the Smoot-Hawley Tariff Act, whereby US tariffs were increased.[329] '*It quickly became a symbol of the "beggar-thy-neighbor" policies of the 1930s.*'[330] It soon created a spillover effect, and many (almost twenty) countries imposed retaliatory measures by raising their tariffs, leading to a contraction in international trade and worsening the economic situation.

1 *Monetary and Economic Conference, London, 1933*

> The severity of the crisis in world trade is known to everyone, and one of the main objects of this Conference is to promote the flow of world trade by reducing the barriers to international commerce such as tariffs, import restrictions, exchange control, subsidies, and the like, which have so disastrously affected the trade of the world.[331]

Countries were eager to abandon the monetary, financial and economic conflict, and cooperate to solve the world crisis. A Preparatory Commission of Experts was formed in 1932 to work on the Monetary and Economic Conference, which was held in London in June-July 1933.[332] One month before the conference, sixty-one states (out of the sixty-four that participated), representing nearly 90% of world trade signed a 'truce',[333] whereby countries agreed not to adopt new measures increasing the barriers to international trade[334] until the end of the conference.[335]

328. Bretton Woods-GATT, 1941-1947. US Department of State Office of the Historian, viewed at: https://history.state.gov/milestones/1937-1945/bretton-woods.
329. '*Originally developed as a means of providing relief to distressed farmers suffering from crop failures and the Great Depression, (...) this measure raised tariffs on a wide range of agricultural and industrial products.*' C. VanGrasstek, *The History and Future of the World Trade Organization*, 2013, p. 42.
330. Protectionism in the Interwar Period, The Smoot-Hawley Tariff Act. US Department of State Office of the Historian, viewed at: https://history.state.gov/milestones/1921-1936/protectionism.
331. League of Nations document C. 435. M. 220. 1933. II. [Conf.M.E.22(l).], 27 July 1933, p. 36.
332. It was formed by: '*(a) One financial and one economic expert from each of the following countries: Germany, Belgium, United Kingdom, China, United States of America, France, India, Italy and Japan.*
    (b) Six experts appointed by the Council of the League of Nations, belonging to the following nations: For financial questions: Poland, Switzerland, Finland; For economic questions: Czechoslovakia, Hungary, Argentine Republic. (c) Two experts appointed by the Bank for International Settlements.
    (d) One expert representing the Rapporteur on financial questions to the Council of the League of Nations (Norway).' *Ibid.*, pp. 3, 41.
333. Telegram from the Chairman of the American Delegation (Hull) to President Roosevelt on 5 August 1933. US Department of State Office of the Historian, Foreign Relations of The United States, Diplomatic Papers, 1933, General, Vol. I., viewed at: https://history.state.gov/historicaldocuments/frus1933v01/d563.
334. League of Nations document C48.12.1933.II [Conf. M.E.I.], p. 605.
335. League of Nations document C. 435. M. 220. 1933. II. [Conf.M.E.22(l).], 27 July 1933, pp. 3, 4.

The Conference was organized in two main Commissions, the Economic Commission and the Monetary and Financial Commission. The Monetary and Financial Commission covered, on the one hand, '*Immediate Measures of Financial Reconstruction*' and, on the other hand, '*Permanent Measures for the Re-establishment of an International Monetary Standard*'.[336] The Economic Commission had four sub-commissions on: (1) Commercial Policy, covering the progressive abolition of trade restrictions and foreign exchange controls, as well as tariff and treaty policy, including the most-favoured-nation regime; (2) Subsidies, to consider direct and indirect subsidies, especially shipping subsidies, and works; (3) Co-ordination of Protection and Marketing, to deal with wheat and other foodstuffs (sugar, wine, coffee, etc.), raw materials (coal, timber, etc.), and industrial and agricultural agreements; and (4) Indirect Protectionism, including marks of origin,[337] veterinary and phytosanitary issues.[338]

During the discussions on commercial policy and subsidies, it was agreed that measures had to be taken for '*the abolition or restriction of Government subsidies and bounties to trade and commerce*'. Some countries requested to distinguish between production and export bounties and subsidies and expressed their reservations regarding '*drawbacks of duty on goods exported, export credits and railway rates for export*'. Particular focus was given to '*shipping subsidies*', which according to the UK memorandum, had 'evil' effects on trade; and combined with, '*dumping to shipping services*', defeated the national treatment provision in navigation treaties.[339] Countries agreed to

336. Acting in their advisory capacity, the conference counted on the work of the Economic and Financial Committees, the Organisation for Communications and Transit, the International Labour Office, the International Institute of Agriculture and the Bank for International Settlements. *Ibid.*

337. A proposal for an agreement on marks of origin (presented by the German delegation and supported by Belgium, the Netherlands and Czechoslovakia) was submitted to a Drafting Committee: '*The essential object of this proposal was threefold: a truce in the sense of an agreement not to introduce new provisions, mitigation of existing provisions, gradual abolition of laws concerning marks of origin.*' The Committee agreed on the following points: '*(1) In the application of their laws and regulations on marks of origin, States must refrain from any discrimination as between the goods of one foreign country and another.*

(2) The laws and regulations on the marking of goods must not have the effect of damaging the goods.

(3) Effective publicity must be given to all provisions relating to the marking of goods. So far as possible, reasonable time must be allowed to those concerned prior to the putting into force of any new measures. (4) I t must always be possible for persons deeming themselves injured by the action of the authorities responsible for the application of the laws and regulations relative to the marking of goods to institute proceedings for redress. (5) It is desirable to explore the practicability of a simplified and uniform nomenclature for the indication of the country of origin.' *Ibid.*, p. 32.

338. *Ibid.*, pp. 5, 6.

339. '*Under Treaties of Commerce and Navigation, to which most countries are parties, there is laid down the most definite national treatment for shipping. Shipping subsidies in their present form constitute a kind of protection which was not contemplated when the present form of these treaties was elaborated. The older methods of flag discrimination are practically nonexistent to-day, but the grant of subsidies on competitive routes really amounts to a dumping of shipping services which tends to render nugatory the navigation provisions of Treaties. It is also contrary to the spirit of the Maritime Ports Convention.*' The UK delegation explanation of the issue of shipping subsidies since World War I: '*Since the War, there has spread the policy of building and running ships, in part or whole at the cost of the State, to compete with and displace in*

exclude '*subsidies from other than Government sources*', i.e., 'unofficial subsidies' from discussions; notwithstanding, several proposals were submitted for further study on the subject.[340]

The work of the Sub-Commission on Commercial Policy, which dealt with quantitative restrictions,[341] tariff policy,[342] and the most-favoured-nation clause,[343] was based on '*the stabilisation, or at any rate the de facto stability, of currencies*'.[344] Nevertheless, given the fluctuations in the exchange rates, while several countries considered it necessary to maintain full liberty of action on quantitative restrictions, foreign exchange control or customs tariffs, others indicated which measures could be taken once stability had been reached. '*This divergence of opinion made unanimous*[345]

international trade ships of other flags. This has produced and maintained tonnage not called for by economic conditions, and has tended to make impossible the operation of the freight market on an economic basis. In conjunction with the decline in world trade, it has disastrously affected the shipbuilding and shipowning interests under all flags. The great excess of sea-carrying power over the quantity of cargo to be carried is in part due to this policy.' *Ibid.*, p. 38.

340. *Ibid.*, pp. 33-40.
341. On quantitative restrictions, various proposals were submitted: '*1.The unconditional and complete abolition within the shortest possible time of all import prohibitions and quotas and of any other arbitrary restrictions; 2.The concurrent abolition of import quotas and exchange control by the simultaneous conclusion of two general conventions so framed as to establish a progressive parallelism between their effects; 3.The conclusion of a convention based on the text of the 1927 Convention for the Abolition of Prohibitions and Restrictions of Imports and Exports, so modified as to adapt it to present circumstances (in particular, a transitional system and a 100 per cent, quota system would be introduced); 4.The conclusion of an immediate truce to restrictive measures was also advocated.*' *Ibid.*, p. 22.
342. '*The need and urgency of reducing excessive customs tariffs were unanimously admitted. However, three different points of views were presented to achieve that goal: (1) A collective or general convention could alone attain the desired result; (2) Customs duties could only be lowered by the conclusion of bilateral treaties; (3) No method should be excluded; that of a general convention and that of bilateral treaties might be adopted concurrently.*' *Ibid.*, p. 23.
343. '*There was a general opinion in favour of the maintenance of the most-favoured-nation clause, in its unconditional and unrestricted form – naturally with the usually recognized exceptions – stressing the points that it represents the basis of all liberal commercial policy; and that any general and substantial reduction of tariffs by the method of bilateral treaties is only possible if the clause is unrestricted, and that this method would avoid the constant resumption of negotiations. However, certain delegations manifested a strong tendency in favour of allowing new exceptions in addition to those hitherto unanimously admitted. (...) Opinions differed very widely, and the following recommendations were made: An exception in favour of collective conventions for the reduction of economic barriers, open to all countries. An exception in favour of agricultural products; An exception in favour of agreements arising out of historic ties between certain countries, subject to a favourable opinion by the Council of the League of Nations; An exception in favour of agreements binding only those countries which undertake to accept a certain regime and to maintain a certain standard of living for their population; An exception in favour of the agreements contemplated at Stresa and in favour of regional and collective agreements concluded under the auspices of the League of Nations; An exception based on reciprocity and equitable treatment.*' *Ibid.*
344. *Ibid.*, p. 22.
345. '*The unanimity rule and (...) the "automaticity principle" proved to be fatal flaws in the design of the League's economic machinery. Not coincidentally, both would be eschewed by the architects of the IMF many years later.*' L.W. Pauly, *The League of Nations and the Foreshadowing of the International Monetary Fund*, Princetown Essays in International Finance No. 201, 1996, p. 19.

agreement impossible.' The Conference entered upon recess '*although the chief portion of its work* [was] *uncompleted*'.[346]

The Monetary and Economic Conference of 1933 was ground-breaking for the development of the multilateral trading system. Despite the League of Nations Monetary and Economic Conference's failure to develop a collective response to the Great Depression,[347] its work towards developing a multilateral agreement was an important departing point for the monetary and financial agreements achieved at Bretton Woods in 1944, and the preparatory work of the ITO Charter and the GATT.[348] With respect to trade remedies, the work elaborated at the 1933 Conference on anti-dumping and countervailing duties was an important reference when the United Nations Preparatory Committee of the International Conference on Trade and Employment met in London in November 1946.[349] Significantly, the 1933 Conference represents the origin of safeguards.

Towards the end of the Conference, the US presented, for discussion and further development, a proposal on commercial policy: A '*possible agreement for a protracted truce against measures restrictive of international trade*'.[350] According to Secretary of State Cordell Hull, a '*continuing truce should serve to restrict new barriers to such instances of evident and unusual necessity as may arise, even while general governmental policy was aimed in the other direction*', as well as serve to progressively reduce existing barriers.[351]

346. League of Nations document C. 435. M. 220. 1933. II. [Conf.M.E.22(l).], 27 July 1933, pp. 22, 41.
347. H. Aufricht, *Guide to League of Nations Publications. A Bibliographical Survey of the Work of the League, 1920-1947*, 1951, pp. 229-30.
348. Message from the US President F. Roosevelt at the end of the Conference: '*Results are not always measured in terms of formal agreements. They can come equally from the free presentation of each nation's difficulties and each nation's methods to meet its individual needs (...) Such interchange, especially if it results in full discussion of all problems and not a few only makes progress more and not less possible in the future. That is why I do not regard the Economic Conference as a failure. Largely because of your tact and perseverance the larger and more permanent problems will continue to be analyzed and discussed. You recognize with me that new adjustments are necessary to meet world and national conditions which have never existed before in history. You can count on our continued efforts towards world rehabilitation because we are convinced that a continuation of the work of the World Economic Conference will result in practical good in many fields of joint endeavor.*' Telegram from the US President F. Roosevelt to the Acting Secretary of State to the Chairman of the American Delegation (Hull) on 26 July 1933. US Department of State Office of the Historian, viewed at: https://history.state.gov/historicaldocuments/frus1933v01/d561.
349. UN document E/PC/T/C.II.48, 11 November 1946, p. 2.
350. American Suggestion for the further Development, during the Recess and Later Stages of the Conference, of a Programme on Commercial Policy League of Nations document C. 435. M. 220. 1933. II. [Conf.M.E.22(l).], 27 July 1933, pp. 40-44.
351. '*It does not attempt to put into legal form of agreement the terms of possible action; the difficulties of this require further discussion among governments. But it does attempt to limit with some degree of precision the exceptions and reservations which may be necessary. It also sets forth the present American attitude towards other matters involved in commercial treaty negotiations, such as the most-favoured-nation principle and the possible special exceptions from that principle that might be allowed by Governments to facilitate agreements for the lowering of trade barriers. I trust that these proposals will turn out to be a useful contribution to the long term plan of attack upon existing trade obstacles. Despite their limitations and imperfections, I am confident that their acceptance in substance would mark an important*

The proposal suggested beginning with the reduction of import duties and the elimination of those restrictions lacking economic justification; in particular, those that had curtailed importation since 1929 or had restricted importation to less than 5% compared to domestic consumption, and those that after having been in place for a considerable period did not increase the domestic production of the protected commodities. Bilateral and multilateral agreements were not to introduce '*new obstacles, direct or indirect, to the movements of international commerce, whether such obstacles are embodied in new legislation or brought into existence by the exercise of administrative or executive power under existing legislation*'.[352]

Nonetheless, exceptions and reservations were also suggested, among which the following were suggested: first, 'for purpose of sanitation, plant and animal protection, morals, etc' (that had been included under Article 4 of the Geneva Convention of 1927); second, importing duties or taxes merely to offset internal excise taxes on competing domestic products; third, on agreed 'regulation of production and/or marketing of natural products'; additional duties on products of countries that refuse to grant equal treatment; 'on goods found to be "dumped" (...) or benefiting directly or indirectly from governmental or other bounties', as well as on 'new or additional duties or restrictions necessitated by governmental measures of an emergency character which - by raising wages, shortening hours and improving conditions of labour - have resulted in increased costs and prices'.[353] This last exception was the 'safeguarding provision', the basis for the 'emergency action' clause that would later be enshrined under GATT Article XIX.

2 *Origin of Safeguards, 1933*

The 'safeguarding provision' incorporated in the US proposal at the 1933 Conference consisted of an exceptional measure to be imposed in case of 'emergency', i.e., exclusively to prevent '*an excessive influx of imports of particular commodities*'. This provision allowed the imposition of '*new or additional duties or restrictions*', in a non-discriminatory manner (among countries that were part of the agreement), under the following circumstances: increase in costs and prices as a result of '*raising wages, shortening hours and improving conditions of labour*'.[354]

Strict conditions would accompany this emergency measure: It would only be in force during the period of the emergency and to prevent drastic increases of imports above the level of such period. Furthermore, the measure was required to neither be '*more than sufficient to meet the emergency*' nor '*reduce foreign trade in the commodities affected below the level of a pre-determined period*'. Prior notice and an opportunity for consultations had to be given before imposing the measure. In case of an

advance towards the restoration of international commerce.' Communication by Mr. Cordell Hull (United States of America) to the President of the Economic Commission. *Ibid.*, p. 41.

352. *Ibid.*, p. 42.
353. *Ibid.*
354. *Ibid.*

unsatisfactory outcome of consultations, countries had the right to renounce the agreement, by invoking this proposed 'safeguarding provision', which read as follows:

> (f) New or additional duties or restrictions necessitated by governmental measures of an emergency character which – by raising wages, shortening hours and improving conditions of labour have resulted in increased costs and prices.
>
> Any new or additional duties or restrictions authorised under the above circumstances shall be imposed only for the purpose of preventing an excessive influx of imports of particular commodities. They should not be more than sufficient to meet the emergency and should continue in force only for the period of the emergency. They should not reduce foreign trade in the commodities affected below the level of a pre-determined period, and should be used only to prevent drastic increases of imports above the level of such period. They should not be imposed or applied in such manner as to discriminate against the trade in the products concerned of any country participating in the truce.
>
> Before exercising the right conferred in this reservation, Governments are to give preliminary notice to the principal foreign countries supplying their imports of the particular commodity, and to allow reasonable opportunity for representation of the viewpoints of such Governments with regard to such duties or restrictions, each Government having the right, in the case of an unsatisfactory result of such consultations, to denounce the agreement with reference to the products of the country availing itself of this safeguarding provision.

An illustration of the limits of actions under the 'safeguarding provision' was presented for discussion:

> New or additional duties or restrictions authorised under the above circumstances shall not be imposed on any commodity unless, during a period of (say) two months, the imports of the commodity shall have exceeded (say) five per cent, of the estimated domestic consumption, and unless they shall have exceeded the average imports during the corresponding months of the three-year period 1930, 1931 and 1932:
>
> (1) By at least (say) ten per cent, in the case of any article of which the imports during the two months period have either exceeded (say) twenty per cent, of domestic consumption, or have constituted a materially larger proportion of domestic consumption than during normal years preceding 1930.
> (2) By at least (say) 25 per cent, in the case of any article of which the imports during the two months period have exceeded (say) 10 per cent, of domestic consumption but have been less than 20 per cent, thereof.
> (3) By at least (say) 50 per cent, in the case of any article of which the imports during the two months period have not exceeded (say) 10 per cent, of domestic consumption.[355]

After the failure of the 1933 Monetary and Economic Conference, this 'safeguarding provision' was further developed by the US and included in its bilateral agreements of the 1940s. The US–Mexico Agreement of 1942 was the first to incorporate the safeguarding provision ('escape clause').[356] Between 1934 and 1945, the US concluded

355. *Ibid.*

356. The escape clause in the US Reciprocal Trade Agreement with Mexico read as follows: '*If as a result of unforeseen developments and of the concession granted on any article enumerated and described in the Schedules annexed to this Agreement, such article is being imported in such increased quantities and under such conditions as to cause or threaten serious injury to domestic*

thirty-two trade agreements, pursuant to the US 1934 Reciprocal Trade Agreement Act (and its extensions),[357] whereby Congress delegated powers to the President to reach agreements aimed at lowering tariffs.[358] In July 1945, Congress approved an extension until June 1948, whereby the US adopted the GATT.[359] During the congressional debate,[360] complaints of injury by industries led the US government (under President Truman from April 1945) to establish the incorporation of an escape clause in every US trade agreement,[361] which was written into statutory law by the US Congress in 1951.[362] The escape clause was also introduced in the US Suggested Charter for an ITO in 1946 as the 'emergency action' provision (Article 29), the basis of GATT Article XIX.

C Conferences During World War II

The outbreak of World War II frustrated the aims of the Monetary and Financial and the Economic Committees of the League of Nations,[363] whose powers and functions were

producers of like or similar articles, the Government of either country shall be free to withdraw the concession, in whole or in part, or to modify it to the extent and for such time as may be necessary to prevent such injury.' Article XI of the US Reciprocal Trade Agreement with Mexico, 23 December 1942.

357. The 1934 Reciprocal Trade Agreement Act was '*at the behest of President Roosevelt's Secretary of State, Cordell Hull*'. J.H. Jackson, *World Trade and the Law of GATT (A Legal Analysis of the General Agreement on Tariffs and Trade)*, 1969, p. 37.
358. J.H. Jackson, *Restructuring the GATT System*, 1990, p. 9.
359. An Act to Extend the Authority of the President under Section 350 of the Tariff Act of 1930 and for other purposes, 59 Stat.410, 19 USC1351-66, 5 July 1945. J.H. Jackson, *World Trade and the Law of GATT (A Legal Analysis of the General Agreement on Tariffs and Trade)*, 1969, p. 37.
360. '*91 Cong. Rec. 4872 (1945) (remarks of Congressman Doughton); Hearings on the Extension of the Reciprocal Trade Agreements Act Before the Senate Finance Comm., 79th Cong., 1st Sess. 84, 86, 90, 179-80, 459 (1945); Hearings on the Extension of the Reciprocal Trade Agreements Act Before the House Comm. On Ways and Means, 79th Cong., 1st Sess. 273 (1945)*'. J.H. Jackson, *World Trade and the Law of GATT (A Legal Analysis of the General Agreement on Tariffs and Trade)*, 1969, p. 553.
361. US Executive Order No. 9832, 25 February 1947.
362. US President Roosevelt's message to Congress recommending the renewal of the authority on 26 March 1945: '*Trade is fundamental to the prosperity of nations, as it is of individuals. All of us earn our living by producing for some market, and all of us buy in some market most of the things we need. We do better, both as producers and consumers, when the markets upon which we depend are as large and rich and various and competitive as possible. The same is true of nations. We have not always understood this, in the United States or in any other country. We have tried often to protect some special interest by excluding strangers' goods from competition. In the long run everyone has suffered...It is also important to remember that imports mean much more than goods for ultimate consumers. They mean jobs and income at every stage of the processing and distribution channels through which the imports flow to the consumer. By reducing our own tariff in conjunction with the reduction by other countries of their trade barriers, we create jobs, get more for our money, and improve the standard of living of every American consumer...The purpose of the whole effort is to eliminate economic warfare, to make practical international cooperation effective on as many fronts as possible, and so to lay the economic basis for the secure and peaceful world we all desire...When this trade-agreements legislation and the other legislation I have recommended to this Congress is adopted, and when the general Organization of the United Nations and their various special agencies, including one on trade, have been created and are functioning, we shall have made a good beginning at creating a workable kit of tools for the new world of international cooperation to which we all look forward.*' US Department of State Bulletin, Vol. 12, 1945, pp. 531-533.
363. From 1933 until the beginning of World War II, the League of Nations held two more Economic Conferences with minor significance: The International Sugar Conference, in 1937; and the

transferred to the United Nations Economic and Social Committee (ECOSOC) in 1945.[364] Nonetheless, during World War II, the willingness not to repeat the mistakes of the 1930s was declared in the Atlantic Charter of 1941 by the US (under President F.D. Roosevelt) and the UK (under Prime Minister W. Churchill), pledging '*to further the enjoyment by all states (...) of access, on equal terms, to the trade and to the raw materials of the world which are needed for their economic prosperity*; [and] *bring about the fullest collaboration between all nations in the economic field with the object of securing, for all, improved labor standards, economic advancement, and social security*'.[365]

Pursuant to the Atlantic Charter, the US and UK agreed under Article VII of their Mutual Aid Agreement of 1942 'not to burden commerce between the two countries, but to promote mutually advantageous economic relations between them and the betterment of world-wide economic relations'. To that end, both countries agreed to begin conversations, 'open to participation by all other countries of like mind', and set forth the following economic objectives: elimination of discriminatory treatment in international trade, reduction of tariffs and other trade barriers, as well as the establishment of domestic and international measures to expand 'production, employment, and the exchange and consumption of goods, which are the material foundations of the liberty and welfare of all peoples'.[366]

European Conference on Rural Life, in 1939. H. Aufricht, *Guide to League of Nations Publications. A Bibliographical Survey of the Work of the League, 1920-1947*, 1951, pp. 218, 230, 250.

364. The United Nations Charter final draft was presented at the San Francisco Conference (in April-June 1945; following Conferences at Bretton Woods in July 1944, at Dumbarton Oaks in August-October 1944, and at Yalta in February 1945), and after being ratified by members, it came into force on 24 October 1945. UN website information, viewed at: https://www.un.org/en/about-us/history-of-the-un/san-francisco-conference.

365. Fourth and fifth clauses of the Atlantic Charter: '*Fourth, they will endeavor, with due respect for their existing obligations, to further the enjoyment by all states, great or small, victor or vanquished, of access, on equal terms, to the trade and to the raw materials of the world which are needed for their economic prosperity; Fifth, they desire to bring about the fullest collaboration between all nations in the economic field with the object of securing, for all, improved labor standards, economic advancement, and social security*', Joint declaration by the President of the United States and the Prime Minister of the United Kingdom, 14 August 1941. US Library of Congress, Digital Collection, United States Treaties and Other International Agreements, United States Treaty Series (1795-1945), compiled by Charles I. Bevans, viewed at: https://www.loc.gov/law/help/us-treaties/bevans/m-ust000003-0686.pdf.

366. Article VII of the Anglo-American Mutual Aid Agreement: '*In the final determination of the benefits to be provided to the United States of America by the Government of the United Kingdom in return for aid furnished under the Act of Congress of March 11, 1941, the terms and conditions thereof shall be such as not to burden commerce between the two countries, but to promote mutually advantageous economic relations between them and the betterment of world-wide economic relations. To that end, they shall include provision for agreed action by the United States of America and the United Kingdom, open to participation by all other countries of like mind, directed to the expansion, by appropriate international and domestic measures, of production, employment, and the exchange and consumption of goods, which are the material foundations of the liberty and welfare of all peoples; to the elimination of all forms of discriminatory treatment in international commerce, and to the reduction of tariffs and other trade barriers; and in general, to the attainment of all the economic objectives set forth in the Joint Declaration made on Aug. 12, 1941, by the President of the United States of America and the Prime Minister of the United Kingdom. At an early convenient date, conversations shall be*

Among the members of the delegations were notable the work of important economists such as J.M. Keynes (who had participated in the preparatory works of the Economic Conference of 1933), J. Meade and L. Robbins, on the UK delegation; and H. Hawkins and H.D. White, Special Assistant to the US Secretary of the Treasury, on the US delegation. Aimed at reaching an agreement on economic objectives towards worldwide prosperity, the UK and US began, in early 1942, to prepare proposals on post-war economic institutions that helped ensure economic and financial stability.[367] Both countries considered that it had to be attained through the expansion of international trade, fixed exchange rates and financial assistance to countries experiencing short-term balance of payments deficits.[368]

Their delegations held discussions in Washington in 1943, which was referred to as a 'seminar' since they were able to discuss it without final governmental approval.[369] With respect to trade, agreement was found on most of the substantive policy issues: prohibition of discrimination, substantial reduction of tariffs, elimination of export subsidies and export taxes, prohibition of quantitative restrictions (except in case of balance-of-payment emergencies), and encouragement for state trading enterprises to operate like private sector enterprises.[370] Further meetings were held bilaterally as well as multilaterally, including the Monetary and Financial Conference, held in Bretton Woods in 1944, which successfully concluded with an agreement of forty-four nations on the creation of the International Monetary Fund (IMF)[371] and the International Bank for Reconstruction and Development (IBRD), soon after called the World Bank.[372] The conference recommended to '*reduce obstacles to international trade and in other ways to promote mutually advantageous international commercial relations*',[373]

---

begun between the two governments with a view to determining, in the light of governing economic conditions, the best means of attaining the above-stated objectives by their own agreed action and of seeking the agreed action of other like-minded governments.' The Anglo-American Mutual Aid Agreement, 28 February 1942. Yale Law School Lillian Goldman Library online, viewed at: https://avalon.law.yale.edu/wwii/angam42.asp#art7.

367. In 1941, J.M. Keynes presented a proposal for an International Clearing Union. Based on it, J. Meade drafted a Proposal for an International Commercial Union in 1942. For a deeper description of J. Meade's proposal, *see* D.A. Irwin, P.C. Mavroidis, A.O. Sykes, *The Genesis of the GATT*, 2008.
368. Bretton Woods-GATT, 1941-1947. US Department of State Office of the Historian, viewed at: https://history.state.gov/milestones/1937-1945/bretton-woods.
369. R.N. Gardner, *Sterling Dollar Diplomacy*, 1956, p. 103.
370. R.E. Hudec, *The GATT Legal System and World Trade Diplomacy*, 1975, p. 8.
371. '*The IMF was charged with overseeing a system of fixed exchange rates centered on the US dollar and gold, serving as a forum for consultation and cooperation and a provider of short-term financial assistance to countries experiencing temporary deficits in their balance of payments... The fixed exchange rate system established at Bretton Woods endured for the better part of three decades; only after the exchange crises of August 1971, when President Richard M. Nixon suspended the dollar's convertibility into gold, and February/March 1973 did floating exchange rates become the norm for the major industrialized democracies.*' Bretton Woods-GATT, 1941-1947. US Department of State Office of the Historian, viewed at: https://history.state.gov/milestones/1937-1945/bretton-woods.
372. '*The IBRD was responsible for providing financial assistance for the reconstruction of war-ravaged nations and the economic development of less developed countries.*' *Ibid.*
373. United Nations Monetary and Financial Conference held at Bretton Woods, 1-22 July 1944.

yet further conferences on trade would be needed until a multilateral trade agreement was reached.[374]

In 1945, the US presented 'Proposals for Expansion of World Trade and Employment',[375] to hold a United Nations (UN) Conference on Trade and Employment, aimed at creating an International Trade Organization (ITO). To this end, the US Suggested Charter for an ITO of the UN was presented in 1946.[376] UN delegations negotiated and redrafted it in four sessions during 1946-1948, which culminated in the UN Conference on Trade and Employment, held in Havana, and resulted in the enactment of the GATT in 1947 and the ITO Charter in 1948.

374. *'One of the most contentious issues was the system of preferential tariffs established among the members of the British Commonwealth in 1932, whereby trade within the Commonwealth was subject to lower tariffs than trade between the Commonwealth nations and the rest of the world. US officials such as Cordell Hull opposed imperial preferences on both ideological and practical grounds – the United Kingdom and Canada, both members of the system, were the United States' two largest trading partners – and called for their abolition; however, many U.K. and other Commonwealth officials favored keeping the preferences, at least until the United States agreed to reduce the high Smoot-Hawley tariffs set in 1930.'* US Department of State Office of the Historian, Bretton Woods-GATT, 1941-1947, viewed at: https://history.state.gov/milestones/1937-1945/bretton-woods.
375. US Department of State, Proposals for Expansion of World Trade and Employment, November 1945.
376. US State Department, Suggested Charter for an International Trade Organization of the United Nations, September 1946.

CHAPTER 5

Preparatory Work of the GATT and ITO Charter, 1945-1948

Chapter 5 explores the evolution of multilateral provisions on trade remedies and subsidies during the preparatory work of the GATT and the ITO Charter, developed between 1945 and 1948. The US Proposals for Expansion of World Trade and Employment of 1945 and Suggested Charter for an International Trade Organization of the United Nations of 1946 served as the basis for the GATT and the ITO Charter, developed in London; New York; Geneva, where the GATT was signed in 1947; and Havana, where the Conference on Trade and Employment culminated with the signature of the ITO Charter in 1948. Since the ITO Charter did not enter into force, the GATT Review Session of 1954-1955 incorporated some amendments into the GATT. Therefore, Section I will address the US Proposals for Expansion of World Trade and Employment and the US Suggested Charter for an ITO, while Section II will focus on the UN preparatory work of the GATT and the ITO Charter up to the current version of GATT provisions on trade remedies and subsidies.

I US MULTILATERAL PROPOSALS FOR AN INTERNATIONAL TRADE ORGANIZATION

The need for the creation of a multilateral institution for trade was recognized at the Bretton Woods Conference in 1944,[377] where the International Monetary Fund and the World Bank were created.[378] In July 1945, the US Reciprocal Trade Agreement Act was renewed for a three-year period. In order to reach a multilateral agreement within this period, the US urged other countries to meet, under the sponsorship of the UN, and

377. J.H. Jackson, *Restructuring the GATT System*, p. 10; J.H. Jackson, *The World Trading System: Law and Policy of International Economic Relations*, 2nd ed., 2000, p. 36.
378. US Bretton Woods Agreement Act, 31 July 1945, viewed at: https://fraser.stlouisfed.org/files/docs/historical/congressional/bretton-woods-agreements-act-1945.pdf.

presented, in November 1945, the Proposals for Expansion of World Trade and Employment '*for consideration by the peoples of the world*' (hereinafter 'US Proposals').[379] At its first meeting on 18 February 1946, the UN ECOSOC adopted a resolution calling for the International Conference on Trade and Employment aimed at drafting the Charter for an International Trade Organization.[380]

To this end, in September 1946, the US presented the Suggested Charter for an International Trade Organization of the United Nations (hereinafter 'US Suggested Charter'),[381] which served as the basis for the UN delegations' work during four sessions: London, 1946; New York and Geneva, 1947; and Havana, 1948. At the end of the third session, on 30 October 1947, the GATT was signed by twenty-three nations.[382] The fourth session, '*the actual United Nations Conference on Trade and Employment*',[383] concluded on 28 March 1948, with the signature of the ITO Charter by fifty-three countries.[384]

The GATT, consisting of provisions on commercial policy, was intended to be part of the ITO Charter and was negotiated in parallel in order to accelerate the agreement on the reduction of tariffs. Nevertheless, since the ITO Charter never came into existence, all the ITO provisions other than on commercial policy (included in the GATT) did not enter into force, e.g., dispute settlement, employment, and restrictive business practices. Some of the amendments made at the Havana Conference to the provisions on commercial policy of the ITO Charter were later incorporated in the GATT, first in 1948 and then at the GATT Review Session of 1954-1955. GATT provisions on trade remedies and subsidies are a redrafted version of the provisions included in the US Proposals of 1945 and the US Suggested Charter of 1946.

A US Proposals for Expansion of World Trade and Employment, 1945

The US Proposals for Expansion of World Trade and Employment was prepared by technical staff within the US government to establish the International Trade Organization, aimed at the UN harmonization of policies on international trade and employment. '*The purpose* [was] *to make real the principle of equal access to the markets and the raw materials of the world, so that the varied gifts of many peoples may exert themselves more fully for the common good. The larger purpose* [was] *to contribute to the effective partnership of the United Nations, to the growth of international confidence and solidarity, and thus to the preservation of the peace.*' Therefore, the Proposals suggested the adoption of '*fair rules of mutual tolerance*' for the existent variety of

379. US Department of State, Proposals for Expansion of World Trade and Employment, 1945.
380. UN ECOSOC Resolution 13. UN document E/22, 18 February 1946.
381. US State Department, Suggested Charter for an International Trade Organization of the United Nations, September 1946.
382. UNTS, Vol. 55, pp. 187-316.
383. J.H. Jackson, *World Trade and the Law of GATT (A Legal Analysis of the General Agreement on Tariffs and Trade)*, 1969, p. 42.
384. UN document E/CONF.2/78, 24 March 1948.

economic systems '*to meet in the market-place without conflict, thus to contribute each to the other's prosperity and welfare*'.[385]

Emphasis was made on the direct contribution of the expansion of trade to attain maximum levels of '*employment, production and consumption*'. Accordingly, further action was required concerning trade barriers and discrimination, which prevent the expansion of multilateral trade and full employment. While '*high and stable levels of employment are a necessary condition for an enlarged volume of trade*', seeking '*employment by prohibiting imports or by subsidizing exports would be harmful and self-defeating*'. Among the problems that prevented the expansion of trade, the following were mentioned: restrictions imposed by governments (in the form of tariffs, quotas, import prohibitions, export licences, and burdensome importing paper-work), as well as by private combines and cartels ('*to obtain the unfair advantage of monopoly*'); the fear of disorder in markets for primary commodities (mainly caused by post-war subsidies); and the irregularity in production and employment, accompanied by the fear of that irregularity.[386]

The US Proposals consisted of six chapters devoted to the organization, its purposes and membership, as well as to each of the tasks the ITO was designed to perform, i.e., commercial policy, restrictive business practices, and international commodity arrangements. Along with other UN existing agencies dealing with labour, agriculture, investment and civil aviation, the ITO was designed to be the '*central international agency to deal with trade*', aimed at serving as an international forum for discussion and improvement; as well as performing, with internal specialization, assigned tasks concerning '*trade barriers, restrictive business practices, and international commodity arrangements*'.[387]

The ITO was designed to consist of 'a Conference, an Executive Board, a Commercial Policy Commission, a Commission on Business Practices, a Commodity Commission, and a Secretariat', to establish the machinery for promoting cooperation on commercial policy; granting members the possibility not to recourse to trade-restrictive measures; eliminating discrimination among members in international trade to facilitate their access 'to the trade and raw materials which are needed for their economic prosperity'; and promoting production and consumption in order to reduce trade barriers.[388]

In order to contribute to the expansion of the world economy, reaching high levels of employment in all countries and creating economic conditions to maintain world peace, the following functions were assigned to the ITO: '*collect, analyze and publish information*'; provide technical assistance; make recommendations to members; and interpret provisions regarding commercial policy, restrictive business practices and intergovernmental commodity arrangements. Furthermore, it would be entrusted to '*make recommendations for international agreements designed to improve*

385. US Department of State, Proposals for Expansion of World Trade and Employment, 1945, pp. 3, 7.
386. *Ibid.*, pp. 8-10.
387. *Ibid.*, p. 7.
388. *Ibid.*, p. 24.

the bases of trade and to assure just and equitable treatment for the enterprises, skills and capital brought from one country to another, including agreements on the treatment of foreign nationals and enterprises, on the treatment of commercial travelers, on commercial arbitration, and on the avoidance of double taxation'.[389]

The chapter on commercial policy established some general provisions, general exceptions, regimes on exchange controls, subsidies, and quantitative trade restrictions. Under the general provisions, members would undertake to, *inter alia*, accord imports no less favourable treatment than to domestic products as well as freedom of transit; eliminate '*excessive requirements regarding marks of origin in so far as they affect products imported from other members*'; give effect to agreed valuation procedures; simplify customs formalities; not to discourage '*directly or indirectly*' the '*importation or consumption of products of other members*' by financing or organizing campaigns or boycotts; publish trade laws and regulations; and establish independent national tribunals '*to review and correct administrative customs action*'. Regarding anti-dumping and countervailing duties, it was proposed that members subscribe to a definition in order to '*properly*' apply such duties on importation.[390]

An emergency action was suggested to temporarily protect producers from sudden and widespread injury. It was suggested to be incorporated in '*undertakings reducing tariffs (...) to cover such contingencies*'. As opposed to the 'safeguarding provision' proposed by the US at the 1933 Conference, in the US Proposals for Expansion of World Trade and Employment, the emergency action was not established along with the general exceptions, those considered necessary to, *inter alia*, protect '*public morals*'; '*human, animal or plant life or health*'; and '*national treasures of artistic, historic or archaeological value*'; as well as those relating to arm's traffic; '*prison-made goods*', etc.[391]

Subsidies granted after the war constituted another main concern due to their devastating effects on world trade. Therefore, the following was proposed: On general subsidies, to inform the ITO of subsidies that either increase exports or reduce imports; and to discuss the limitation of subsidies, including '*any form of internal income or price support*', with other members of the ITO. On export subsidies, '*not to take any action which would result in the sale of a product in export markets at a price lower than the comparable price charged for the like product to buyers in the home market, due allowance being made for differences in conditions and terms of sale, for differences in taxation, and for other differences affecting price comparability*'. When, pursuant to ITO procedures, the supply of a commodity was considered a '*burdensome world surplus*', agreement by either producers or consumers was suggested in order to increase consumption and reduce production.[392]

A special reference was made to state trading, encouraging members to commit to grant equal treatment to other members; ensure that only commercial considerations, '*such as price, quality, marketability, transportation and terms of purchase or*

389. *Ibid.*, pp. 11, 23, 24.
390. *Ibid.*, p. 12.
391. *Ibid.*, pp. 13, 18.
392. *Ibid.*, pp. 5, 15, 16.

sale', influence sales and purchases of state trading enterprises; negotiate a maximum protective margin between the '*landed price*' and the price in the home market of a state monopoly product, regardless of its origin; and, in case of having a complete state monopoly of foreign trade, consult with the ITO and agree with other members to purchase (on a non-discriminatory basis) an aggregate amount of their products.[393]

Cartels as well as governmental restrictions on production or exportation were recognized to take '*unfair advantage of consumers*'. The US Proposals emphasized that, by dividing the market among members of a cartel, the damages not only fall on new and small businesses, but also '*levy an unjust toll upon consumers*'. Restrictive business practices were considered to have a harmful effect on competition and trade, occasionally '*even more destructive of world trade*' than governmental restrictions. Therefore, a chapter was devoted to restrictive business practices, whereby members were suggested to develop an agreement, as well as continuing the effectiveness of national legislation aimed at their elimination or prevention. To this end, a special agency within the ITO was proposed to request information from members in order to examine the facts and make recommendations, which would be enforceable by members. In the US, it would '*continue to be by judicial proceedings under antitrust laws*'.[394]

B US Suggested Charter for an International Trade Organization, 1946

In this line, the US Suggested Charter was presented, in September 1946, 'a middle way between the code too rigid to withstand strain and the near anarchy which would be likely in the absence of any code'. Reliance was put upon the ITO 'to reconcile the need for international discipline with the aversion of the member countries to irrevocable commitments and to submission to rigid rules'.[395] Accordingly, the US Suggested Charter can be considered the first draft charter of a multilateral trade organization, serving as the basis for the UN work on drafting the ITO Charter, signed in 1948.

Based on the US Proposals, the US Suggested Charter included the following chapters: I. Purposes; II. Membership; III. Employment Provisions; IV. General Commercial Policy; V. Restrictive Business Practices; Intergovernmental Commodity Arrangements; VII. Organization.[396] The chapter on commercial policy, which would become the GATT in 1947, included detailed provisions on trade remedies. The anti-dumping and countervailing duty provisions were established under Article 11 and the safeguard provision under Article 29.

393. '*Unless the product is subject to rationing, the monopoly should offer for sale such quantities of the product as will be sufficient to satisfy the full domestic demand.*' *Ibid.*, p. 17.
394. Among restrictive business practices were included '*combinations or agreements to fix prices and terms of sale, divide markets or territories, limit production or exports, suppress technology or invention, exclude enterprises from particular fields, or boycott or discriminate against particular firms*'. *Ibid.*, pp. 4-6, 19.
395. J. Viner, Conflicts of Principle in Drafting a Trade Charter, *Foreign Affairs*, Vol. 25, No. 4, 1947, pp. 612-628 at 628 https://doi.org/10.2307/20030068.
396. US State Department, Suggested Charter for an International Trade Organization of the United Nations, September 1946, pp. v-vii.

The anti-dumping provision was based on the US Antidumping Act of 1921. The countervailing duty provision was very similar to the US countervailing duty provision under the Tariff Act of 1930, except for the injury requirement. Article 11 of the US Suggested Charter, establishing both anti-dumping and countervailing duties provisions, required injury for the imposition of duties. Notwithstanding some changes were added during the preparatory work of the GATT and the ITO Charter (1946-1948), GATT Article VI is very similar to Article 11 of the US Suggested Charter, which read as follows:

> Article 11. Antidumping and Countervailing Duties
> 1. No antidumping duty shall be imposed on any product of any Member country imported into any other Member country in excess of an amount equal to the margin of dumping under which such product is being imported. For the purposes of this Article, the margin of dumping shall be understood to mean the amount by which the price of a product exported from one country to another is less than (a) the comparable price charged for the like or similar product to buyers in the domestic market of the exporting country, or, (b) in the absence of such domestic price, the highest comparable price at which the like or similar product is sold for export to any third country, or, (c) in the absence of (a) and (b), the cost of production of the product in the country of origin; with due allowance in each case for differences in conditions and terms of sale, for differences in taxation, and for other differences affecting price comparability.
> 2. No countervailing duty shall be imposed on any product of any Member country imported into any other Member country in excess of an amount equal to the estimated bounty or subsidy ascertained to have been granted, directly or indirectly, on the production or export of such product in the country of origin or exportation.
> 3. No product of any Member country imported into any other Member country shall be subject to antidumping or countervailing duty by reason of the exemption of such product from duties or taxes imposed in the country of origin or exportation upon the like product when consumed domestically.
> 4. No product of any Member country imported into any other Member country shall be subject to both antidumping and countervailing duty to compensate for the same situation of dumping or export subsidization.
> 5. Each Member undertakes that as a general rule it will not impose any antidumping duty or countervailing duty on the importation of any product of other Member countries unless it determines that the dumping or subsidization, as the case may be, under which such product is imported, is such as to injure or threaten to injure a domestic industry, or is such as to prevent the establishment of a domestic industry.[397]

The provision on safeguard measures, under Article 29 of the US Suggested Charter, was titled '*Emergency Action on Imports of Particular Products*', and was established in the same section as the provision on consultation and nullification or impairment. The first paragraph of Article 29 of the US Suggested Charter mirrored the escape clause that the US included in the 1942 US–Mexico agreement[398] (and all other bilateral agreements since 1945) with the only replacement of 'concessions' by

397. *Ibid.*, pp. 5, 6.
398. Article XI of the US Reciprocal Trade Agreement with Mexico, 23 December 1942.

'obligations'. This first paragraph of Article 29 would later become GATT Article XIX.1(a). The second paragraph of Article 29 of the US Suggested Charter would later constitute part of paragraphs 2 and 3 of GATT Article XIX. The safeguard provision under Article 29 of the US Suggested Charter read as follows:

> Article 29: Emergency Action on Imports of Particular Products
> 1. If, as a result of unforeseen developments and of the effect of the obligations incurred under this Chapter, including the tariff concessions granted pursuant to Article 18, any product is being imported into the territory of any Member in such increased quantities and under such conditions as to cause or threaten serious injury to domestic producers of like or similar products, the Member shall be free to withdraw the concessions, or suspend the obligation, in respect of such product, in whole or in part, or to modify the concessions to the extent and for such time as may be necessary to prevent such injury.
> 2. Before any Member shall take action pursuant to the provisions of paragraph 1 of this Article, it shall give notice in writing to the Organization as far as in advance as may be practicable and shall afford the Organization, and the other Members having a substantial interest as exporters of the product concerned, an opportunity to consult with it in respect of the proposed action. If an agreement among the interested Members with respect to the proposed action is not reached, the Member which proposes to take the action shall, nevertheless, be free to do so, and if such action is taken the other affected Member shall then be free, within sixty days after such action is taken, to suspend on sixty days' written notice to the Organization the application to the trade of the Member taking such action, of any of the obligations or concessions under this Chapter the suspension of which the Organization does not recommend against.[399]

Notwithstanding that Articles 11 and 29 of the US Suggested Charter were the only ones dealing with trade remedies, intrinsically related to countervailing duties is the discipline on subsidies; hence, the provision on subsidies under the US Suggested Charter requires special consideration. Article 25 of the US Suggested Charter established the following obligations to members:

(a) notification of a subsidy (including any form of income or price support), which operates to increase the exportation or reduce importation; as well as the commitment to discuss the limitation of the subsidy in case of causing 'serious injury' to another member;
(b) prohibition of direct or indirect export subsidies or another system that allows exporting at 'a price lower than the comparable price charged for the like product to buyers in the domestic market';
(c) prohibition of subsidies on the exportation of products that have the effect of granting a share of world trade in excess of the share of 'the previous representative period'; and
(d) in cases in which a product may become in a burdensome world surplus, consultation 'with a view of reaching an intergovernmental commodity

399. US State Department, Suggested Charter for an International Trade Organization of the United Nations, September 1946, pp. 29, 30.

agreement' in order to adopt 'measures to increase consumption and reduce production through the diversion of resources from uneconomic production'.[400]

As the US Proposals, the US Suggested Charter devoted a section to '*State Trading*' (Articles 26-28), the origin of GATT Article XVII '*State Trading Enterprises*'. A state trading enterprise was considered to be any enterprise over which a '*substantial measure of control*' is exercised, directly or indirectly, by a member government. Members were mandated to establish or maintain state enterprises to accord non-discriminatory treatment to other countries' commerce, and to provide '*specific and detailed information*' to other members about the operation of the enterprise regarding its external purchases and sales, which shall '*be influenced solely by commercial considerations, such as price, quality, market-ability, transportation and terms of purchase or sale*' (Article 26).

In case Members established or maintained a monopoly of the importation or exportation of individual products, they shall enter into negotiations with other Members in order to set a maximum margin (i.e., the price difference between home market and foreign suppliers) regarding import and/or export monopolies (Article 27). In cases of complete state monopoly of import trade, an aggregate amount of products to be imported shall be negotiated and would be subject to periodic adjustment (Article 28).[401] Although this clause was not maintained in the final draft of the ITO Charter, it foreshadowed a technique that was later incorporated in some Protocols of Accessions to the GATT,[402] e.g., Yugoslavia and Poland.[403]

Remarkably, the US Suggested Charter also included a Chapter (V) on '*Restrictive business practices*' (Articles 34-40).[404] Notwithstanding this chapter was not included in the GATT, which only consisted of provisions on commercial policy, it was maintained in the ITO Charter, signed at the Havana Conference in 1948.[405] The chapter on restrictive business practices of the US Suggested Charter was aimed at preventing commercial practices from frustrating the purpose of the aimed trade organization, i.e., promoting the expansion of production and trade, as well as maintaining a high level of real income in all countries. Specifically, the objective was preventing '*commercial enterprises*' from undertaking practices that would '*restrain competition, restrict market access or foster monopolistic control in international trade*'. The term '*commercial enterprises*' referred to '*all persons and entities conducting*

400. *Ibid.*, pp. 18-20.
401. *Ibid.*, pp. 20-22.
402. J.H. Jackson, *World Trade and the Law of GATT (A Legal Analysis of the General Agreement on Tariffs and Trade)*, 1969, pp. 362-364.
403. '*Poland shall, with effect from the date of this Protocol, undertake to increase the total value of its imports from the territories of contracting parties by not less than 7 per cent per annum.*' GATT document L/2851, 19 September 1967, p. 9.
404. US State Department, Suggested Charter for an International Trade Organization of the United Nations, September 1946, pp. 25-29.
405. Chapter V of the ITO Charter (Articles 46-54). UN document E/CONF.2/78, 24 March 1948.

business, including such entities in which there is a government interest as well as agencies of government conducting trade'.[406]

The Organization was authorized to receive and investigate complaints, assist in consultations, request information from members, determine whether the restrictive practice had harmful effects on trade, prepare recommendations for action by members, conduct studies, call consultative conferences in the field, etc. It provided obligations for countries aimed at preventing commercial enterprises within their jurisdiction from engaging in trade-restrictive practices. To this end, within their jurisdiction, members were entrusted to carry on investigations '*to inform the Organization about the restrictive business practices, consult other members, follow recommendations of the Organization in taking action to terminate and prevent the recurrence of restrictive business practices*'.[407]

The US Suggested Charter '*could no doubt be improved upon, but not at the pleasure of the United States, and not without strong opposition from American sources. If adopted it will bring some, though by no means all, (...) order in the international trade field (...). If it is rejected, (...) the consequences are clearly indicated: a return to the systematic economic warfare which prevailed in the 1930's, with its political tensions, its economic wastefulness, and its favorable setting for the launching by desperate leaders, on behalf of despairing peoples, of ventures fatal to the world at large as well as to themselves. The International Trade Organization Charter [was] the only available safeguard against such a development*'.[408]

II UN CONFERENCE ON TRADE AND EMPLOYMENT, 1946-1948

A month after the US Suggested Charter was presented, the UN began the preparatory work of the ITO Charter, which culminated with its signature at the Conference on Trade and Employment, in Havana, in March 1948. Previously, the Preparatory Committee met in London, New York and Geneva, where the GATT was signed in October 1947. The four sessions were held as follows:

406. '*Combinations, agreements or other arrangements which*
   a. *fix prices r terms or conditions to be observed in dealing with others in the purchase or sale of any product or service.*
   b. *exclude enterprises from any territorial market or field of business activity, allocate or divide any territorial market or field of business activity, allocate costumers, or fix sales or purchase quotas, except as such arrangements are only a part of regular marketing arrangements between a particular enterprise and its distributions with respect to its own products and are not designed to reduce competition between that enterprise and its competitors;*
   c. *boycott or discriminate against particular enterprises.*
   d. *limit production or fix production quotas;*
   e. *suppress technology or invention, whether patented or unpatented;*
   f. *extend the use of rights under patents, trade-marks or copyrights to matters not properly within the scope, or to products or services which are not the immediate subject, of the authorized grant.*' US State Department, Suggested Charter for an International Trade Organization of the United Nations, September 1946, pp. 25, 26 (Article 34).
407. *Ibid.*, p. 28 (Article 37).
408. J. Viner, Conflicts of Principle in Drafting a Trade Charter, *Foreign Affairs*, Vol. 25, No. 4, 1947, pp. 612-628 at 628 https://doi.org/10.2307/20030068.

(1) First Session of the Preparatory Committee, London, 15 October-26 November 1946.
(2) Drafting Committee of the Preparatory Committee, New York, 20 January-25 February 1947.
(3) Second Session of the Preparatory Committee, Geneva, 10 April-30 October 1947. Signature of the GATT.[409]
(4) Conference on Trade and Employment, Havana, 21 November 1947-24 March 1948. Signature of the ITO Charter.[410]

The First Session of the Preparatory Committee, held in London from 15 October to 26 November 1946, was also known as the London Conference.[411] Based on the US Suggested Charter, the London Conference was divided into five committees: (i) Employment and Economic Activity, (ii) General Commercial Policy, (iii) Restrictive Business Practices, (iv) Inter-governmental Commodity Arrangements, and (v) Administration and Organization.[412]

The London Conference highlighted the need to reach a multilateral trade agreement 'directed towards the reduction of tariffs and the elimination of preferences'. To avoid keeping them 'in abeyance pending action by the International Conference on Trade and Employment and the adoption of the Charter by national legislatures', the agreed tariff schedules would be incorporated in the GATT. To this end, multilateral negotiations were proposed to be held in Geneva from April 1947. The GATT was designed to be signed and made public at the close of the tariff negotiations, and brought into force as soon as possible, and 'legally independent of the Charter'.[413]

The GATT was regarded as an instrument to give effect to certain provisions of the ITO Charter. Accordingly, the GATT would conform to the principles of the Charter, and none of its provisions would prevent the operation of the ITO. The GATT would include those provisions '*considered essential to safeguard the value of the tariff concessions and such other provisions as may be appropriate*'. Therefore, the Preparatory Committee decided that the provisions on commercial policy would be drawn up for the GATT, which was entrusted to Committee II.[414] '*The deliberations of this committee, therefore, are the most important for the purpose of interpreting GATT.*'[415]

During the London Conference, attention was devoted to protective measures. While the use of tariffs was permitted without exceeding the (voluntarily) negotiated

409. Final Act adopted at the conclusion of the Second Session of the Preparatory Committee of the United Nations Conference on Trade and Employment. Signed at Geneva, on 30 October 1947. UNTS, Vol. 55, pp. 187-316.
410. UN document E/CONF.2/78, 24 March 1948.
411. J.H. Jackson, *The Jurisprudence of GATT & the WTO, Insights on Treaty Law and Economic Relations*, 2002, p. 22; J.H. Jackson, *World Trade and the Law of GATT (A Legal Analysis of the General Agreement on Tariffs and Trade)*, 1969, p. 42.
412. United Nations Economic and Social Council, Report of the First Session of the Preparatory Committee of the United Nations Conference on Trade and Employment. UN document EPCT/33, 31 October 1946, pp. 3, 9-18.
413. *Ibid.*, pp. 4, 48-51.
414. *Ibid.*, pp. 9-18, 48-51.
415. J.H. Jackson, *World Trade and the Law of GATT (A Legal Analysis of the General Agreement on Tariffs and Trade)*, 1969, p. 42.

tariff bindings, and the discussion focused on determining the kind of protective measures to be used for promoting development, the Preparatory Committee recognized that the US Suggested Charter provided a certain degree of '*freedom to use subsidies*'. However, the problem was related to other forms of protection other than subsidies and unbound tariffs. The concern was determining ways for members to obtain a limited release from the assumed obligations with other members.[416] Therefore, while some of the provisions of the US Suggested Charter were redrafted at the London Conference in order to be incorporated into the ITO Charter, other provisions (Articles 15-23), including anti-dumping and countervailing duties, required further consideration and were left to be (re)drafted at a later stage.[417]

Between the First and Second Sessions of the Preparatory Committee, the 'Drafting Committee' met in Lake Success, New York, from 20 January to 25 February 1947. At this meeting, the first full draft of the GATT (New York draft) was developed by the Sub-Committee on Tariff Negotiations.[418] The discussion centred on which provisions on commercial policy of the ITO Charter were to be included in the GATT, and the decision was to select those that '*were necessary for the protection of the tariff concessions to be negotiated*'.[419]

Since the GATT was designed to be a 'specific trade agreement within the broader institutional context of the ITO Charter' while the ITO 'would furnish the necessary organizational and secretariat support for GATT',[420] the 'Drafting Committee' included in the first GATT draft (New York draft) a commitment whereby members would 'observe, and make effective to the fullest extent of their authority, all of the principles and provisions' of the draft Charter, i.e., including the provisions under chapters on 'Employment'; 'Demand, and Economic Activity'; 'Economic Development'; 'Restrictive Business Practices'; and 'Inter-governmental Commodity Arrangements'.[421]

The Second Session of the Preparatory Committee was held in Geneva from 10 April to 30 October 1947. Considered to be '*the principal meeting*',[422] it attained two endeavours, the preparation of the ITO Charter and the GATT, which were, in turn, subdivided. The preparatory work for the ITO Charter was divided into the substantive part and the procedural and organizational part. The embodiment of the GATT included, on the one hand, the negotiations on tariff reduction and, on the other hand,

416. UN document EPCT/33, 31 October 1946, p. 8.
417. Article 15: '*National Treatment on Internal Taxation and Regulation*'; Article 16: '*Freedom of Transit*'; Article 17: '*Antidumping and Countervailing Duties*'; Article 18: '*Tariff Valuation*'; Article 19: '*Customs Formalities*'; Article 20: '*Marks of Origin*'; Article 21: '*Publication and Administration of Trade Regulations - Advance Notice of Restrictive Regulations*'; Article 22: '*Information, Statistics and Trade Terminology*', Article 23: '*Boycotts*'. *Ibid.*, p. 28.
418. United Nations - Economic and Social Council - Drafting Committee of the Preparatory Committee of the United Nations Conference on Trade and Employment - Draft General Agreement on Tariffs and Trade, UN document E/PC/T/C.6/85, 15 February 1947, p. 1.
419. J.H. Jackson, *World Trade and the Law of GATT (A Legal Analysis of the General Agreement on Tariffs and Trade)*, 1969, p. 43.
420. *Ibid.* UN documents E/PC/T/33, 31 October 1946, pp. 22-25; Report of the Drafting Committee of the Preparatory Committee of the United Nations Conference on Trade and Employment, E/PC/T/34, 5 March 1947, p. 45.
421. UN document E/PC/T/C.6/85, 15 February 1947, p. 38.
422. J.H. Jackson, *Restructuring the GATT System*, p. 10.

the drafting of the Agreement. Much of the latter would be drawn from the ITO Charter provisions on commercial policy. Following a discussion regarding which articles from the ITO Charter should be included in the GATT, the decision was that the GATT would incorporate only those provisions that would normally be found in commercial treaties.[423] At the end of the Geneva Conference, on 30 October 1947, twenty-three nations signed the Final Act of the GATT.[424] Technically, it never came into force,[425] but was applied by a Protocol of Provisional Application on 1 January 1948.[426] The signature of eight specified countries before 15 November 1947 permitted the application of the GATT.[427]

The fourth and last session, the actual Conference on Trade and Employment, was held in Havana from 21 November 1947 to 24 March 1948. It concluded with the signature of the ITO Charter by fifty-three countries. Besides the chapter on commercial policy, the ITO Charter included chapters on: Economic Development and Reconstruction; Restrictive Business Practices; Inter-governmental Commodity Agreements; the ITO; Settlement of Differences; and General Provisions.[428] The objective of agreeing to the establishment of a multilateral trade organization was achieved, and an interim Commission for the ITO (ICITO) was established to bring the ITO into force. Meanwhile, several changes made at the Havana Conference on the commercial policy provisions of the ITO Charter were later incorporated into the GATT in 1948.[429]

Nevertheless, the US Congress indicated it would not approve it, and the ITO never came into existence.[430] For this reason, the GATT Review Session of 1954-1955 introduced some of the changes made to the provisions on commercial policy of the ITO Charter at the Havana Conference (that had not been incorporated in the GATT in 1948). Additionally, this GATT Review Session was seen as an occasion to draft a

423. J.H. Jackson, *World Trade and the Law of GATT (A Legal Analysis of the General Agreement on Tariffs and Trade)*, 1969, pp. 43, 44.
424. '*The Governments of the Commonwealth of Australia, the Kingdom of Belgium, the United States of Brazil, Burma, Canada, Ceylon, the Republic of Chile, the Republic of China, the Republic of Cuba, the Czechoslovak Republic, the French Republic, India, Lebanon, the Grand-Duchy of Luxemburg, the Kingdom of the Netherlands, New Zealand, the Kingdom of Norway, Pakistan, Southern Rhodesia, Syria, the Union of South Africa, the United Kingdom of Great Britain and Northern Ireland, and the United States of America.*' UNTS, Vol. 55, pp. 187-316 at 188.
425. J.H. Jackson, *The Jurisprudence of GATT & the WTO, Insights on Treaty Law and Economic Relations*, 2002, p. 20.
426. UNTS, Vol. 55, pp. 187-316 at 308.
427. The Governments of the Commonwealth of Australia, the Kingdom of Belgium (in respect of its metropolitan territory), Canada, the French Republic (in respect of its metropolitan territory), the Grand Duchy of Luxemburg, the Kingdom of the Netherlands (in respect of its metropolitan territory), the United Kingdom of Great Britain and Northern Ireland (in respect of its metropolitan territory), and the United States. UNTS, Vol. 55, pp. 187-316 at 188, 194, 308.
428. United Nations Conference on Trade and Employment – Held at Havana, Cuba – From 21 November 1947, to 24 March 1948 - Final Act and Related Documents. UN document E/CONF.2/78, 24 March 1948.
429. J.H. Jackson, *World Trade and the Law of GATT (A Legal Analysis of the General Agreement on Tariffs and Trade)*, 1969, p. 50.
430. J.H. Jackson, *Restructuring the GATT System*, p. 12; J.H. Jackson, *The World Trading System: Law and Policy of International Economic Relations*, 2nd ed., 2000, p. 38.

charter for a simpler organization, the Organization for Trade Cooperation; however, it resulted in a second failed attempt at the US Congress.[431]

These failures in constituting a trade organization had unavoidable consequences in the drafting of the GATT. Some commercial policy provisions of the ITO Charter entrusted the ITO with multilateral decisions, which implied a unique and impartial voice. In the GATT, 'Organization' was replaced by 'CONTRACTING PARTIES', requiring consensus among all GATT Contracting Parties. As an illustration, Article 34.6 of the ITO Charter, on third-country dumping,[432] required the ITO to waive the injury requirement for a member to impose anti-dumping duties. GATT Article VI.6, as well as ADA Article 14, entrusts 'CONTRACTING PARTIES' with the decision of waving the injury requirement, which entails unanimity; hence, the affected country has to agree with the imposition of the duties on its products, something really unlikely.

In this line, through the different preparatory sessions of the GATT and the ITO Charter, the following general (and common) amendments were introduced into the provisions of the US Suggested Charter. The reference to the 'Organization' in the US Suggested Charter was replaced by 'Committee' in the first GATT draft at New York, and by 'CONTRACTING PARTIES' in the GATT at Geneva, which has been maintained in the current version. The ITO Charter, signed at Havana, maintained the reference to the 'Organization', which never came into force. Similarly, the reference to 'Member' in the US Suggested Charter became 'Contracting Party' in the GATT. Following the establishment of the WTO in 1994, the term 'Member' has been reintroduced in the WTO Agreements.

With respect to trade remedies and subsidies, the Preparatory Committee of the GATT and ITO Charter based their work on the provisions of the US Suggested Charter. Interestingly, some reference was made to the work of the League of Nations Conference of 1933.[433] As a general statement, the Preparatory Committee maintained the main aspects of these provisions under the US Suggested Charter. After multilateral discussions on the provisions on trade remedies and subsidies, amendments were

431. J.H. Jackson, *World Trade and the Law of GATT (A Legal Analysis of the General Agreement on Tariffs and Trade)*, 1969, pp. 50, 51. GATT documents L/261-69; L/189, 1954.

432. Article 34.6 ITO Charter: '*No Member shall levy any anti-dumping or countervailing duty on the importation of any, product of another Member country unless it determines that the effect of the dumping or subsidization, as the case may be, is such as to cause or threaten material injury to an established domestic industry, or is such as to retard materially the establishment of a domestic industry. The Organization may waive the requirements of this paragraph so as to permit a Member to levy an anti-dumping or countervailing duty on the importation of any product for the purpose of offsetting dumping or subsidization which causes or threatens material injury to an industry in another Member country exporting the product concerned to the importing Member country.*'

433. '*The statement of the United States Delegate that price should be defined in terms of circumstances in the exporting country clarified the intention of a definition which the United States had submitted to the World Conference in 1933*' UN document E/PC/CII/54, 16 November 1946, p. 2.

incorporated through the four sessions held in London, New York, Geneva and Havana during 1946-1948.[434]

Since the US Suggested Charter provisions on trade remedies and subsidies have been presented above, in order to show their normative evolution, the next sections will depart from the first GATT draft (the New York draft),[435] notwithstanding relevant discussions that were previously held at the London Conference will be highlighted. Due to the fact that the signature of the GATT preceded the ITO Charter, the amendments incorporated into these GATT provisions after the Havana Conference (mainly at the GATT Review Session of 1954-1955) will also be hereby described. In order to better illustrate the normative evolution of each provision on trade remedies and subsidies until the current framework, each of the provisions will be analysed separately following chronological order.

Anti-dumping and countervailing duties, both enshrined under Article 11 of the US Suggested Charter, have been maintained together under GATT Article VI; thus, they will be explored together. The provision on subsidies will follow due to the intrinsic relationship with countervailing duties, and their later inclusion in the Agreement on Subsidies and Countervailing Measures. Afterwards, the provision on safeguards will be succeeded by a last section devoted to 'restrictive business practices'.

A Anti-dumping and Countervailing Duties

Inspired by the Antidumping Act of 1922 and the countervailing duty provision of the US Tariff Act of 1930, the (first) multilateral provision on anti-dumping and countervailing duties was incorporated under Article 11 of the US Suggested Charter for an ITO in 1946. During the next decade, the provision was amended during the preparatory work of the GATT and the ITO Charter, and lastly at the GATT Review Session of 1954-1955. Since then, it has been maintained under GATT Article VI.

1 London, 1946; New York, 1947: First GATT Draft

At the Report of the First Session of the Preparatory Committee, held in London, the consideration and drafting of the provision on anti-dumping and countervailing duties were reserved for a later stage,[436] notwithstanding, the Technical Sub-Committee held discussions on the subject.[437] The majority of countries considered that '*such duties*

434. UN documents: London Report, E/PC/T/33, 31 October 1946; GATT draft at Lake Success, New York, E/PC/T/C.6/85, 15 February 1947; GATT, signed at Geneva in 1947, UNTS, Vol. 55, pp. 187-316 at 194; ITO Havana Charter, E.CONF.2/78, 24 March 1948.
435. The Sub-Committee was of the opinion that the draft Agreement was not made public, but merely passed to the Second Session of the Preparatory Committee as a working paper. UN document E/PC/T/C.6/85, 15 February 1947, p. 2.
436. UN document E/PC/T/33, 31 October 1946, p. 28.
437. UN Preparatory Committee of the International Conference on Trade and Employment Committee II, Discussion of Anti-dumping and Countervailing Duties, UN document E/PC/T/C.II/48, 11 November 1946, pp. 1-17.

may properly be applied' under certain circumstances, whereas the UK made a reservation stating '*that all anti-dumping and countervailing duties should be prohibited*'.[438]

During the discussions, some countries complained that '*Japanese prices had been low because of low labour standards, exchange manipulation, and the use of subsidies*', and considered other forms of dumping other than price dumping, i.e., '*dumping by means of devaluation and dumping based on a low standard of living in the producing country*', while others, such as Belgium, claimed that there was a '*tendency to describe any unfair practice as dumping*'.[439] The US provided for clarification on Article 11 of the US Suggested Charter, claiming that it only permitted measures to counteract price dumping, which '*would obligate members not to impose anti-dumping duties with respect to the other three types*',[440] i.e., social, service and exchange dumping.[441] After discussing it, the Technical Sub-Committee decided not to include the other three forms of dumping, but to submit the matter for consideration to the Drafting Committee at New York.

Overall, a common view on the subject of anti-dumping was absent, and the variety of opinions was as wide as the number of countries involved in the talks; hence, the most significant contributions are hereby presented. With respect to the injury requirement, Czechoslovakia suggested adding '*some guarantee against arbitrary action*'. Australia and South Africa suggested to delete from the injury requirement the clause '*or is such as to prevent the establishment of a domestic industry*'. Following some questions raised by the Netherlands regarding the procedure to justify the measures, the US clarified that '*the normal procedure would be to place the burden of proof on the party complaining*'. France considered that the decision on whether the duties were justified should rest with the Organization, after hearing the countries concerned. Australia proposed that the '*criteria for the imposition of anti-dumping and countervailing duties should include: (i) A determination of actual or potential injury by an independent administrative authority; (ii) Optional and not mandatory application of these duties, (iii) Appeal to the ITO by any member aggrieved by any action of another member under this Article*'. South Africa was not in favour of requiring prior authorization by the Organization, but agreed on assigning an appeal process against the imposition of anti-dumping and countervailing duties to a central authority. On its part, New Zealand made a reservation to immediately impose anti-dumping duties.[442]

In view of the lack of agreement, further discussions and the drafting of the provisions were left for a later stage, at the Drafting Committee meeting in Lake Success, New York, from 20 January to 15 February 1947, when the first draft of the

438. UN document E/PC/CII/54, 16 November 1946, pp. 1-16.
439. *Ibid.*, pp. 1-3.
440. UN document E/PC/T/C.II/48, 11 November 1946, p. 1.
441. Jackson explained that these forms of dumping referred to the following: Social dumping – prison or sweated labour; service dumping – freight; and exchange dumping – manipulation of currency. J.H. Jackson, *World Trade and the Law of GATT (A Legal Analysis of the General Agreement on Tariffs and Trade)*, 1969, p. 404.
442. UN documents E/PC/T/C.II/48, 11 November 1946, pp. 11, 15, 16; E/PC/CII/54, 16 November 1946, pp. 15, 16.

GATT was released.[443] Based on Article 11 of the US Suggested Charter, the provision on anti-dumping and countervailing duties incorporated minor changes. A last paragraph (6) was added at the request of Cuba, but other countries claimed it did not involve any modification to their obligations under the Charter.[444] Therefore, it was later deleted and was not included in the GATT draft of 30 October 1947.[445] Other incorporations were suggested, such as permitting quantitative restrictions to offset subsidization, favouring other measures besides anti-dumping and countervailing duties, inserting '*is less by more than five per cent*' to determine the margin of dumping, prohibiting countervailing duties on products with preferential treatment, etc. None of these suggestions were inserted in the article.[446] With respect to broadening the scope of anti-dumping duties to cover other forms of dumping, Australia suggested the incorporation of another paragraph (7),[447] whose inclusion was not accepted by the US. The Drafting Committee rejected its inclusion in the first draft of the GATT (New York draft),[448] but submitted it for consideration at the Second Session,[449] where it was definitely rejected. At the end of the Drafting Committee meeting in New York, the first GATT draft provision on anti-dumping and countervailing duties read as follows:

> 1. No anti-dumping duty or charge[450] shall be imposed on any product of the territory of any contracting party[451] imported into the territory of any other contracting party in excess of an amount equal to the margin of dumping under which such product is being imported. For the purposes of this Article, the margin of dumping shall be understood to mean the amount by which the price of the product exported from one country to another is less than
>   (a) the comparable price charged for the like product to buyers in the domestic market of the exporting country, or, in the absence of such domestic price, either

443. UN document E/PC/T/C.6/85, 15 February 1947.
444. Article IV.6 of the first draft of the GATT of 15 February 1947: '*Nothing in this Article shall preclude contracting parties from incorporating in a regulatory commodity agreement conforming to the principles of Chapter VII of the draft Charter for an International Trade Organization provisions prohibiting, as between the contracting parties to such a commodity agreement, the use of anti-dumping duties in cases in which dumping, within the meaning of paragraph 1 of this Article, may be permitted under the terms of such an agreement.*' UN document E/PC/T/C.6/85, 15 February 1947, pp. 7, 21.
445. UNTS, Vol. 55, pp. 187-316 at 212-217.
446. UN document E/PC/T/34, 5 March 1947, p. 13.
447. '*Any contracting state maintaining restrictions against forms of dumping other than "price dumping", e.g., freight dumping or dumping by means of depreciation of currency, shall only impose such, dumping duties where it has determined after enquiry that the method and extent of dumping against which action is taken is such as to injure or threaten to injure an established domestic industry.*' E/PC/T/C.6/55, 5 February 1947, p. 22. '*Any Member maintaining restrictions on forms of dumping other than "price dumping", e.g., freight dumping or dumping by means of depreciation of currency, shall only impose such dumping duties where it has determined after enquiry that the method and extent of dumping against which action is taken is such as to injure or threaten to injure an established domestic industry.*' UN document E/PC/T/34, 5 March 1947, p. 13.
448. UN document E/PC/T/C,6/55, 5 February 1947, p. 22.
449. UN document E/PC/T/34, 5 March 1947, p. 13.
450. The US Suggested Charter did not include 'or charge'.
451. US Suggested Charter referred to 'Member country'. At New York, in the first GATT draft, it was replaced by 'contracting party'.

(b) the highest comparable price at which the like product is sold for export to any third country in the ordinary course of commerce, or
(c) the cost of production of the product in the country of origin plus a reasonable addition for selling cost and profit;[452] with due allowance in each case for differences in conditions and terms of sale, for differences in taxation, and for other differences affecting price comparability,

2. No countervailing duty shall be imposed on any product of the territory of any contracting party imported into the territory of another contracting party in excess of an amount equal to the estimated bounty or subsidy determined to have been granted, directly or indirectly, on the production or export of such product in the country of origin or exportation. The term 'countervailing duty' shall be understood to mean an additional duty imposed for the purpose of off-setting any bounty or subsidy bestowed, directly or indirectly, upon the manufacture, production or exportation of any merchandise.[453]
3. No product of the territory of any contracting party imported into the territory of any other contracting party shall be subject to anti-dumping or countervailing duty by reason of the exemption of such product from duties or taxes imposed in the country of origin or exportation upon the like product when consumed domestically, or by reason of the refund of such duties or taxes.[454]
4. No product of the territory of any contracting party imported into the territory of any other contracting party shall be subject to both anti-dumping and countervailing duties to compensate for the same situation of dumping or export subsidization.
5. No contracting party shall impose any anti-dumping or countervailing duty or charge on the importation of any product of the territories of other contracting parties unless it determines that the effect of the dumping or subsidization, as the case may be, is such as materially to injure or threaten to injure an established domestic industry, or is such as to prevent the establishment of a domestic industry.
6. Nothing in this Article shall preclude contracting parties from incorporating in a regulatory commodity agreement conforming to the principles of Chapter VII of the draft Charter for an International Trade Organization provisions prohibiting, as 'between the contracting parties to such a commodity agreement, the use of anti-dumping duties in cases in which dumping, within the meaning of paragraph 1 of this Article, may be permitted under the terms of such an agreement'.[455]

The New York draft maintained an article from the US Suggested Charter, providing for the publication and administration of trade regulations, as well as the advance notice of restrictive regulations. In case of import restrictions, advance notice was required thirty days before giving effect to the restrictive measure, yet anti-dumping and countervailing duties were explicitly excluded from it.[456] The exception was not kept in the GATT after the Geneva Conference in 1947.

452. The sentence '*plus a reasonable addition for selling cost and profit*' was not in the US Suggested Charter.
453. This last sentence concerning the interpretation of the term 'countervailing duty' was not in the US Suggested Charter.
454. At the London Session, the sentence '*or by reason of the refund of such duties or taxes*' was added to para. 3 (the addition was approved in the NY draft). UN document E/FC/T/C.6/55, 15 February 1947, p. 20.
455. UN document E/PC/T/C.6/85, 15 February 1947, pp. 6, 7.
456. *Ibid.*, p. 10.

2 *Second Session of the Preparatory Committee, Geneva, 1947: The GATT*

During the Second Session, 'the principal meeting', held in Geneva from 10 April to 30 October 1947,[457] the Preparatory Committee endeavoured the drafting of both the GATT and the ITO Charter, as well as entered into multilateral negotiations on tariff reductions. The resulting bound tariffs were incorporated in the GATT, which was signed by twenty-three countries on 30 October 1947.[458]

With respect to the discussions concerning which provisions should be incorporated in the GATT, only one month before the signature of GATT, the US reiterated that the provision on anti-dumping and countervailing duties was not essential to the Agreement; therefore, it suggested its deletion from the GATT.[459] Nevertheless, the article on anti-dumping and countervailing duties was redrafted; some clarifications and paragraphs were incorporated into GATT Article VI.[460]

Regarding anti-dumping duties, paragraph 1(a) clarified that, when determining the margin of dumping, prices have to be compared '*in the ordinary course of trade*'. An interpretative note regarding paragraph 1 was incorporated and has since then been maintained. It read as follows:

> Hidden dumping by associated houses (that is, a sale by an importer at a price below that corresponding to the price invoiced by an exporter with whom the importer is associated, and also below the price in the exporting country) constitutes a form of price dumping.

With respect to the provision prohibiting countervailing duties in excess of the amount of the bounty or subsidy, the then paragraph 2 incorporated '*including any special subsidy to the transportation of a particular product*'.[461] The following interpretative note was added, and has been maintained in the current version of GATT Article VI (with a minor change due to the change in the number of paragraphs):

> Multiple currency practices can in certain circumstances constitute a subsidy to exports which may be met by countervailing duties under paragraph 2 or can constitute a form of dumping by means of a partial depreciation of a country's currency which may be met by action under paragraph 1 of this Article. By 'multiple currency practices' is meant practices by governments or sanctioned by governments.

Moreover, two new paragraphs were introduced at the end of GATT Article VI, which correspond to the current first sentence of paragraph 6(b) and paragraph 7. The first paragraph aimed at facilitating the imposition of duties in case of injury caused to a third country, i.e., to offset the dumping or subsidization that has caused or threatened material injury to an industry in a third country. It read as follows:

---

457. J.H. Jackson, *Restructuring the GATT System*, p. 10.
458. UNTS, Vol. 55, pp. 187-316.
459. UN document E/PC/T/TAC/PV/10, 4 September 1947, p. 45.
460. UNTS, Vol. 55, pp. 187-316 at 212-217.
461. *Ibid.*, p. 212.

> The CONTRACTING PARTIES may waive the requirements of this paragraph so as to permit a contracting party to levy an anti-dumping or countervailing duty on the importation of any product for the purpose of offsetting dumping or subsidization which causes or threatens material injury to an industry in the territory of another contracting party exporting the product concerned to the territory of the importing contracting party.[462]

This paragraph would have accomplished its aim of facilitating the imposition of duties only if the ITO had come into existence, since the ITO Charter entrusted 'the Organization' with waiving the injury requirement. Under the current wording of the paragraph, the waiver must be agreed by 'CONTRACTING PARTIES', i.e., consensus; hence, it is difficult to imagine that the affected country would agree on the imposition of the duties on its products.

Concerning the imposition of duties on a third country, the Preparatory Committee introduced another paragraph at the end of the article, which was neither incorporated in the ITO Charter nor the subsequent versions of the GATT. This paragraph intended to emphasize that anti-dumping and countervailing duties could merely be imposed to offset dumping or subsidization:

> No measures other than anti-dumping or countervailing duties shall be applied by any contracting party in respect of any product of the territory of any other contracting party for the purpose of offsetting dumping or subsidization.[463]

The second paragraph added at the Geneva Conference (current paragraph 7) incorporated a presumption of non-determination of material injury in cases where dumping occurs under a '*system of stabilization of domestic prices*'. According to it, countries substantially interested may determine, by consultations, that there is no material injury in cases where the product has been exported at higher prices than sold in the domestic market, or in those where the system has not resulted in the '*unduly*' stimulation of exports or otherwise seriously prejudiced other countries. The term 'product' was replaced by 'commodity' under the ITO Charter and has been maintained in the current version of GATT Article VI.7. The paragraph read as follows:

> A system for the stabilization of the domestic price or of the return to domestic producers of a primary commodity, independently of the movements of export prices, which results at times in the sale of the product for export at a price lower than the comparable price charged for the like product to buyers in the domestic market, shall be considered not to result in material injury within the meaning of paragraph 5 of this Article, if it is determined by consultation among the contracting parties substantially interested in the product concerned:
>
> (a) that the system has also resulted in the sale of the product for export at a price higher than the comparable price charged for the like product to buyers in the domestic market, and

462. *Ibid.*, p. 214.
463. Ibid., p. 216. It included an interpretative note: '*The obligations set forth in paragraph 7, as in the case of other obligations under this Agreement, are subject to the provisions of Article XIX.*'

(b) that the system is so operated, either because of the effective regulation of production or otherwise, as not to stimulate exports unduly or otherwise seriously prejudice the interests of other contracting parties.[464]

3 *The ITO Charter, Havana 1947-1948: The GATT Review Session, 1954-1955*

At the Havana Conference, the actual Conference on Trade and Employment, the Preparatory Committee completed the drafting of the ITO Charter, which was signed on 24 March 1948. Modifications were incorporated into Article 34 of the ITO Charter, on anti-dumping and countervailing duties.[465] Notwithstanding the ITO Charter never came into force, the following amendments made at the Havana Conference were incorporated under GATT Article VI.[466]

First, a definition of dumping and the requirement of injury were introduced in the first sentence of paragraph 1:

> The contracting parties recognize that dumping, by which products of one country are introduced into the commerce of another country at less than the normal value of the products, is to be condemned if it causes or threatens material injury to an established industry in the territory of a contracting party or materially retards the establishment of a domestic industry.[467]

The changes of the Preparatory Committee into the provision on anti-dumping and countervailing duties at the Havana Conference resulted in an alteration in the numbering of paragraphs under its Article 34, which were later incorporated in the GATT in 1948 and have been maintained in the current version of GATT Article VI. The first paragraph, concerning anti-dumping duties, was divided into two paragraphs. As a result, the numbering of the paragraphs in the article changed, e.g., the former paragraph 2 regarding countervailing duties was renumbered as 3. The first sentence of the new paragraph 2, establishing that the amount of the duty may not be greater than the margin of dumping, was redrafted as follows:

> In order to offset or prevent dumping, a contracting party may levy on any dumped product an anti-dumping duty not greater in amount than the margin of dumping in respect of such product. For the purposes of this article, the margin of dumping is the price difference determined in accordance with the provisions of paragraph 1.

In addition, the ITO Charter included a new interpretative note to the provision on anti-dumping and countervailing duties, regarding paragraphs 2 and 3. This new interpretative note was later incorporated in the current GATT Article VI (along with

464. *Ibid.*, p. 214. The term 'product' of this paragraph was changed by 'commodity' in the ITO Charter and this modification has been maintained in the current GATT version. UN document E.CONF.2/78, 24 March 1948, p. 28.
465. UN document E.CONF.2/78, 24 March 1948, pp. 27-28 (Article 34).
466. Article VI was amended by the Protocol modifying the GATT Part II and Article XXVI, which was signed at Geneva, on 14 September 1948. UNTS, Vol. 62, pp. 86-60.
467. UN document E.CONF.2/78, 24 March 1948, p. 27 (Article 34).

the two notes inserted at the Geneva Conference and two more that would be included at the GATT Review Session of 1954-1955). The new interpretative note to paragraphs 2 and 3 read as follows:[468]

> As in many other cases in customs administration, a Member may require reasonable security (bond or cash deposit) for the payment of anti-dumping or countervailing duty pending final determination of the facts in any case of suspected dumping or subsidization.

Since the ITO Charter did not come into force, the GATT was reviewed in 1954-1955, when changes were exclusively introduced to paragraph 6 of GATT Article VI, concerning dumping or subsidy in a third country. The GATT Review Session of 1954-1955 was the last time GATT Article VI was amended. A second sentence to subparagraph (b), an interpretative note to it, and a third subparagraph (c) were added to paragraph 6. This incorporation was requested by Australia and New Zealand and recommended by the Working Party. The additions to paragraph 6 read as follows:

> (b) (...) The CONTRACTING PARTIES shall waive the requirements of sub-paragraph (a) of this paragraph, so as to permit the levying of a countervailing duty, in cases in which they find that a subsidy is causing or threatening material injury to an industry in the territory of another contracting party exporting the product concerned to the territory of the importing contracting party.
>
> In exceptional circumstances, however, where delay might cause damage which would be difficult to repair, a contracting party may levy a countervailing duty for the purpose referred to in subparagraph (b) of this paragraph without the prior approval of the CONTRACTING PARTIES; Provided that such action shall be reported immediately to the CONTRACTING PARTIES and that the countervailing duty shall be withdrawn promptly if the CONTRACTING PARTIES disapprove.

The following interpretative note to paragraph 6(b) was included in the GATT: 'Waivers under the provisions of this sub-paragraph shall be granted only on application by the contracting party proposing to levy an anti-dumping or countervailing duty, as the case may be.'

It provides that CONTRACTING PARTIES shall (not may) allow a country [A] to impose countervailing duties (no anti-dumping) in cases in which it finds that the subsidy of a second country [B] causes or threatens to cause material injury to an industry of a third country [C]. Compared to the first sentence of subparagraph (b), this allows a country to initiate a countervailing duty investigation in a third country and impose provisional countervailing duties without approval of the CONTRACTING PARTIES, provided it is immediately reported and approved. As mentioned above, since 'the Organization' under the ITO Charter became 'CONTRACTING PARTIES' under the GATT, without this last amendment to paragraph 6, the provision would have remained invalidated due to the reduced possibility that it is approved by consensus, i.e., that the affected country approves the imposition of duties on its products.

468. *Ibid.*, p. 112 (Annex P, Interpretative Note *Ad* Article 34).

Besides the interpretative note to paragraph 6(b), a new interpretative note was incorporated into paragraph 1 regarding anti-dumping. This note permits to disregard domestic prices in the exporting country. This construction of the normal value requires that two circumstances exist in the exporting country: a monopoly of its trade and the fixation of prices by the State. This interpretative note would be later used to construct the normal value of imports from the so-called *non-market economies*, not only in anti-dumping, but also in countervailing duty proceedings:

> It is recognized that, in the case of imports from a country which has a complete or substantially complete monopoly of its trade and where all domestic prices are fixed by the State, special difficulties may exist in determining price comparability for the purposes of paragraph 1, and in such cases importing contracting parties may find it necessary to take into account the possibility that a strict comparison with domestic prices in such a country may not always be appropriate.

During the Preparatory Conferences of the GATT and the ITO, the idea of entrusting an independent (multilateral) authority, the Organization, with the verification and authorization of the imposition of duties was suggested. That has already been in force in 1902, when the Brussels Sugar Convention entrusted an independent permanent commission to verify the existence and amount of subsidies prior to the imposition of countervailing duties. Nevertheless, the political pressure to protect the domestic industry prompted some countries (Australia and New Zealand, which had anti-dumping and countervailing duty laws) to reject this suggestion. Furthermore, during the discussions of the Preparatory Committee, some countries (the UK and the US) repeatedly manifested that the anti-dumping and countervailing duty provision was not essential to the GATT; hence, some countries suggested its deletion from the GATT.

B Subsidies

Due to their intrinsic relation with countervailing duties, it is essential to provide an overview of the evolution of the provision on subsidies throughout the preparatory work of the GATT and the ITO Charter. Enshrined under GATT Article XVI, the provision on subsidies was drawn upon Article 25 of the US Suggested Charter.

1 London, New York and Geneva Conferences, 1946-1947: The GATT

At the First Session in London, the Preparatory Committee held long discussions regarding the provision on subsidies under Article 25 of the US Suggested Charter, which was redrafted at London and New York. At the latter, Brazil and New Zealand requested the non-inclusion of the provisions on export subsidies in the GATT. For this reason, the GATT provision on subsidies merely mandated the notification of subsidies and consultations to limit them in case of causing '*serious prejudice*' to other members:

General Undertaking Regarding Subsidies

> If any contracting party grants or maintains any subsidy, including any form or income of price support, which operates directly or indirectly to increase exports of any product from, or to reduce imports of any product into its territory, the contracting party shall notify the Committee in writing as to the extent and nature of the subsidization, as to the estimated effect of the subsidization on the quantity of the affected product or products imported into or exported from the territory of the contracting party and as to the conditions making the subsidization necessary. In any case in which it is determined, by consultation through the Committee among the contracting parties having an important interest in the trade in the product concerned, that serious prejudice to the interest of any other contracting party is caused or threatened by any such subsidization, the contracting party granting the subsidization shall, upon request, discuss with the other contracting party or contracting states concerned, or with the Committee, the possibility of limiting the subsidization.[469]

The Drafting Committee clarified that this first paragraph applied to 'cases in which the subsidy operates, "directly or indirectly", to increase exports or reduce imports of any product and can thus not be interpreted as being confined to subsidies operating directly to affect trade in the product under consideration'. Compared to Article 25 of the US Suggested Charter, the Drafting Committee had replaced the term 'anticipated effect' by 'estimated effect' in the first sentence 'in order to remove the possible impression that the effect of a subsidy on trade could be accurately predicted'.[470] This paragraph constituted the subsidies provision under GATT Article XVI as of the signature of the GATT in 1947, when the term 'Committee' was replaced by 'CONTRACTING PARTIES', and 'conditions' by 'circumstances'.[471]

Provisions on export subsidies were not included in the GATT, but maintained in the ITO Charter. The Drafting Committee clarified that these provisions on export subsidies were not an alternative to the provision on general subsidies[472] and discussed these provisions under paragraphs 2-6 of Article 30 of the New York draft ITO Charter (which would later become Articles 26-28 in the ITO Charter, signed at Havana in 1948).

As seen above, Article 25 of the US Suggested Charter prohibited export subsidies (or any other system) that allowed '*a price lower than the comparable price charged for the like product to buyers in the domestic market*'.[473] With respect to this provision, the Drafting Committee introduced an exception for primary products, conditioned on the compliance of two requirements: that they had also resulted in exporting at higher prices than the domestic market, and that the system had not stimulated exports unduly or otherwise seriously prejudiced the interest of other Members. Under these two conditions, the Drafting Committee established that a '*system for the stabilization*

469. UN document E/PC/T/C.6/85, 15 February 1947, pp. 1, 25.
470. UN document E/PC/T/34, 5 March 1947, p. 26.
471. UN document E/PC/T/C.6/85, 15 February 1947, p. 25; UNTS, Vol. 55, pp. 187-316 at 250.
472. The provision on general subsidies was established under Article 30.1 in the New York draft for the ITO Charter and later under Article 25 in the ITO Charter signed in 1948.
473. US State Department, Suggested Charter for an International Trade Organization of the United Nations, September 1946, p. 19.

of the domestic price or of returns to domestic producers of a primary product' would not constitute a subsidy on exportation (Article 30.3 of the New York draft ITO Charter and Article 27.1 of the ITO Havana Charter).[474]

The other prohibition of export subsidies under Article 25 of the US Suggested Charter affected any product having the effect of acquiring a share of world trade in a product in excess of the share during a previous representative period. In this case, the 'Drafting Committee' decided to keep its application on any product, '*whether on primary or nonprimary commodities, whenever such subsidies are permitted under this Article*' (Article 30.5 of the New York ITO Charter draft and Article 28 of the ITO Havana Charter).[475] Therefore, with respect to this prohibition of export subsidies (on products having the effect of acquiring a share of world trade in excess of the previous representative period), the ITO Charter did not distinguish between primary and non-primary products. The provisions on export subsidies in the New York draft for the ITO Charter (Article 30, paragraphs 2-6) read as follows:

> 2. (a) No Member shall grant, directly or indirectly, any subsidy on the exportation of any product, or establish or maintain any other system, which results in the sale of such product for export at a price lower than the comparable price charged for the like product to buyers in the domestic market, due allowance being made for differences in the conditions and terms of sale, for differences in taxation, and for other differences affecting price comparability, provided that this shall not prevent any Member from exempting exported products from duties or taxes imposed in respect of like products when consumed domestically, from remitting such duties or taxes which have accrued, or from using the proceeds of such duties or taxes to make payments to domestic producers;[476]
>
> (b) Members shall give effect to the provisions of this paragraph at the earliest practicable date, but in any event not later than three years from the day on which this Charter enters into force. If any Member considers itself unable to make the provisions of this paragraph effective in respect of any specified product or products upon the expiration of such period, such Member shall, at least three months before the expiration of such period, give to the Organization notice in writing requesting a specific extension of the period and accompanied by a complete analysis of the system in question and the facts justifying it. It shall then be determined whether the extension requested should be made.
>
> 3. A system for the stabilization of the domestic price or of returns to domestic producers of a primary product, which results over a period in the sale of the product for export at a price lower than the comparable price charged for the like product to buyers in the domestic market, may be determined not to involve a subsidy on exportation under the terms of paragraph 2 of this Article

474. UN document E/PC/T/34, 5 March 1947, p. 26. This exception would be later included under the current version of GATT Article VI.7 as a presumption not to constitute material injury.
475. *Ibid.*, p. 27.
476. At the New York meeting of the Drafting Committee, one delegate requested to record his opinion on this paragraph, stating that it '*should not be interpreted so as to prevent countries far removed from world market to sell their products at current world market prices even though these may be lower than the prices charged in the domestic market, such action not being the result of a direct or indirect subsidy or of the establishment of any other system*' (Article 30.2 of the New York draft later became Article 26 of the ITO Charter). *Ibid.*, p. 26.

if it has also resulted over a period in the sale of the product for export at a price higher than the comparable price charged for the like product to domestic buyers, and if the system is so operated, either because of the effective limitation of production or otherwise, as not to stimulate exports unduly or otherwise seriously prejudice the interest of other Members.

4. (a) In any case of subsidization of a primary commodity, if a Member considers that its interests are seriously prejudiced by the subsidy or if the Member granting the subsidy considers itself unable to comply with the provisions of paragraph 2 of this Article within the time limit laid down therein, the difficulty may be determined to be a special difficulty of the kind referred to in Chapter VII [Inter-governmental commodity arrangements], and in that event the procedure laid down in that Chapter shall be followed;
   (b) If it is determined that the measures provided for in Chapter VII have not succeeded, or do not promise to succeed, within a reasonable period of time, in removing or preventing the development of a burdensome world surplus of the primary product concerned, the requirements of paragraph 2 of this Article shall cease to apply in respect of such product as from the effective date of such determination and shall not be re-applied in respect of such product until a date determined in accordance with procedures approved by the Organization.[477]
5. Notwithstanding the provisions of paragraph 2 and sub-paragraph 4 (b) of this Article, no Member shall grant any subsidy on the exportation of any product which has the effect of acquiring for that Member a share of world trade in that product in excess of the share which it had during a previous representative period, account being taken insofar as practicable of any special factors which may have affected or may be affecting the trade in that product. The selection of a representative period for any product and the appraisal of any special factors affecting the trade in the product shall be made initially by the Member granting the subsidy, Provided that such Member shall, upon the request of any other Member having an important interest in the trade in that product, or upon the request of the Organization, consult promptly with the other Member or with the Organization regarding the need for an adjustment of the base period selected or for the re-appraisal of the special factors involved.
6. Any determination required by or appropriate to the operation of this Article shall be made under procedures established by the Organization in accordance with paragraph 4 of Article 66.[478]

These provisions on export subsidies under Article 30 of the New York draft ITO Charter were redrafted under Articles 26-28 of the ITO Charter, signed in Havana, where some changes were introduced and incorporated into the GATT following the Review Session in 1954-1955.[479]

477. Two delegates suggested to delete the avoidance of the obligation to cease providing export subsidies resulting '*in the sale of such product for export at a price lower than the comparable price charged for the like product to buyers in the domestic market*' (Article 30.4(b) of the New York and Article 27.3 of ITO Charter at Havana). *Ibid.*, p. 27.
478. *Ibid.*, pp. 25-27.
479. UN document E.CONF.2/78, 24 March 1948, pp. 23, 24 (Article 25-28).

2 *The ITO Charter, Havana, 1948*

Article 26 of the Havana ITO Charter, *'Additional Provisions on Export Subsidies'*,[480] divided into four paragraphs, maintained the prohibition of export subsidies which resulted in sale on exportation at a lower price than the comparable price charged for the like product to buyers in the domestic market (under former paragraph 2 of Article 30 of the New York draft ITO Charter).[481]

The exception for primary products was maintained under Article 27 of the Havana ITO Charter, *'Special Treatment of Primary Commodities'*,[482] which, divided into five paragraphs, incorporated paragraphs 3 and 4 of Article 30 of the New York

---

480. Article 26 of the ITO Charter: '*Additional Provisions on Export Subsidies*

1. *No Member shall grant, directly or indirectly, any subsidy on the export of any product, or establish or maintain any other system, which subsidy or system results in the sale of such product for export at a price lower than the comparable price charged for the like product to buyers in the domestic market, due allowance being made for differences in the conditions and terms of sale, for differences in taxation, and for other differences affecting price comparability.*
2. *The exemption of exported products from duties or taxes imposed in respect of like products when consumed domestically, or the remission of such duties or taxes in amounts not in excess of those which have accrued, shall not be deemed to be in conflict with the provisions of paragraph 1. The use of the proceeds of such duties or taxes to make payments to domestic producers in general of those products shall be considered as a case under Article 25.*
3. *Members shall give effect to the provisions of paragraph 1 at the earliest practicable date but not later than two years from the day on which this Charter enters into force. If any Member considers itself unable to do so in respect of any particular product or products, it shall, at least three months before the expiration of such period, give notice in writing to the Organization, requesting a specific extension of the period. Such notice shall be accompanied by a full analysis or the system in question and the circumstances justifying it. The Organization shall then determine whether the extension requested should be made and, if so, on what terms.*
4. *Notwithstanding the provisions of paragraph 1, any Member may subsidize the exports of any product to the extent and for such time as may be necessary to offset a subsidy granted by a non-Member affecting the Member's exports of the product. However, the Member shall, upon the request of the Organization or of any other Member which considers that its interests are seriously prejudiced by such action, consult with the Organization or with that Member, as appropriate, with a view to reaching a satisfactory adjustment of the matter.'*

481. This article included an exception to this prohibition in order to offset a subsidy granted by a non-member that affected the member's exports of the product. Nevertheless, this provision was never incorporated into the GATT.

482. Article 27 of the ITO Charter: '*Special Treatment of Primary Commodities*

1. *A system for the stabilization of the domestic price or of the return to domestic producers of a primary commodity, independently of the movements of export prices, which results at times in the sale of the commodity for export at a price lower than the comparable price charged for the like commodity to buyers in the domestic market, shall be considered not to involve a subsidy on export within the meaning of paragraph 1 of Article 26, if the Organization determines that (a) the system has also resulted, or is so designed as to result, in the sale of the commodity for export at a price higher than the comparable price charged for the like commodity to buyers in the domestic market: and (b) the system is so operated, or is designed so to operate, either because of the effective regulation of production or otherwise, as not to stimulate exports unduly or otherwise seriously prejudice the interests of other Members.*

draft ITO Charter. Nevertheless, it entrusted the Organization with the determination of the two requirements, i.e., that products had been sold on exportation at higher prices than in the domestic market and that the system had not unduly stimulated exports or otherwise seriously prejudiced the interest of other Members. In other words, authorization by an independent multilateral body was necessary to grant subsidies on the exportation of primary products.

Article 28, '*Undertaking regarding Stimulation of Exports of Primary Commodities*',[483] covered the prohibition of export subsidies having the effect of maintaining or acquiring more than '*an equitable share of world trade*', term that replaced a share of world trade '*in excess of the share which it had during a previous representative period*'

---

2. *Any Member granting a subsidy in respect of a primary commodity shall co-operate at all times in efforts to negotiate agreements, under the procedures set forth in Chapter VI, with regard to that commodity.*
3. *In any case involving a primary commodity, if a Member considers that its interests would be seriously prejudiced by compliance with the provisions of Article 26, or if a Member considers that its interests are seriously prejudiced by the granting of any form of subsidy, the procedures set forth in Chapter VI may be followed. The Member which considers that its interests are thus seriously prejudiced shall, however, be exempt provisionally from the requirements of paragraphs 1 and 3 of Article 26 in respect of that commodity, but shall be subject to the provisions of Article 28.*
4. *No Member shall grant a new subsidy or increase an existing subsidy affecting the export of a primary commodity, during a commodity conference called for the purpose of negotiating an inter-governmental control agreement for the commodity concerned unless the Organization concurs, in which case such new or additional subsidy shall be subject to the provisions of Article 28.*
5. *If the measures provided for in Chapter VI have not succeeded, or do not promise to succeed, within a reasonable period of time, or if the conclusion of a commodity agreement is not an appropriate solution, any Member which considers that its interests are seriously prejudiced shall not be subject to the requirements of paragraphs 1 and 3 of Article 26 in respect of that commodity, but shall be subject to the provisions of Article 28.'*

483. Article 28 of the ITO Charter: '*Undertaking regarding Stimulation of Exports of Primary Commodities*

1. *Any Member granting any form of subsidy, which operates directly or indirectly to maintain or increase the export of any primary commodity from its territory, shall not apply the subsidy in such a way as to have the effect of maintaining or acquiring for that Member more than an equitable share of world trade in that commodity.*
2. *As required under the provisions of Article 25, the Member granting such subsidy shall promptly notify the Organization of the extent and nature of the subsidization, of the estimated effect of the subsidization on the quantity of the affected commodity exported from its territory, and of the circumstances making the subsidization necessary. The Member shall promptly consult with any other Member which considers that serious prejudice to its interests is caused or threatened by the subsidization.*
3. *If, within a reasonable period of time, no agreement is reached in such consultation, the Organization shall determine what constitutes an equitable share of world trade in the commodity concerned and the Member granting the subsidy shall conform to this determination.*
4. *In making the determination referred to in paragraph 3, the Organization shall take into account any factors which may have affected or may be affecting world trade in the commodity concerned, and shall have particular regard to:*
   (a) *the Member country's share of world trade in the commodity during a previous representative period;*
   (b) *whether the Member country's share of world trade in the commodity is so small that the effect of the subsidy on such trade is likely to be of minor significance;*

(under the former Article 30.5 of the New York draft ITO Charter). Furthermore, the scope of application of this prohibition was narrowed and applied only to primary products. In case such subsidies caused serious prejudice (or threat thereof), Article 28 provided for consultation, whose negative result would lead the Organization to determine the '*equitable share*', and the member would be obliged to conform to this determination. Notably, this prohibition of export subsidies disappeared for non-primary products. Since the ITO Charter did not enter into force, the provisions on export subsidies were redrafted and incorporated into GATT Article XVI following the Review Session of 1954-1955.

3 *The GATT Review Session, 1954-1955*

The GATT Review Session of 1954-1955 incorporated Articles 26-28 into four new paragraphs under GATT Article XVI, '*Section B – Additional Provisions on Export Subsidies*', and six interpretative notes. An interpretative note to GATT Article XVI (Article 26.2 of the ITO Charter) clarified that the exemption of exported products from duties or taxes, or their remission (not in excess), is not considered a subsidy.[484] Two interpretative notes were added to the new Section B, on export subsidies. The first permits the use of multiple rates of exchange, pursuant to provisions of the IMF Agreement.[485] The second defines a primary product.[486]

The four new paragraphs recognize that export subsidies may have harmful effects on other countries and include the obligation to cease export subsidies on primary products, which result in '*having more than an equitable share of world export trade in that product*' (under paragraph 3); and on non-primary products, which result in the sale on exportation at a price lower than in the domestic market (under paragraph 4).[487] Three other interpretative notes were added to paragraphs 3 and 4. The new paragraphs, with their respective interpretative notes, read as follows:

(c) *the degree of importance of the external trade in the commodity to the economy of the Member country granting, and to the economies of the Member countries materially affected by, the subsidy;*
(d) *the existence of price stabilization systems conforming to the provisions of paragraph 1 of Article 27;*
(e) *the desirability of facilitating the gradual expansion of production for export in those areas able to satisfy world market requirements of the commodity concerned in the most effective and economic manner, and therefore of limiting any subsidies or other measures which make that expansion difficult.*'

484. '*The exemption of an exported product from duties or taxes borne by the like product when destined for domestic consumption, or the remission of such duties or taxes in amounts not in excess of those which have accrued, shall not be deemed to be a subsidy.*'
485. '*1. Nothing in Section B shall preclude the use by a contracting party of accordance with the Articles of Agreement of the International Monetary Fund.*'
486. '*2. For the purposes of Section B, a "primary product" is understood to be any product of farm, forest or fishery, or any mineral, in its natural form or which has undergone such processing as is customarily required to prepare it for marketing in substantial volume in international trade.*'
487. The Agreement on Subsidies and Countervailing Measures abolished the distinction between primary and non-primary products, prohibiting all export subsidies (ASCM Article 3).

Section B – Additional Provisions on Export Subsidies

2. The contracting parties recognize that the granting by a contracting party of a subsidy on the export of any product may have harmful effects for other contracting parties, both importing and exporting, may cause undue disturbance to their normal commercial interests, and may hinder the achievement of the objectives of this Agreement.
3. Accordingly, contracting parties should seek to avoid the use of subsidies on the export of primary products. If, however, a contracting party grants directly or indirectly any form of subsidy which operates to increase the export of any primary product from its territory, such subsidy shall not be applied in a manner which results in that contracting party having more than an equitable share of world export trade in that product, account being taken of the shares of the contracting parties in such trade in the product during a previous representative period, and any special factors which may have affected or may be affecting such trade in the product.[488]
4. Further, as from 1 January 1958 or the earliest practicable date thereafter, contracting parties shall cease to grant either directly or indirectly any form of subsidy on the export of any product other than a primary product which subsidy results in the sale of such product for export at a price lower than the comparable price charged for the like product to buyers in the domestic market. Until 31 December 1957 no contracting party shall extend the scope of any such subsidization beyond that existing on 1 January 1955 by the introduction of new, or the extension of existing, subsidies.
5. The CONTRACTING PARTIES shall review the operation of the provisions of this Article from time to time with a view to examining its effectiveness, in the light of actual experience, in promoting the objectives of this Agreement and avoiding subsidization seriously prejudicial to the trade or interests of contracting parties.

Under GATT Article XVI.4, primary products are totally exempted from the prohibition on subsidies upon exportation at a lower price than the comparable price

488. The second Interpretative Notes to para. 3 was based on Article 27.1 of the ITO Charter. Interpretative notes *Ad* Article XVI. 3 read as follow:

‘1. *The fact that a contracting party has not exported the product in question during the previous representative period would not in itself preclude that contracting party from establishing its right to obtain a share of the trade in the product concerned.*

2. *A system for the stabilization of the domestic price or of the return to domestic producers of a primary product independently of the movements of export prices, which results at times in the sale of the product for export at a price lower than the comparable price charged for the like product to buyers in the domestic market, shall be considered not to involve a subsidy on exports within the meaning of paragraph 3 if the CONTRACTING PARTIES determine that:*
   (a) *the system has also resulted, or is so designed as to result, in the sale of the product for export at a price higher than the comparable price charged for the like product to buyers in the domestic market; and*
   (b) *the system is so operated, or is designed so to operate, either because of the effective regulation of production or otherwise, as not to stimulate exports unduly or otherwise seriously to prejudice the interests of other contracting parties.*

Notwithstanding such determination by the CONTRACTING PARTIES, operations under such a system shall be subject to the provisions of paragraph 3 where they are wholly or partly financed out of government funds in addition to the funds collected from producers in respect of the product concerned.’

charged to buyers in the domestic market, while the ITO Charter had established two requirements for such exemption, which the Organization was entrusted to determine.[489] GATT Article XVI.4 included a 'standstill' obligation until 1958, expected to last while countries reached an agreement on the prohibition of all non-primary products.[490] Pursuant to paragraph 5, since an agreement was not reached, CONTRACTING PARTIES extended the application of the standstill provision through a declaration that was annually extended between 1957 and 1960.[491] A Declaration Giving Effect to the Provisions of GATT Article XVI.4 entered into force on 14 November 1962. Nevertheless, it was merely adopted by seventeen Contracting Parties.[492] Therefore, GATT Article XVI.4 was only applicable to those seventeen signatories and inoperative for most GATT Contracting Parties for thirty years (1964-1994).[493]

C Safeguard Measures ('*Emergency Action*')

As the provisions on subsidies, anti-dumping and countervailing duties, the emergency action provision of the US Suggested Charter evolved throughout the preparatory work of the GATT and the ITO Charter until its current version under GATT Article XIX.

1 London, 1946; New York, 1947: First GATT Draft

During the First Session of the Preparatory Committee, held in London in 1946, the US explained that the 'emergency action' under Article 29 of the US Suggested Charter

489. The distinction between export subsidies on primary and non-primary products has continued. Following the Uruguay Round, non-primary (industrial) products are subject to the Agreement on Subsidies and Countervailing Measures, whereby all export subsidies are prohibited (ASCM Article 3). Primary products are regulated by the Agreement on Agriculture, which provided for a reduction commitment on export subsidization. It was not until the Nairobi Ministerial Conference in 2015 that WTO Members reached an agreement to eliminate agricultural export subsidies over specific deadlines. It provided for an immediate elimination for developed Members, while developing countries and least developed countries were allowed to maintain export subsidies on marketing costs as well as on internal transport and freight charges (pursuant to Article 9.4 of the Agreement on Agriculture) until 2023 and 2030, respectively. WTO document MIN (15)/45, 21 December 2015.
490. Interpretative Note to GATT Article XVI. 4: '*The intention of paragraph 4 is that the contracting parties should seek before the end of 1957 to reach agreement to abolish all remaining subsidies as from January 1985; or, failing this, to reach agreement to extend the application of the standstill until the earliest date thereafter by which they can expect to reach such agreement.*'
491. The Declaration on the Extension of the Standstill Provisions of Article XVI.4 of the GATT was adopted on 30 November 1957 (6S/24); first extension, 22 November 1958 (7S/30); second extension, 19 November 1959 (8S/25); third extension, 19 November 1960 (9S/33). The third extension (9S/33) expired at the end of 1963. Seeking that Article XVI.4 of the GATT was applicable to all Contracting Parties, the Second Declaration on the Extension of the Standstill Provisions of Article XVI.4 of the GATT (12S/50) was presented for adoption, but it was only signed by one Contracting Party and allowed to expire on 31 December 1967. GATT documents COM.TD/72, 17 March 1970; L/2137, 17 February 1964, p. 3; L/2854/Rev.l, 13 October 1967, pp. 4-5.
492. GATT document L/1380, 1 November 1960, Annex I, pp. 4-5.
493. Austria, Belgium, Canada, Denmark, France, Germany, Italy, Japan, Luxembourg, the Netherlands, New Zealand, Norway, Southern Rhodesia, Sweden, Switzerland, the United Kingdom, and the United States. GATT document PROT/2. Rev.3, 1967, para. 42.01.

consisted of an exceptional action to safeguard the right given to the other parties in the agreement, as well as to prevent abuse of that right. To invoke the emergency action, prior notification and consultation with the Organization as well as with any interested country were required. If no agreement on the notified action was reached, after sixty days, the country was free to take action. In that case, under the approval of the Organization, and after sixty days from the written notice, the affected country was allowed to suspend any obligation or concessions to the country that had invoked the clause in the first place.[494]

The US reiterated the need to incorporate the safeguard provision '*in a document or an agreement or charter of this kind*'. Notwithstanding the UK considered it necessary to include an '*escape provision*', it desired to confine the scope of the emergency action to the tariff field and not to leave it applicable to '*quantitative restrictions, subsidies, State trading, and indeed it seems, all the commercial policy obligations of the Charter*'. The UK highlighted its apprehension towards such a broad provision, arguing it might '*seriously impair the value of the Charter as a whole, and (...) undermine the confidence in its effectiveness*'.[495]

The safeguard provision was amended by the Preparatory Committee at the London Conference and maintained in the first GATT draft by the Drafting Committee at New York. More specifically, the following three sentences were introduced. In the first paragraph, an explanatory sentence was inserted in brackets to extend the application of the provision to products receiving preference. The Preparatory Committee explained that this inserted language clarified that '*members invoking Article may withdraw or modify concessions in respect of preferences as well as concessions in respect of tariffs and obligations regarding quantitative restrictions, etc*'. Moreover, the Preparatory Committee divided the second paragraph of Article 29 of the US Suggested Charter into two paragraphs, thus creating a third new paragraph. Two new provisions were incorporated, one at the end of paragraph 2, permitting the imposition of safeguard measures without prior consultation; and the other one, at the end of the new paragraph 3, allowing the Organization to authorize counteraction above the equivalent to the original action.[496]

The provision inserted in paragraph 2 permitted, under critical and exceptional circumstances, the provisional imposition of safeguard measures without prior consultation, notwithstanding requiring it immediately after taking the action. During the discussions in London, as well as in New York, three delegates expressed the undesirability of permitting action without prior consultation even in emergency circumstances. One of them argued that if action was taken without prior consultation, counteraction by the affected member should be allowed without delays caused by requesting permission from the Organization.[497]

The provision added to paragraph 3 allowed the Organization to authorize counteraction, suspension of either concessions or obligations, above the equivalent

494. UN document. E/PC/T/C.II/PV/7, 1 November 1946, p. 3.
495. *Ibid.*, pp. 4-6.
496. UN document E/PC/T/C.34, 5 March 1947, pp. 29-30.
497. UN documents E/PC/T/33, 31 October 1946, p. 10.; E/PC/T/C.34, 5 March 1947, pp. 29-30.

action originally taken. The Preparatory Committee clarified this provision was intended to prevent disproportionate counteraction, hence allowing the Organization to permit '*severe counteraction in cases of abuse of the privileges granted by the Article*'.[498]

The provision on safeguard measures in the first GATT draft maintained the incorporations added at the London Conference, which have been underlined below. The Drafting Committee substituted the term 'Organization' by 'Committee', and '*In serious cases*' by '*In cases of abuse*'.[499] The safeguard provision of the first GATT draft read:

> Emergency Action on Imports of Particular Products
>
> 1. If, as a result of unforeseen developments and of the effect of any obligations incurred under or pursuant to this Agreement, any product is being imported into the territory of any contracting party in such increased quantities and under such conditions as to cause or threaten serious injury to domestic producers of like or directly competitive products (or, in the case of a product which is the subject of a concession with respect to a preference, is being imported under such conditions as to cause or threaten serious injury to producers in a territory which receives or received such preference), the contracting party shall be free to suspend the obligation in respect of such product in whole or in part, or to withdraw or modify the concession.
> 2. Before any contracting party shall take action pursuant to the provisions of paragraph 1, it shall give notice in writing to the Committee[500] as far in advance as may be practicable and shall afford the Committee and those contracting parties having a substantial interest as exporters of the product concerned, an opportunity to consult with it in respect of the proposed action. In critical and exceptional circumstances such action may be taken provisionally without prior consultation Provided that consultation shall be effected immediately following upon the taking of such action.[501]
> 3. If agreement among the interested contracting parties with respect to the action is not reached, the contracting party which proposes to take or continue the action, shall, nevertheless, be free to do so, and if such action is taken or continued, the affected contracting parties shall then be free, not later than sixty days after such action is taken, to suspend, upon the expiration of thirty days from the date of which written notice of such suspension is received by the Committee, the application to the trade of the contracting party taking such action, of such substantially equivalent obligations or concessions under this Agreement the suspension of which the Committee does not disapprove. In cases of abuse the Committee may authorize an affected contracting party to suspend concessions or obligations in addition to those which may be substantially equivalent to the action originally taken.[502]

498. *Ibid.*, p. 10. The Drafting Committee referred to this provision in the ITO Charter draft, considering it reasonable to require a two-thirds majority for the Organization's action under the last sentence of the safeguard provision. UN document E/PC/T/34, 5 March 1947, p. 63.
499. UN document E/PC/T/C.6/85, 15 February 1947, p. 29.
500. The US Suggested Charter read 'Organization'. In the Lake Success, NY, GATT draft it was replaced by 'Committee'.
501. At the Geneva Conference, the adjective 'exceptional' was removed and has been maintained under GATT Article XIX.2.
502. UN document E/PC/T/C.6/85, 15 February 1947, pp. 28-29.

2 *The GATT, Geneva, 1947; the ITO Charter, Havana, 1948; GATT Review Session, 1954-1955*

At Geneva, the Preparatory Committee redrafted the safeguard provision before the signature of the GATT in 1947. The term 'Committee' in the New York draft was replaced by 'CONTRACTING PARTIES' in the final draft of the GATT and has remained in the current version of GATT Article XIX. Additionally, amendments were made in two of the three provisions that had been inserted at London, which were redrafted and separated into new subparagraphs. Under the first paragraph, the Preparatory Committee redrafted the sentence inserted in brackets at the London Conference, whereby the action was extended to products under preference, and moved it to a new paragraph 1(b). Since then, it has been maintained under GATT Article XIX.1(b).

The second change introduced at Geneva was eliminating the provision that had been added at London at the end of paragraph 3, establishing the authorization requirement to counteract above the equivalent original action. Instead, a new subparagraph 3(b) grants the affected country the discretion to suspend concessions or obligations '*as may be necessary to prevent or remedy the injury*' in cases where the original action had been taken without prior consultation (pursuant to paragraph 2) and '*delay would cause damage difficult to repair*', i.e., emergency retaliation. In case another country had taken action without prior consultation, the affected country can suspend concessions or other obligations at discretion and without prior consultation.[503] The new subparagraph 3(b) has been maintained under current GATT Article XIX.3(b), which reads as follows:

> (b) Notwithstanding the provisions of sub-paragraph (a) of this paragraph, where action is taken under paragraph 2 of this Article without prior consultation and causes or threatens serious injury in the territory of a contracting party to the domestic producers of products affected by the action, that contracting party shall, where delay would cause damage difficult to repair, be free to suspend, upon the taking of the action and throughout the period of consultation, such obligations or concessions as may be necessary to prevent or remedy the injury.

Contrary to subparagraph 3(a), which provides for retaliation '*to the trade of the contracting party*' that had taken action, i.e., on a discriminatory basis; subparagraph 3(b) allows the suspension of concessions or obligations without implying or specifying retaliation against the trade of the particular country. Concerning this 'ambiguity' of the relationship of subparagraphs 3(a) and 3(b), the Preparatory Committee added, at Havana, an interpretative note to the safeguard provision under the ITO Charter, clarifying that subparagraph 3(b), as well as subparagraphs 1(a) and 1(b), must be applied on a non-discriminatory basis '*and that such action should avoid, to the fullest extent possible, injury to other supplying Member countries*'.[504]

503. UNTS, Vol. 55, pp. 187-316 at 258-262.
504. UN document E.CONF.2/78, 24 March 1948, p. 113 (Annex P, Interpretative Note *Ad* Article 40).

Furthermore, at the Havana Conference, the Preparatory Committee introduced some other modifications to the article on safeguards (Article 40 of the ITO).[505] In the first paragraph, the adverb *'relatively'* was added to modify the quantification of the increase of imports, i.e., *'in such relatively increased quantities'*. In paragraph 2, *'critical circumstances'* was replaced by *'in circumstances of special urgency'*. Moreover, a fourth paragraph was added not to consult with ITO Members that were not GATT Contracting Parties the withdrawal or modification of concessions, which would exclude the obligations under the ITO Charter.[506] Nevertheless, none of these modifications were introduced in the GATT Article XIX. Further amendments were suggested at the GATT Review Session of 1954-1955, but rejected and not incorporated into GATT Article XIX,[507] except the replacement of *'obligations or concessions'* with *'concessions or other obligations'*.[508]

Overall, the amendments incorporated during the preparatory work of the GATT rendered looser the safeguard provision, hence facilitating the imposition of safeguard measures under GATT Article XIX (compared to Article 29 of the US Suggested Charter). Alleging that it would safeguard the concessions given to other parties to the agreement, the provision on safeguards was considered essential in the GATT, unlike anti-dumping and countervailing duty provisions, whose deletion was even suggested. However, since the GATT already provides for the possibility to invoke the 'nullification or impairment clause' under GATT Article XXIII, it can arguably be discussed whether the safeguard provision was essential to the GATT.

D Restrictive Business Practices

Intrinsically related to trade remedies and subsidies is the chapter on restrictive business practices of the US Suggested Charter (Chapter V, Articles 34-40) which was maintained in the ITO Charter. Since the GATT only included provisions on commercial policy and the ITO Charter did not enter into force, this chapter was never in force. Nevertheless, the Preparatory Committee recognized the importance of regulating restrictive business practices in order to safeguard the objectives of the organization.[509] Therefore, discussions on these provisions were held during the preparatory work of the ITO Charter in London, New York, Geneva and Havana.

505. *Ibid.*, pp. 31-32 (Article 40).
506. *'4. Nothing in this Article shall be construed*

(a) to require any Member, in connection with the withdrawal or modification by such Member of any concession negotiated pursuant to Article 17, to consult with or obtain the agreement of Members others than those Members which are contracting parties to the General Agreement on Tariffs and Trade, or (b) to authorize any Member which is not a contracting party to that Agreement, to withdraw from or suspend obligations under this Charter by reason of the withdrawal or modification of such concession.'

507. GATT document W.9/193, pp. 12-13, 11 February 1955 (Review Working Party II on Tariffs, Schedules and Customs Administration – Articles I, II, III, XIX and XXIV – Statement of Recommendations Submitted by Sub-Group B to Working Party II).
508. GATT document W.9/236, 2 March 1955 (Legal and Drafting Committee – Drafting Changes to Articles XXVI, I, II, 14, IV, XI, XIX, XXIV, XXV, and XXVII – Annexes A, C, F, G, and H).
509. UN document EPCT/33. 31 October 1946, pp. 18, 19.

At the London Conference, the Preparatory Committee considered that the Organization had a main role in examining restrictive practices, including laws and procedures related to them; and that complaints regarding restrictive business practices could be received not only from members, but also from organizations, enterprises and persons, with the prior approval of a responsible government. The Preparatory Committee focused on consultation and investigation procedures, emphasizing the role of the Organization in requesting information, investigating, determining the existence of harmful effects and recommending remedial measures to prevent the maintenance or recurrence of restrictive business practices. The Preparatory Committee highlighted the relevance of these provisions, the absence of which would drive countries to resort to restrictive action on trade and production.[510]

The ITO Charter, signed at Havana, established the provisions on restrictive business practices under Chapter V (Articles 46-54), whereby members were mandated to cooperate with the Organization to prevent harmful effects on trade and production caused by practices aimed at restraining competition, limiting access to markets or fostering monopolistic control by public or private commercial enterprises.[511] As the US Suggested Charter, the ITO Charter provided for procedures on consultation and investigation; obligations of members to coordinate with other members and the organization; cooperative remedial arrangements; special procedures with respect to services; and authorization for the Organization to request information from countries, conduct studies and organize conferences on the subject.

After having reviewed the evolution of trade remedy laws during the preparatory work of the GATT and ITO Charter, it can be concluded that the three provisions were included in the GATT with the (exclusive) aim of protecting domestic industries. Through the three trade remedy laws, protection to the domestic industry is attained by unilateral means. Therefore, the incorporation of trade remedy laws into the GATT and the ITO Charter seems an attempt to guarantee a multilateral trade agreement and organization with protectionist means, i.e., including protectionist means to prevent protectionism.

Contrary, the only means to ensure compliance with a multilateral trade agreement is establishing a judicial mechanism. Accordingly, the protection for domestic industries that countries attain by unilaterally imposing trade remedies should in its stead be a judicial protection whereby multilateral trade rules are interpreted and enforced by an independent and objective body. The idea of establishing a higher authority that verified the existence of the condemned action,[512] and authorized countermeasures, as it occurred in the case of the Brussels Sugar Convention of 1902, seems to be in line with the aims of a multilateral trade agreement and organization; nonetheless, the ITO Charter, which provided for a dispute settlement mechanism, never entered into force; and thus, an independent and multilateral authority (ITO) was absent to decide on the imposition of trade remedies.

510. *Ibid.*
511. Article 46 of the ITO Charter. UN document E/CONF.2/78, 24 March 1948.
512. GATT Article VI does not condemn 'dumping' although it allows countries to impose anti-dumping duties.

Furthermore, the trade-restrictive effects of trade remedies were in contradiction with the provisions on restrictive business practices under the ITO Charter. Agreeing to multilateral provisions on restrictive business practices seems to be a better solution than the GATT provisions on trade remedy laws, whereby countries are permitted to impose unilateral measures. While provisions on restrictive business practices were never incorporated in the GATT, trade remedy laws were developed during the GATT period, i.e., since 1947 to 1994. The next chapter will explore the evolution of trade remedy laws throughout the main GATT negotiations rounds, i.e., Kennedy, Tokyo and Uruguay.

CHAPTER 6

Trade Remedy Laws Through Main GATT Negotiations Rounds, 1948-1994

This chapter explores the normative evolution of multilateral trade remedy laws and subsidy disciplines through the main GATT negotiations rounds, including the enactment of the 1967 Anti-dumping Code, as a result of the Kennedy Round; its repeal by the 1979 Anti-dumping Code, and the development of the Subsidies and Countervailing Measures Code, and Decision on Safeguards, following the Tokyo Round; as well as the creation of the WTO Agreements on Subsidies and Countervailing Measures, Anti-dumping, and Safeguards. An overview of the GATT disputes concerning trade remedy laws and subsidies is included to better understand the normative evolution of certain provisions until their current version.

The Second Session of the Preparatory Committee, held in Geneva in 1947, was the first multilateral trade negotiation on tariff reduction, where twenty-three countries, accounting for '*80 percent of world trade*', agreed to reduce tariffs on an MFN basis.[513] The resulting bound tariffs, with a trade value of USD 10 billion, were annexed to the GATT. Following the signature of the GATT, seven more negotiation rounds took place during the GATT period (1948-1994): Annecy, 1949; Torquay, 1950; Geneva, 1956; Dillon, 1961; Kennedy, 1962-1967; Tokyo, 1973-1979; and Uruguay, 1986-1994.[514] During the first five negotiation rounds, GATT Contracting Parties mainly focused on tariff negotiations. It was not until the sixth round, the Kennedy Round (1962-1967), that non-tariff barriers (NTBs) became part of trade negotiations.

While GATT Contracting Parties reached further tariff reductions,[515] they increased protection through the imposition of non-tariff barriers. '*Many domestic*

513. D.A. Irwin, The GATT in Historical Perspective, *The American Economic Review*, Vol. 85, No. 2, 1995, pp. 323-328 at 325.
514. J.H. Jackson, *Restructuring the GATT System*, p. 37.
515. Value of trade covered in GATT negotiations rounds: Geneva (1947): USD 10 billion; Geneva (1956): USD 2.5 billion; Dillon (1961): USD 4.9 billion; Kennedy (1962-1967): USD 40 billion; Tokyo (1973-1979): USD 155 billion; Uruguay (1986-1994): USD 3,700 billion. In J.H. Jackson,

producer interests began turning to a variety (more than a thousand) of non-tariff barriers as a way to minimize the competition from imports, since tariffs would no longer provide that type of protection.'[516] Anti-dumping and countervailing duties became a major concern among GATT Contracting Parties. Therefore, after the GATT Review Session of 1954-1955, the GATT Secretariat was requested to prepare studies and reports on different national legislation on anti-dumping and countervailing duties,[517] following which CONTRACTING PARTIES decided that further studies should be conducted.[518] A group of experts presented two reports, whereby they recommended a moderate use of anti-dumping and countervailing duties, recalled their exceptional and temporary nature to deal with specific cases of injury, and warned that immoderate use of these measures would reduce the efforts made since World War II to remove trade barriers.[519]

As a result, trade remedies and subsidies became important subjects during multilateral trade negotiation rounds, resulting in the development of specific agreements: At the Kennedy Round (1962-1967), the 1967 Anti-dumping Code (1967 AD Code)[520] was enacted. During the Tokyo Round (1973-1979), the 1979 Anti-dumping Code (1979 AD Code)[521] and the first Subsidies and Countervailing Measures Code (SCM Code)[522] were developed. Part of the results of the Uruguay Round (1986-1994) were the Agreements on Anti-dumping (ADA), Subsidies and Countervailing Measures (ASCM), and Safeguards (ASG).[523] Compared to the Kennedy and Tokyo Round Codes, the Uruguay Round Agreements are part of the WTO Agreement, hence, binding on all WTO Members.[524]

This section will focus on the evolution of multilateral trade remedy rules throughout the last GATT negotiating rounds (Kennedy, Tokyo and Uruguay), i.e., the enactment of the different GATT/WTO agreements on subsidies, anti-dumping and countervailing duties, and safeguard measures. A selection of the main GATT dispute settlement reports concerning trade remedies and subsidies will be included for a

---

Restructuring the GATT System, p. 37; J.H. Jackson, *The World Trade Organization, Constitution and Jurisprudence*, Chatham House Papers, 1998, p. 21.

516. J.H. Jackson, *Restructuring the GATT System*, p. 37; J.H. Jackson, *The World Trade Organization, Constitution and Jurisprudence*, Chatham House Papers, 1998, p. 21.
517. GATT documents L/409, 22 September 1955; L/479, 27 March 1956; L/552, 16 October 1956; L/548, 11 October 1956; L/555, 18 October 1956; L/712, 23 October 1957.
518. GATT documents L/908, 11 November 1958.
519. GATT documents L/978, 24 April 1959; L/1141, 29 January 1960.
520. Agreement on the Implementation of Article VI of the General Agreement on Tariffs and Trade, signed on 30 June 1967. GATT document, BISD, 15th Supp., 1968, pp. 24-35.
521. Agreement on the Implementation of Article VI of the General Agreement on Tariffs and Trade, signed on 12 April 1979, GATT document LT/TR/A/1.
522. Agreement on Interpretation and Application of Articles VI, XVI and XXIII of the General Agreement on Tariffs and Trade. GATT document LT/TR/A/3, signed on 30 June 1979.
523. The Uruguay Round renegotiated and adopted the following Agreements (on): Anti-dumping, Subsidies and Countervailing Measures, Safeguards, Agriculture, Customs Valuation, Textiles and Clothing, Sanitary and Phytosanitary, Technical Barriers to Trade, Trade-Related Investment Measures, Preshipment Inspection, Rules of Origin, and Import Licensing. J.H. Jackson, *The World Trade Organization, Constitution and Jurisprudence*, Chatham House Papers, 1998, p. 39.
524. The Marrakech Agreement Establishing the World Trade Organization, whereby GATT Contracting Parties became WTO Members.

twofold purpose: first, to better understand the problems arising from their application, and second, to explore the relationship between the GATT dispute settlement reports and the normative evolution.

During the GATT period (1948-1994), a total of 316 disputes were brought to the GATT, of which almost 120, i.e., almost 40%, concerned trade remedies or subsidies. As a matter of course, before the enactment of the different Agreements, disputes regarding trade remedy laws and subsidies were brought to the GATT by invoking GATT Articles VI, XVI and XIX. Therefore, disputes have been divided between those brought to the GATT before and after the Tokyo Round Codes. Although the GATT Review Session of 1954-1955 showed there was evidence of displeasure regarding Contracting Parties' anti-dumping procedures,[525] only two complaints regarding anti-dumping duties were submitted to the GATT before the 1967 AD Code and no disputes occurred while it was in force. Among the rest of the disputes brought to the GATT before the Tokyo Round, two concerned countervailing duties, eight regarded safeguard measures, and (at least) seventeen involved subsidies.[526] Following the enactment of the Tokyo Round Codes in 1980,[527] disputes concerning anti-dumping and countervailing duties exponentially increased, accounting for around forty on anti-dumping;[528] and thirty on countervailing duties, of which three disputes combined both anti-dumping and countervailing duties.[529] The number of disputes regarding subsidies remained stable following the SCM Code in 1980, accounting for around twenty-one disputes.[530] After 1982, no complaint concerning safeguard measures (GATT Art. XIX) was submitted to the GATT.[531]

I RESULTS OF THE KENNEDY ROUND AND GATT DISPUTES FROM 1948 TO 1980

The Kennedy Round (1962-1967) '*made little dent on the plethora of ingenious nontariff barriers that not only are causing complaints and pressures for retaliation among nations, but are eagerly sought by protectionist forces*'.[532]

525. GATT documents L/409, 22 September 1955; L/479, 27 March 1956; L/552, 16 October 1956; L/548, 11 October 1956; L/555, 18 October 1956; L/712, 23 October 1957.
526. *See* Appendix I: Table including GATT disputes on trade remedies and subsidies before the enactment of the Tokyo Round Codes, 1948-1980.
527. J.H. Jackson, W. Davey, *Legal Problems of International Economic Relations, Cases, Materials and Text*, 2nd ed., 1986, pp. 665-669.
528. Ten of which concluded with the issuance of a GATT Panel report (*see* Appendix III: Table including GATT disputes on anti-dumping duties after the 1979 AD Code).
529. Fifteen of which concluded with the issuance of a GATT Panel report (*see* Appendix II: Table covering GATT disputes concerning subsidies and countervailing duties after the entry into force of the SCM Code).
530. Five of which concluded with the issuance of a GATT Panel report.
531. Last, GATT disputes regarding safeguard measures terminated in the consultation proceeding:

    Austria – Restrictions on Imports of Video Tape Recorders (GD/117). Complainant: Japan. GATT document L/5119, 25 February 1981. *Switzerland – Imports of Table Grapes* (GD/136). Complainant: EEC-10, GATT document L/5371, 29 September 1982.

532. J.H. Jackson, *World Trade and the Law of GATT (A Legal Analysis of the General Agreement on Tariffs and Trade)*, 1969, p. 229.

A Anti-dumping

1 GATT Disputes on Anti-dumping, 1948-1980

Before the 1967 AD Code was developed at the Kennedy Round, two disputes regarding anti-dumping duties were submitted to the GATT, thus invoking GATT Article VI: *Sweden – AD Duties* in 1955 and *Canada – Potatoes* in 1962. These two cases show how, from the beginning of the history of the application of GATT Article VI, the methodology used in anti-dumping proceedings to determine the margin of dumping was used to manipulate the result of the calculation, hence, increasing the anti-dumping duties. In both cases, prices in the country of origin were ignored and the normal value was constructed in order to find 'dumping'. In the first case, Sweden ignored prices in Italy and fixed a minimum export price; while, in the second case, Canada ignored prices in the US and determined a 'value for duty'.

Sweden – AD Duties was submitted to the GATT by Italy in 1954,[533] alleging the inconsistency of Swedish anti-dumping regulations with GATT Article VI.[534] A Swedish decree established the imposition of anti-dumping duties on products imported under a minimum fixed price. As a result, imports of nylon stocking from Italy imported at a lower price than the minimum price fixed by Sweden were subject to anti-dumping duties. Italy raised a complaint against the discrimination that anti-dumping duties caused to low-cost producers compared to high-cost producers, by making the former lose their price advantage.[535] The Panel[536] considered the argument not to be entirely convincing and stated that GATT Article VI does neither oblige an importing country to impose anti-dumping duties in cases of dumping nor '*to treat in the same manner all suppliers*' who resort to dumping.[537]

Notwithstanding the absence of competence by the Panel to deal with Swedish legal procedures before customs authorities or the courts, it considered that the

533. In 1954, Italy was one of the founding members of the European Coal and Steel Community (ECSC), whereas Sweden did not become an EU member until 1995. As a result, trade barriers (in particular, anti-dumping duties) were not eliminated among the two countries by the time of the dispute.
534. *Swedish Anti-dumping Duties* (GD/23). GATT documents L/215, 29 July 1954; L/328, 23 February 1955.
535. The argument was developed as a hypothesis: High-cost producers could 'subsidize' their exportation in order to lower the price to the Swedish fixed price and enter the Swedish market without the imposition of anti-dumping duties. However, if the low-cost producers did not recourse to dumping practices, but exported at an equal or higher price than the Swedish minimum fixed price, they would lose the price advantage. '*If, in order to meet the changed conditions of the competition*', low-cost producers were to resort to dumping practices, the anti-dumping duties would be imposed even if the amount of dumping were lower than in the case of high-cost producers. GATT document L/328, 23 February 1955, paras 2, 7.
536. There was specific authority in GATT for a Working Party or a Panel. '*The Working Party consisted of the two disputants and three other nations (...) The step from Working Party to panel in dispute handling may seem innocuous, but it is very significant in that it represents a step towards greater respect for objective international legal obligations and a step away from the political bargaining among nations.*' J.H. Jackson, *World Trade and the Law of* no *GATT (A Legal Analysis of the General Agreement on Tariffs and Trade)*, 1969, pp. 173, 174.
537. GATT document L/328, 23 February 1955, para. 8.

Swedish decree reversed the burden of proof, allowing customs authorities not to demonstrate the existence of dumping *'or even to establish a prima facie case of dumping'*. The Panel concluded that the Swedish regulation was neither inconsistent with GATT Article VI nor with the most-favoured-nation clause, enshrined under GATT Article I; yet it recognized that the administration of such a system *'might easily run into conflict with those obligations'*.[538]

In 1962, the US brought the case *Canada – Potatoes*[539] to the GATT, complaining against the imposition of 'value for duty' (anti-dumping duties) on potatoes under the Canadian Customs Act. In October 1962, Canada had mandated the application of anti-dumping duties on fresh potatoes, over the tariff concession that Canada had granted to US potatoes in 1957. In cases where prices in the exporting country had declined *'as a result of the season or the marketing period'*, the Canadian Minister was entrusted the discretion to ignore prices in the country of origin (normal value) and to determine the amount of the *'value for duty'*.[540]

The Panel concluded that, in the ordinary course of trade, there was no difference between the price of potatoes when exported and when destined for domestic consumption in the US, i.e., no dumping; therefore, Canadian anti-dumping duties were not justified under GATT Article VI.1(a). Furthermore, by imposing *'an additional charge above the bound import duty'*, Canada had failed to carry out its obligations under GATT Article II.1(a). Finally, the Panel suggested that CONTRACTING PARTIES recommended the withdrawal of the additional charge on imports of potatoes, *'or to effect any other satisfactory adjustment of the impaired benefit accruing to the United States'*.[541] Canada adopted the report[542] and both countries agreed to a mutual solution.[543]

These two cases reflect certain parallel with both the origins of the first anti-dumping provision, enacted by Canada in 1904, and the methodologies currently applied by several WTO members in anti-dumping proceedings, particularly, the construction of the normal value under ADA Article 2.2 and the reversal of the burden of proof under the (expired) Section 15 of the Protocol of Accession of China to the

538. *Ibid.*, paras 15-17.
539. *Exports of Potatoes to Canada* (GD/67). Complainant: US. GATT documents L/1927, 16 November 1962; SR.20/13, 16 November 1962; L/1968, 2 January 1963.
540. According to the 1958 Canadian legislation amending the Customs Act, anti-dumping duties were imposed on fresh fruit or vegetable if the export value was lower than the 'value for duty', *'to be the average value, weighted as to quantity, at which like fresh fruits or vegetables were imported during the three-year period immediately preceding the date of shipment to Canada'*. *'The season in many parts of* [the US] *was advanced on the Canadian production season. At the time Canadian producers were only beginning to market their fruit and vegetables, the United States' season was often at its peak and, accordingly, prices were normally at their lowest level for the season (...) The marketing season was often short and changes in supply could result in wide fluctuations in price over a very short period.'* GATT document L/1927, 16 November 1962, paras 1-3.
541. *'The Panel felt that the problem for Canadian potato producers due to imports of potatoes from the United States was caused by specific climatic differences which could in certain years give rise to exceptional difficulties.'* GATT documents L/1927, 16 November 1962, paras 17-19.
542. GATT document SR.20/13,16 November 1962.
543. GATT document L/1968, 2 January 1963.

WTO. These were the sole cases on anti-dumping brought to the GATT before the enactment of the 1979 AD Code as a result of the Tokyo Round.

2 *Results of Kennedy Round: Anti-dumping Code, 1967*

The Kennedy Round was aimed at reaching comprehensive trade negotiations, on tariffs and non-tariff barriers, to liberalize world trade.[544] It featured the largest tariff reduction until that date,[545] and affected a much larger segment of world trade than any previous negotiation round.[546] Concerning non-tariff barriers, GATT Contracting Parties recognized that anti-dumping should not constitute an unjustifiable obstacle to international trade and considered it desirable to provide for '*equitable and open*' rules on anti-dumping '*in order to provide greater uniformity and certainty*'. Therefore, at the Kennedy Round, GATT Contracting Parties enacted the first Anti-dumping Code, the 1967 AD Code.[547]

The 1967 AD Code consisted of seventeen Articles, which established definitions and procedures to impose anti-dumping duties. It set forth rules for determining dumping, material injury, threat of material injury, and material retardation; investigation and administration procedures; duties and provisional measures; and action on behalf of a third country. The 1967 AD Code entered into force on 1 July 1968, merely obliging those GATT Contracting Parties having accepted it (Article 13). When the Tokyo Round began in 1973, all GATT Contracting Parties – including the incorporated European Economic Community (EEC) – were parties to the 1967 AD Code.[548] Notwithstanding they committed to ensure the conformity of their laws, regulations and administrative procedures with its provisions, the 1967 AD Code '*was not very successful*'. Notably, while it was in force, no dispute was submitted to the GATT regarding anti-dumping duties.

Among the provisions that caused more dissent after its entry into force were those relating to the determination of injury to the domestic industry, whereby dumped

544. '*The success of the European program of trade liberalization, capped by the formation of the EEC in 1958, prompted the United States once again to initiate multilateral trade negotiations. Aiming to reduce the EEC's common external tariff, Congress gave the president authority to reduce tariffs up to 50 percent.*' D.A. Irwin, The GATT in Historical Perspective, *The American Economic Review*, Vol. 85, No. 2, 1995, pp. 323-328 at 326.
545. Value of trade covered in GATT negotiations rounds: Geneva (1947): USD 10 billion; Geneva (1956): USD 2.5 billion; Dillon (1961): USD 4.9 billion; Kennedy (1962-1967): USD 40 billion; Tokyo (1973-1979): USD 155 billion; Uruguay (1986-1994): USD 3,700 billion. In J.H. Jackson, *Restructuring the GATT System*, p. 37; J.H. Jackson, *The World Trade Organization, Constitution and Jurisprudence*, Chatham House Papers, 1998, p. 21.
546. J.W. Evans, *The General Agreement on Tariffs and Trade*, International Organization, Vol. 22, No. 1, 1968, pp. 72-98 at 88.
547. Agreement on Implementation of Article VI of the General Agreement on Tariffs and Trade, in the Protocols 1964-1967 Trade Conference, GATT document, BISD, 15th Supp., 1968, pp. 24-35.
548. Austria, Belgium, Canada, Czechoslovakia, Denmark, European Economic Community, Finland, France, Germany, Greece, Hungary, Italy, Japan, Luxembourg, Malta, the Netherlands, Norway, Portugal, Spain, Sweden, Switzerland, the United Kingdom, the United States and Yugoslavia. GATT documents L/3167, 17 January 1969; L/3167/Rev.4, 24 August 1973; L/3167/Rev.5, 3 October 1975.

products had to be *'demonstrably the principal cause'*, including the definition of 'domestic industry' referred to as *'the domestic producers as a whole of the like products or to those of them whose collective output of the products constitutes a major proportion of the total domestic production of those products'*, except in cases where the market was divided within a country and producers to each market were treated as separate industries, requiring *'injury to all or almost all of the total production of the product in the market as defined'*.[549] This injury provision, requiring dumped imports to be the principal cause of injury, caused implementation issues in some GATT Contracting Parties. As a result, the injury provision is where its successor, the 1979 AD Code, mainly differs from the 1967 AD Code.

Particularly notorious was the case of the US, where it was not fully implemented.[550] The US Senate acted to suspend the participation in the code,[551] for restricting the discretion of the US International Tariff Commission *'in performing its duties and functions under the Antidumping Act, 1921'*,[552] to determine injury.[553] The House of Representatives dissented from the Senate, but they reached a compromise whereby the provisions of the 1967 AD Code were applied only to the extent that they neither limited the USITC discretion in the injury determination, nor conflicted with the Antidumping Act of 1921.[554] In other words, the USITC was permitted to ignore the 1967 AD Code and continue applying the US Antidumping Act of 1921.[555] As a result, it *'adopted a new de minimis standard, under which positive findings increased dramatically'*, although the trend was reversed soon afterwards.[556] Similarly, certain areas of the 1967 AD Code were omitted in the EEC, since negotiators were uncertain of their power to bind Member States on certain subjects and preferred to avoid *'constitutional challenge'*. Therefore, the 1967 AD Code was revised at a late stage of

549. 1967 AD Code Articles 3 and 4.
550. J.H. Jackson, J-V. Louis, M. Matsushita, Implementing the Tokyo Round: Legal Aspects of Changing International Economic Rules, *Michigan Law Review*, Vol. 81, No. 2, 1982, pp. 267-397 at 268, 273 https://doi.org/10.2307/1288518.
551. US Senate (90th Congress, 2nd Session), Renegotiation Amendments Act of 1968, Report No. 1385, 11 July 1968, viewed at: https://www.finance.senate.gov/imo/media/doc/Rpt90-1385.pdf.
552. US House of Representatives (90th Congress, 2nd Session), Conference Report on Renegotiation Amendment Act of 1968, 3 October 1968, viewed at: https://www.finance.senate.gov/imo/media/doc/ConfRpt90-1951.pdf; J.H. Jackson, W. Davey, *Legal Problems of International Economic Relations, Cases, Materials and Text*, 2nd ed., 1986, p. 672.
553. J.H. Jackson, W. Davey, *Legal Problems of International Economic Relations, Cases, Materials and Text*, 2nd ed., 1986, pp. 672-673.
554. Title II of Public Law 90-634, approved on 24 October 1968, 82 Stat., p. 1347, viewed at: https://www.govinfo.gov/content/pkg/STATUTE-82/pdf/STATUTE-82-Pg1345.pdf; R. Long, United States Law and the International Anti-dumping Code, *International Lawyer*, Vol. 3 No. 3, 1969, pp. 463-489.
555. J.W. Evans, Subsidies and Countervailing Duties in the GATT, *Maryland Journal of International Law*, Vol. 3, No. 1, 1977, pp. 211-245 at 229.
556. *'Between 1964 and 1967, only 28% of the Tariff Commission decisions found injury; from 1968 to 1970, injury was found in nearly 86% of the cases decided (...) from January 1974 through October 1975, the Commission found injury in 11 of 16 cases; it has not repeated its earlier application of the de minimis standard. Nevertheless, the post-1968 practice, if repeated, would differ radically from the position endorsed by the GATT membership in 1959, when they adopted the report of the Group of Experts.' Ibid.*, p. 228. GATT document BISD, 9th Supp., 1961, p. 200.

the Tokyo Round of multilateral trade negotiations and repealed by the 1979 AD Code.[557]

B Subsidies and Countervailing Duty Disputes, 1948-1980

Prior to the enactment of the SCM Code in 1980, GATT Article XVI was invoked in seventeen GATT disputes, of which eleven concluded in the issuance of a Panel report. Two of them occurred before the GATT Review Session of 1954-1955, i.e., when GATT Article XVI did not include provisions on export subsidies. Among the other nine reports, one also interpreted the provision on countervailing duties, established under GATT Article VI (the only report concerning countervailing duties before the SCM Code).[558] These GATT disputes show the different application of GATT Article XVI before the GATT Review Session of 1954-1955, when it merely provided for the obligation to notify subsidies and discuss their limitation in case of causing serious prejudice, and after the provisions on export subsidies were included, distinguishing between primary and non-primary products.

1 Subsidies Disputes Before the GATT Review Session of 1954-1955

The absence of provisions on export subsidies in the GATT is reflected in the first two GATT reports concerning disputes on subsidies. In the first case, *Australia – Ammonium Sulphate*, an export subsidy was challenged by invoking GATT Article XXIII, on nullification and impairment. In the second case, *US – Sultanas*, the respondent (the US) decided not to cease subsidization although CONTRACTING PARTIES recommended a mutually agreed solution.

In the *Australia – Ammonium Sulphate* case,[559] Chile submitted a complaint against Australia for removing the subsidy from a fertilizer while leaving the subsidy on another type of fertilizer, almost interchangeable with the former. Previously, in 1947, Australia had granted a tariff-free concession to Chile on nitrate of soda. When Australia removed the subsidy on nitrate of soda in 1949, it maintained the subsidy on sulphate of ammonia (both being nitrogenous fertilizers, with almost interchangeable uses). Australian action '*resulted in upsetting the competitive relationship between sodium nitrate and ammonium sulphate*'; hence, imports of nitrate of soda from Chile decreased.[560]

557. J.H. Jackson, J-V. Louis, M. Matsushita, Implementing the Tokyo Round: Legal Aspects of Changing International Economic Rules, *Michigan Law Review*, Vol. 81, No. 2, 1982, pp. 267-397 at 268, 273 https://doi.org/10.2307/1288518.
558. *United States – Suspension of Customs Liquidation Regarding Certain Japanese Consumer Electronic Products* (GD/98). Complainant: Japan. GATT document L/4508, 6 June 1977.
559. *Australia – Subsidy on Ammonium Sulphate* (GD/5). Complainant: Chile. GATT document CP.4/39, 31 March 1950. Other GATT related documents CP.3/61, 27 July 1949; CP.4/SR21, 3 April 1950; CP.5/SR.6, 6 November 1950; CP.5/SR.6/Corr.1, 6 November 1950.
560. GATT document CP.4/39, 31 March 1950, paras 1-6.

The Working Party[561] found no breach of GATT Articles I, III or XVI since Australia was neither obligated to subsidize the first type of fertilizer nor obligated, at that point, to remove the subsidy. Nevertheless, it found that the Australian measure had nullified or impaired (GATT Article XXIII) the tariff concession (on nitrate of soda) that Australia had granted to Chile in 1947. Without the intention of implying that the Australian measure was '*unreasonable*', the Working Part explained that during the 1947 negotiations, Chile could not have been expected '*to have foreseen such action or the reasons which led to it*' and concluded that there was a prima facie case that the value of a concession previously granted had been impaired.[562]

As a result of this case, during the GATT Review Session of 1954-1955, CONTRACTING PARTIES agreed with respect to subsidies that '*a contracting party which has negotiated a concession under Article II may be assumed, for the purpose of Article XXIII, to have a reasonable expectation, failing evidence to the contrary, that the value of the concession will not be nullified or impaired by the contracting party which granted the concession by the subsequent introduction or increase of a domestic subsidy on the product concerned*'.[563] For this reason, GATT Article XXIII was interpreted, along with Articles VI and XVI, in the SCM Code and the ASCM.

The other GATT dispute report concerning subsidies before the GATT Review Session of 1954-1955, *US – Sultanas*,[564] followed complaints submitted in 1952 by Greece and Turkey against US subsidies on sultanas. Pursuant to the then GATT Article XVI, Contracting Parties were merely obliged to notify the subsidy and discuss its limitation with other Contracting Parties in case of causing serious prejudice to them. Therefore, CONTRACTING PARTIES could solely recommend parties to enter into consultations with a view to cease the subsidies, and the US decided it would not relinquish subsidies on sultanas shortly.[565]

561. '*The Working Party consisted of the two disputants and three other nations.*' J.H. Jackson, *World Trade and the Law of GATT (A Legal Analysis of the General Agreement on Tariffs and Trade)*, 1969, p. 173.
562. Before the GATT Review Session of 1954-1955, Article XVI only obliged Contracting Parties to notify their subsidies. As the Working Party stated: '*The situation in this case is different from that which would have arisen from the granting of a new subsidy on one of the two competing products. In such a case, given the freedom under the General Agreement of the Australian Government to impose subsidies and to select the products on which a subsidy would be granted, it would be more difficult to say that the Chilean Government had reasonably relied on the continuation of the same treatment for the two products.*' GATT document CP.4/39, 31 March 1950, paras 7-12.
563. GATT document, BISD, 3rd Supp., 1955, para. 13.
564. *United States Export Subsidy on Sultanas* (GD/17). Complainants: Greece and Turkey. GATT documents L/146, L/146/Add.1, 30 September 1953 (Greece); L/148, 30 September 1953(Turkey). Other GATT related documents (consultations) L/39, 3 October 1952 (Greece), L/45, 10 October 1952 (Turkey).
565. Interestingly, few years later, when the third (and last before the GATT Review Session) complaint regarding subsidies was brought in GATT, a mutual solution was agreed between the parties, Turkey and Italy, before a report was issued. Turkish Import Taxes and Export Bonuses (GD/24). Complainant: Italy. GATT documents L/214, 30 July 1954; SR.9/40, SR.9/40/Corr1., 2 March 1955 (Mutually agreed solution).

2 *Subsidies Disputes after GATT Review Session of 1954-1955*

A completely different result arose from GATT disputes on subsidies taking place after the GATT Review Session of 1954-1955, when provisions on export subsidies were incorporated into GATT Article XVI. Those provisions distinguished between export subsidies on primary and non-primary products. Between 1955 and 1980, when the SCM entered into force, the GATT issued nine reports on disputes concerning export subsidies, of which three involved primary products (GATT Article XVI.3), and six regarded non-primary products (GATT Article XVI.4).

a *GATT Article XVI.3: Export Subsidies on Primary Products*

GATT dispute settlement reports interpreting GATT Article XVI.3,[566] concerning export subsidies on primary products, reflect the difficulty of applying the concept of '*more than an equitable share of world export trade*'. In the first dispute, *France – Wheat Exports*,[567] Australia submitted, in 1956, a complaint against a French export subsidy on wheat and wheat flour, alleging displacement of Australian trade in these products in Ceylon, Indonesia and Malaya (including Singapore). The Panel recalled that during the discussions at both Havana and the GATT Review Session, '*equitable share*' was not meant to refer to trade in a product in individual markets, but to the share in world export trade of that particular product. In determining 'equitable share', '*any special factors affecting world trade in the products*' should be taken into account, particularly '*the exporting country's share of world trade in those products during a previous representative period*'.[568]

The Panel found that Australian supplies, particularly of wheat flour, had been displaced to a large extent by French supplies in the South East Asian countries. This was supported by evidence (based on statistics) of the following two facts, occurring from 1954 to 1958: First, France had increased its share of exports of wheat flour to the South East Asian countries, while Australia had decreased it. Second, in the South East Asian countries combined, the share of imports from France had increased while the import share from Australia had decreased. According to the Panel, subsidies had contributed to the increase in France's exports of wheat flour, and the French share of world export trade in wheat flour was more than equitable. Therefore, it recommended

566. GATT Article XVI.3. '*Accordingly, contracting parties should seek to avoid the use of subsidies on the export of primary products. If, however, a contracting party grants directly or indirectly any form of subsidy which operates to increase the export of any primary product from its territory, such subsidy shall not be applied in a manner which results in that contracting party having more than an equitable share of world export trade in that product, account being taken of the shares of the contracting parties in such trade in the product during a previous representative period, and any special factors which may have affected or may be affecting such trade in the product*'.
567. *French Assistance to Exports of Wheat and Wheat Flour* (GD/36). Complainant: Australia. GATT document L/924, 20 November 1958. Other GATT relevant documents IC/SR.38, 19 May 1958; SR.13/20, 21 November 1958; L/1323, L/1548, SCM/W/48, 24 October 1960.
568. GATT document L/924, 20 November 1958, paras 1-7, 15.

that France avoid creating adverse effects on Australia's exports of flour to South East Asian markets through the system of payment to exporters of wheat and wheat flour.[569]

GATT Article XV.3 was invoked by Australia and Brazil in their complaints against EEC refunds on exports of sugar.[570] The Panel in *EEC – Sugar Exports* could not conclude that the EEC increased share of sugar exports resulted in the EEC '*having more than an equitable share of world export trade*' in sugar, in terms of GATT Article XVI.3, yet the EEC system of refunds on exports of sugar constituted a form of subsidy, subject to GATT Article XVI.1. The Panel concluded that the EEC system of granting refunds on sugar exports, notwithstanding notified, had contributed to depress sugar prices in the world market, constituting serious prejudice to both Australia and Brazil, and was a '*permanent source of uncertainty in world sugar markets*', constituting a threat of serious prejudice in terms of GATT Article XVI.1.[571]

b GATT Article XVI.4: Export Subsidies on Non-primary Products

GATT Article XVI.4, concerning export subsidies on non-primary products, was invoked in six GATT dispute settlement reports, of which one did not conclude whether the trade interests of the complainant had been adversely affected,[572] and another one also involved countervailing duties (thus, it is presented in the section below). The other four concerned subsidies through income taxes by the US, *US – DISC*, and three EEC-6 countries, *France, Belgium, Netherlands – Income Tax*, which were brought to the GATT in 1972. In the *US – DISC* case, the EEC-6 complained about the US domestic international sales corporations (DISCs) alleging it operated as an export subsidy.[573] A few months later, the US lodged three complaints against income tax practices maintained by France, Belgium, and the Netherlands.[574] The Panel in the four disputes

569. France had increased its share of exports of wheat flour to the three countries from 13% in 1953-1954 to 34% in 1957-1958, Australian share had fallen from 64% to 50% in the same periods, and that while the proportion of total imports of wheat flours in the Southeast Asian markets had, in the case of France, increased from 0.7% in 1954 to 46% in the first half of 1958, in the case of Australia it fell from 83% to 37%. GATT document L/924, 20 November 1958, paras 12, 19, 23.
570. *EEC – Refunds on Exports of Sugar – Complaint by Australia* (GD/102). GATT document L/4833, 25 October 1979. Other relevant GATT documents C/M/128, C/M/128/Corr.1, 18 October 1978 (consultations); C/M/135, 6 November 1979 (adoption of report). *EEC – Refunds on Exports of Sugar – Complaint by Brazil* (GD/103). GATT document L/5011, 7 October 1980. Adoption of report: GATT documents C/M/144, C/M/144/Corr.1, 10 November 1980.
571. GATT documents L/4833, 25 October 1979, pp. 30, 32 (Australia); L/5011, 7 October 1980, pp. 29, 30 (Brazil).
572. A report was also issued regarding a dispute on export subsidies on tobacco granted by the US, but there was no conclusion on whether the trade interests of Malawi and other countries had been adversely affected by the US subsidies on tobacco. *United States – Export Subsidy on Unmanufactured Tobacco* (GD/75). Complainant: Malawi. GATT document L/2925, 20 November 1967. Other GATT related documents L/2715, 5 December 1966; L/2856, 23 October 1967; L/2925/Add.1, 4 December 1967; SR.24/13, 21 November 1967.
573. *United States – Income Tax Legislation (DISC)* (GD/83). Complainant: EEC 6. GATT document L/4422, 2 November 1976. Other GATT related documents L/3851, 4 February 1972; C/M/154, 8 December 1981.
574. *Income Tax Practices Maintained by France* (GD/85). Complainant: US. GATT document L/4423, 2 November 1976. Other relevant GATT documents L/3860, 24 May 1972; C/M/154,

found that the US DISCs legislation, as well as the French, Belgian and Dutch tax practices, constituted export subsidies, having effects inconsistent with GATT Article XVI.4; hence, a '*prima facie case of nullification or impairment*' of benefits that contracting parties were entitled to expect under the GATT.[575]

3 *Countervailing Dispute Before the SCM Code: GATT Articles VI and XVI.4*

The only GATT dispute settlement report[576] concerning a dispute on countervailing duties issued before the SCM Code entered into force in 1980 was the *Zenith Case*,[577] in which GATT Article VI.4 and the Interpretative Note to GATT Article XVI were interpreted following Japan's complaint against the US customs' suspension of appraisement and liquidation of Japanese electronic products in order to eventually impose countervailing duties.

In 1970, Zenith Radio Corporation submitted a petition to the US Secretary of the Treasury to impose countervailing duties on electronic products from Japan, alleging that the remission or exemption of consumption taxes upon exportation '*amounted to a payment or bestowal of bounties or grants*', which resulted in a final negative countervailing duty determination. Following a summons filed by Zenith Radio Corporation, the US Court of Customs reversed, in 1977, the US Secretary of the Treasury's decision, directing the imposition of countervailing duties equal to the bounties or grants.[578] Pending the final outcome, customs officers were entrusted to suspend the appraisement and liquidation of the Japanese electronic products, as well as introduce '*a procedure under which entries and warehouse withdrawals* [could] *only*

7-08 December 1981. *Income Tax Practices Maintained by Belgium* (GD/86). Complainant: US. GATT document L/4424, 2 November 1976. Other relevant GATT documents L/3860, 24 May 1972; C/M/154, 7-8 December 1981. *Income Tax Practices Maintained by the Netherlands* (GD/87). Complainant: US. GATT document L/4425, 2 November 1976. Other relevant GATT documents L/3860, 24 May 1972; C/M/154, 7-8 December 1981.

575. GATT documents L/4422, 2 November 1976, paras 69, 74, 80 (US); L/4423, 2 November 1976, paras 48, 53, 58 (France); L/4424, 2 November 1976, paras 35, 40, 45 (Belgium); L/4425, 2 November 1976, paras 35, 40, 45 (the Netherlands).
576. In 1978, the EEC-9 brought a complaint against US countervailing duties, but it terminated in the consultation proceeding, i.e., a panel was not composed. *United States – Application of Countervailing Duties* (GD/104). Complainant: EEC-9. GATT document L/4745, 7 December 1978.
577. *United States – Suspension of Customs Liquidation Regarding Certain Japanese Consumer Electronic Products* (GD/98). Complainant: Japan. GATT document L/4508, 6 June 1977.
578. The Trade Act of 1974, amending the Tariff Act of 1930, established judicial review in cases of negative countervailing duty determinations. The US Treasury decided that '*no bounty or grant within the meaning of Section 303 was being paid or bestowed upon the manufacture, production, or exportation of the Japanese electronic products concerned*'. GATT document L/4508, 6 June 1977, paras 3, 4. In 1979, the competence was transferred from the Department of the Treasury to the Department of Commerce. The US Tariff Act of 1930 did not require the existence of injury for the imposition of countervailing duties.

be made if bonds in amounts equal to the estimated countervailing duties [were] *submitted*'. The US appealed the case to the Court of Customs and Patent Appeals.[579]

Meanwhile, a GATT Working Party was established. All but one of the members of the GATT Working Party agreed that Japanese practice was in conformity with GATT provisions and that the eventual US imposition of countervailing duties on Japanese electronic products would be in contravention of both GATT Article VI.4 and the Note to GATT Article XVI. The EEC expressed its concern about the US Court of Customs decision, highlighting excerpts from the US Administration Brief to the Court of Customs and Patent Appeals to emphasize that the US Treasury had interpreted the remission of taxes on consumption as not countervailable since 1898. The EEC also emphasized *the risk of a future supplementary charge on imports of between 5 and 20 per cent which, if applied, would be clearly contrary to GATT*'. Concerned about the proliferation of countervailing duties for world trade while the Tokyo Round of multilateral trade negotiations was taking place, the Working Party requested the urgent transmission of its report to the GATT Council '*for expeditious consideration*'.[580]

C Safeguards Disputes, 1948-1994

Among the eight GATT disputes in which GATT Article XIX was invoked, three either terminated in consultations[581] or the request was withdrawn,[582] and another was questioned to be considered a dispute.[583] The four GATT dispute settlement reports are of significant relevance due to the three conditions established under GATT Article XIX.1, the non-discriminatory application of safeguard measures; and retaliation by the affected country under paragraph 3.

Interestingly, the first dispute in the history of the GATT concerned emergency action under GATT Article XIX; notwithstanding, the invocation of GATT Article XXIII prevented the imposition of safeguard measures. More specifically, pursuant to GATT Article XXIII, Cuba requested, in 1948, CONTRACTING PARTIES to authorize an emergency action against the increase in imported quantities of US nylon stockings, hollow tyres, inner tubes for motor vehicles and lorries, and textiles (trimmings,

579. '*The amounts of the bonds required were estimated to be in the range of US$200 to US$300 million according to 1976 trade figures.*' GATT document L/4508, 6 June 1977, paras 4, 5, 9.
580. *Ibid.*, paras 11, 12, 15, 17, 18.
581. *Austria – Restrictions on Imports of VideoTape Recorders* (GD/117). Complainant: Japan. GATT document L/5119, 25 February 1981.
Switzerland – Imports of Table Grapes (GD/136). Complainant: EEC-10. GATT document L/5371, 29 September 1982.
582. *EEC – Emergency Action on Table Apples* (GD/78). Complainant: Australia. GATT documents L/3385, 3 April 1970; C/M/63, L/3385/Add.1, 15 July 1970 (Withdrawal of the request).
583. In 1956, there was a dispute in which Germany invoked Article XIX. Nevertheless, there was no interpretation of Article XIX in the GATT report: *Greek Increase of Bound Duty* (GD/38). Complainant: Germany. GATT document L/580, 9 November 1956. Other relevant GATT documents L/575, 10 October 1956; L/765, 29 November 1957; L/765, 29 November 1957. '*The "Greek Increase of Bound Duty" (GD/38) (also known as "Greek Gramophones") was discussed by a group of customs experts and its status could, therefore, be questioned as not being a GATT dispute.*' GATT document SR.11/12, 10 November 1956. World Trade Organization, GATT disputes: 1948-1995, Vol. 1: Overview and one-page case summaries, 2020, p. 32, footnote 97.

ribbons, gallons, coloured woven textiles, etc.).[584] The Working Party recommended a solution that did not impair GATT rights or obligations of Cuba or the US, to which they mutually agreed,[585] and which was incorporated in the Cuban Schedule.[586]

One of the most significant GATT disputes regarding safeguards was the Hatters' Fur case, *US – Fur Felt Hats*.[587] In 1950, the US withdrew the concession granted, at Geneva in 1947, on imports of ladies' fur felt hats; hence, Czechoslovakia brought a complaint to the GATT. The Working Party found that there was no conclusive evidence to determine that the US had breached its GATT obligations and was '*entitled to the benefit of any reasonable doubt*',[588] while Czechoslovakia had '*failed to establish that no serious injury has been sustained or threatened*'. It concluded that action under GATT Article XIX is of an emergency character and should be of limited duration.[589] The Working Party examined each of the three conditions that had to be fulfilled to justify the right to withdraw concessions under GATT Article XIX.1.

First, with respect to the increase in quantities, the Working Party found, based on the available data, that imports of ladies' fur felt hats had substantially increased from 1948 to the first half of 1950 as compared with 1946 and 1947. Second, notwithstanding the US alleged existence of '*unforeseen developments*', it admitted that the increase in imported quantities of fur felt hats was caused by a change of (ladies') hat style. Members of the Working Party, except the US representative, agreed with Czechoslovakia that a change in the fashion of hats did not constitute an unforeseen development. The Working Party considered that the term should be interpreted to mean '*developments occurring after the negotiation of the relevant tariff concession which it would not be reasonable to expect that the negotiators of the country making the concession could and should have foreseen at the time when the concession was negotiated*'. Third, the Working Party recognized that the increase in imports caused (or threatened to cause) some adverse effects to the US industry; nevertheless, it considered not to have sufficient evidence to determine the existence of serious injury (or threat therefor). Recourse to GATT Article XIX was permitted in case where '*a new*

584. GATT document CP.2/W12, 8 September 1948.
585. *Report of Working Party 7 on the Cuban Schedule* (GD/1). Complainant: US. GATT document CP.2/43, 13 September 1948. Other relevant GATT documents CP.2/W.12 19 August 1948; CP.2/SR.25, 14 September 1948; CP.3/SR.29, 29 June 1949.
586. GATT document CP.5/45, 12 December 1950.
587. *Assured Life of Tariff Concessions with regard to Article XIX/US – Fur Felt Hats* (GD/9). Complainant: Czechoslovakia. Respondent: US. GATT document CP/106, 27 March 1951. Other relevant GATT documents: CP.5/22, CP.5/SR.14, 10 November 1950; CP.6/SR.19, CP.6/SR.19/Corr.1, 22 October 1951 (adoption of report).
588. '*It almost appears that a mere rapid increase in the proportion of imports to the domestic production would make invocation of Article XIX justifiable, especially when all benefit of doubt goes to the party invoking it. The net result is to render tariff concessions and other GATT obligations less stable. The need to re-examine Article XIX with a view to obtaining greater stability of trade concessions was mentioned in a 1963 GATT report, but no follow-up occurred.*' J.H. Jackson, *World Trade and the Law of GATT (A Legal Analysis of the General Agreement on Tariffs and Trade)*, 1969, p. 563. Report of the Working Party on Procedures for Tariff Reductions. GATT document L/2002, 30 April 1963, p. 13.
589. GATT document CP/106, 27 March 1951, paras 30, 49, 50.

or novel type of imported product is replacing the customary domestic product to a degree which causes or threatens serious injury to domestic producers'.[590]

GATT Article XIX was also interpreted in *German Import Restrictions*.[591] Until 1957, Germany had been entitled to impose import restrictions. After the expiry of the period, in 1959, several Contracting Parties brought a joint consultation, pursuant to GATT Article XXII, against Germany's maintenance of import restrictions, alleging not to be permitted under GATT Article XIII. In case the circumstances alleged by Germany existed, they argued that Germany should invoke the emergency protective action under GATT Article XIX. Furthermore, they complained that the German '*unilateral control*' deprived other Contracting Parties from taking counteraction under GATT Article XIX.3, i.e., imposing safeguards in case their '*interests were affected by such emergency action*'. Moreover, Contracting Parties clarified that GATT Article XIX did not permit the imposition of quantitative restrictions '*to combat low-priced imports or to protect expanding industries*', and that safeguard measures would be applied in a non-discriminatory fashion.[592]

The non-discriminatory application of safeguard measures was interpreted in the last GATT dispute regarding GATT Article XIX, *Norway – Textiles*. In 1978, Hong Kong submitted a complaint against Norwegian safeguard measures, in the form of quantitative restrictions, on nine textile imports.[593] Previously, Hong Kong's textile products had been subject to a restrictive bilateral agreement with Norway, yet the negotiations for the renewal of the bilateral agreement were not successful. After concluding long-term bilateral agreements with six other textile-supplying countries, aimed at acceding to the Multi Fibre Agreement, Norway imposed a quota system without allocating a share for imports from Hong Kong. The Panel concluded that Norwegian action under GATT Article XIX was inconsistent with GATT Article XIII, which provides for a non-discriminatory administration of quantitative restrictions, and recommended Norway to either terminate the safeguard measure (quota system) or allocate a share to Hong Kong consistently with GATT Article XIII.[594]

590. *Ibid.*, paras 6, 8, 9, 11, 28, 30.
591. *German Import Restrictions* (GD/55). Complainants: Australia, Austria, Canada, Denmark, Greece, India, New Zealand, Norway, Pakistan, Sweden, the UK, the US, Czechoslovakia, Japan. GATT document L/966, 10 April 1959. Consultations: GATT document L/949, 21 November 1958.
592. Australia, Austria, Canada, Czechoslovakia, Denmark, India, Japan, New Zealand, Sweden, Norway, the UK and the US. GATT document L/966, 10 April 1959, paras 2, 21, 37.
593. *Norway – Restrictions on Imports of Certain Textile Products* (GD/100) Complainant: Hong Kong. GATT document L/4959, 24 March 1980. Other relevant GATT documents L/4671, 1 March 1978 (consultations); C/M/141, 18 June 1980 (adoption of report).
594. GATT documents L/4671, 1 March 1978, paras 5, 15, 16, 18.

II RESULTS OF THE TOKYO ROUND, 1973-1979, AND THE URUGUAY ROUND, 1986-1994

The Tokyo Round (1973-1979) constituted '*the first major negotiating round to make non-tariff barriers the priority objective of the negotiation*',[595] since trade policy had shifted from being 'tariff-centred' to focus on 'managed trade', which included (sectorial) trade arrangements, such as the Multifibre Arrangement, and trade remedies.[596] As a result of the Tokyo Round, GATT Contracting Parties enacted several agreements,[597] known as the 'Tokyo Round Codes'.[598] Regarding trade remedy laws, the Subsidies and Countervailing Measures (SCM) Code was produced; the 1967 Anti-dumping Code was amended and repealed by the new 1979 Anti-dumping Code (1979 AD Code); and a Decision on Safeguard Action for Development Purposes was adopted.[599] The Tokyo Round Codes and Decision only applied to GATT Contracting Parties that had signed them. They would later be renegotiated and repealed by the respective Agreements resulting from the Uruguay Round.[600]

The SCM Code was an important objective of the Tokyo Round. As a consequence of its development, some provisions of the 1967 AD Code were amended (e.g., the injury provision). The intention was to provide the same interpretation to the GATT Article VI, on anti-dumping and countervailing duties. Therefore, this section will begin with the history of the adoption of the SCM Code and the disputes that were brought to the GATT after its entry into force. Since the 1967 AD Code was amended and repealed as a consequence of the development of the SCM Code, the new 1979 AD Code and its effect on GATT disputes will follow the former. Then, the Decision on Safeguards will be presented. No GATT dispute settlement report on safeguards was issued after the Tokyo Round.

---

595. J.H. Jackson, *The World Trade Organization, Constitution and Jurisprudence*, Chatham House Papers, 1998, p. 21.
596. R.C. de Grey, The Decay of the Trade Relations Systems, in R.H. Snape (ed.), *Issues in World Trade Policy: GATT at the Crossroads*, 1986, pp. 17-31 at 17.
597. '*Ten major agreements and several "understandings" resulted from the negotiations. Because of the difficulty of amending the GATT, none of the nontariff agreements or understandings were incorporated into the GATT system as a technical change to the text of GATT. Instead, most of the MTN agreements are "stand-alone" treaty instruments. The "understandings" of the "Group Framework" negotiations were adopted by the GATT Contracting Parties as "decisions". The relationship of these agreements and decisions to the GATT itself is not a simple subject*', J.H. Jackson, J-V. Louis, M. Matsushita, Implementing the Tokyo Round: Legal Aspects of Changing International Economic Rules, *Michigan Law Review*, Vol. 81, No. 2, 1982, pp. 267-397 at 272 https://doi.org/10.2307/1288518.
598. Tokyo Round Codes: Anti-dumping, Subsidies and Countervailing duties, Civil Aircraft, Customs Valuation, Government Procurement, Import Licensing, Technical Barriers to Trade. In the Tokyo Round, GATT Contracting Parties also adopted an Understanding on Dispute Settlement; the International Dairy Agreement; the Arrangement regarding Bovine Meat; a Declaration on Balance of Payments; and Decisions on Safeguards, and on Differential and More Favourable Treatment, Reciprocity and Fuller Participation of Developing Countries.
599. Decision on Safeguard Action for Development Purposes, GATT document LT/TR/D/2, 28 November 1979.
600. WTO Agreement on Anti-dumping (ADA), Agreement on Subsidies and Countervailing Measures (ASCM), and the first Agreement on Safeguards (ASG). Compared to the Tokyo Round Codes, these WTO Agreements apply to all WTO Members.

A Subsidies and Countervailing Duties at the Tokyo Round

Increased attention was devoted to subsidies and countervailing duties during the Tokyo Round. Subsidies had been adopted by governments to restore the competitive advantage after having dismantled other trade-distorting measures. Subsidies had become one of the most frequently used and controversial instruments of commercial policy, an important instrument of protection. Under the impact of a recessionary world economy, governments had embarked on massive funding to, *inter alia*, promote exports, prop up ailing industries or stimulate consumer demand. In some sectors, world trade was being conducted more on the basis of competitive subsidization.[601] Therefore, negotiating countries reflected apprehension that the progress made in other trade areas was threatened by competitive subsidization and rules that regulated subsidies and countervailing duties were considered '*both incomplete and equivocal*'.[602]

Among the Tokyo Round Codes, the SCM Code '*certainly was the most difficult to negotiate*'.[603] A central objective was to design a framework of rules to cope with increasing problems in these areas.[604] Nevertheless, an essential divergence of views among Contracting Parties prevented compromise on disciplining domestic subsidies, as well as tightening rules for imposing countervailing duties, which were '*increasing and expanding*'.[605] Subsidies as well as countervailing duties were critical and contentious issues.[606]

Regarding subsidies, even the definition of subsidy caused disagreement among Contracting Parties.[607] There was '*no consensus on the purposes of such a discipline and the possible function of trade impact in such rules*'.[608] One of the major difficulties was to differentiate between subsidies that distorted world trade and deprived other countries of trade opportunities, and those aimed at pursuing social and economic

601. Report by the Director General of the GATT. General Agreement on Tariffs and Trade, *Multilateral Negotiations, Statement by GATT Director-General on Tokyo Round*, reprinted in International Legal Materials, Vol. 18; No. 3, 1979, pp. 553-576 at 569.
602. J.W. Evans, Subsidies and Countervailing Duties in the GATT, *Maryland Journal of International Law*, Vol. 3, No. 1, 1977, pp. 211-245 at 211.
603. J.H. Jackson, J-V. Louis, M. Matsushita, Implementing the Tokyo Round: Legal Aspects of Changing International Economic Rules, *Michigan Law Review*, Vol. 81, No. 2, 1982, pp. 267-397 at 273 https://doi.org/10.2307/1288518.
604. R. Rivers, J. Greenwald, The Negotiation of a Code on Subsidies and Countervailing Measures: Bridging Fundamental Policy Differences, *Law and Policy in International Business* Vol. 11, No. 4, 1979, pp. 1447-1496 at 1494.
605. J. Bourgeois, The GATT Rules for Industrial Subsidies and Countervailing Duties and the New GATT Round-The Weather and the Seeds, in E.U. Petersmann, M. Hilf (eds), *The New GATT Round of Multilateral Trade Negotiations: Legal and Economic Problems*, Studies in Transnational Economic Law, Vol. 5, 1988, pp. 219-235 at 231.
606. J.H. Jackson, W. Davey, *Legal problems of International Economic Relations, Cases, Materials and Text*, 2nd ed., 1986, pp. 723, 724.
607. *Ibid.*
608. There were two schools: the Injury-Only School and the Anti-Distortion School. J. Bourgeois, The GATT Rules for Industrial Subsidies and Countervailing Duties and the New GATT Round-The Weather and the Seeds, in E.U. Petersmann, M. Hilf (eds), *The New GATT Round of Multilateral Trade Negotiations: Legal and Economic Problems*, Studies in Transnational Economic Law, Vol. 5, 1988, pp. 219-235 at 231, 232.

policies.[609] Some industrialized countries focused on reducing trade-distorting subsidies, while others' concern was limiting the imposition of countervailing duties. Developing countries united in efforts to prevent both subsidies and countervailing duties restraints from being equally applicable to them.[610]

With respect to countervailing duties, many Contracting Parties were concerned about the US absence of material injury requirement to the domestic industry caused by subsidized imports. To them, the US acceptance and implementation of the causal link requirement '*was the crux of the negotiations*'. GATT Contracting Parties that signed the SCM Code agreed to permit the imposition of countervailing duties both through GATT Article VI, under the material injury criterion, and GATT Article XXIII action, requiring authorization by the Committee. Nevertheless, some participants claimed that the latter option, which only required 'serious prejudice' under GATT Article XVI, facilitated the imposition of countervailing duties as compared with the material injury requirement of GATT Article VI. Furthermore, the possibility of imposing provisional measures under GATT Article XXIII was an issue that caused much discussion. Notwithstanding signatories recognized the need for quick action, '*many countries could not accept that such unilateral action be taken in the absence or prior examination by an international body*'.[611]

1 *Subsidies and Countervailing Measures Code, 1979*

The SCM Code was aimed at interpreting GATT Article VI, with respect to countervailing duties; GATT Article XVI, on subsidies; and GATT Article XXIII, on nullification or impairment, only with respect to subsidies and countervailing duties. The enactment of the SCM had a threefold aim, ensuring that subsidies would not prejudice the interest of other Contracting Parties, making relief available for adversely affected producers, and not unjustifiably impeding international trade through countervailing duties.[612] It provided '*only a framework of rights and obligations within which to solve the problems of the future. It* [did] *not prescribe the solutions for such problems*'.[613] The SCM Code entered into force on 1 January 1980 for Contracting Parties having accepted it,[614]

609. J.H. Jackson, W. Davey, *Legal Problems of International Economic Relations, Cases, Materials and Text*, 2nd ed., 1986, pp. 723, 724.
610. J.W. Evans, Subsidies and Countervailing Duties in the GATT, *Maryland Journal of International Law*, Vol. 3, No. 1, 1977, pp. 211-245 at 212.
611. J.H. Jackson, W. Davey, *Legal Problems of International Economic Relations, Cases, Materials and Text*, 2nd ed., 1986, p. 730.
612. GATT document LT/TR/A/3, pp. 51-80 at 51.
613. R. Rivers, J. Greenwald, The Negotiation of a Code on Subsidies and Countervailing Measures: Bridging Fundamental Policy Differences, *Law and Policy in International Business*, Vol. 11, No. 4, 1979, pp. 1447-1496 at 1495.
614. Few countries signed the SCM Code due to the controversy regarding subsidies. These countries were: Argentina, Australia, Austria, Brazil, Canada, Chile, Colombia, Egypt, the European Economic Community, Finland, Hong Kong, India, Indonesia, Israel, Japan, Korea, New Zealand, Norway, Pakistan, the Philippines, Sweden, Switzerland, Turkey, US and Uruguay. G.N. Horlick, P.A. Clarke, The Agreement on Subsidies and Countervailing Measures, in G.N. Horlick (ed.), *World Trade Organization and International Trade Law: Antidumping, Subsidies and Trade Agreements*, 2014, pp. 217-272 at 222.

committing to ensure the conformity of their laws, regulations and administrative procedures.[615]

The SCM Code consisted of nineteen articles distributed in seven different parts. Provisions on countervailing duties were established under Part I (Articles 1 to 6) while subsidies were regulated under Part II (Articles 7 to 13). The rest of the SCM Code set out provisions for developing countries, which received some special treatment (Article 14); special situations, permitting to disregard prices in the subsidizing country provided it had a monopoly of its trade and prices were fixed by the State (Article 15);[616] the Committee (Article 16), as well as conciliation and dispute settlement procedures applying to both subsidies and countervailing duties proceedings (Articles 17 and 18). An updated version of the illustrative list of prohibited export subsidies (originally adopted by Contracting Parties in 1960 for the purposes of GATT Article XVI.4) was annexed to the SCM Code.[617]

Concerning subsidies, the SCM Code reflected disagreement among Contracting Parties, who recognized that while subsidies promote social and economic objectives, they may cause adverse effects to the interests of other parties, which they committed to avoid (SCM Code Article 8). This was particularly the case of subsidies other than export subsidies, some forms of which were merely enumerated by the SCM Code (SCM Code Article 11). Export subsidies were prohibited except for certain primary products, maintaining the limit of GATT Article XVI.3, i.e., '*more than an equitable share of world export trade*', and providing for clarification on the application of this concept (SCM Code Articles 9 and 10). Consultations, conciliation and dispute settlement procedures included, as a last resort, countermeasures, provided that adverse effects were found to exist and that they had previously been authorized by the Committee (SCM Code Articles 12, 13, 17, 18).

With regard to countervailing duties, the SCM Code set out procedures for the investigation (SCM Code Article 2), determination of injury (SCM Code Article 6), consultations (SCM Code Article 3), and imposition of provisional and definitive measures (SCM Code Articles 4 and 5). Remarkably, the initiation of the investigation was permitted also ex officio, and authorities were allowed to offer price undertakings to exporters. The SCM Code provided for the determination of a causal link (through an objective examination of the volume of subsidized imports and their effect on domestic producers), and the non-attribution effect of other factors that may also cause injury or

615. Signed on 30 June 1979. GATT document LT/TR/A/3, pp. 51-80 at 75.
616. SCM Code Article 15 permitted Contracting Parties the alternative use of anti-dumping or countervailing duties proceedings when injury was caused by imports from a country with a situation described under Interpretative Note 2 *Ad* Article VI.1, i.e., having a monopoly of its trade and prices fixed by the State. This interpretative note referred only to anti-dumping. Nevertheless, SCM Code Article 15 transposed such situation to countervailing duties. It provided that the margin of dumping or amount of subsidy could be determined by disregarding prices in the country of origin, and either using third-country prices or constructing the value.
617. J.H. Jackson, W. Davey, *Legal Problems of International Economic Relations, Cases, Materials and Text*, 2nd ed., 1986, p. 728.

threat thereof.[618] The term 'domestic industry' was defined as producers accounting for a major proportion of the total domestic production, except where the production was divided into two or more competitive markets.

2 *GATT Disputes after the SCM Code, 1980-1994*

After the entry into force of the SCM Code in 1980, the number of disputes regarding subsidies and countervailing duties increased. From 1980 to 1994, around twenty-one disputes on subsidies and twenty-eight on countervailing duties were brought to the GATT.[619] The most important cases regarding the impact of the application of the new rules and further normative evolution will be highlighted below.

a GATT Disputes Regarding Subsidies

Among the twenty-one disputes regarding subsidies that were brought to the GATT following the entry into force of the SCM Code, most of them terminated in the consultations proceeding. A GATT dispute settlement report was issued solely in five cases, of which one interpreted GATT Article XVI (not the SCM Code).[620] The other four cases concern US complaints against EEC subsidies. Some of these cases illustrate how issues regarding the distinction between export subsidies on primary and non-primary products, under GATT Article XVI, persisted despite the SCM Code intended to provide for clarification, as case *EEC – Pasta Subsidies*. Indeed, one of the difficulties the Panel encountered in *EEC – Wheat Flour Subsidies* was to assess whether the subsidy effected a '*more than an equitable share of world export trade*' for the granting contracting party. Two of the cases, the Oilseeds cases, show how subsidies could put at risk the non-discrimination principle.

In the *EEC – Wheat Flour Subsidies* case, the US submitted a complaint against EEC subsidies on wheat and wheat flour,[621] alleging EU subsidies had resulted in '*more than an equitable share of the world export trade*' in these products, with prices materially below those of other suppliers in the market, inconsistently with SCM Code

618. The injury requirement mirrored the provision included in the 1979 AD Code, which lowered the 1967 AD Code requirement to demonstrate that imports were the principal cause of injury.
619. See Appendix II: Table including GATT disputes on subsidies and countervailing duties after the entry into force of the SCM Code.
620. *EEC – Canned Fruit* was '*the only case involving the application of the concept of non-violation impairment to subsidies under Article XVI*'. The Report of the Panel was not adopted due to disagreement between the parties (US and EU) regarding the '*application of the concept of impairment to subsidies and on its consequences as regards the balance of rights and obligations arising from Articles II and XVI*'. GATT document L/6627, 14 December 1989, para. 67. *EEC – Production Aids Granted on Canned Peaches, Canned Pears, Canned Fruit Cocktail and Dried Grapes* (GD/129). Complainant: US. GATT document L/5778, 20 February 1985. Other relevant GATT documents: L/5306, 25 February 1982 (consultations); C/M/195, C/M/195/Corr.1, 12 February 1986 (mutually agreed solution).
621. *European Economic Community – Subsidies on Export of Wheat Flour* (GD/122). Complainant: US. GATT document SCM/42, 21 March 1983. Another relevant GATT document: SCM/10, 29 September 1981.

Article 10.[622] Based on GATT Article XVI.3, Contracting Parties committed not to grant export subsidies on primary products if they resulted in granting *'more than an equitable share of world export trade'*, a concept that SCM Code Article 10 intended to clarify. Nevertheless, the Panel could neither determine the existence of market displacement (SCM Code Article 10.2) nor conclude whether EEC export subsidies had resulted in prices materially below those of suppliers to the same market (SCM Code Article 10.3).[623] Contrary to the *French – Wheat Exports* case (of 1958),[624] in which only GATT Article XVI was interpreted, the Panel in *EEC – Wheat Flour Subsidies* found itself unable to conclude whether or not subsidies on wheat resulted in a *'more than an equitable share of world export trade'*.

Accordingly, pursuant to GATT Article XVI.2, the Panel found that EEC subsidies on exports of wheat flour could have caused undue disturbance to the normal commercial interests of the US, resulting in a drop of sales opportunities; hence, it recommended that the EEC made *'greater efforts to limit the use of subsidies on the exports of wheat flour'*.[625] Finally, the Panel considered that problems of export subsidies *'could only be found in making the pertinent provisions of the Code more operational, stringent and effective in application'*, requiring attention in, *inter alia*, the following two areas: First, the concept of *'more than equitable share'*, requiring the establishment of a *'clear and more common understanding'* of the concept and rendering it *'more operational'*. Second, whether *'international understandings*

622. SCM Code Article 10: *'Export subsidies on certain primary products*

1. *In accordance with the provisions of Article XVI:3 of the General Agreement, signatories agree not to grant directly or indirectly any export subsidy on certain primary products in a manner which results in the signatory granting such subsidy having more than an equitable share of world export trade in such product, account being taken of the shares of the signatories in trade in the product concerned during a previous representative period, and any special factors which may have affected or may be affecting trade in such product.*
2. *For purposes of Article XVI:3 of the General Agreement and paragraph 1 above:*
   (a) *"more than an equitable share of world export trade" shall include any case in which the effect of an export subsidy granted by a signatory is to displace the exports of another signatory bearing in mind the developments on world markets;*
   (b) *with regard to new markets traditional patterns of supply of the product concerned to the world market, region or country, in which the new market is situated shall be taken into account in determining "equitable share of world export trade";*
   (c) *"a previous representative period" shall normally be the three most recent calendar years in which normal market conditions existed.*
3. *Signatories further agree not to grant export subsidies on exports of certain primary products to a particular market in a manner which results in prices materially below those of other suppliers to the same market.'*

623. In words of the Panel: *'highly artificial levels and conditions of trade in wheat flour, the complexity of developments in the markets, including the interplay of a number of special factors, the relative importance of which it was impossible to assess, and, most importantly, the difficulties inherent in the concept of "more than-equitable share"'*. GATT document SCM/42; 21 March 1983, paras 5.3-5.5.

624. *French Assistance to Exports of Wheat and Wheat Flour* (GD/36). Complainant: Australia. GATT document L/924, 20 November 1958.

625. GATT document SCM/42; 21 March 1983, para. 5.7.

relating to sales on other than commercial terms' adequately complemented and supported export subsidies.[626]

Since the concept of '*more than equitable share of world export trade*' rule under SCM Code Article 10 solely applied to primary products (based on GATT Article XVI.3), determining whether the subsidy was granted to a primary or non-primary product became an issue. It was reflected in the case *EEC – Pasta Subsidies*,[627] where the question was to determine whether EEC subsidies on exports of pasta constituted a subsidy on a primary product, subject to the '*more than equitable share*' rule under SCM Code Article 10, or a non-primary product, prohibited under SCM Code Article 9.[628] The EEC pasta makers received a refund on the exportation of pasta equivalent to the wheat content, which the US claimed to be inconsistent with SCM Code Article 9, including its footnote 29 in relation to Note *Ad* GATT Article XVI.2.[629]

The Panel reminded that, according to SCM Code Article 9 footnote 29 in relation to Note *Ad* GATT Article XVI.2, a primary product was '*a product of farm, forest or fishery in its natural form or which has undergone such processing as is customarily required to prepare it for marketing in substantial volume in international trade*'.[630] The majority of the members of the Panel found that EEC subsidies on pasta constituted subsidies on non-primary products, and thus were inconsistent with SCM Code Article 9.[631] Nevertheless, one member of the Panel dissented, considering that subsidization of processed agricultural exports was permitted under the GATT and that Contracting Parties signatories to the SCM Code '*had in no way affected the status quo with respect to processed agricultural products*'.[632]

The other two GATT dispute settlement reports on subsidies after the entry into force of the SCM Code concerned US complaints against EEC subsidies on oilseeds and related animal-feed proteins. In the *EEC – Oilseeds I* case, the EEC was requested to

626. GATT document SCM/42; 21 March 1983, para. 5.9.

627. *EEC – Subsidies on Export of Pasta Products* (GD/128). Complainant: US. GATT document SCM/43, 19 May 1983. Another relevant GATT document: SCM/Spec/8, 18 February 1982.

628. Article 9: '*Export subsidies on products other than certain primary products*

1. *Signatories shall not grant export subsidies on products other than certain primary products.*
2. *The practices listed in points (a) to (l) in the Annex are illustrative of export subsidies Footnote: 'For purposes of this Agreement "certain primary products" means the products referred to in Note Ad Article XVI of the General Agreement, Section B, paragraph 2, with the deletion of the words "or any mineral"'.*

629. GATT document SCM/43, 19 May 1983, para. 1.1.

630. '*For purposes of this Agreement "certain primary products" means the products referred to in Note Ad Article XVI of the General Agreement, Section B, paragraph 2, with the deletion of the words "or any mineral"*'. SCM Code Footnote 29 in relation to GATT Note *Ad* Article XVI.2. GATT document SCM/43, 19 May 1983, para. 4.5.

631. GATT document SCM/43, 19 May 1983, para. 4.14.

632. *Ibid.*, para. 5.5. '*The dissent clearly has a point. Can you imagine the EC accepting the SCM if it had anticipated this decision?*' J.H. Jackson, W. Davey, *Legal Problems of International Economic Relations, Cases, Materials and Text*, 2nd ed., 1986, p. 744.

bring the challenged Regulations into conformity with the GATT as well as recommended to eliminate the impairment caused to the US.[633] Following the EEC amendment to the contested Regulation, the US initiated the *EEC – Oilseeds II* dispute, claiming that the EEC new system did not comply with the recommendations and rulings.[634]

The *EEC – Oilseeds I* case was submitted to the GATT in 1988 by the US, complaining against EEC Regulations that provided for payments and subsidies granted to processors and producers of oilseeds and related animal-feed proteins.[635] The Panel found that payments were granted to seed processors who purchased oilseeds originating in the Community. According to it, the mere exposure of imported products to a risk of discrimination constituted, by itself, a form of discrimination. Therefore, the Panel considered EEC Regulations to be inconsistent with GATT Article III.4.[636]

Furthermore, in light of GATT Article XXIII, the Panel examined whether EEC subsidies to producers of oilseeds had nullified or impaired US benefits. At the Dillon Round in 1962, the EEC had granted duty-free tariff concessions for oilseeds. As a result of EEC enlargements, and establishment of the common external tariff, these concessions had been extended and applied at negotiations pursuant to GATT Article XXIV.6 in 1986/87. The Panel found that, in all negotiations to that date, the duty-free tariff bindings for oilseeds had been maintained under GATT Article XXIV.6 and concluded that the US maintained the protection of reasonable expectations accruing to it under the duty-free tariff concessions, which had been initially negotiated in 1962.[637]

The EEC suggested that the Panel revised '*these decisions in the light of a particular interpretation of a Code accepted by a portion of the contracting parties*', to which the Panel replied by recalling the preamble of the SCM Code, whose purpose was '*to apply fully and interpret*' GATT Articles VI, XVI and XXIII. Moreover, it emphasized that SCM Code Article 8.4[638] should be interpreted '*in conformity with the decisions of the CONTRACTING PARTIES rather than, as the Community suggests*'.[639]

---

633. *European Economic Community – Payments and Subsidies Paid to Processors and Producers of Oilseeds and Related Animal-Feed Proteins* (GD/191). Complainant: US. GATT document L/6627, 14 December 1989. Other relevant GATT documents: L/6328, 19 February 1988, 19 April 1988 (consultations); C/M/238, C/M/238/Corr.1, 25 January 1990 (adoption of report).
634. *Follow up on the Panel Report 'European Economic Community – Payments and Subsidies Paid to Processors and Producers of Oilseeds and Related Animal-Feed Proteins'* (GD/262). Complainant: US. GATT document DS28/R, 31 March 1992. Other relevant GATT documents: DS28/1, December 1992 (consultations); C/M/257, C/M/257/Corr.1, 19 June 1992 (adoption of report).
635. It included '*rapeseed, sunflowerseed and soyabeans and related meals, peas, beans, lupines and skim milk powder. The main products in question are soyabeans, rapeseed, sunflowerseed and the meals derived from these oilseeds*'. GATT document L/6627, 14 December 1989, para. 7.
636. *Ibid.*, para. 142.
637. GATT document L/6627, 14 December 1989, paras 131, 143, 145, 146.
638. SCM Article 8.4 read as follows:

> The adverse effects to the interests of another signatory required to demonstrate nullification or impairment or serious prejudice may arise through
>
> (a) the effects of the subsidized imports in the domestic market of the importing signatory,
> (b) the effects of the subsidy in displacing or impeding the imports of like products into the market of the subsidizing country, or

In the *EEC – Oilseeds II* case, notwithstanding the EEC claimed that the new oilseed system was intended to eliminate the former system's inconsistency with GATT Article III.4 (i.e., granting payments to oilseed processors on the condition of purchasing Community oilseeds), the Panel found that the benefits accruing to the US under the zero-tariff binding for oilseeds continued to be impaired under the new EEC Regulation. Consequently, the Panel recommended the EEC to act expeditiously in order to either eliminate the impairment to the US by modifying the new system or renegotiate its tariff concessions for oilseeds under GATT Article XVIII. In addition, the Panel suggested CONTRACTING PARTIES to consider further action under GATT Article XXIII.2 in case the dispute was not resolved expeditiously and the US requested it.[640]

b Disputes Regarding Countervailing Duties, 1980-1994

The number of GATT disputes regarding countervailing duties increased following the entry into force of the SCM Code in 1980. Nevertheless, during the GATT period, countervailing duties were applied much less frequently than anti-dumping duties. The US, EEC, Canada and Australia were the main anti-dumping users, albeit the imposition of countervailing duties was mainly a '*US phenomenon*'.[641] While the SCM Code was in force, around twenty-eight disputes regarding countervailing duties were submitted to the GATT. Half of the disputes terminated in consultations. A GATT dispute settlement report was issued in the other fourteen cases, of which four terminated with a mutually agreed solution, followed by the withdrawal of the requests.[642] Among the other ten GATT dispute settlement reports, seven have been selected due to the impact of the application of the SCM Code or their consequences in

(c) the effects of the subsidized exports in displacing the exports of like products of another signatory from a third country market.

639. GATT document L/6627, 14 December 1989, para. 154.
640. GATT document DS28/R, 31 March 1992, para 88.
641. For instance, according to the data collected by the GATT Committee on Subsidies and Countervailing Measures, the number of US countervailing cases from 1974 to 1986 accounted for 313. Since the entry into force of the SCM Code in 1980 until 1984, the US initiated 139 investigations, of which fifty-six terminated in provisional and thirty in definitive countervailing duties. During the same period, the EEC initiated five investigations, of which three resulted in definitive duties. No other country imposed definitive countervailing duties from 1980 to 1984. During this period, provisional measures were imposed by Chile (9), Australia (8) and Canada (7). J.H. Jackson, W. Davey, *Legal Problems of International Economic Relations, Cases, Materials and Text*, 2nd ed., 1986, p. 727.
642. Reports regarding previous withdrawal of requests:

(1) *United States – Imposition of Countervailing Duty without Injury Criterion/Industrial Fasteners Imported from India* (GD/115). Complainant: India. GATT document C/M/152, 3 November 1981; Other relevant GATT documents: L/5028, 22 September 1980 (consultations); L/5062/Add.1, 25 September 1981 (adoption of report, mutually agreed solution, withdrawal of the request).
(2) *United States – Measures Affecting the Export of Softwood Lumber from Canada* (GD/164). Complainant: Canada. GATT document SCM/83, 25 May 1987. Other relevant GATT documents: SCM/73, 4 June 1986 (no finding in light of mutually agreed solution);

the further evolution of the rules.[643] The seven selected disputes concern complaints submitted by the EEC, the US and Canada against the imposition of countervailing duties by the US or Canada.

Four of the seven GATT dispute settlement reports interpreted SCM Code Article 6, concerning the definition of industry and the determination of injury. The definition of industry under paragraphs 5, 6 and 7 of SCM Code Article 6 was interpreted in two disputes, *US - Wine and Grape Products* and in *Canada - Manufacturing Beef CVD*. The determination of injury, under paragraphs 1, 2, 3 and 4 of SCM Code Article 6, was interpreted in the *Canada - Grain Corn* dispute and in the first countervailing duty case mandating the reimbursement of duties, the *US - Canadian Pork*. With respect to the other three disputes, the Panel in the *US - Softwood Lumber II* case interpreted SCM Code Articles 2, 4 and 5 and in the *US - Lead and Bismuth I* dispute, SCM Code Articles 1 and 4. The *US - Norwegian Salmon CVD* case has been placed in the anti-dumping section along with the dispute on anti-dumping duties on salmon from Norway, the *US - Norwegian Salmon AD* case. All these cases influenced the evolution of the SCM Code into the SCM Agreement developed at the Uruguay Round (1986-1994).

In the *US - Wine and Grape Products* case, the EEC complained against the US amendment of the definition of industry (incorporated in the US Trade and Tariff Act). Following the US imposition of countervailing duties on wine and grape products, the question became whether growers of grapes and wine producers were part of the same

SCM/M/34, SCM/M/34/Corr.1, 3 June 1987 (adoption of report); CM/83, 30/12/1986 (mutually agreed solution).

(3) *United States - Measures Affecting the Export of Pure and Alloy Magnesium from Canada* (GD/256). Complainant: Canada. GATT document SCM/174, 9 August 1993. Other relevant GATT documents: SCM/M/56, 5 September 1991 (consultations); SCM/174, 7 July 1993 (withdrawal of request).

(4) Australian Customs Amendment Act 1991 and Countervailing Duty Proceeding Concerning Imports of Glacé Cherries from France and Italy (GD/265) Complainant: EEC 12. GATT document: SCM/178, 28 October 1993. Other relevant GATT documents; SCM/178, 18 October 1993 (adoption of report, mutually agreed solution, withdrawal of the request).

643. The three disputes not selected for the purpose of this section were two cases brought to the GATT by Brazil against US countervailing duties on footwear, and the EEC complaint against countervailing duties imposed by Brazil on milk powder:

US - Non-Rubber Footwear, in which US countervailing duties were found consistent with the SCM Code. *United States - Collection of Countervailing Duties on Non-Rubber Footwear from Brazil* (GD/187) Complainant: Brazil. GATT document SCM/94, 4 October 1989. Other relevant GATT documents: SCM/M/35, 27-28 October 1987 (consultations); SCM/M/73, 13 June 1995 (adoption of report);

US - MFN Footwear, in which US measures were found inconsistent with GATT Article I.1. due to the Generalized System of Preferences. *United States - Denial of Most-Favoured Nation Treatment as to Non-Rubber Footwear from Brazil* (GD/233). Complainant: Brazil. GATT document DS18/R, 10 January 1992. Other relevant GATT documents: DS18/1, 7 August 1990 (consultations); C/M/257, C/M/257/Corr.1, 19 June 1992 (adoption of report);

Brazil - EEC Milk, on which the measures were found inconsistent with SCM Code Articles 5 and 6. *Brazil - Imposition of Provisional and Definitive Countervailing Duties on Milk Powder and Certain Types of Milk from the European Economic Community* (GD/271). Complainant: EEC 12. GATT document SCM/179, SCM/179/Corr.1, 27 January 1994. Other relevant GATT documents: SCM/149, 23 June 1992; 6 July 1992; SCM/151, 1 January 1992 (consultations); SCM/M/69, 28 April 1994 (adoption of report).

industry in the US.[644] The Panel interpreted the definition of industry in the light of paragraphs 5, 6 and 7 of the SCM Code Article 6 and considered that a separate identification of wine-grapes production from wine production was possible.[645] The Panel supported its conclusion with the fact that, prior to the amendment of the definition of industry, the USITC had determined not to include grape growers in the wine production industry in countervailing duty investigations. Consequently, there were two separate industries in terms of SCM Code Article 6.6.[646]

Moreover, the Panel rejected an interpretation of the definition of 'domestic industry', under the SCM Code Article 6.5, which concerned countervailing duties, in the light of SCM Code Article 9, which prohibited the use of export subsidies on non-primary products. In this line, the Panel recalled that the two provisions had different origins (GATT Articles VI and XVI, respectively) and that they served separate purposes. Furthermore, the Panel held that the definition of domestic industry, under SCM Code Article 6.5 and GATT Article VI, should be interpreted narrowly, '*because they permitted action of a nature otherwise prohibited by Article I*', i.e., an exception to the most-favoured-nation principle. Accordingly, the Panel concluded that the provision added to the US Tariff Act was inconsistent with SCM Code Article 6.5, and thus, the US had not acted in conformity with SCM Code Article 19.5, which mandated the conformity of national laws with the SCM Code.[647]

644. *United States – Definition of Industry Concerning Wine and Grape Products* (GD/153). Complainant: EEC-10. GATT document SCM/71, 24 March 1986. Other relevant GATT documents: SCM/54, 29 November 1984 (consultations); SCM/M/59, 28 April 1992 (adoption of report).

645. SCM Code Article 6.5: '*In determining injury, the term "domestic industry" shall, except as provided in paragraph 7 below, be interpreted as referring to the domestic producers as a whole of the like products or to those of them whose collective output of the products constitutes a major proportion of the total domestic production of those products, except that when producers are related to the exporters or importers or are themselves importers of the allegedly subsidized product the industry may be interpreted as referring to the rest of the producers*'.

SCM Code Article 6.6: '*The effect of the subsidized imports shall be assessed in relation to the domestic production of the like product when available data permit the separate identification of production in terms of such criteria as: the production process, the producers' realization, profits. When the domestic production of the like product has no separate identity in these terms the effects of subsidized imports shall be assessed by the examination of the production of the narrowest group or range of products, which includes the like product, for which the necessary information can be provided*'.

SCM Code Article 6.7: '*In exceptional circumstances the territory of a signatory may, for the production in question, be divided into two or more competitive markets and the producers within each market may be regarded as a separate industry if (a) the producers within such market sell all or almost all of their production of the product in question in that market, and (b) the demand in that market is not to any substantial degree supplied by producers of the product in question located elsewhere in the territory. In such circumstances injury may be found to exist even where a major portion of the total domestic industry is not injured provided there is a concentration of subsidized imports into such an isolated market and provided further that the subsidized imports are causing injury to the producers of all or almost all of the production within such market*'.

646. GATT document SCM/71, 24 March 1986, p. 10.

647. *Ibid.*, paras 4.5, 4.6.

In the other dispute in which the definition of industry was interpreted, *Canada – Manufacturing Beef CVD*, the EEC submitted a complaint against Canadian countervailing duties imposed on boneless manufacturing beef from the EEC.[648] Canada had considered a petition by cattle producers and included them in the Canadian beef industry to determine the threat of injury caused by EEC imports of beef. Canada claimed a flexible definition of domestic industry, arguing that it was the intention of signatory parties expressed under SCM Code Article 6.7, and that some governments objected to an interpretation based on the '*like product*' for being too narrow. The Panel examined the standing of the petitioners and the definition of industry applied by Canada in the countervailing duty proceeding. In its view, '*any principle justifying the Canadian exception would open the door to claims of standing by a substantial number of other input suppliers*', and referred to the negotiating history as well as the text of the SCM Code to interpret it.[649]

The Panel emphasized that SCM Code Article 2.1 and both paragraphs 5 and 7 of SCM Code Article 6 were drawn or copied verbatim from the 1967 AD Code,[650] and recalled that, during the Kennedy Round of trade negotiations, countries agreed to require that '*complaints must normally be filed on behalf of the relevant industry as a whole, and not (...) by any party which considered itself injured*'. At the Kennedy Round, the UK disagreed with the view of Canada and the US since it would give '*every complainant a chance to prove its case*'.[651] Moreover, the Panel emphasized that signatories of the SCM Code recognized that countervailing duties also imposed a burden on trade, and that its overall objective was to find a balance between the injury caused by subsidies and the injury caused by remedies to them. '*Thus, the fact that subsidies may be causing a particular injury does not by itself establish that the Code meant to provide a remedy for it.*'[652] The Panel concluded that signatories of the SCM Code did not intend to provide for a so flexible interpretation of '*domestic industry*' under its Article 6.7 as to consider input suppliers as producers, pointing out that the only way to adopt such an interpretation would have been by amending the SCM Code.[653] Accordingly, the Panel found that the Canadian interpretation of '*producer*' was inconsistent with the SCM Code.

In the *Canada – Grain Corn* case, the Panel also interpreted the determination of injury under SCM Code Article 6. In 1987, the US brought the case to the GATT, alleging that Canadian countervailing duties on imports of corn were inconsistent with the

648. *Canada – Imposition of Countervailing Duties on Imports of Manufacturing Beef from the EEC* (GD/160). Complainant: EEC 10. GATT document SCM/85, 13 October 1987. Another relevant GATT document: SCM/75, 30 October 1985.
649. GATT document SCM/85, 13 October 1987, paras 1, 5.11, 5.12.
650. *Ibid.*, paras 5.9, 5.11.
651. Statement by the UK delegation in the negotiation of the 1967 AD Code (at the Kennedy Round): '*The conditions governing the initiation and acceptance of applications for anti-dumping action determine to a large extent the number of anti-dumping cases which arise and the number which are eventually dismissed because full investigations show that action is not justified. In the view of the United Kingdom, therefore, it is of crucial importance that these conditions should be such as to reduce to the minimum the number of unnecessary anti-dumping investigations, and thereby prevent unjustifiable disruption of trade.*'
652. GATT document SCM/85, 13 October 1987, paras 5.6, 5.9.
653. *Ibid.*, para. 5.13.

mentioned article.[654] The Panel concluded that Canada failed to submit evidence that US subsidized imports were the cause of material injury, notwithstanding *'a general decline in world market prices resulting from a* [US] *subsidy may* [have] *cause*[d] *serious problems to* [Canadian] *producers'*. Consequently, Canada's determination of injury was found inconsistent with SCM Code Article 6.1-4[655] and recommended Canada to bring the measure into conformity with it.[656] In addition, the Panel recalled that in case subsidies had caused *'injury, nullification or impairment, or serious prejudice'*, SCM Code Article 13.4 provided for procedures to address it.

The *US - Canadian Pork* case was the first countervailing duty case in which the Panel recommended the reimbursement of duties.[657] Canada submitted a complaint against US countervailing duties on imports of live swine and fresh, chilled and frozen

654. *Canada – Injury Determination on Grain Corn from the United States* (GD/179) Complainant: US. GATT documents SCM/140, 21 February 1992; SCM/140/Corr.1, 26 February 1992. Other relevant GATT documents: SCM/82, 30 April 1987; SCM/M/58 26 March 1992 (adoption of the report).

655. SCM Code Article 6, paras 1-4: *Determination of injury*:

> A determination of injury for purposes of Article VI of the General Agreement shall involve an objective examination of both (a) the volume of subsidized imports and their effect on prices in the domestic market for like products and (b) the consequent impact of these imports on domestic producers of such products.
> With regard to the volume of subsidized imports the investigating authorities shall consider whether there has been a significant increase in subsidized imports, either in absolute terms or relative to production or consumption in the importing signatory. With regard to the effect of the subsidized imports on prices, the investigating authorities shall consider whether there has been a significant price undercutting by the subsidized imports as compared with the price of a like product of the importing signatory, or whether the effect of such imports is otherwise to depress prices to a significant degree or prevent price increases, which otherwise would have occurred, to a significant degree. No one or several of these factors can necessarily give decisive guidance.
> The examination of the impact on the domestic industry concerned shall include an evaluation of all relevant economic factors and indices having a bearing on the state of the industry such as actual and potential decline in output, sales, market share, profits, productivity, return on investments, or utilization of capacity; factors affecting domestic prices; actual and potential negative effects on cash flow, inventories, employment, wages, growth, ability to raise capital or investment and, in the case of agriculture, whether there has been an increased burden on Government support programmes. This list is not exhaustive, nor can one or several of these factors necessarily give decisive guidance.
> It must be demonstrated that the subsidized imports are, through the effects of the subsidy, causing injury within the meaning of this Agreement. There may be other factors which at the same time are injuring the domestic industry, and the injuries caused by other factors must not be attributed to the subsidized imports.

656. GATT documents SCM/140, 21 February 1992, paras 5.2.10., 6.2.

657. '*Either reimburse the countervailing duties corresponding to the amount of the subsidies granted to producers of swine or to make a subsidy determination which meets the requirements of Article VI:3 and reimburse the duties to the extent that they exceed an amount equal to the subsidy so determined to have been granted to the production of pork.*' GATT document DS7/R (formerly issued as L/6721), 18 September 1990, para. 5.2. As it had previously occurred in the anti-dumping case *New Zealand – Finnish Transformers*, the first case in which the GATT mandated the reimbursement of duties.

pork from Canada.[658] The Panel found that the US had determined the existence of Canadian subsidy on pork equal to the amount granted to producers of swine, based on two factors, '*the substantial dependence of the demand for swine on the demand for pork and the limited value added in the production of swine into pork*'. According to the Panel, subsidies granted to producers of swine could not justify that the decrease in prices of swine paid by producers of pork was '*equivalent to the full amount of the subsidy*' and that resulted in prices of swine below the level of '*other commercially available sources of supply*'.[659] Therefore, it considered that the determination of the existence of the subsidy was not based on '*all relevant economic factors*' required under SCM Code Article 6.3; hence, US countervailing duties were found to be inconsistent with that provision.[660]

A very relevant countervailing duty case in the history of the GATT is the *US – Softwood Lumber II* case, brought by Canada against US measures on imports of softwood lumber.[661] The Panel analysed whether the evidence of a threat of injury was sufficient to justify the initiation of an investigation (SCM Code Article 2.1), the imposition of provisional measures (SCM Code Article 5.1), or action following the other party's violation of an undertaking (SCM Code Article 4.6). Prior to this dispute, Canada had brought a case to the GATT regarding US countervailing duties on softwood lumber from Canada, which terminated with a mutually agreed solution in 1986,[662] a Memorandum of Understanding (MoU), whereby Canada collected a charge on exports of softwood lumber (subject to reduction or elimination depending on the increase of stumpage or other production charges), until Canada terminated it on 4 October 1991 (five years later).[663] Following Canada's termination of the MoU, the US took two actions against Canada. First, on 4 October 1991, i.e., the same day the MoU was terminated, the US suspended liquidation and imposed bonding requirements.

---

658. *United States – Countervailing Duties on Fresh, Chilled and Frozen Pork from Canada* (GD/220). Complainant: Canada. GATT document L/6721, 18 September 1990. Other relevant GATT documents: DS7/1, 19 September 1989 (consultations); C/M/251, 11 July 1991 (adoption of report).
659. GATT document L/6721, 18 September 1990, para. 4.10.
660. GATT Article VI.3. '*No countervailing duty shall be levied on any product of the territory of any contracting party imported into the territory of another contracting party in excess of an amount equal to the estimated bounty or subsidy determined to have been granted, directly or indirectly, on the manufacture, production or export of such product in the country of origin or exportation, including any special subsidy to the transportation of a particular product. The term "countervailing duty" shall be understood to mean a special duty levied for the purpose of offsetting any bounty or subsidy bestowed, directly, or indirectly, upon the manufacture, production or export of any merchandise.*'
661. *United States – Measures Affecting Imports of Softwood Lumber from Canada* (GD/258). Complainant: Canada. GATT document SCM/162, 19 February 1993. Other relevant GATT documents: SCM/W/251, 16 October 1991 (consultations); SCM/M/67, SCM/M/67/Corr.1, 27 October 1993 (adoption of report).
662. *United States – Measures Affecting the Export of Softwood Lumber from Canada* (GD/164). Complainant: Canada. GATT document SCM/83, 25 May 1987. Other relevant GATT documents: SCM/73, 4 June 1986 (no finding in light of mutually agreed solution); SCM/M/34, SCM/M/34/Corr.1, 3 June 1987 (adoption of report); CM/83, 30 December 1986 (mutually agreed solution).
663. It was concluded on 30 December 1986 and terminated on 4 October 1991. GATT document SCM/162, 19 February 1993, paras 7, 313.

Second, a few days later, on 31 October 1991, the US initiated a countervailing duty investigation on imports of softwood lumber from Canada.[664]

The Panel considered that, since Canada had terminated the MoU, there was sufficient evidence of threat of material injury to the US industry to initiate a countervailing duty investigation. Accordingly, the Panel concluded that the US initiation of the investigation was consistent with SCM Code Article 2.1. Nevertheless, the Panel found that, when the MoU was terminated, there was not sufficient evidence of threat of material injury to justify the US imposition of provisional measures, and since there had not been '*a preliminary affirmative finding*', the US imposition of provisional measures was inconsistent with SCM Code Article 5.1.[665] Furthermore, the Panel considered that US action, following Canada's termination of the MoU, could not be justified under SCM Code Article 4.6,[666] which provided for cases in which there had been a violation of an undertaking.[667] Accordingly, the Panel recommended that the US released bonds, refunded any cash deposits, and terminated the suspension of liquidation of entries and the bonding requirement. In this case, the reimbursement of the duties imposed was also recommended by the Panel.[668]

In the *US – Lead and Bismuth I* case, the Panel interpreted US measures in the light of SCM Code Articles 1 and 4.2.[669] In 1993, the EEC-12 submitted a complaint against US countervailing duties on certain hot-rolled lead and bismuth carbon steel products from Germany, France and the UK.[670] The US consideration of debt forgiveness and equity infusions as countervailable subsidies was found erroneous and countervailing measures inconsistent with SCM Code Article 1 footnote 4, whereby

664. *Ibid.*
665. SCM Code Article 5.1: '*Provisional measures may be taken only after a preliminary affirmative finding has been made that a subsidy exists and that there is sufficient evidence of injury as provided for in Article 2, paragraph 1 (a) to (c). Provisional measures shall not be applied unless the authorities concerned judge that they are necessary to prevent injury being caused during the period of investigation.*'
666. SCM Code Article 4.6: '*Authorities of an importing signatory may require any government or exporter from whom undertakings have been accepted to provide periodically information relevant to the fulfilment of such undertakings, and to permit verification of pertinent data. In case of violation of undertakings, the authorities of the importing signatory may take expeditious actions under this Agreement in conformity with its provisions which may constitute immediate application of provisional measures using the best information available. In such cases definitive duties may be levied in accordance with this Agreement on goods entered for consumption not more than ninety days before the application of such provisional measures, except that any such retroactive assessment shall not apply to imports entered before the violation of the undertaking.*'
667. GATT document SCM/162, 19 February 1993, paras 303-325, 326-410.
668. *Ibid.*, paras 414-415. The reimbursement of the duties had already been ordered in two previous cases, first, in *New Zealand – Finnish Transformers*, involving anti-dumping duties, and, second, in US – *Canadian Pork*, regarding countervailing duties.
669. SCM Code Article 4. 2: '*No countervailing duty shall be levied on any imported product in excess of the amount of the subsidy found to exist, calculated in terms of subsidization per unit of the subsidized and exported product.*'
670. *United States – Definitive Affirmative Injury Determinations Concerning Certain Carbon Steel Flat Products from Several Member States of the EEC* (GD/280). Complainant: EEC-12. GATT document: SCM/185 15 November 1994. Other relevant GATT documents: SCM/159, 2 February 1993; SCM/159/Add.1, 12 February 1993 (consultations).

countervailing duties were aimed at '*off-setting any bounty or subsidy bestowed directly or indirectly upon the manufacture, production or export of any merchandise*'.[671]

In the case of Germany, the Panel concluded that since the US Department of Commerce (USDOC) had considered debt forgiveness by private German banks as a subsidy, US countervailing duties were inconsistent with SCM Code footnote 4 of Article 1. In the absence of a subsidy, the Panel found that the US measure was also inconsistent with SCM Code Article 4.2.[672] In the case of the UK[673] and France,[674] the Panel concluded that the US measure was inconsistent with both SCM Code Articles 1 and 4.2, when the USDOC treated equity infusions as grants; and inconsistent with Article 1, when the USDOC provided an inadequate explanation of its evaluations of prospects of the BSC (UK) and the Usinor Sacilor (France), for considering them '*not equityworthy*' during certain years and '*creditworthy*' only in the case of Usinor Sacilor.[675]

Before the Uruguay Round (1986-1994), the SCM Code was considered inadequate since it had not resolved issues regarding subsidies and countervailing duties. A report released by the GATT Secretariat stated that a failing in the world economy was due to, *inter alia*, the increasing use of subsidies and abuse of countervailing duties.[676] Therefore, the Uruguay Round was launched with the mandate to improve, *inter alia*, '*GATT disciplines relating to all subsidies and countervailing measures that affect international trade.*'[677]

3 *WTO Agreement Subsidies and Countervailing Measures, 1994*

At the Uruguay Round, several delegations emphasized the need to deal effectively with both disciplines due to their interrelationship, aimed at finding efficient solutions,

671. SCM Code Article 1, footnote 4: '*The term "countervailing duty" shall be understood to mean a special duty levied for the purpose of offsetting any bounty or subsidy bestowed directly or indirectly upon the manufacture, production or export of any merchandise, as provided for in Article VI:3 of the General Agreement.*'
672. GATT document SCM/185 15 November 1994, paras 372-404.
673. In the particular case of the UK, the Panel found that the US measure was also inconsistent with Article 1 since a '*pass through*' of subsidies from BSC to UES was considered a subsidy on the production of merchandise by UES. Therefore, US action was inconsistent with Article 4.2 as well. *Ibid.*, paras 404-430.
674. Regarding the case of France, the Panel concluded that the US had acted inconsistently with Articles 1 and 4.2 for the following USDOC actions: first, insufficient explanation of its reliance on the facts available for determining the basis for the calculation of the discount rate applied; second, allocation of subsidies exclusively to domestic production in France, without providing parties for an adequate opportunity to submit evidence; third, failing to provide sufficient explanation for allocating certain subsidies an average useful life of assets of fifteen years. *Ibid.*, paras 581-646.
675. *Ibid.*, paras 494-558.
676. General Agreement on Tariffs and Trade, Report of Eminent Persons on Problems Facing the International Trade System, *International Legal Materials*, Vol. 24, No. 3, 1985, pp. 716-744 at 735.
677. General Agreement on Tariffs and Trade, Ministerial Declaration on the Uruguay Round of Multilateral Trade Negotiations, *International Legal Materials*, Vol. 25, No. 6, 1986, pp. 1623-1627 at 1626.

and resolving conceptual issues existing even before the Tokyo Round. GATT Contracting Parties pointed out that the abuse of countervailing duties resulted from the perception of fading subsidies discipline, which was criticized for lacking economic policy basis in certain instances; some rules on subsidies were weak and others vague. Countervailing duty rules presented loopholes that permitted unilateral interpretations and practices, resulting in arbitrariness, harassment, and uncertainty for exporters. Developing countries were particularly affected despite the efforts. Nevertheless, some delegations considered it to be a problem not only of inadequacy of rules, but also of inobservance by governments.[678]

The US and the EU, the two major players during the Uruguay Round negotiations, differed in their view on 'the appropriateness of the use of subsidies, their effects on international trade, and beyond that, on what should be the role of governments in the economy'. Most of the negotiations on the Agreement on Subsidies and Countervailing Measures (ASCM) focused on bringing the US and EU positions together, with Canada aiming at protecting itself from US countervailing duties, and the developing countries claiming special and differential treatment.[679] 'Worries about this text focus on the ambiguity of several "exceptions" clauses which could lead to abuse.'[680]

Unlike the SCM Code, which applied to its signatories, the ASCM applies to all WTO Members.[681] Compared to the SCM Code, which consisted of nineteen articles, the ASCM contains thirty-two articles.[682] The new Agreement includes definitions of subsidy (ASCM Article 1), specificity (ASCM Article 2), and serious prejudice (ASCM

678. Some of issues identified by some delegations were: '*definition of a countervailable subsidy (including the question of specificity), distinction between subsidies and other measures (including the concept of incentives for development or structural adjustment), measurement of the amount of a subsidy, issues related to the initiation and conduct of investigation (standing of petitioners, injury threshold, information available), imposition of countervailing duties (insignificant subsidy, marginal suppliers), injury (cumulation, cross-cumulation, criteria), definition of industry, definition of sale*'. GATT documents MTN.GNG/NG10/2, 10 June 1987; MTN.GNG/NG10/1, 16-17 March 1987.
679. G. Depayre, Subsidies and Countervailing Measures after the Uruguay Round: An Overview, in J. Bourgeois, F. Berrod, E. Gippini Fournier (eds), *The Uruguay Round Results, A European Lawyers' Perspective: Proceedings of an International Conference Held at the College of Europe, Bruges*, 1999, pp. 247-254 at 255. For a description of countervailing duty provisions and their differences with respect to the then US law and practice, *see* G.N. Horlick, P.A. Clarke, The 1994 WTO Subsidies Agreement, *World Competition*, Vol. 17, No. 4, 1994, pp. 41-54 https://doi.org/10.54648/woco1993024.
680. J.H. Jackson, *The World Trade Organization, Constitution and Jurisprudence*, Chatham House Papers, 1998, p. 3.
681. The ASCM is part of Final Act Embodying the Results of the Uruguay Round of Multilateral Trade Negotiations, 15 April 1994. UNTS, Vol. 1867, p. 14. The single undertaking approach '*definitively brings to an end the possibility of "à la carte" acceptance of agreements, means that in time all trading partners will be subject to the same rules even if there are initially transition periods for less developed countries*', J. Leflon, Uruguay Round Comments: A View from UNICE, in J. Bourgeois, F. Berrod, E. Gippini Fournier (eds), *The Uruguay Round Results: A European Lawyers' Perspective*, 1995, pp. 59-65 at 60.
682. For a detailed discussion on each provision of the ASCM, *see* G.N. Horlick, P.A. Clarke, The Agreement on Subsidies and Countervailing Measures, in G.N. Horlick (ed.), *World Trade Organization and International Trade Law: Antidumping, Subsidies and Trade Agreements*, 2014, pp. 217-272. For a negotiating history of the ASCM, *see* G.N. Horlick, A Personal History of the WTO Subsidies Agreement, *Journal of World Trade*, Vol. 47, No. 2, 2013, pp. 447-452 https://doi.org/10.54648/trad2013014.

Article 6). A subsidy is defined as the benefit conferred through a financial contribution granted by the government or any public body within the territory, or any form of income or price support (in the sense of GATT Article XVI). To be countervailable, a subsidy must be specific. A subsidy is deemed specific if its access is limited (*de iure* or *de facto*) to a particular enterprise or industry, group of them, or a geographical region, within the jurisdiction of the granting authority.

The ASCM classifies subsidies into three categories, which are often referred to through the example of traffic lights (red, yellow and green): Red-prohibited (ASCM Articles 3 and 4), yellow-actionable (ASCM Articles 5 to 7), and green-non-actionable (ASCM Articles 8 and 9). The ASCM prohibits export subsidies (as the SCM Code) as well as import-substitution subsidies, i.e., subsidies contingent upon the use of domestic over imported products. Prohibited subsidies are considered by definition specific (ASCM Article 2.3). Actionable subsidies are specific subsidies which cause adverse effects to the interest of other Members, i.e., injury or threat thereof, nullification or impairment, or serious prejudice. Non-actionable subsidies are non-specific subsidies, and until 1999, certain specific subsidies for research and development, environmental, and regional programmes that met the conditions listed under ASCM Article 8.2.[683]

A dispute settlement procedure is established for prohibited subsidies (ASCM Article 4) and actionable subsidies (ASCM Article 7). In both cases, the WTO DSB can authorize countermeasures. Countervailing duties can be imposed on specific (either prohibited or actionable) subsidies if they cause injury or threat thereof (ASCM Articles 10-23). The ASCM permits the parallel invocation of both dispute settlement and countervailing duty proceedings. Nevertheless, to offset the effect of a subsidy in the importing country, only one form of relief is permitted, i.e., either countervailing duties (pursuant to ASCM Articles 10-23) or countermeasures (pursuant to ASCM Article 4, in case of prohibited; or 7, for actionable subsidies). Non-actionable subsidies are exempted from countervailing duties or the dispute settlement procedure.[684] In case a non-actionable subsidy results in adverse effects to another Member, the ASCM provides for consultations and recourse to the Committee. When the subsidizing country does not follow the recommendation of the Committee, the latter may authorize the affected Member to take countermeasures.

The ASCM amended the procedures to impose countervailing duties (ASCM Articles 10 to 23), requiring specific time limits, due process and transparency. ASCM Article 11 provides that investigations be concluded within eighteen months from the initiation. Before the investigation, the administering authority is required to determine that a written application includes sufficient evidence of a subsidy, its amount (when possible), and a causal link between the subsidy and the alleged injury.[685] Moreover,

683. ASCM Articles 8 and 9 expired five years after the entry into force of the ASCM (ASCM Article 31).
684. Nevertheless, those proceedings can be invoked in case subsidies under Article 8.2 (for research and development programmes) are not notified. *See* ASCM Note 35.
685. In case of ex officio initiation of investigation by the authorities, the ASCM also requires evidence of causal link, together with the existence of subsidy and injury (as provided by SCM Code Article 2.1).

it must be determined on the basis of positive evidence that the application is requested '*by or on behalf of the domestic industry*', i.e., supported by at least 25% of the total production of the like product, and by more than 50% of those that express either support or opposition to the application. A subsidy that amounts to less than 1% (2% for developing Members)[686] ad valorem is considered *de minimis*.

The methodology to calculate the benefit of the subsidy is left to WTO Members (ASCM Article 14).[687] The causal link between the subsidized imports and the injury requires that authorities examine '*all relevant evidence*' before them, which includes '*any known factors*' other than the subsidized imports that are injuring the domestic industry. In other words, the ASCM provides for an explicit examination of the 'known' non-attributable factors when determining injury (ASCM Article 15.5). It allows for a cumulative assessment of injury of imports from different countries, provided that imports from each country amount to more than *de minimis* and the volume is not negligible and '*that* [cumulation]*is appropriate in light of the conditions of competition*' (ASCM Article 15.3). A sunset provision was incorporated to limit the duration of the countervailing duty to five years, unless continuation or recurrence of the injury is determined in a review before the mentioned deadline (ASCM Article 21). Remarkably, judicial review of countervailing duty determinations is provided for (ASCM Article 23).

The ASCM includes provisions on the Committee on Subsidies and Countervailing Measures, and the subsidiary bodies it may set up, such as the Permanent Group of Experts (PGE), which may be requested to assist a panel or give confidential advisory opinions concerning the nature of a subsidy in place or proposed to be introduced (ASCM Article 24). The systems of notifications and surveillance were strengthened (ASCM Articles 25 and 26). Some special and differential treatment is provided for developing country Members, which were required to progressively phase out export subsidies (ASCM Article 27). In addition, the ASCM establishes transitional arrangements, including for Members transforming from a centrally planned into a market, free-enterprise economy (ASCM Articles 28 and 29).

B Anti-dumping after the Tokyo Round

1 Anti-dumping Code, 1979

Notwithstanding that it was not among the objectives of the Tokyo Round, the 1967 AD Code was revised and repealed by a new code, the 1979 AD Code. It '*was a somewhat watered-down version of the 1967 Code that the Treasury Department had contended was consistent with US law. The changes in procedure, however, were fundamental in*

686. ASCM Article 27.10.
687. The ASCM merely provides for some guidance and requires that the methodology be provided for in national legislation or implementing regulation.

nature'.[688] The 1979 AD Code entered into force on 1 January 1980 for eight Contracting Parties – including the EEC – having accepted it.[689] The acceptance of the code was open for those countries that had provisionally acceded to the GATT and those countries that had deposited their instrument of accession.[690] By December 1993, twenty-one more countries had accepted the 1979 AD Code.[691]

The most significant modification that the 1979 AD Code introduced concerned the provision on the determination of injury, under AD Codes Article 3. The 1967 AD Code[692] required dumped imports to be the 'principal cause' of injury, whereas the 1979 AD Code replaced that requirement by 'causing injury'. This new provision on the determination of injury mirrored SCM Code Article 6, i.e., in case of subsidization. As a matter of fact, the first four paragraphs of 1979 AD Code Article 3 were practically identical to the SCM Code Article 6. '*This may have been an unfortunate step, since the two subjects, although seemingly parallel, differ substantially in their underlying policy foundations. Dumping involves activity by particular, often private, firms. Subsidy*

688. J.H. Jackson, W. Davey, *Legal Problems of International Economic Relations, Cases, Materials and Text*, 2nd ed., 1986, p. 675.
689. Contracting Parties having accepted the 1979 AD Code before its entry into force on 1 January 1980: EEC, US, UK, Switzerland, Sweden, Norway, Canada and Austria. Brazil signed it before 1 January 1980, but on a condition, which made the acceptance effective in May 1980. GATT document LEG/1/Supp. 15, 1993, Ch. 16 'Multilateral Trade Negotiations 1973-1979', Section 158.
690. GATT document LT/TR/A/1, 12 April 1979, pp. 127-145 at 143.
691. Contracting Parties having accepted the 1979 AD Code after its entry into force on 1 January 1980: Yugoslavia, Spain, the Slovak Republic, Singapore, Romania, Poland, Pakistan, New Zealand, Colombia, Mexico, the Republic of Korea, Japan, India, Hungary, Hong Kong, Finland, Egypt, the Czech Republic, Brazil, Australia, Argentina. GATT document LEG/1/Supp. 15, 1993, Ch. 16 'Multilateral Trade Negotiations 1973-1979', Section 158.
692. First paragraphs of Article 3 of the 1967 AD Code: '*Determination of Injury*
    (a) *A determination of injury shall be made only when the authorities concerned are satisfied that the dumped imports are demonstrably the principal cause of material injury or of threat of material injury to a domestic industry or the principal cause of material retardation of the establishment of such an industry. In reaching their decision the authorities shall weigh, on one hand, the effect of the dumping and, on the other hand, all other factors taken together which may be adversely affecting the industry. The determination shall in all cases be based on positive findings and not on mere allegations or hypothetical possibilities. In the case of retarding the establishment of a new industry in the country of importation, convincing evidence of the forthcoming establishment of an industry must be shown, for example that the plans for a new industry have reached a fairly advanced stage, a factory is being constructed or machinery has been ordered.*
    (b) *The valuation of injury – that is the evaluation of the effects of the dumped imports on the industry in question – shall be based on examination of all factors having a bearing on the state of the industry in question, such as: development and prospects with regard to turnover, market share, profits, prices (including the extent to which the delivered, duty-paid price is lower or higher than the comparable price for the like product prevailing in the course of normal commercial transactions in the importing country), export performance, employment, volume of dumped and other imports, utilization of capacity of domestic industry, and productivity; and restrictive trade practices. No one or several of these factors can necessarily give decisive guidance.*
    (c) *In order to establish whether dumped imports have caused injury, all other factors which, individually or in combination, may be adversely affecting the industry shall be examined, for example: the volume and prices of undumped imports of the product in question, competition between the domestic producers themselves, contraction in demand due to substitution of other products or to changes in consumer tastes.*'

activity, in contrast, is basically governmental activity, and can stem from legitimate internal social policies being pursued by the government.'[693]

Other relevant changes were incorporated into the 1979 AD Code: Inclusion of a time limit of one year on investigations (Article 5); expansion of rules on price undertakings (Article 7), which incorporated a requirement of 'satisfaction' by investigating authorities upon receipt of voluntary undertakings by exporters to revise their prices or cease exportation; and the introduction of three new articles devoted to developing countries (Article 13); the Committee (Article 14); and consultation, conciliation and dispute settlement (Article 15).[694] The final provisions established the obligation for parties to notify amendments in their anti-dumping laws or regulations (Article 16).

2 GATT Disputes on Anti-dumping after the Tokyo Round

Following the entry into force of the 1979 AD Code, Finland submitted a complaint to the GATT against New Zealand's imposition of anti-dumping duties on electronic transformers. Nonetheless, since New Zealand was not a signatory of the 1979 AD Code, the Panel based its considerations on GATT Article VI, paragraphs 1, 2 and 6(a). *New Zealand – Finnish Transformers*[695] was the first GATT dispute settlement report in the history of the GATT in which the reimbursement of the duties previously collected was recommended by the Panel.[696]

From April to July 1982, a New Zealand import licence had inhibited the entrance of the two Finnish electric transformers. Thereafter, New Zealand reopened an anti-dumping investigation on Finnish transformers and imposed anti-dumping duties. In order to calculate the margin of dumping, New Zealand constructed the normal value on the basis of GATT Article VI (b) (ii),[697] *'in the absence of a domestic price in Finland for custom-built transformers of this kind'*. In 1984, Finland complained against New Zealand's anti-dumping duties on the two transformers. The Panel found that Finland had not provided for all the necessary cost elements for New Zealand to have carried out *'a meaningful cost-of-production calculation the basis of the information*

693. J.H. Jackson, J-V. Louis, M. Matsushita, Implementing the Tokyo Round: Legal Aspects of Changing International Economic Rules, *Michigan Law Review*, Vol. 81, No. 2, 1982, pp. 267-397 at 274 https://doi.org/10.2307/1288518.
694. GATT document LT/TR/A/1, 12 April 1979, pp. 140-141.
695. *New Zealand – Imports of Electrical Transformers from Finland* (GD/150). Complainant: Finland. GATT document L/5814, 19 June 1985. Other relevant GATT documents: C/M/180, 11 July 1984 (consultations); C/M/191, 17-19 July 1985 (adoption of report).
696. GATT document L/5814, 19 June 1985, paras 3.9, 4.1, 4.14.
697. GATT Article VI(b)(ii): '*For the purposes of this Article, a product is to be considered as being introduced into the commerce of an importing country at less than its normal value, if the price of the product exported from one country to another (...)*
    (b) in the absence of such domestic price, is less than either (...)
    (ii) the cost of production of the product in the country of origin plus a reasonable addition for selling cost and profit.'

supplied by the exporter alone', and thus, New Zealand had appropriately calculated the cost on the basis '*of price elements obtained from other sources*'.[698]

Nevertheless, with respect to the matter of material injury, the Panel found that the injury suffered by the New Zealand industry on transformers was due to the '*lack of new orders, diminishing orders on hand in certain product categories, declining profitability, a large increase in imports and considerable uncertainty as to new orders*'. In addition, it observed that the two Finnish transformers, which constituted an almost insignificant part of the increase in imports, had not caused the alleged injury. Furthermore, the Panel considered that the Finnish exporter had not attempted to increase sales; hence, the imposition of anti-dumping duties could not be based on the threat of material injury. Since New Zealand had not been able to demonstrate that the importation of the two Finnish transformers had caused material injury to its industry, the imposition of anti-dumping duties was found inconsistent with GATT Article VI.6(a). The Panel established that the measure constituted a prima facie nullification or impairment and recommended the reimbursement of the duties.[699]

US – Swedish Steel[700] was the first GATT case in which the 1979 AD Code was interpreted, particularly its Article 5, on the initiation of the investigation. In 1988, Sweden submitted a complaint against the US imposition of anti-dumping duties on imports of seamless stainless steel hollow products from Sweden. The Panel examined whether the investigation was initiated '*on behalf of the industry affected*', under 1979 AD Code Article 5.1.[701] According to its footnote 9, 'industry' shall be interpreted as defined in 1979 AD Code Article 4. The Panel considered that, before opening an investigation, authorities were required to examine '*whether the person or entity who made a request for the opening of an investigation acted on behalf of the industry affected*', and such a request required the approval or authorization of the affected industry before the initiation of the investigation. The evidence submitted by the US was found to be insufficient to prove that the investigation was initiated on behalf of the domestic industry; hence, the US action was considered inconsistent with 1979 AD Code Article 5.1.[702]

This provision was also interpreted in the *US – Cement* case,[703] brought to the GATT in 1990 by Mexico. The Panel examined whether the US anti-dumping investigation on imports of grey portland cement and cement clinker from Mexico was '*initiated upon a written request by or on behalf of the industry affected*', pursuant to

698. GATT document L/5814, 19 June 1985, paras 1, 2, 4.2.
699. *Ibid.*, paras 4.7, 4.9, 4.10, 4.14.
700. *United States – Imposition of Anti-dumping Duties on Imports of Seamless Stainless Steel Hollow Products from Sweden* (GD/204) Complainant: Sweden. GATT document ADP/47, 20 August 1990. Another relevant GATT document: ADP/38, 14 July 1988.
701. 1979 AD Code Article 5.1. '*An investigation to determine the existence, degree and effect of any alleged dumping shall normally be initiated upon a written request by or on behalf of the industry affected. The request shall include sufficient evidence of (a) dumping; (b) injury within the meaning of Article VI of the General Agreement as interpreted by this Code and (c) a causal link between the dumped imports and the alleged injury.*'
702. GATT document ADP/47, 20 August 1990, paras 5.9, 5.10, 5.14, 5.23.
703. *United States – Anti-dumping Duties on Grey Portland Cement and Cement Clinker from Mexico* (GD/237). Complainant: Mexico. GATT document ADP/82, 7 September 1992. Another relevant GATT document: ADP/51, 24 October 1990.

1979 AD Code Article 5.1. A petition to initiate an anti-dumping investigation of grey portland cement and cement clinker from Mexico was filed by the Ad Hoc Committee, representing a number of domestic producers from Arizona, New Mexico, Texas and Florida. In the petition, the Ad Hoc Committee claimed it accounted for a '*majority of domestic production of grey portland cement in each of the regional markets at issue*', and included a list of members and other producers in the two regional industries. Petitioners alleged that the two regional domestic industries (one in Arizona, New Mexico and Texas, and the other in Florida) could be considered as a single region for the purposes of 1979 AD Code Article 5.1 ('affected industry') in relation to Articles 3 and 4. The petitioners' certified claim that '*they represented a majority of the regional production*' was the only evidence to prove that the investigation was requested '*by or on behalf of the affected industry*'. Notwithstanding the Panel found support of the petition by a majority of regional producers, '*accounting for about 62 per cent of the production in the regional market (as finally determined) had supported the petition, and producers accounting for 4 per cent of the production in that market had opposed it*', this information was neither sought by the USDOC nor provided to it by the USITC at any time during the investigation.[704]

Pursuant to 1979 AD Code Article 5.1 in relation to Articles 3 and 4, the Panel considered that the requirement '*on behalf of the industry affected*' (under Article 5.1) differed depending on whether the market was regional or national. In the case of a national market, evidence of support by '*a major proportion of the total domestic production of those products*' (Article 4.1) would meet the requirement under Article 5.1 ('*industry affected*') to initiate an investigation. In cases in which a regional market existed in exceptional circumstances, established under (Article 4.1.ii), evidence of support by '*producers of all or almost all of the production within such market*' would be required to initiate an investigation '*on behalf of the industry affected*' (Article 5.1).[705]

Following this distinction, the Panel concluded that, in order to initiate an investigation in the case of a regional market, authorities were required to satisfy themselves that the petition was authorized or approved by '*producers of all or almost all of the production within such market*' (Article 4.1.ii) and rejected that producers that accounted for a majority of the market could represent producers '*of all or almost all of the production*' in the regional market. Moreover, the Panel found that US investigating authorities could not have had, prior to the initiation, '*adequate grounds to believe*' (i.e., did not satisfy themselves) that all or almost all of the producers in the regional market had approved or authorized the petition. Therefore, the Panel concluded that

704. The US stated that the US Department of Commerce did not verify or ascertain the level of support or approval for the petition, which stated that the petitioners accounted for a majority of the production in the relevant region and included a list of other producers, without their approval or disapproval regarding the petition. The policy of the US Department of Commerce was to presume the existence of approval unless a majority of the domestic industry indicated their opposition. GATT document ADP/82, 7 September 1992, paras 1, 2.3, 5.32, 5.33.

705. *Ibid.*, para. 5.26.

the US initiation of the anti-dumping investigation was inconsistent with 1979 AD Code Article 5.1.[706]

In 1991, Sweden submitted a complaint against the US review of anti-dumping duties (established under 1979 AD Code Article 9.2), *US – Swedish Steel Plate*.[707] In 1985 and 1987, the USITC had dismissed two requests for review made by Sweden, concluding that the need for the initiation of a review was not substantiated by the information on either '*the purchase in 1976 of a steel mill in New Castle, Indiana by a predecessor of the Swedish exporter*' or '*the changed structure of the Swedish stainless steel plate industry and on the free-trade agreements between Sweden and the EC*'. The Panel found that the USITC decision not to initiate a review was '*based on factually incorrect data*' concerning the first request and lacked sufficient evidence and adequate explanation regarding the second request. Therefore, the Panel concluded that the US action was inconsistent with 1979 AD Code Article 9.2.[708]

US anti-dumping duties were also the object of a dispute initiated in 1991, the *US - Norwegian Salmon AD* case,[709] brought to the GATT along with a complaint against US countervailing duties, the *US – Norwegian Salmon CVD* case.[710] Following petitions from the US Coalition for Fair Atlantic Salmon Trade, consisting of domestic producers of fresh and chilled Atlantic salmon, the USDOC initiated anti-dumping and countervailing duties investigations in 1990. The disputes were examined separately, but to better compare them, the dispute on countervailing duties has been included in this section. While the Panel found that US countervailing duties were consistent with the SCM Code, US anti-dumping duties were considered inconsistent with 1979 AD Code Articles 2.4, 2.6 and 6.8.

In the countervailing duty case, *US – Norwegian Salmon CVD*, the Panel found that over the majority of all domestic production of Atlantic salmon had approved the petition as of the date of the initiation; therefore, it concluded that USDOC initiated the countervailing duty investigation '*on behalf of the industry affected*', in a manner consistent with SCM Code Article 2.1. Furthermore, the Panel concluded that the USDOC's calculation of the amount of subsidies was consistent with SCM Code Article 4.2, and the imposition of countervailing duties was in conformity with the provision on regional development programmes under SCM Code Article 11.[711]

In the anti-dumping duty case, *US – Norwegian Salmon AD*, the Panel found that while US measures were consistent with 1979 AD Code Articles 3, 5.1, 6.1, 8.3 and 9.1,

706. *Ibid.*, paras 5.31, 5.32, 5.34.
707. *United States – Anti-dumping Duties on Imports of Stainless Steel Plate from Sweden* (GD/247). Complainant: Sweden. GATT documents ADP/117, 24 February 1994, ADP/117/Corr.1, 30 March 1994. Another relevant GATT document: ADP/56, 6 May 1991.
708. GATT documents ADP/117, 24 February 1994, para. 439.
709. *United States – Imposition of Anti-dumping Duties on Imports of Fresh and Chilled Atlantic Salmon from Norway* (GD/251). Complainant: Norway. GATT document ADP/87, 30 November 1992. Other relevant GATT documents: ADP/57, 17 June 1991(consultations); ADP/M/44, 25-26 April 1994 (adoption of report).
710. *United States – Imposition of Countervailing Duties on Imports of Fresh and Chilled Atlantic Salmon from Norway* (GD/249). Complainant: Norway. GATT document SCM/153, 4 December 1992. Other relevant GATT documents: SCM/115, 10 June 1991 (consultations); SCM/M/69, 28 April 1994 (adoption of report).
711. GATT document SCM/153, 4 December 1992, paras 232, 233, 241, 244, 250, 350, 351.

the US determination of dumping was inconsistent with 1979 AD Code Articles 2.4 and 2.6. Therefore, the Panel found that the US imposition of anti-dumping duties on imports of fresh and chilled salmon from Norway was inconsistent with US obligations under the 1979 AD Code, and recommended the US reconsideration of the determination of dumping in a manner consistent with 1979 AD Code Articles 2.4 and 2.6, based on the following grounds.[712]

In order to calculate the '*cost of production in the country of origin*', the US used a methodology based on sampling. Notwithstanding that the 1979 AD Code did not provide for the use of sampling, the Panel examined whether the US methodology contravened 1979 AD Code Article 2.4.[713] The Panel considered that the results obtained with this procedure '*would not be significantly different than the results obtained through an investigation of the total population of Norwegian salmon farms*'; nevertheless, the USDOC failed to consider '*the question of the number of farms to be included in the samples (...) to ensure that these samples would be representative*', hence concluded that the US acted inconsistently with 1979 AD Code Article 2.4.[714]

Furthermore, the Panel noted that the USDOC had used the sample to compute a single average figure '*to be included in the calculation of the constructed normal values of most of the exporters under investigation*'. In six of the seven salmon farms in the sample, the actual verified costs of production per kg significantly differed. With regard to the remaining salmon farm included in the sample, Nordsvalaks, '*which allegedly had failed to provide certain information*', the USDOC enjoyed its right to choose '*the facts available*'. As a result, Nordsvalaks was imputed the '*highest cost of production figure found for any other farm in the sample*'. According to the Panel, when determining the costs of production of Nordsvalaks, the USDOC '*should have considered how its choice of "the facts available" (...) would affect the representativeness of the results of the sample*'. Nevertheless, the Panel found no indication that the USDOC had considered how the representativeness of the sample was affected by its determination of the cost of production of Nordsvalaks '*on the basis of the fact available*', pursuant to 1979 AD Code Article 6.8.[715] Therefore, also in this respect, the Panel concluded that the US acted inconsistently with 1979 AD Code Article 2.4.[716]

712. GATT document ADP/87, 30 November 1992, paras 595-597.

713. 1979 AD Code Article 2.4. '*When there are no sales of the like product in the ordinary course of trade in the domestic market of the exporting country or when, because of the particular market situation, such sales do not permit a proper comparison, the margin of dumping shall be determined by comparison with a comparable price of the like product when exported to any third country which may be the highest such export price but should be a representative price, or with the cost of production in the country of origin plus a reasonable amount for administrative, selling and any other costs and for profits. As a general rule, the addition for profit shall not exceed the profit normally realized on sales of products of the same general category in the domestic market of the country of origin.*'

714. GATT document ADP/87, 30 November 1992, paras 414, 426.

715. 1979 AD Code Article 6.8. '*In cases in which any interested party refuses access to, or otherwise does not provide, necessary information within a reasonable period or significantly impedes the investigation, preliminary and final findings, affirmative or negative, may be made on the basis of the facts available.*'

716. GATT document ADP/87, 30 November 1992, paras 23, 450.

In addition, the Panel examined whether the US had established a fair comparison between the export price and the normal value, pursuant to 1979 AD Code Article 2.6,[717] and found that the US had compared the constructed normal value across different weight categories of salmon with export prices which varied by weight category. In its allegation, the USDOC claimed that prices of Atlantic salmon per kg varied by weight category, while the costs of production per kg did not vary by weight. The Panel interpreted the '*fair comparison between the export price and the domestic price*' provision under 1979 AD Code Article 2.6 in a manner that applied to normal values based on prices, as well as to constructed normal values. Accordingly, it found that the USDOC had failed to explain why the difference in weight categories was considered not to be a relevant factor to construct normal values, and to properly consider whether the difference in weight categories affected the comparability between constructed normal values and export prices; hence, the US acted inconsistently with 1979 AD Code Article 2.6.[718]

Notably, the Panel interpreted the injury provision under 1979 AD Code Article 3.4, whereby it must be demonstrated that dumped imports were causing injury[719] and concluded that the US determination of material injury was consistent with it.[720] According to the Panel, if investigating authorities were required '*to continue to collect data up to the time of the final determination*', other provisions of the 1979 AD Code would be undermined, such as 1979 AD Code Article 6.2,[721] regarding interested parties' rights to access information used by investigating authorities. Therefore, in order to adequately protect the procedural rights of interested parties, the Panel considered that the determination of material injury shall be based on a defined record of facts before the investigating authorities.

In the *EC – Audio Cassettes* case,[722] the Panel also interpreted 1979 AD Code Article 2.4 and 2.6, regarding the determination of dumping. In 1991, Japan brought a

717. 1979 AD Code Article 2.6. '*In order to effect a fair comparison between the export price and the domestic price in the exporting country (or the country of origin) or, if applicable, the price established pursuant to the provisions of Article VI:1 (b) of the General Agreement, the two prices shall be compared at the same level of trade, normally at the ex-factory level, and in respect of sales made at as nearly as possible the same time. Due allowance shall be made in each case, on its merits, for the differences in conditions and terms of sale, for the differences in taxation, and for the other differences affecting price comparability. In the cases referred to in paragraph 5 of Article 2 allowance for costs, including duties and taxes, incurred between importation and resale, and for profits accruing, should also be made.*'
718. GATT document ADP/87, 30 November 1992, paras 471, 472.
719. 1979 AD Code Article 3.4 '*It must be demonstrated that the dumped imports are, through the effects of dumping, causing injury within the meaning of this Code. There may be other factors which at the same time are injuring the industry, and the injuries caused by other factors must not be attributed to the dumped imports.*'
720. GATT document ADP/87, 30 November 1992, para. 580.
721. 1979 AD Code Article 6.2. '*The authorities concerned shall provide opportunities for the complainant and the importers and exporters known to be concerned and the governments of the exporting countries, to see all information that is relevant to the presentation of their cases, that is not confidential as defined in paragraph 3 below, and that is used by the authorities in an anti-dumping investigation, and to prepare presentations on the basis of this information.*'
722. *EEC – Imposition of Anti-dumping Duties on Imports of Audio Cassettes from Japan* (GD/253). Complainant: Japan. GATT documents ADP/136, 28 April 1995, ADP/136/Corr.1, 8 June 1995. Other relevant GATT documents: ADP/79, July 1991, October 1991, December 1991, April 1992(consultations).

complaint to the GATT against the EEC's imposition of anti-dumping duties on audio cassettes. Following a petition from the Chemical Manufacturers' Federation, on behalf of certain EEC producers of audio cassettes, the EEC initiated an investigation based on its then Basic Regulation (EEC Council Regulation 2423/88),[723] and imposed provisional and definitive anti-dumping duties on imports of audio cassettes originating in Japan, Hong Kong and the Republic of Korea.[724]

With regard to the methodology used by the EEC to determine dumping, the Panel found that the EEC had constructed certain normal values by, on the one hand, allocating '*an amount for selling, administrative and selling costs*' on a cost-of-manufacture basis, and, on the other hand, derived an amount for profit for the three kinds of 'normal' type cassettes from '*data relating to sales of all sales of the like product by that exporter in the Japanese market*'. The Panel concluded that the EEC methodology to construct the normal value was consistent with 1979 AD Code Article 2.4. Concerning the EEC's averaging methodology, the Panel considered that it did not contravene 1979 AD Code Article 2.1. Nevertheless, it considered that the information before the Panel did not permit it to conclude that the averaging methodology had been inconsistent with the '*fair comparison*' obligation derived from 1979 AD Code Article 2.1 and 2.6.[725]

Furthermore, the Panel examined whether the EEC had established a 'fair comparison' between the normal value and the export price, pursuant to 1979 AD Code Article 2.6. While the EEC included selling, marketing and promotion expenses to construct the normal value, it deducted all advertising expenses related to sales in the EEC to construct an export price, resulting in an increase in the margin of dumping. The EEC alleged that the level of trade of '*the sales department/company of the Japanese producer, adjusted to deduct all direct expenses*' in Japan was equivalent to the domestic sales network or sales subsidiary in the EEC. According to the EEC Regulation, establishing the imposition of definitive duties, when sales were made to subsidiary companies, the EEC constructed certain export prices '*by deducting certain expenses and an amount for profit from the price paid by an independent purchaser (recital 17)*'. The Panel concluded that the EEC had acted inconsistently with 1979 AD Code Article 2.6 for using a methodology that resulted in differences, which could affect price comparability, hence recommended the EEC to bring its Basic Regulation into conformity with it.[726]

More specifically, the majority of the members of the Panel considered that the EEC had failed to make 'due allowance on its merits for differences in indirect selling expenses, and with respect to profits related to differences in the functions performed by the seller in the domestic and export markets'. Nevertheless, with regard to profits (i.e., 'profits related to differences in the functions performed by the seller in the domestic and export market'), one of the members of the Panel dissented with the

723. EEC Council Regulation 2423/88 of 11 July 1988 on protection against dumped or subsidized imports from countries not members of the European Economic Community.
724. EEC Commission Regulation 3262/90 and EEC Council Regulation 1251/91. GATT documents ADP/136, 28 April 1995, paras 7, 8.
725. GATT documents ADP/136, 28 April 1995, paras 454, 456.
726. *Ibid.*, paras 9, 107, 384, 458-460.

majority. According to the dissenting member, the Panel did not have sufficient information to conclude that the EEC failed to make adjustments regarding profits in order to ensure a fair comparison and thus 'could not conclude that the EEC had not made a fair comparison, or that it was precluded from doing so by its Basic regulation'. A comparison could have been deemed to be fair if the EEC had complied with the requirements under 1979 AD Code Article 2.6, i.e., 'same level of trade, normally at the ex-factory level, and in respect of sales made at as nearly as possible the same time'. Consequently, since the EEC had not selected 'the appropriate level of trade for domestic and export sales', it failed to 'effect a fair comparison', inconsistently with 1979 AD Code Article 2.6.[727]

3 *WTO Agreement on Anti-dumping, 1994*

The Agreement on Anti-dumping, as part of the WTO Agreement, is binding on all WTO Members, unlike the 1967 and 1979 AD Codes, which were independent international treaties.[728] An overall difference between the Anti-dumping Agreement and the 1979 AD Code is the '*greater degree of specificity and detail*' of new rules concerning, *inter alia*, the determination of dumping and the investigation proceeding. Nevertheless, it '*still leaves room for significant differences in approach to the enforcement of anti-dumping laws*', such as the public interest clause, the non-imposition of the lesser duty rule, or the freedom of choosing between imposing duties and reaching price undertakings.[729] Consisting of eighteen articles, the Agreement on Anti-dumping incorporated the sixteen articles comprising the 1979 AD Code, most of which were amended, and two new provisions, regarding public notice and explanation of determinations (ADA Article 12), and judicial review (ADA Article 13). The main modifications incorporated in the ADA are hereby presented.[730]

With regard to the determination of dumping, ADA Article 2 introduced the possibility of treating sales below cost as '*not being in the ordinary course of trade*', thereby disregarding them to determine the normal value (paragraph 2.2.1). This

727. *Ibid.*, paras 455, 462, 465, 467.
728. The ADA is part of the Uruguay Round results, accepted by all WTO Members under the 'single undertaking' approach, '*which definitively brings to an end the possibility of 'à la carte' acceptance of agreements, means that in time all trading partners will be subject to the same rules even if there are initially transition periods for less developed countries*'. J. Leflon, Uruguay Round Comments: A View from UNICE, in J. Bourgeois, F. Berrod, E. Gippini Fournier (eds), *The Uruguay Round Results: A European Lawyers' Perspective*, 1995, pp. 59-65 at 60.
729. M. Koulen, The New Anti-dumping Code Through its Negotiating History, in J. Bourgeois, F. Berrod, E. Gippini Fournier (eds), *The Uruguay Round Results, A European Lawyers' Perspective: Proceedings of an International Conference Held at the College of Europe, Bruges*, 1999, pp. 151-232 at 194, 195.
730. For a detailed discussion on the negotiating history and major provisions of the ADA, *see* G.N. Horlick, E.C. Shea, The World Trade Organization Antidumping Agreement, *Journal of World Trade*, Vol. 29, No. 1, 1995, pp. 5-32 https://doi.org/10.54648/trad1995001. For a detailed explanation of the ADA and its comparison with the 1979 AD Code, *see* M. Koulen, The New Anti-dumping Code Through its Negotiating History, in J. Bourgeois, F. Berrod, E. Gippini Fournier (eds), *The Uruguay Round Results, A European Lawyers' Perspective: Proceedings of an International Conference Held at the College of Europe, Bruges*, 1999, pp. 151-232.

requires that at least 20% of sales are below cost or that the weighted-average selling price is below the weighted-average per unit costs (Note 5). The protection of companies in start-up situations was incorporated by requiring authorities to adjust costs (paragraph 2.2.1.1.), yet a definition of start-up is lacking. Authorities are permitted to calculate profit margins based on selected sales (paragraph 2.2.2), through the legitimation of the much-criticized EU practice of inflating margins of dumping.[731] More specific rules are established to ensure a fair comparison, *inter alia*, by limiting the practice of countries to compare a weighted-average normal value with individual transactions in cases where authorities find, and explain, '*hidden dumping*', i.e., that high export prices hide low export prices (paragraph 4).

Concerning the determination of material injury, ADA Article 3 presents four amendments, namely the use of cumulation when assessing the effects of imports from several countries (paragraph 3); '*the magnitude of the margin of dumping*' as a factor to be considered in the examination of the impact of imports (paragraph 4); emphasis in the obligation of authorities to examine both all relevant evidence before them in order to determine the causal link (between the dumped imports and injury) and other known factors (paragraph 5); as well as a list of factors to determine the existence of threat of material injury (paragraph 7).

Concerning the proceedings of the investigation, the rules relating to the initiation and subsequent investigation were amended with the intention to bring transparency, fairness and protection '*against frivolous claims*'.[732] ADA Article 5.8 introduced a *de minimis* margin of dumping (2% of the export price) and a negligible import share in the injury determination (3% from a single country, unless countries collectively account for more than 7%). ADA Article 6 strengthened the rights of parties participating in an investigation, circumscribing the conditions under which investigating authorities may rely on the best available information (to reach provisional or definitive determinations); providing for control of such information (under Annex II); and including a provision to require that samples be '*statistically valid*' or cover '*the largest percentage of the volume of the exports* [that] *can reasonably be investigated*'.

With respect to the application of anti-dumping duties and price undertakings, compared to the AD 1979 AD Code, ADA Articles 7 to 11 extended rules on provisional and definitive measures, their duration, retroactivity and price undertakings. Notably, ADA Article 11.3 incorporated a sunset clause, limiting the duration of anti-dumping duties to five years, unless authorities determine, through a review before the five-year deadline, that the termination of the duties would result in the continuation or recurrence of dumping and injury. A remarkable provision was introduced under ADA Article 9.3.3., whereby authorities are permitted to deduct anti-dumping duties from the export price when constructing the export price (i.e., in cases of 'hidden dumping' by association between the exporter and importer), and the importer is required to

731. G.N. Horlick, E.C. Shea, The World Trade Organization Antidumping Agreement, *Journal of World Trade*, Vol. 29, No. 1, 1995, pp. 5-32 at 26 https://doi.org/10.54648/trad1995001.
732. *Ibid.*, p. 23.

demonstrate that it has also *'raised its prices by the full amount of the dumping margin'*.[733]

Under ADA Article 17, the procedure on 'conciliation' is absent. One of the most controversial unresolved issues during the Uruguay Round was the standard of review to be applied by panels.[734] A *sine qua non* condition for the US was the incorporation of ADA Article 17.6,[735] which provides for an interpretation of the ADA consistent with *'customary rules of interpretation of public international law'*, and establishes that, where ADA provisions admit *'more than one permissible interpretation'*, the anti-dumping measure must be found consistent with the ADA. Nonetheless, the claim that *'more than one permissible interpretation'* exists *'may conflict with the normal standards of treaty interpretation'*,[736] established in the Vienna Convention on the Law of Treaties.[737]

C Safeguard Measures after the Tokyo Round

1 Decision on Safeguards, 1979

At the Tokyo Round, GATT Contracting Parties were unable to reach an agreement on safeguard measures,[738] *'due to divergences between the countries of the North and the*

733. *Ibid.*, p. 27.
734. M. Koulen, The New Anti-dumping Code Through its Negotiating History, in J. Bourgeois, F. Berrod, E. Gippini Fournier (eds), *The Uruguay Round Results, A European Lawyers' Perspective: Proceedings of an International Conference Held at the College of Europe, Bruges*, 1999, pp. 151-232 at 226.
735. ADA Article 17.6 reads: *'In examining the matter referred to in paragraph 5:*

    (i) in its assessment of the facts of the matter, the panel shall determine whether the authorities' establishment of the facts was proper and whether their evaluation of those facts was unbiased and objective. If the establishment of the facts was proper and the evaluation was unbiased and objective, even though the panel might have reached a different conclusion, the evaluation shall not be overturned;
    (ii) the panel shall interpret the relevant provisions of the Agreement in accordance with customary rules of interpretation of public international law. Where the panel finds that a relevant provision of the Agreement admits of more than one permissible interpretation, the panel shall find the authorities' measure to be in conformity with the Agreement if it rests upon one of those permissible interpretations.'

736. G.N. Horlick, E.C. Shea, The World Trade Organization Antidumping Agreement, *Journal of World Trade*, Vol. 29, No. 1, 1995, pp. 5-32 at 30 https://doi.org/10.54648/trad1995001.
737. Under the rubric *'General rule of interpretation'*, Article 31 the Vienna Convention on the Law of Treaties establishes: *'1. A treaty shall be interpreted in good faith in accordance with the ordinary meaning to be given to the terms of the treaty in their context and in the light of its object and purpose.(...) 3. There shall be taken into account, together with the context: (...) (b) any subsequent practice in the application of the treaty which establishes the agreement of the parties regarding its interpretation.'* Article 32 includes a supplementary means of interpretation, *'the preparatory work of the treaty and the circumstances of its conclusion'* where the meaning is left *'ambiguous or obscure'*. Article 33 reads: *'when a comparison of the authentic texts discloses a difference of meaning which the application of articles 31 and 32 does not remove, the meaning which best reconciles the texts, having regard to the object and purpose of the treaty, shall be adopted'*.
738. J.H. Jackson, *The World Trade Organization, Constitution and Jurisprudence*, Chatham House Papers, 1998, p. 3.

countries of the South',[739] which was considered a *'failure'*.[740] GATT Contracting Parties, however, adopted a Decision on *'Safeguard Action for Development Purposes'* (hereinafter 'Decision on Safeguards'),[741] aimed at granting less-developed countries additional flexibility in the procedural rules to modify or withdraw concessions to achieve *'programmes and policies of economic development aimed at raising the standard of living of the people'*. The Decision provided less-developed countries the possibility to impose, immediately after notification, a provisional safeguard measure to achieve development objectives. Specifically, the Decision on Safeguards allowed less-developed countries to deviate from certain provisions under GATT Article XVIII (Section A and paragraphs 14, 15, 17 and 18 of Section C), whereby less-developed countries were required to notify CONTRACTING PARTIES and enter into consultations with them within thirty days (paragraph 15) and concur in such measure within ninety days (paragraph 17).

2 *WTO Agreement on Safeguards, 1994*

After the Tokyo Round, no GATT dispute settlement report was issued concerning safeguard measures (GATT Art. XIX).[742] At the Uruguay Round (1986-1994), GATT Contracting Parties recognized the need to clarify and reinforce the discipline of emergency actions under GATT Article XIX and to eliminate safeguard measures outside multilateral control. Furthermore, they identified the need to enhance competition and the importance of structural adjustment.[743] Therefore, as part of the Uruguay Round results, an Agreement on Safeguards, binding on all WTO Members, was reached.

Consisting of fourteen articles, the Agreement on Safeguards sets out procedures on the conditions for the imposition of measures, including the non-discriminatory application (ASG Article 2); the investigation (ASG Article 3), determination of serious injury, including the existence of a causal link and non-attribution analysis (ASG Article 4); application of both provisional and definitive safeguards (ASG Articles 5 and 6); duration of the measures, establishing a maximum period of four years, renewable for another period following a review (ASG Article 7); retaliation, prohibiting recourse

739. T. Flory, The Agreement on Safeguards, in J. Bourgeois, F. Berrod, E. Gippini Fournier (eds), *The Uruguay Round Results, A European Lawyers' Perspective: Proceedings of an International Conference Held at the College of Europe, Bruges*, 1999, pp. 265-271 at 266.

740. GATT document, The Tokyo Round of Multilateral Trade Negotiations, Vol. II. Supplementary Report, January 1980, pp. 14-17. '*One of the failures of the Tokyo Round in 1979 was its inability to achieve an agreement on safeguard and escape clause measures.*' J.H. Jackson, *The World Trade Organization, Constitution and Jurisprudence*, Chatham House Papers, 1998.

741. GATT document L/4897, 28 November 1979.

742. Last GATT disputes regarding safeguard measures terminated in the consultation proceeding:

   Austria – Restrictions on Imports of Video Tape Recorders (GD/117). Complainant: Japan. GATT document L/5119, 25 February 1981.
   Switzerland – Imports of Table Grapes (GD/136). Complainant: EEC-10, GATT document L/5371, 29 September 1982.

743. Preamble of the Agreement on Safeguards. UNTS, Vol. 1869, p. 154.

to it during three years in case of an absolute increase in imports (ASG Article 8); special rules for developing country Members regarding both exportation and importation (ASG Article 9); elimination of pre-existing safeguard measures no later than five years (ASG Article 10); prohibition and elimination of certain measures,[744] such as voluntary export restraints (VERs) and other safeguard import or export arrangements (ASG Article 11); notification, consultation, and other obligations (ASG Article 12); surveillance and dispute settlement (ASG Articles 13 and 14).

Notwithstanding that the new Agreement on Safeguards was considered to contain improvements regarding the imposition of safeguard measures, certain inefficiencies were maintained, and the adjustment problem was introduced (preamble and ASG Article 7.1). Among the improvements, the Agreement on Safeguards provides for a stricter framework to impose safeguards, with refined criteria and specific time periods. More importantly, it introduced the progressive elimination of voluntary export restraints (VERs) and similar measures (ASG Article 11). This provision was expected to bring '*greater transparency and legal certainty*', despite the fact that the Agreement on Safeguards did not list these measures, hence, maintaining the difficulty of identifying and eliminating them.[745]

The Agreement on Safeguards enshrined the non-discrimination principle (ASG Article 2.2), yet permitted a customs union to impose safeguards as a single unit and on behalf of a member (footnote 1). While this was considered an improvement for the then EC, providing it with '*greater effectiveness and swiftness when injury has been found in connection with the territory of one Member State*', it is arguably the opposite for the multilateral trading system. The Agreement on Safeguards has been criticized for the absence of, *inter alia*, a definition of authorized safeguards, since GATT Article XIX implicitly allows the imposition of customs duties and quotas; precision in the selection criteria when allocating quotas (ASG Article 5.2); differentiation in relation to the categories of developing countries, contrary to the ASCM; and judicial review, unlike in anti-dumping and countervailing duty proceedings.[746]

744. According to footnote 4 of the Agreement on Safeguards, '*Examples of similar measures include export moderation, export-price or import-price monitoring systems, export or import surveillance, compulsory import cartels and discretionary export or import licensing schemes, any of which afford protection.*'
745. T. Flory, The Agreement on Safeguards, in J. Bourgeois, F. Berrod, E. Gippini Fournier (eds), *The Uruguay Round Results, A European Lawyers' Perspective: Proceedings of an International Conference Held at the College of Europe, Bruges*, 1999, pp. 265-271 at 267, 268.
746. *Ibid.*

PART III

Trade Remedy Laws, Subsidies and Competition in the XXI Century

> No country could enjoy economic and political stability in a world which would not itself be orderly in the economic sense (...) To maintain orderliness in such a world, progress in overall stability, requires continuous adjustment to the continuous flow of change and novelty.[747]

This third part of the book consists of a comprehensive proposal aimed at enhancing the multilateral trading system. It consists of a comprehensive multilateral solution that encompasses the amendment of subsidy disciplines, abolition of trade remedy laws (countervailing and anti-dumping duties, and safeguard measures), incorporation of an agreement on competition law and trade-restrictive practices, and the inclusion of labour and environmental standards within the WTO Agreement. A multilateral solution based on welfare economics is in the interest of each and all WTO Members, the environment, and individuals around the globe. Furthermore, on the basis of the historical research, a multilateral approach, in contrast to a plurilateral approach,[748] is considered the best (and the only proper) for this endeavour.

747. J. Tumlir, GATT Rules and Community Law, in M. Hilf, F. Jacobs, E.U. Petersmann, *The European Community and the GATT*, 1986, pp. 1-22 at 1.

748. '*Arthur Dunkel (...) stated: "The tendency toward bilateralism and sectorialism on trade policy is the greatest present danger both politically and economically to order and prosperity in the world economy".*' R.C. de Grey, *Trade Policy and the System of Contingency Protection in the Perspective of Competition Policy*, 1986, p. 9.

Introduction: A Plurilateral Rather Than Multilateral Solution? Abolition of Trade Remedies in FTAs and Customs Unions: GATT Articles VI, XIX and XXIV.8

WTO Members are permitted, under GATT Article XXIV, to establish free trade agreements (FTAs) or customs unions aimed at '*increasing freedom of trade (...) and not to raise barriers to the trade of other contracting parties with such territories*'.[749] GATT Article XXIV.8, in its paragraphs (a)(i) and (b), provides for the internal elimination of trade-restrictive measures and regulations, '*except, where necessary, those permitted under Articles XI, XII, XIII, XIV, XV and XX*'. Therefore, GATT Articles VI and XIX are not included in GATT Article XXIV.8 as justifying the maintenance of trade barriers within FTAs or customs unions. In other words, neither anti-dumping or countervailing duties, nor safeguards are included among these excepted measures, permitted to be imposed within FTAs or customs unions. '*The increasing importance of non-tariff barriers and of administered protection, however, argues for a more rigorous application of the requirements of GATT Article XXIV.*'[750]

Nevertheless, free trade agreements and customs unions notified over the years to the GATT/WTO have nearly always maintained the possible application of anti-dumping, countervailing and safeguards provisions among their members,[751] inconsistently with GATT Article XXIV.8. Recent cases include the FTAs signed after Brexit by the UK with the EU and with New Zealand. The EU-U.K. Trade and Cooperation

749. GATT Article XXIV.4: '*The contracting parties recognize the desirability of increasing freedom of trade by the development, through voluntary agreements, of closer integration between the economies of the countries parties to such agreements. They also recognize that the purpose of a customs union or of a free-trade area should be to facilitate trade between the constituent territories and not to raise barriers to the trade of other contracting parties with such territories.*'
750. M. Hart, Dumping and Free Trade Areas, in J.H. Jackson, E.A. Vermulst (eds), *Antidumping Law and Practice: A Comparative Study*, 1990, pp. 326-342 at 333.
751. *Ibid.*, pp. 329-330.

Agreement consists of a regression of the economic integration progress (i.e., 'economic disintegration'). It includes a provision on trade remedies (Article 32), whereby both parties affirm their rights and obligations under GATT Articles VI and XIX, and related WTO Agreements (ADA, ASCM and ASG).[752] Notably, these measures had not been imposed between the UK and other EU Members since the 1970s. The U.K.-New Zealand Agreement also includes a chapter on trade remedies, whereby both countries agree to retain WTO rights and obligations with respect to subsidies, anti-dumping and countervailing duties, and safeguard measures.[753] In addition, it establishes a bilateral safeguard mechanism, which is per se inconsistent with the non-discriminatory application of GATT Article XIX.1.

Since GATT Article XXIV.8 does not list GATT Articles VI and XIX as exceptional measures to be imposed within WTO Members of an FTA or a customs union, the question of whether the imposition of trade remedies is consistent with GATT Article XXIV.8 has been raised since the early days of the GATT. Gobbi Estrella and Horlick consider that the abolition of trade remedies within FTAs or customs unions is mandatory to qualify as FTA or customs union under GATT Article XXIV.8, and thus, those FTAs or customs unions that allow the application of trade remedies are '*illegitimate departures of MFN that lack justification on the basis of Article XXIV of the GATT*'.[754] According to them, as well as Lockhart and Mitchell,[755] the WTO Appellate Body confirmed this interpretation of GATT Article XXIV.8 in the *Textiles – Turkey* ruling,[756] by establishing that '*members of a customs union may maintain, where*

752. Trade and Cooperation Agreement between the EU and the U.K., OJEU, L.149, 30 April 2021, pp. 10-2539 at 52-54.
753. U.K. Department for International Trade, Policy paper U.K.-New Zealand FTA negotiations: agreement in principle, 20 October 2021, viewed at: https://www.gov.uk/government/publications/uk-new-zealand-free-trade-agreement-negotiations-agreement-in-principle/uk-new-zealand-fta-negotiations-agreement-in-principle.
754. A.T. Gobbi Estrella, G.N. Horlick, Mandatory Abolition of Anti-dumping, Countervailing Duties and Safeguards in Customs Unions and Free-Trade Areas Constituted Between World Trade Organization Members: Revisiting a Long-Standing Discussion in Light of the Appellate Body's Turkey-Textiles Ruling, *Journal of World Trade*, Vol. 40, No. 5, 2006, pp. 909-944 at 910, 911, 944.
755. '*While not a definitive ruling on this issue, (...) the Appellate Body would read the bracketed phrase as containing an exclusive list of ORRCs that may be maintained in an RTA.*' N.J.S. Lockhart, A.D. Mitchell, Regional Trade Agreements Under GATT 1994: An Exception and Its Limits, in N.J.S. Lockhart, A.D. Mitchell, *Challenges And Prospects For The WTO*, 2005, pp. 217-239 at 232.
756. A.T. Gobbi Estrella and G.N. Horlick found that neither consensus had ever been reached '*nor a definite clarification had been provided by the DSB*' on the application of trade remedies in FTAs and customs unions, under GATT Article XXIV.8, until the WTO Appellate Body's *Turkey-Textiles* ruling '*endorsed the first interpretation*' on the subject. Matsushita, Schoenbaum and Mavroidis claimed that the WTO DSB had '*held that parties to a PTA may impose safeguards against other parties to the PTA*' in each of the discriminatory safeguard cases, '*where a WTO Member that was a party to a RTA applied a safeguard measure and excluded imports originating in their RTA partners from the scope of the safeguard*', i.e., in *Argentina-Footwear (EC)*, *US – Wheat Gluten*, *US – Lamb*, *US – Line Pipe* and *US – Steel Safeguards*. M. Matsushita, T.J. Schoenbaum, P.C. Mavroidis, *The World Trade Organization: Law, Practice and Policy*, Oxford, 2003, p. 363. Cited in A.T. Gobbi Estrella, G.N. Horlick, Mandatory Abolition of Anti-dumping, Countervailing Duties and Safeguards in Customs Unions and Free-Trade Areas Constituted Between World Trade Organization Members: Revisiting a

necessary, in their internal trade, certain restrictive regulations of commerce that are otherwise permitted under Articles XI through XV and under Article XX of the GATT 1994'.[757] In the particular case of safeguard measures, this departure from the MFN principle is also inconsistent with GATT Article XIX.

I RELATION OF GATT ARTICLE XIX WITH GATT ARTICLE XXIV: SAFEGUARD MEASURES IN FTAS AND CUSTOMS UNIONS

The relation between GATT Articles XIX and XXIV was unsettled before the Uruguay Round.[758] Some GATT Contracting Parties exempted parties to FTAs from safeguards, alleging GATT Article XXIV.8(b) justified the discriminatory application of safeguards (e.g., FTAs between the EC and Austria, Iceland, Portugal, Sweden and Switzerland). Nevertheless, in those days, most Contracting Parties disagreed that '*the invocation of Article XXIV permitted the discriminatory application of Article XIX*' and interpreted GATT Article XIX to mean that '*safeguard action would be taken on a strictly most-favoured-nation basis*'. This interpretation was in line with the GATT Secretariat's study on GATT Article XIX, which highlighted that '*the clear intent of the drafters of Article XIX was that it should be non-discriminatory in its application*'.[759]

Following this non-discriminatory interpretation of GATT Article XIX.1, parties to FTAs or customs unions were not allowed to exempt other parties to the FTA or customs union from the application of safeguards, i.e., were obliged to impose safeguard measures also to their FTAs/custom unions' parties. Since GATT Article XIX is not listed as a permitted exception under GATT Article XXIV.8(a)(i) and (b), the imposition of safeguards within parties to FTAs or customs unions would be inconsistent with GATT Article XXIV.8. As a result, GATT Articles XIX.1 and XXIV.8 would render impossible for parties to FTAs or customs unions the imposition of safeguard measures. Nonetheless, no GATT Contracting Party/WTO Member has ever challenged the consistency of existing FTAs or customs unions which provide for the imposition of safeguards (or more broadly, trade remedies) within parties, with GATT Article XXIV.8. On the contrary, it seems to be accepted by WTO Members that FTAs do not fulfil the requirement under GATT Article XXIV.8(b).

Furthermore, following the Uruguay Round, customs unions are permitted to impose safeguard measures, *inter alia*, as a single unit, i.e., in a discriminatory manner (ASG footnote 1), while the non-discriminatory application of safeguards is provided for within FTAs (ASG Article 2.2).[760] Nonetheless, due to the worldwide proliferation of FTAs, customs unions are also part of FTAs; hence, they are not allowed to impose safeguards consistently with GATT Article XXIV.8(b), whereby the imposition of

Long-Standing Discussion in Light of the Appellate Body's Turkey-Textiles Ruling, *Journal of World Trade*, Vol. 40, No. 5, 2006, pp. 909-944 at 911, 912.

757. *Turkey – Restrictions on Imports of Textile and Clothing Products* (DS34). WTO document DS34/AB/R, 19 November 1999, para. 48.

758. M. Koulen, The Non-discriminatory Interpretation of GATT Article XIX.1. A Reply, *Legal Issues of Economic Integration*, Vol. 10, No. 2, 1983, pp. 87-111.

759. GATT document L/4679, 5 July 1978, paras 23-26 (under Section VII).

760. ASG footnote 1. *See* Ch. 10.

safeguards is not permitted within parties, as well as GATT Article XIX.1 and ASG Article 2.2, whereby safeguards must be applied on a non-discriminatory basis. Accordingly, WTO Members that are parties to FTAs are not allowed to impose safeguard measures consistently with those provisions.

II RELATION OF GATT ARTICLE VI WITH GATT ARTICLE XXIV: ANTI-DUMPING AND COUNTERVAILING DUTIES IN FTAS AND CUSTOMS UNIONS

The relation of GATT Articles VI and XXIV.8 is different from the case of GATT Article XIX since the application of anti-dumping and countervailing duties is discriminatory per se. GATT Article VI constitutes an exception to the non-discrimination principles, enshrined in GATT Articles I and III (most-favoured-nation and national treatment principles). Accordingly, if WTO Members that are parties to FTAs or customs unions exempt, pursuant to GATT Article XXIV.8(a)(i) and (b), their parties from the application of anti-dumping and countervailing duties, it would be consistent with GATT Article VI. In other words, WTO Members can eliminate anti-dumping and countervailing duties within their FTAs or customs unions, pursuant to GATT Article XXIV.8, while imposing them externally (i.e., on non-parties to the FTA/customs union) without violating GATT Article VI.

Indeed, some FTAs and customs union have eliminated their internal anti-dumping duties (and replaced them with competition rules), consistently with GATT Article VI. Besides the well-known case of the EU, Australia and New Zealand signed the Closer Economic Relations Agreement, whereby the use of anti-dumping duties and safeguards has been precluded since 1990; yet the use of countervailing duties is still possible between both countries, which is not in conformity with GATT Article XXIV.8(a)(i).[761]

As opposed to the multilateral abolition of trade remedy laws, the problem of eliminating trade remedies through GATT Article XXIV.8(a)(i) and (b) would be that while anti-dumping and countervailing duties would be eliminated within FTAs and customs unions, this may result in the tendency of creating blocks between FTAs or customs unions, for protectionist purposes. Unlike the non-discriminatory application of GATT Article XIX.1 (as interpreted by the GATT Secretariat, and established under ASG Article 2.2), the discriminatory nature of GATT Article VI permits that, even where parties to FTAs or customs unions eliminate anti-dumping and countervailing duties among themselves, pursuant to GATT Article XXIV.8(a)(i) and (b), anti-dumping and countervailing duties could be legally imposed on imports from non-parties to the FTAs or customs unions; hence, this possibility may tend to create blocks in the international trading system.

For this reason, the elimination of trade remedies within FTAs and customs unions pursuant to an interpretation of GATT Article XXIV.8(a)(i) and (b) as an

761. Australian Government Productivity Commission, Australia's Anti-dumping and Countervailing System, Report No. 48, 2009.

exhausting list does not seem an advisable solution. Therefore, in order to prevent that anti-dumping and countervailing duties may continue to be imposed also between FTAs or customs unions, the advisable solution is a complete elimination of trade remedies through the abolition of GATT Articles VI and XIX. In addition, while some plurilateral agreements or customs unions have provided for the elimination of trade remedies within the parties and incorporated competition rules (e.g., Australia and New Zealand),[762] and even subsidies rules (e.g., the EU), this plurilateral/regional solution cannot guarantee a situation of Pareto's optimum, whereby global welfare is enhanced. Furthermore, a plurilateral solution, far from harmonizing rules, tends to create blocs among countries, and thus promote discrimination:

> The great political virtue of multilateralism, far exceeding in importance its economic virtues, is that it makes it economically possible for most countries, even if small, poor and weak, to live in freedom and with chances of prosperity without having to come to special terms with some Great Power.[763]

762. *See* Sections 6A and 99A of the New Zealand's Commerce Act 1986.
763. J. Viner, Conflicts of Principle in Drafting a Trade Charter, *Foreign Affairs*, Vol. 25, No. 4, 1947, pp. 612-628 at 626 https://doi.org/10.2307/20030068.

CHAPTER 7
Subsidies

This chapter explores the need to amend the WTO rules on subsidies in order to address certain issues in the multilateral trading system. It is suggested to approach the subsidy disciplines from the perspective of welfare economics. Instead of focusing solely on production, it is proposed that multilateral rules on subsidies should include an economic analysis of the effects of subsidies on consumption, which should be enforced through multilateral procedures. To this end, some amendments to the WTO rules on subsidies, i.e., GATT Article XVI and the ASCM, are hereby proposed.

I JUSTIFICATION OF THE NEED TO REFORM RULES ON SUBSIDIES

Since Adam Smith's criticism of mercantilism in *The Wealth of Nations*, there is evidence that subsidies have been used to promote exports as well as to restrain imports. By making subsidized products more competitive, subsidies can affect international trade by displacing products in third-country markets and/or substituting imports in the domestic market of the subsidizing country.[764] Due to this twofold effect of subsidies in international trade, subsidies may be used as a protectionist device, i.e., to restrain imports and/or promote exports. When countries have competed in providing subsidies (especially in certain situations, such as the recent COVID-19 pandemic),[765] the advantage that they might have enjoyed has been offset. It is

764. J.H. Jackson, *The World Trade and The Law of The GATT*, 1969, p. 365; G.N. Horlick, John Jackson and the development of GATT-WTO Subsidies Rules, in M. Bronckers, R. Quick (eds), *New Directions in International Economic Law: Essays in Honour of John H. Jackson*, 2000, pp. 177-184 at 177. J.H. Jackson, World Trade Rules and Environmental Policies: Congruence or Conflict?, *Washington and Lee Law Review*, Vol. 49, No. 4, 1992, pp. 1227-1278 at 1246.
765. '*The COVID-19 pandemic generated a massive expansion in fiscal policy, appropriately so, but many of the subsidies are firm- or activity-specific and thus may distort international competition.*' B. Hoekman, P.C. Mavroidis, WTO Reform: Back to the Past to Build for the Future, *Global Policy*, Vol. 12, No. 3, 2021, pp. 5-12 at 6 https://doi.org/10.1111/1758-5899.12924.

undesirable and inefficient that countries resort to the use of subsidies as a protectionist device.[766]

Subsidies may distort international trade in the manner described above, yet they may also correct distortions in markets,[767] i.e., subsidies can, under certain circumstances, generate a social benefit. Therefore, the difficulty for the multilateral trading system lies in identifying trade-distorting subsidies and disciplining them. The existing WTO rules have been criticized for doing *'a poor job at identifying protectionist subsidies'*,[768] and the importance of improving the subsidies rules has been highlighted.[769] Furthermore, after countries resorted to subsidies to mitigate the global financial crisis of 2007, the strengths and weaknesses of the WTO subsidy disciplines were unveiled, and experts in the field presented proposals to improve them.[770]

More recently, the need to revisit multilateral rules on subsidies has been shared by academics, practitioners, as well as WTO Members. Concerned about the so-called *China Inc. issue*,[771] the US, Japan and the EU engaged in developing a joint proposal to reform WTO subsidy disciplines.[772] The US complaints against the WTO AB's interpretations partly involve the ASCM, particularly state-owned enterprises (SOEs) or

766. A similar effect can also be produced with import protection, such as the spillover effect in raising tariffs created in the 1930s following the US Smoot-Hawley Act, or the recent US–Sino 'trade war'.
767. H.G. Johnson, Optimal Trade Intervention in the Presence of Domestic Distortions, in R.E. Baldwin et al. (eds), *Trade, Growth and the Balance of Payments, Trade, Growth, and the Balance of Payments: Essays in Honor of Gottfried Haberler*, 1965, pp. 3-34.
768. A.O. Sykes, The Questionable Case for Subsidies Regulation: A Comparative Perspective, Stanford University School of Law, Law & Economics Research Paper Series, Paper No. 380, 2009, p. 38.
769. K. Bagwell, R.W. Staiger, Will International Rules on Subsidies Disrupt the World Trading System?, *American Economic Review*, Vol. 96, No. 3, 2006, pp. 877-895 https://doi.org/10.1257/aer.96.3.877.
770. G.N. Horlick, P.A. Clarke, WTO Subsidies Discipline During and after the Crisis, *Journal of International Economic Law*, Vol. 13, No. 3, 2010, pp. 859-874 https://doi.org/10.1093/jiel/jgq043. B. Hoekman, Subsidies and Spillovers in a Value Chain World: New Rules Required?, *E15Initiative*, International Centre for Trade and Sustainable Development (ICTSD) and World Economic Forum (WEF), 2015; G.N. Horlick, P.A. Clarke, Rethinking Subsidy Disciplines for the Future. E15 Task Force on Rethinking International Disciplines: Policy Options Paper, *E15Initiative*, ICTSD and WEF, 2016; K. Maskus, Research and Development Subsidies: A Need for WTO Disciplines? *E15Initiative*, ICTSD and WEF, 2015.
771. M. Wu, The China, Inc, Challenge to Global Trade Governance, *Harvard International Law Journal*, Vol. 57, 2016, pp. 1001-1063.
772. In 2000, the EU, the US and Japan published a joint statement to amend the ASCM, including the following modifications: The term 'public body', interpreted by the WTO Appellate Body as requiring to possess, exercise or be *'vested with governmental authority'*, is suggested to include State Enterprises. ASCM Article 25 is proposed to consider subsidies as prohibited for not being notified. ASCM Article 3.1, on prohibited subsidies, is suggested o include: unlimited guarantees; subsidies to an insolvent or ailing enterprise in the absence of a credible restructuring plan; subsidies to enterprises unable to obtain long-term financing or investment from independent commercial sources operating in sectors or industries in overcapacity; and certain direct forgiveness of debt. In cases where the subsidizing Member's market is distorted, WTO Members would be allowed to use 'proper benchmark' in the subsidy determination, including the use of 'out-country prices', i.e., to disregard prices in the subsidizing country. ASCM Article 6.3 is suggested to include an additional type of serious prejudice related to capacity. Moreover, the reversal of the burden of proof is proposed for certain subsidies, i.e., the subsidizing Member shall demonstrate that no serious negative trade or capacity effects

'*public body*'.[773] Some scholars have argued that the US unilateral measures imposed from 2018 have been aimed at addressing 'competitive distortions', driven by its perception of the inadequacy of certain WTO Agreements and the Protocol of Accession of China to the WTO. Furthermore, as a result of the economic stimulus measures in response to the pandemic,[774] and the recent amendment of the US and EU subsidies regulations,[775] the need to improve the WTO rules on subsidies has gained in importance.

II RETHINKING THE MULTILATERAL SUBSIDY DISCIPLINES

Reforming multilateral rules on subsidies is essential to create legal certainty and address legal loopholes. Nevertheless, an amendment to the ASCM requires an objective analysis of the real problems, rather than addressing complaints against particular WTO members (e.g., China). Multilateral rules on subsidies should take into account the diversity of economic systems on a non-discriminatory basis.

A Production and Consumption

Multilateral rules on subsidies have not been founded on welfare economics, but were established with the following twofold aim: to prevent subsidies from being used as a protectionist device and to discipline the imposition of countervailing measures to offset another country's subsidies. As it occurred in the mercantilist system, where production, and not consumption, was considered '*the ultimate end and object of all industry and commerce*',[776] multilateral rules on subsidies have focused on the effects of subsidies on production, without taking into account their effects on consumption.

In the mercantilist system, bounties on exportation and restrictions on importation were used to satisfy the interest of producers, whereas consumers were obliged to pay, first, the tax to fund the bounty/subsidy (on exportation),[777] and second, the implicit tax arising from the higher price of the product in the domestic market. The interests of consumers were generally sacrificed to attain a positive balance of trade, i.e., excess of exports over imports. Nevertheless, the wealth of all and each nation

---

exist, having to withdraw the subsidy otherwise. USTR, Joint Statement of the Trilateral Meeting of the Trade Ministers of Japan, the U.S and the EU, 14 January 2020.

773. D. Ahn, Why Reform Is Needed: WTO 'Public Body' Jurisprudence, *Global Policy*, Vol. 12, No. 3, 2021, pp. 61-70 https://doi.org/10.1111/1758-5899.12929.
774. '*The COVID-19 pandemic generated a massive expansion in fiscal policy, appropriately so, but many of the subsidies are firmor activity-specific and thus may distort international competition*', B. Hoekman, P.C. Mavroidis, WTO Reform: Back to the Past to Build for the Future, *Global Policy*, Vol. 12, No. 3, 2021, pp. 5-12 at 10 https://doi.org/10.1111/1758-5899.12924.
775. US Regulations Improving and Strengthening the Enforcement of Trade Remedies Through the Administration of the Antidumping and Countervailing Duty Laws, US Federal Register, Vol. 89, No. 58, 25 March 2024, pp. 20766-20841. EU Regulation 2022/2560 of the European Parliament and of the Council of 14 December 2022 on foreign subsidies distorting the internal market, OJEU, L.330, 23 December 2022.
776. A. Smith, *The Wealth of Nations*, [1776], 2000, p. 877.
777. '*Bounties upon production, however, have been very rarely granted.*' A. Smith, *The Wealth of Nations*, [1776], 2000, p. 677.

should be attained, according to Adam Smith, through the balance of produce and consumption.[778]

Centring the political economy on the balance of trade neither made sense in the XVIII century,[779] nor does nowadays, when there is generally no coincidence between '*State, territory and firms*'.[780] Country A may subsidize a company established in country B whose workers may not necessarily be nationals of country B. However, subsidization by country A would be at the expense of its taxpayers. Moreover, a request to impose countervailing duties by country B may be requested by a company owned by a national of country A. In this case, the benefit of the company is to the detriment of consumers in country B. These situations are not hypothetical. It has been the case of Bombardier, the Canadian aircraft manufacturer, that sold the majority of shares of the production of certain aircraft to the Airbus plant in Alabama in order to avoid US countervailing duties. Also, the EU has imposed countervailing duties on certain imports produced in Egypt and Indonesia, supposedly benefitting from Chinese subsidies.[781]

This focus merely on production may create an absurd situation, which could result from the sum of the two previous situations. A company owned by nationals of country A receives a subsidy from country A, but it is established in country B, where it requests the imposition of countervailing duties (to the detriment of consumers in B). An illustrative case would be a Chinese-owned company that receives a subsidy from China to produce polysilicon in Germany, produces solar cells in the EU or the US, and petitions the EU Commission or the USDOC for the imposition of countervailing duties on imports of solar cells. This company would be producing polysilicon by benefitting from Chinese taxpayers while raising prices of solar cells to the detriment of EU/US consumers.

Since WTO rules require that the financial contribution be granted within the territory of the subsidizing Member, these situations do not fall under the ASCM definition of subsidy. Once the financial contribution of a WTO Member is granted outside its territory, a legal loophole is created. Accordingly, in order to protect producers established within its territory, some WTO Members suggest amending the rules on subsidies to deal with the above situations by permitting the imposition of countervailing duties even if the subsidy is granted outside the jurisdiction of the subsidizing country. This would broaden the scope of current WTO rules on countervailing duties, and thus, adversely affect consumers in the importing country.

778. '*Consumption is the sole end and purpose of all production; and the interest of the producer ought to be attended to only so far as it may be necessary for promoting that of the consumer. The maxim is so perfectly self evident that it would be absurd to attempt to prove it.*' A. Smith, *The Wealth of Nations*, [1776], 2000, pp. 652, 877.
779. A. Smith, *The Wealth of Nations*, [1776], 2000, p. 587.
780. F. Snyder, *The EU, the WTO and China: Legal Pluralism and International Trade Regulation*, 2010, p. 138.
781. Commission Implementing Regulation (EU) 2020/776, OJEU, L 189/1, 15 June 2020. *See* article dealing with this issue by S.J. Evenett, J.D. Sud, E.A. Vermulst, The European Union's New Move Against China: Countervailing Chinese Outward Foreign Direct Investment, *Global Trade and Customs Journal*, Vol. 15, No. 9, 2020, pp. 413-422 https://doi.org/10.54648/gtcj2020081.

A revision of current multilateral rules on subsidies is proposed hereby with the objective of taking into account the effects of subsidies also on consumers, as well as the environment, and balancing their effects on the different affected parties. This would apply to both production and consumption subsidies, on goods - including both primary and industrial - and services. In other words, multilateral rules on subsidies should aim at global welfare. Therefore, the objective of those multilateral rules on subsidies should be to distinguish between welfare-enhancing and welfare-reducing subsidies.

Besides the fact that some current situations in the international trading system did not exist in the past and need to be regulated, such as the suggestion to extend subsidy disciplines to services, or the lack of coincidence between subsidizing state and territory, certain issues have been maintained or created during the history of multilateral negotiations on subsidies. Therefore, the endeavour of amending WTO rules on subsidies requires a historical overview of multilateral provisions on subsidies.

B Evolution of Subsidy Rules in Multilateral Trade Negotiations

The evolution of the multilateral rules on subsidies illustrates that the GATT provisions on subsidies were the result of negotiations among countries, where certain producers have exerted political pressure and Contracting Parties have defended their particular interests during negotiations. Multilateral rules on subsidies have been influenced by the need for consensus at those negotiations and the GATT dispute settlement reports; hence, they are not based on welfare economics.

As seen in Part II, subsidies provisions under GATT Article XVI were redrafted from Article 25 of the US Suggested Charter. During the Preparatory Conferences of 1947, Brazil and New Zealand requested to exclude the provisions on export subsidies from the GATT; notwithstanding, they were maintained in the ITO Charter. For this reason, GATT Article XVI merely provided for the notification of subsidies until the GATT Review Session of 1954-1955 incorporated the ITO Charter provisions on export subsidies. As a result, GATT dispute settlement reports differed before and after the application of provisions on export subsidies. Furthermore, unlike the subsidies provisions under the US Suggested Charter, GATT Article XVI distinguishes between primary and non-primary products. In addition, the role of an independent authority (the ITO) became absent in the GATT.

The first two GATT dispute settlement reports on subsidies reflect the fact that Contracting Parties were not bound by any rules on export subsidies. In the first case, *Australia – Ammonium Sulphate*,[782] since GATT Article XVI had not yet incorporated those provisions (from the ITO Charter), the effect of an export subsidy had to be challenged by invoking GATT Article XXIII, on nullification and impairment. For this reason, following the Tokyo Round, the SCM Code included the interpretation of GATT

782. *Australia – Subsidy on Ammonium Sulphate* (GD/5). Complainant: Chile. GATT document CP.4/39, 31 March 1950. Other GATT related documents CP.3/61, 27 July 1949; CP.4/SR21, 3 April 1950; CP.5/SR.6, 6 November 1950; CP.5/SR.6/Corr.1, 6 November 1950.

Article XXIII, along with Articles VI and XVI. In the second case, *US – Sultanas*,[783] notwithstanding CONTRACTING PARTIES recommended a mutually agreed solution, the US decided not to cease subsidization.

In the GATT Review Session of 1954-1955, provisions on export subsidies were inserted under GATT Article XVI, which provided for a different treatment of export subsidies on primary and non-primary products. While its paragraph 3 established the obligation to cease export subsidies on primary products that result in '*having more than an equitable share of world export trade in that product*' (e.g., *France – Wheat Exports*[784] and *EEC – Sugar Exports),*[785] paragraph 4 included a standstill provision prohibiting export subsidies on non-primary products sold on exportation at a lower price than in the domestic market (e.g., *US – DISC* and *France – Belgium – Netherlands – Income Tax*).[786]

The regulatory disparity between primary and non-primary products was the result of negotiations, which was first reflected in the ITO Charter, and then in the GATT. Nevertheless, the original provisions on the prohibition of export subsidies under the US Suggested Charter of 1946 did not distinguish between primary and non-primary products, but prohibited export subsidies which resulted in exporting at a lower price than the price charged '*to buyers in the domestic market*', as well as those that had the effect of acquiring a world share over a previous representative year.[787]

Concerning the first prohibition, i.e., export at a lower price than the price charged '*to buyers in the domestic market*', the New York draft for an ITO Charter added an exception for primary products, conditioned on the compliance with two requirements, first, exporting also at a higher price than the comparable price charged '*to buyers in the domestic market*', and second, causing no prejudice. With respect to the second prohibition, i.e., having the effect of acquiring a share of world trade, it was reduced to primary products under the Havana ITO Charter, which introduced the term '*more than an equitable share of world trade*'. This regulatory distinction between primary and non-primary products was introduced under GATT Article XVI in the

783. *United States Export Subsidy on Sultanas* (GD/17). Complainants: Greece and Turkey. GATT documents L/146, L/146/Add.1, 30 September 1953 (Greece); L/148, 30 September 1953(Turkey). Other GATT related documents (consultations) L/39, 3 October 1952 (Greece), L/45, 10 October 1952 (Turkey).

784. *French Assistance to Exports of Wheat and Wheat Flour* (GD/36). Complainant: Australia. GATT document L/924, 20 November 1958.

785. *EEC – Refunds on Exports of Sugar – Complaint by Australia* (GD/102). GATT document L/4833, 25 October 1979. Other relevant GATT documents C/M/128, C/M/128/Corr.1, 18 October 1978 (consultations); C/M/135, 6 November 1979 (adoption of report). *EEC – Refunds on Exports of Sugar – Complaint by Brazil* (GD/103). GATT document L/5011, 7 October 1980. Adoption of report: GATT documents C/M/144, C/M/144/Corr.1, 10 November 1980.

786. GATT documents L/4422, 2 November 1976, para. 69 (US); L/4423, 2 November 1976, para. 48 (France); L/4424, 2 November 1976, para. 35 (Belgium); L/4425, 2 November 1976, para. 35 (the Netherlands).

787. In addition, in case a product may become in burdensome world surplus, the Organization would invite members to '*consult with each other with a view to the adoption of measures to increase consumption and to reduce production through the diversion of resources from uneconomic production, or with a view to seeking, if necessary, the conclusion of an intergovernmental commodity agreement*'. Article 25.3 of the US Suggested Charter of 1946.

GATT Review Session of 1954-1955, and it has continued all along multilateral negotiations on export subsidies.

As a result of the Tokyo Round negotiations, the SCM Code prohibited export subsidies for non-primary products and maintained the '*more than equitable share*' rule under GATT Article XVI.3 for primary products. This distinction proved to be particularly problematic in the dispute *EEC – Pasta Subsidies*, in which the majority of the members of the Panel considered that pasta was a non-primary product, whose subsidy on exportation was prohibited (under SCM Code Article 10). A dissenting opinion argued that subsidization of processed agricultural exports was permitted subject to the '*more than equitable share*' rule (under GATT Article XVI.3 and SCM Code Article 9). This distinction with regard to export subsidies on primary and non-primary products resulted in different findings in the disputes *France – Wheat Exports* and *EEC – Pasta Subsidies*.

The exception provided for primary products has not been easily applied in practice. Although SCM Code Article 10.2 incorporated a more precise application of the '*more than an equitable share of world export trade*' concept,[788] the Panel in *EEC – Wheat Flour Subsidies* found itself unable to apply this concept and resolve whether subsidies on wheat resulted in a '*more than an equitable share of world export trade*',[789] unlike the *French – Wheat Exports* case of 1958, in which only GATT Article XVI.3 was interpreted.

The distinction between primary and non-primary products was incorporated in 1947 and has been maintained through multilateral negotiations on export subsidies. Indeed, as a result of the Uruguay Round negotiations, WTO Members accepted reducing commitments, in quantity and value terms, of subsidized exports of agricultural (primary) products under the Agreement on Agriculture, while the prohibition on export subsidies under the ASCM applies merely to industrial (non-primary) products. It was not until the Ministerial Conference at Nairobi in 2015 that WTO Members reached an agreement to eliminate agricultural export subsidies over specific deadlines.[790]

This regulatory distinction between primary and non-primary products reflects the negotiators' defence of agricultural producers' interests and the strength of the farmers' lobby. Notably, the US Suggested Charter provided for the possibility to adopt measures to reach a balance between consumption and production in case a '*specified*' product became in burdensome world surplus,[791] whereas no reference to consumption is found in the later provisions on export subsidies.[792]

788. J.H. Jackson, W. Davey, *Legal Problems of International Economic Relations, Cases, Materials and Text*, 2nd ed., 1986, p. 731.
789. *European Economic Community – Subsidies on Export of Wheat Flour* (GD/122). Complainant: US. GATT document SCM/42, 21 March 1983.
790. While developed Members had to immediately eliminate them, developing countries and least developed countries were allowed to maintain export subsidies on marketing costs as well as on internal transport and freight charges (pursuant to Article 9.4 of the Agreement on Agriculture) until 2023 and 2030, respectively. WTO document MIN (15)/45, 21 December 2015.
791. In case a product may become in burdensome world surplus, the Organization would invite members to '*consult with each other with a view to the adoption of measures to increase*

Another important element was eroded, namely the role of an independent authority, the Organization (ITO). Its significant role was eliminated from multilateral rules on subsidies when the ITO Charter failed to enter into force. The US Suggested Charter had entrusted the ITO with the determination of '*equitable share*', to which the member concerned was obliged to conform. Furthermore, the ITO was to be responsible for determining the existence of the two requirements for exporting primary products at a lower price than the comparable charged '*to buyers in the domestic market*'. Therefore, it was envisaged that an independent multilateral body (the ITO) would supervise and authorize subsidies on the exportation of primary products.

III AMENDMENTS TO WTO RULES ON SUBSIDIES

A ASCM Article 3 and GATT Article III.8(b): Effect of Subsidies

The ASCM, covering merely subsidies on industrial products, prohibits, first, subsidies contingent upon import substitution; and second, upon export performance (ASCM Article 3.1). Subsidies '*exclusively to domestic producers*' are permitted under GATT Article III.8(b) as an exception to the national treatment principle (despite that, if deemed specific, they could also be offset with either unilateral countervailing duties or multilaterally authorized countermeasures).[793] Notably, a subsidy to domestic producers may have the same effect as an import-substitution subsidy or an export subsidy.[794]

In the first case, a subsidy to a domestic producer can have an equivalent effect to a subsidy contingent upon the use of a domestic product (even if it is *de facto* and not *de iure*, i.e., not specified by the law, as in the Oilseeds cases).[795] As a result, instead of granting a subsidy to buyers contingent upon the use of domestic over imported goods, which is prohibited under ASCM Article 3.1(b), a WTO Member may decide to grant a subsidy to sellers/producers, which would be permitted under GATT Article III, e.g., the case of US subsidization of batteries under the Inflation Reduction Act. On the one hand, if the US granted subsidies on electric cars contingent upon the import substitution of electric batteries produced in China with batteries produced in the US, it would be inconsistent with the ASCM. On the other hand, if subsidies were granted to domestic producers of batteries in the US, this would be consistent with GATT

---

consumption and to reduce production through the diversion of resources from uneconomic production, or with a view to seeking, if necessary, the conclusion of an intergovernmental commodity agreement'. Article 25.3 of the US Suggested Charter of 1946.

792. The approach in multilateral trade negotiation rounds has been on the balance of trade, i.e., exportation and importation, rather than on the balance of production and consumption.
793. Since the 'peace clause' under Article 13 of the Agreement on Agriculture expired in 2003, it is now possible to also offset subsidies on agricultural products pursuant to the ASCM.
794. '*Indeed, a per unit subsidy to all domestic buyers of a good can be completely equivalent in its effects to an equal per unit subsidy to all domestic sellers – net output of domestic producers, net imports, and net price to buyers will be exactly the same under competitive conditions.*' A.O. Sykes, The Economics of WTO Rules on Subsidies and Countervailing Measures, John M. Olin Program in Law and Economics Working Paper No. 186, 2003, p. 19.
795. A.O. Sykes, The Questionable Case for Subsidies Regulation: A Comparative Perspective, Stanford University School of Law, Law & Economics Research Paper Series, Paper No. 380, 2009, p. 37.

Article III, but the effect in the substitution of electric batteries imported from China would be the same. Therefore, subsidy disciplines should focus on the effect of subsidies (in the market). Moreover, since the prohibition under ASCM Article 3.1(b) merely applies to industrial subsidies, a regulatory distinction is created between primary and non-primary products, resulting in a discrimination between producers of agricultural and industrial products. Accordingly, the current regulatory distinction between primary and non-primary products should be eliminated. More generally, subsidy disciplines should cover both primary and non-primary products.

In the second case, while the ASCM Article 3.1(a) prohibits subsidies contingent upon export performance, subsidies to domestic producers, which may have the same effect as an export subsidy, are permitted under the exception in GATT Article III.8.b. As a matter of fact, all subsidies on production may result in subsidies on exportation. Therefore, it is important to regulate all subsidies on production, including subsidies to producers. Notably, the prohibition under ASCM Article 3.1(a) merely applied to industrial subsidies until WTO Members agreed in 2015 to eliminate agricultural export subsidies over specific deadlines.[796] The prohibition on export subsidies should continue to apply to both primary and non-primary products.

B ASCM Article 1: Definition of Subsidy

Throughout the history of multilateral trade negotiations, different views of Contracting Parties on subsidies and countervailing duties gave rise to difficulties in reaching an agreement. As a factual matter, one of the achievements of the ASCM was the definition of 'subsidy', which was lacking from the SCM Code (enacted after the Tokyo Round).[797] According to ASCM Article 1, a subsidy is deemed to exist if a benefit is conferred through a financial contribution granted by a government or any public body within the territory of a Member, or any form of income or price support (in the sense of GATT Article XVI). The inclusion of '*within the territory*' has, however, created a legal loophole discussed above.

Therefore, the need arises to regulate governmental financial contributions outside the territory. Under the ASCM, if the government of a WTO Member (A) grants an actionable subsidy to certain enterprises within its territory, another WTO Member (B) can countervail it. This can create an incentive for the funded enterprises to move their production from the territory of WTO Member A to B to avoid the imposition of countervailing duties.[798] Nonetheless, the subsidy can continue, and may create the same distortion to international competition, although it will not be considered a 'subsidy' under the ASCM anymore. In the absence of rules for such a situation, some WTO Members have opted to apply the ASCM as if a subsidy outside the territory of the subsidizing country were considered a subsidy (e.g., EU countervailing duties imposed

796. WTO document MIN (15)/45, 21 December 2015.
797. G.N. Horlick, P.A. Clarke, WTO Subsidies Discipline During and after the Crisis, *Journal of International Economic Law*, Vol. 13, No. 3, 2010, pp. 859-874 at 860 https://doi.org/10.1093/jiel/jgq043.
798. *See* Bombardier and Airbus in Alabama, or China's Belt and Road Initiative.

on Chinese funding in Egypt), or to enact legislation to address subsidies provided outside the territory.[799] Similarly, '*domestic industry*' is a concept not valid in a globalized world.

C Criteria to Classify Subsidies

The ASCM classifies subsidies into three categories: prohibited, actionable and non-actionable subsidies. The classification of subsidies was conditioned by the possibility of countervailing them. Since GATT Article VI permits offsetting subsidization when it causes or threatens material injury to an industry, if the definition of subsidy were too broad, the possibility of (legally) imposing countervailing duties would be increased. To prevent the liberal trading system from being undermined, it has been necessary to either use a restricted definition of subsidy or define a '*subset*' of the broader set to be subject to trade responsc measures.[800]

1 Specificity

The criterion to classify subsidies was aimed at restricting the scope of countervailing duties to certain subsidies. The 'specificity' test was selected to determine whether subsidies are countervailable or not. A subsidy is deemed to be specific if it (or its access) is limited (*de iure* or *de facto*) to a particular enterprise or industry, or a group of them. Therefore, the 'specificity test' determines whether a subsidy has been granted in a discriminatory manner. In other words, the criterion is based on the number of enterprises or industries benefitting from the financial contribution. The specificity rule under ASCM Article 2 had its origin in SCM Code Article 11.3,[801] whereby GATT Contracting Parties recognized that subsidies granted for the promotion of social and economic policy objectives may be aimed at '*giving an advantage to certain enterprises*', and the 1980 *Polish Golf Carts* anti-dumping case.[802]

---

799. For instance, the US has repealed the transnational subsidies regulations, which prevented allegations of transnational subsidies, Regulations Improving and Strengthening the Enforcement of Trade Remedies Through the Administration of the Antidumping and Countervailing Duty Laws, US Federal Register, Vol. 89, No. 58, 25 March 2024, pp. 20766-20841 at 20826-20827. On its part, the EU has enacted regulation to investigate foreign subsidies and redress the distortions that arise in the internal market concerning any economic activity, including concentrations and public procurement procedures, EU Regulation 2022/2560 of the European Parliament and of the Council of 14 December 2022 on foreign subsidies distorting the internal market, OJEU, L.330, 23 December 2022.

800. J.H. Jackson, World Trade Rules and Environmental Policies: Congruence or Conflict?, *Washington and Lee Law Review*, Vol. 49, No. 4, 1992, pp. 1227-1278 at 1247.

801. G.N. Horlick, P.A. Clarke, The Agreement on Subsidies and Countervailing Measures, in G.N. Horlick (ed.), *World Trade Organization and International Trade Law: Antidumping, Subsidies and Trade Agreements*, 2014, pp. 217-272 at 221.

802. The Polish national factory, where carts were produced, imported parts (constituting 79% of the cost of the cart) from market economies. In a US official visit to the factory, Jackson asked which of the six official currency exchange rates was being used by the factory when buying the imported parts. Jackson's question brought Hudec and Horlick to the conclusion that '*in a world of floating exchange rates, a subsidy given equally to everyone within an economy had no*

Specific subsidies are either actionable or prohibited. Prohibited subsidies are export subsidies and import-substitution subsidies. Regardless of whether they are specific or not, they are considered to be specific, according to ASCM Article 2.3. Actionable subsidies are specific subsidies that cause adverse effects to the interest of other Members, i.e., injury or threat thereof, nullification or impairment, or serious prejudice, pursuant to ASCM Article 5. Non-specific subsidies are non-actionable (permitted). Nonetheless, until 1999, certain specific subsidies for research and development, environmental, and regional programmes that met the conditions listed under ASCM Article 8.2 were considered non-actionable subsidies.[803]

In case subsidies are specific, i.e., prohibited or actionable, the ASCM permits invoking in parallel both dispute settlement and countervailing procedures; yet only one form of relief, i.e., unilateral countervailing duties (ASCM Articles 10-23), or (multilaterally authorized) countermeasures (ASCM Article 4, for prohibited; or Article 7, for actionable subsidies), is permitted to offset the effect of the subsidy in the importing country (ASCM Note 35). Countervailing duties can be imposed on specific subsidies when they cause injury (or threat thereof) to the industry of the importing country. Non-actionable subsidies are exempted from those procedures and measures.[804]

2 *Welfare and Environmental Assessment of Subsidies*

The classification of subsidies should be based on economic principles. To illustrate the need, the following situation may occur under the current distinction, based on the specificity test. A non-specific subsidy on the sale of fossil fuels to a wide variety of users[805] would be non-actionable, i.e., permitted, while a specific subsidy on a product used in renewable energies would be considered actionable or even prohibited. Promoting an environmentally friendly policy, on the one hand, while subsidizing fossil fuels, and even imposing countervailing duties (or other trade remedies) on goods that are used in renewable energies, on the other hand, is incoherent. The classification of subsidies should be based on principles of welfare economics.

---

effect on comparative advantage within that country'. G.N. Horlick, John Jackson as a Resource for Scholars and Others, *Journal of International Economic Law*, Vol. 19, No. 2, 2016, pp. 401-402 https://doi.org/10.1093/jiel/jgw040.

803. Until the end of 1999, certain specific subsidies for research and development, environmental, and regional programmes that met the conditions listed under ASCM Article 8.2 were considered non-actionable. ASCM Articles 8 and 9 expired five years after the entry into force of the ASCM, pursuant to ASCM Article 31.

804. Nevertheless, those proceedings can be invoked in case subsidies under Article 8.2 (for research and development programmes) are not notified. In case a non-actionable subsidy results in adverse effect to another Member, the ASCM provides for consultations and recourse to the Committee. If the recommendation by the Committee is not followed by the subsidizing country, it may authorize the requesting Member to take countermeasures.

805. P. Gass, et al., Raising Ambition Through Fossil Fuel Subsidy Reform: Greenhouse Gas Emissions Modelling Results from 26 Countries, The International Institute for Sustainable Development, 2019.

The particular case of environmental subsidies needs special consideration since they '*could have enough positive social benefit to justify trade distortions*',[806] especially nowadays. During the Uruguay Round,[807] discussions were held to permit environmental friendly subsidies, and thus exempting them from countervailing duties or other trade obligations.[808] Experts in the field recognized the importance of reviving discussions on the incorporation of environmental subsidies.[809] Besides eliminating trade remedies on the so-called environmental goods (as this book suggests),[810] the permissibility of subsidies on these products might be worth exploring on a case-by-case basis by experts taking into account global production and consumption.

The ASCM prohibits import-substitution subsidies based on the non-discrimination principle. Subsidies contingent upon the use of domestic over imported products violate the national treatment principle enshrined under GATT Article III. WTO rules on subsidies should include utmost consistency with the non-discrimination principle, whether they apply to agricultural or industrial products. In other words, the non-discrimination principle should govern to the maximum extent as possible multilateral rules on subsidies. The ASCM also prohibits export subsidies; however, it has been recognized that this prohibition on export subsidies should also apply to agricultural goods as well as be extended to services.[811] Furthermore, the prohibition on export subsidies is insufficient since it is almost impossible to control that a production subsidy will not indirectly become an export subsidy. Indeed, according to some scholars, virtually all non-export subsidies provided by larger WTO members are granted on products '*known to be exported*'.[812] Hence, it is important to further discipline production subsidies.

Multilateral rules that distinguish whether a subsidy is permitted, prohibited, or actionable provide legal certainty. The difficult question is what criteria should be used to determine whether subsidies should be permitted or not. A reconsideration of the classification of subsidies based on welfare and environmental economics is hereby

806. G.N. Horlick, Trade Remedies and Development of Renewable Energy, Clean Energy Technologies and the Trade System: Proposals and Analysis, *E15Initiative*, ICTSD and WEF, 2013, pp. 69-73 at 71.
807. '*The entire topic of subsidy law and the environment was actively discussed during the Uruguay Round, and the result was a time-limited "trial period" of a very limited exemption from CVD law for certain environmental subsidies (as well as for certain research and development and regional subsidies) in Article 8 of the ASCM.*' G.N. Horlick, Trade Remedies and Development of Renewable Energy, Clean Energy Technologies and the Trade System: Proposals and Analysis, *E15Initiative*, ICTSD and WEF, 2013, pp. 69-73 at 71.
808. J.H. Jackson, World Trade Rules and Environmental Policies: Congruence or Conflict? *Washington and Lee Law Review*, Vol. 49, No. 4, 1992, pp. 1227-1278 at 1248.
809. G.N. Horlick, Trade Remedies and Development of Renewable Energy, Clean Energy Technologies and the Trade System: Proposals and Analysis, *E15Initiative*, ICTSD and WEF, 2013, pp. 69-73 at 71.
810. *See* Ch. 12.
811. A.O. Sykes, The Economics of WTO Rules on Subsidies and Countervailing Measures, John M. Olin Program in Law and Economics Working Paper No. 186, 2003, pp. 26, 27. G.N. Horlick, P.A. Clarke, WTO Subsidies Discipline During and after the Crisis, *Journal of International Economic Law*, Vol. 13, No. 3, 2010, pp. 859-874, at 872 https://doi.org/10.1093/jiel/jgq043.
812. G.N. Horlick, P.A. Clarke, WTO Subsidies Discipline During and after the Crisis, *Journal of International Economic Law*, Vol. 13, No. 3, 2010, pp. 859-874 at 873 https://doi.org/10.1093/jiel/jgq043.

proposed. The same criterion, based on principles of welfare economics, should permit distinguishing between permitted and prohibited in order to provide legal certainty. The aim is to determine if a subsidy (e.g., on fossil fuels) should be permitted or not based on its economic effects rather than on the specificity test. Therefore, efficiency should be the basis for determining the permissibility of subsidies.

Accordingly, certain subsidies might be allowed in case their net global welfare effects are positive compared with the economic effects of trade distortions. In certain cases, subsidies might need to be conditional on a period; thus, they could be subject to authorization. In this case, the role of experts in the field is essential. Current ASCM Article 24 establishes that a Permanent Group of Experts (PGE) may be requested to assist a panel or give confidential advisory opinions concerning the nature of a subsidy in place or proposed to be introduced. It would be useful if experts in the field conducted an assessment and analysis of the global welfare effects of subsidies currently provided by WTO Members. In this line, a list of both prohibited and permitted subsidies could be added to the WTO Agreement (as it occurs with the non-exhaustive list of prohibited subsidies under ASCM Annex I).

To grant as much legal certainty as possible, the distinction between permitted and prohibited subsidies would require an objective analysis undertaken by independent experts in the field. The Agreement may incorporate a test based on welfare economics that permits the classification of subsidies, taking into account the benefits and adverse effects of subsidies on, *inter alia*, producers, consumers, and the environment. A monitoring and revision of permitted subsidies would be needed, where the WTO Secretariat (e.g., Trade Policy Review mechanism) might act ex officio. To have coherent multilateral rules on subsidies that are based on welfare economics, it is essential to create a system whereby rules are enforced without the possibility of unilaterally offsetting subsidies, as the experience of the Sugar Conventions of 1864 and 1902 has shown. Therefore, a multilateral procedure would be available for all types of subsidies, with the sole recourse to authorized countermeasures. Accordingly, this book suggests the abolition of (unilateral) countervailing duties.[813]

813. *See* Ch. 8.

CHAPTER 8

Countervailing Duties

This chapter questions the unilateral imposition of countervailing duties. To that end, it explores the economic and legal rationale of countervailing duties, as well as lessons learnt from the history of the multilateral provisions on countervailing duties.

I ECONOMIC AND LEGAL RATIONALE

The raîson d'être of countervailing duties is to offset foreign subsidization. In general, however, subsidized imports benefit importers and consumers in the importing country. As the rest of the trade remedies, countervailing duties merely aim at protecting domestic producers without taking into account their market-distorting effects.

The adverse welfare effects of countervailing duties are identical to those of tariffs, as Trebilcock and Sykes have shown.[814] A tariff distorts the prices of the protected products in the importing country, triggering importers and consumers to substitute other ('*socially costlier*') products for the protected ones.[815] Since they constitute a permitted exception to the MFN principle, they are imposed in a discriminatory manner. Remarkably, countervailing duties are imposed in addition to tariffs, being permitted to exceed the tariff binding without any limit (even above 500% ad valorem).[816]

---

814. M.J. Trebilcock, Is the Game Worth the Candle: Comments on a Search for Economic and Financial Principles in the Administration of US Countervailing Duty Law, *Law and Policy in International Business*, Vol. 21, No. 4, 1990, pp. 723-738. A.O. Sykes, Second-Best Countervailing Duty Policy: A Critique of the Entitlement Approach, *Law and Policy in International Business*, Vol. 21, No. 4, 1990, pp. 699-722.
815. J. Tumlir, *Protectionism: Trade Policies in Democratic Societies*, 1985, p. 7.
816. *See*, for instance, Ch. 1, Section I: US countervailing duties on crystalline silicone photovoltaic (CSPV) cells from China (Solar I). Following a sunset review (US Federal Register 10431, 9 March 2018), and an administrative review in 2021, the US increased countervailing duties up to 528% (US Federal Register 48393, 30 August 2021).

Countervailing duties have been considered '*unnecessary and economically inefficient, harmful to neglected consumer interests, and arrogant in the face of a world consensus favoring the use of domestic subsidies in appropriate instances*'.[817] Since subsidized imports constitute a national welfare gain,[818] some economic scholars find it '*difficult to justify countermeasures against subsidized imports in general*' if the policy maxim of the importing nation is its welfare.[819] Jackson considered that countervailing duties can serve to discourage wasteful subsidies and thus enhance global welfare;[820] therefore, they 'should be permitted'.[821] This argument has, nevertheless, been rebutted by Sykes, according to whom countervailing duties '*have no systematic value in discouraging wasteful subsidy practices*'.[822] Additionally, countervailing duties only constitute a remedy for one of the three possible effects of subsidies,[823] the effects in the importing country,[824] but in neither the exporting country nor a third country.[825] They '*are simply one more arrow in the quiver of import-competing industries that seek protection*',[826] and their use as a protectionist device has only increased over the years. Due to their lack of economic rationale, the abolition of unilateral countervailing duty laws '*might best serve the national economic interest*',[827] as well as the global economy. A multilateral rather than unilateral remedy may better serve as a deterrent to wasteful subsidies.

817. W.N. Eskridge Jr., Dynamic Interpretation of Economic Regulatory Legislation (Countervailing Duty Law), *Law and Policy in International Business*, Vol. 21, No. 4, 1990, pp. 663-698 at 698.
818. Some scholars have considered that the appropriate response to subsidized imports is a '*thank-you note to the embassy*'. Jackson considered that the 'thank you-note' approach is only justified if the goal is national welfare but not global welfare. The quote has been attributed to Paul Krugman. A.O. Sykes, The Economics of WTO Rules on Subsidies and Countervailing Measures, John M. Olin Program in Law and Economics Working Paper No. 186, 2003, p. 9. J.H. Jackson, Perspectives on Countervailing Duties, *Law and Policy in International Business*, Vol. 21, No. 4, 1990, pp. 739-762 at 754.
819. A.O. Sykes, The Questionable Case for Subsidies Regulation: A Comparative Perspective, Stanford University School of Law, Law & Economics Research Paper Series, Paper No. 380, 2009, p. 3.
820. J.H. Jackson, *The World Trading System: Law and Policy of International Economic Relations*, 2nd ed., 2000, Ch. 11.
821. J.H. Jackson, Perspectives on Countervailing Duties, *Law and Policy in International Business*, Vol. 21, No. 4, 1990, pp. 739-762 at 743.
822. A.O. Sykes, The Economics of WTO Rules on Subsidies and Countervailing Measures, John M. Olin Program in Law and Economics Working Paper No. 186, 2003, pp. 26, 27.
823. Subsidies may have effects on the importing country, the exporting country and a third country. J.H. Jackson, *The World Trading System: Law and Policy of International Economic Relations*, 2nd ed., 2000, p. 258.
824. Countervailing duties may be beneficial to a large importing country when, in the absence of 'its optimal tariff', the subsidized imports are harmful to it. A.O. Sykes, The Questionable Case for Subsidies Regulation: A Comparative Perspective, Stanford University School of Law, Law & Economics Research Paper Series, Paper No. 380, 2009, p. 3.
825. G.N. Horlick, John Jackson and the Development of GATT/WTO Subsidies Rules in M. Bronckers, R. Quick (eds), *New Directions in International Economic Law, Essays in Honour of J.H. Jackson*, 2000, pp. 177-184 at 184.
826. A.O. Sykes, The Economics of WTO Rules on Subsidies and Countervailing Measures, John M. Olin Program in Law and Economics Working Paper No. 186, 2003, pp. 26, 27.
827. A.O. Sykes, Countervailing Duty Law: An Economic Critique, *Columbia Law Review*, Vol. 89, No. 2, 1989, pp. 199-263 https://doi.org/10.2307/1122821.

From a legal point of view, countervailing duties constitute a form of *lex talionis* (talion law). This conception of unilaterally achieving justice or '*fairness*' has been the origin of some issues concerning multilateral rules on subsidies. As it has been shown in the previous chapter, the possibility of unilaterally deciding on the imposition of countervailing duties (GATT Article VI) has conditioned the development of current multilateral subsidy disciplines under the ASCM. In other words, subsidies have been classified based on the appropriateness of the unilateral action. With a functioning dispute settlement body, allowing WTO members to unilaterally decide on the imposition of countervailing duties lacks legal rationale. The establishment of a multilateral proceeding should be the only available option regardless of the classification of subsidies.

Therefore, in line with the views of Barceló,[828] Evans,[829] Horlick,[830] Sykes,[831] and Trebilcock,[832] this book suggests eliminating the unilateral recourse to countervailing duties. An independent multilateral body, such as a (permanent) group of experts, should determine the existence and distorting effect of a subsidy, as well as authorize, where appropriate, the eventual imposition of countermeasures by the affected country. Implementing this proposal would require nullifying GATT Article VI with respect to countervailing duties, as well as amending the ASCM.

II COUNTERVAILING DUTY PROVISIONS IN TRADE AGREEMENTS BEFORE THE GATT

Since 1865, some European countries included 'anti-bounty' clauses (i.e., commitments not to grant bounties) in their commercial treaties. In the absence of an enforcement mechanism (even in the form of a penalty to offset bounties), the 'anti-bounty' clauses proved to be ineffective and inadequate. The Sugar Convention of 1864 provided for the elimination of bounties in the form of excessive refunds of excises and drawbacks on sugar exports. Nevertheless, due to the lack of compliance by some members, it became inoperative and ceased to be in force in 1875.[833]

While further international conferences were held (without success) to reach a solution for the increase of drawbacks and bounties on sugar,[834] some countries enacted the first countervailing duty provisions in national legislation during the

828. J.J. Barceló III, The Two-Track Subsidies Code: Countervailing Duties and Trade Retaliation, in J. Quinn, P. Slayton, *Non-tariff Barriers After the Tokyo Round*, 1982, pp. 121-152.
829. J.W. Evans, Subsidies and Countervailing Duties in the GATT, *Maryland Journal of International Law*, Vol. 3, No. 1, 1977, pp. 211-245 at 244.
830. G.N. Horlick, P.A. Clarke. Rethinking Subsidy Disciplines for the Future. E15 Task Force on Rethinking International Disciplines – Policy Options Paper, *E15Initiative*, ICTSD and WEF, 2016, p. 7.
831. A.O. Sykes, The Economics of WTO Rules on Subsidies and Countervailing Measures, John M. Olin Program in Law and Economics Working Paper No. 186, 2003, pp. 25-27.
832. M.J. Trebilcock, Is the Game Worth the Candle: Comments on a Search for Economic and Financial Principles in the Administration of US Countervailing Duty Law, *Law and Policy in International Business*, Vol. 21, No. 4, 1990, pp. 723-738 at 732.
833. J. Viner, *Dumping: A Problem in International Trade*, 1923, pp. 168, 179.
834. G. Martineau, The Brussels Sugar Convention, *The Economic Journal*, Vol. 14, No. 53, 1 March 1904, pp. 34-46 at 39 https://doi.org/10.2307/2220737.

1890s.[835] Beginning with the US, which introduced a countervailing duty provision in 1890 to offset export subsidies on refined sugar, countervailing duty laws soon spread around the globe and covered all imports that received export subsidies, first in Belgium, in 1892, followed by the US, in 1897.[836]

The first multilateral trade agreement that incorporated a countervailing duty provision was the Brussels Sugar Convention of 1902, whereby the main sugar-producing countries in Europe, except Russia,[837] committed to abolishing bounties on sugar.[838] The agreement included a multilateral enforcement mechanism, whereby a supranational permanent commission was entrusted, *inter alia*, to verify the existence and estimate the amount of the bounty, as well as to authorize the imposition of countervailing duties on imported 'bounty-fed' sugar. The commission's decisions were binding on members, subject to an appeal process. The final decision by the commission was 'executory' within two months.

Nevertheless, the imposition of countervailing duties gave rise to some concern among members of the Brussels Sugar Convention. While some members defended free trade and the MFN principle, protectionist policies increased in other countries before World War I. Particularly, in 1908, Great Britain submitted its reservations with respect to the imposition of countervailing duties on the grounds that it violated the MFN clause. Hence, it renewed its mandate on the condition of not imposing countervailing duties; albeit, it committed not to re-export products made by subsidized sugar to other members of the Convention, until 1912, when it withdrew from the Convention. Meanwhile, France enacted its first countervailing duty provision in 1910 and, along with Italy, withdrew from the Brussels Sugar Convention in order to increase the tariff protection of the sugar industries during the World War. The Treaty of Versailles expelled Germany from the Convention, which had become ineffective.[839]

835. Except the UK, whose debate in the House of Commons included the following question: '*Is a duty to countervail a bounty consistent with free trade?*' The Crown ruled that imposing countervailing duties against imports of subsidized sugar would violate the MFN clause of its commercial treaties. G. Martineau, The Brussels Sugar Convention, *The Economic Journal*, Vol. 14, No. 53, 1 March 1904, pp. 34-46 at 37 https://doi.org/10.2307/2220737. D.A. Irwin, Multilateral and Bilateral Trade Policies in the World Trading System: An Historical Perspective, in J. De Melo, A. Panagariya, *New Dimensions in Regional Integration*, 1993, pp. 90-119 at footnote 15.
836. India in 1899, Serbia in 1904, Spain in 1906, France and Japan in 1910, British South Africa in 1914, and Portugal and New Zealand in 1921. J. Viner, *Dumping: A Problem in International Trade*, 1923, pp. 169-171.
837. The Brussels Sugar Convention was signed, on 5 March 1902, by Germany, Austria, Hungary, Belgium, Spain, France, Great Britain, Italy, the Netherlands and Sweden (Sweden and Norway). Concluding protocol of the Convention, included in B. Taylor, The Brussels Sugar Convention, *The North American Review*, Vol. 190, No. 646, pp. 347-358, September 1909, p. 352. In 1907, Russia joined the Convention with reservations. J. Viner, *Dumping: A Problem in International Trade*, 1923, p. 181.
838. Furthermore, countries agreed to limit the surtax on sugar ('surtax', i.e., '*difference between the rate of duty or taxation to which foreign sugars are subjected and that imposed on the home product*'). They also incorporated the MFN clause, by which they committed to reciprocally bind their lowest import rate (tariff) on sugar.
839. J. Viner, *Dumping: A Problem in International Trade*, 1923, pp. 183-185.

The outcome of World War I discouraged multilateralism and countervailing duty provisions expanded in national legislations.[840] The US countervailing duty law developed in 1922 laid the foundations of the countervailing duty provision established under Article 11 of the US Suggested Charter of 1946 and GATT Article VI.[841] In 1922, the US broadened the scope of countervailing actions to cover both production and export subsidies, as well as official and unofficial subsidies (i.e., from governmental and non-governmental sources).[842] This US countervailing duty provision did not include injury to the domestic industry as a requirement to impose countervailing duties.[843] Nevertheless, the injury requirement was incorporated in the US Suggested Charter (Article 11.5) for both anti-dumping and countervailing duties[844] and in GATT Article VI.5 (then, GATT Article VI.6).

III GATT ARTICLE VI

GATT Article VI was based on Article 11 of the US Suggested Charter, which was negotiated and redrafted during the preparatory work of the GATT and the ITO Charter (London, New York, Geneva and Havana, 1946-1948), although the UK opposed and the US disregarded its inclusion. The UK stated that '*countervailing duties should be prohibited*' and the US reiterated that the provision was not essential to the GATT, suggesting its deletion only one month before the signature of the GATT.[845]

Despite the fact that the countervailing duty provision remained very similar under GATT Article VI, overall, the changes introduced during the preparatory work rendered the countervailing duty provision more protectionist.[846] Exceptionally, the Preparatory Committee introduced a new (7th) paragraph in the GATT 1947 prohibiting the imposition of other measures than countervailing duties to offset subsidization. An interpretative note to this paragraph included provisions of GATT Article XIX -safeguard measures.[847] Nevertheless, this paragraph was removed at the GATT Review Session of 1954-1955.[848]

840. Czechoslovakia was the only country that enacted a countervailing duty provision that specifically referred to labour standards. '*In 1926, the Government authorised duties on goods produced under "unfavourable social conditions of labour" that threatened domestic production.*' S. Charnovitz, The Influence of International Labour Standards on the World Trading Regime: A Historical Overview, *International Labour Review*, Vol. 126, No. 5, 1987, pp. 565-584 at 577.
841. The countervailing duty provision included in the GATT was based on the US countervailing duty provision under the Tariff Act of 1930.
842. J. Viner, *Dumping: A Problem in International Trade*, 1923, p. 169.
843. The US countervailing duty law was amended by the US Trade Agreements Act of 1979 to incorporate injury in order to comply with the US obligations under the SCM Code, drafted in the Tokyo Round.
844. US State Department, Suggested Charter for an International Trade Organization of the United Nations, September 1946.
845. UN documents E/PC/CII/54, 16 November 1946, p. 16; E/PC/T/TAC/PV/10, 4 September 1947, p. 45.
846. More additions were suggested, such as permitting quantitative restrictions to offset subsidization, but they were not incorporated into the draft provision. UN document E/PC/T/C.6/85, 15 February 1947.
847. UNTS, Vol. 55, pp. 187-316 at 216, 296.
848. This paragraph was absent in both the ITO Charter and the consolidated version of the GATT after the GATT Review Session of 1954-1955.

The main changes to the provision, which have remained under GATT Article VI, are hereby presented. Under certain circumstances, '*multiple currency practices*' (by '*governments or sanctioned by governments*') may be considered a countervailable export subsidy.[849] In addition, members of the Preparatory Committee included the possibility of requiring bond or cash deposits for the payment of countervailing duties '*in any case of suspected subsidization*'.[850] These amendments were incorporated as interpretative notes.

Moreover, Contracting Parties incorporated the possibility to impose countervailing duties in the case where subsidization has caused material injury (or threat thereof) to the industry of a third country that '*exported the product to importing contracting party*' (GATT Article VI.6.b).[851] This provision permits an importing country (A) to 'protect' its industry in case the subsidization of another country (B) has caused injury (or threat thereof) to the industry of a third country (C). This exemption from the injury requirement to the domestic industry for imposing countervailing duties is conditioned on a waiver granted by the CONTRACTING PARTIES (GATT Article VI.6.b first sentence). Since the provision requires consensus, a Contracting Party/WTO Member would unlikely accept the imposition of countervailing duties on its products.[852]

Therefore, following the petition from Australia and New Zealand, the GATT Review Session of 1954-1955 introduced a provision mandating CONTRACTING PARTIES to waive the injury requirement to the domestic industry for imposing countervailing duties on a third country (second sentence of GATT Article VI.6.b).[853] An interpretative note was included to clarify that the waivers (under subparagraph 6.b) shall be requested by the country imposing the countervailing duty. Furthermore, another subparagraph was added to permit, in exceptional circumstances, the imposition of countervailing duties without the waiver '*where delay might cause damage which would be difficult to repair*', subject to later approval by CONTRACTING PARTIES (GATT Article VI.6.c).[854]

IV THE SCM CODE AND ASCM

Before the entry into force of the Subsidies and Countervailing Measures Code (SCM Code) in 1980, only one GATT dispute settlement report was issued, the *Zenith Case*.[855] Nevertheless, countervailing duties were among the most contentious issues during

849. UNTS, Vol. 55, pp. 187-316 at 296.
850. UN document E.CONF.2/78, 24 March 1948, p. 113 (Annex P, Interpretative Note *Ad* Article 40).
851. UNTS, Vol. 55, pp. 187-316 at 214.
852. Under the ITO Charter, 'the Organization' was entrusted to grant the waiver.
853. The only difference between the first and second sentences of GATT Article VI.6.b is the use of the modal verb 'shall' instead of 'may'.
854. The second sentences of subparas 6.b and 6.c only apply to countervailing duties, but not to anti-dumping duties.
855. *United States – Suspension of Customs Liquidation Regarding Certain Japanese Consumer Electronic Products* (GD/98). Complainant: Japan. GATT document L/4508, 6 June 1977. Appraisement and liquidation of Japanese electronic products were suspended by the US (pending final decision to impose countervailing duties). The US alleged that Japanese

the Tokyo Round (1973-1979) for being '*increasing and expanding*'.[856] Divergence of views among Contracting Parties prevented, *inter alia*, the tightening of rules on countervailing duties. Notwithstanding the aim of the SCM Code was to ensure that countervailing duties did not '*unjustifiably impede international trade*',[857] its provisions on countervailing duties tended to favour protectionist interests. More specifically, in the SCM Code lies the origin of key issues, namely, the possibility of opting between imposing countervailing duties or an authorized countermeasure to offset the effects of (foreign) subsidization; the ex officio initiation of a countervailing duty investigation; the alternative to reach undertakings (SCM Code Article 4); and the calculation of the subsidy by construction of the value or comparison with prices in a third country, in '*special situations*' established under Note 2 *Ad* paragraph 1 of GATT Article VI, i.e., where the exporting country has a monopoly of its trade and its domestic prices are fixed by the State (SCM Code Article 15).

A Unilateral Countervailing Duties or Authorized Countermeasures

The SCM Code, which interpreted GATT Articles VI, XVI and XXIII, permitted the imposition of countervailing duties or countermeasures authorized by the SCM Committee (GATT Article XXIII).[858] Compared to the 'material injury' requirement under GATT Article VI, these authorized countermeasures required 'serious prejudice', pursuant to GATT Article XVI, or 'nullification of impairment', established under GATT Article XXIII.[859] Some Contracting Parties expressed concern about facilitating the imposition of countervailing duties in this manner.[860]

The imposition of countermeasures (SCM Code Article 13) was based on the dispute settlement procedure (SCM Code Article 18). The SCM Committee was responsible for determining whether the subsidy under complaint had caused '*injury, nullification or impairment, or serious prejudice*', making recommendations, and if the latter were not followed, authorizing countermeasures. Nevertheless, this multilateral procedure was not applied for the imposition of countervailing duties. The SCM Code allowed Contracting Parties to resort to unilateral remedies against foreign subsidization in case of injury to the domestic industry, provided there was evidence of a causal

---

remission or exemption of consumption taxes constituted the payment of a bounty within the meaning of the countervailing duty law. The US measure was found inconsistent with GATT Article VI.4.

856. J. Bourgeois, The GATT Rules for Industrial Subsidies and Countervailing Duties and the New GATT Round: The Weather and the Seeds, in E.U. Petersmann, M. Hilf, *The New GATT Round of Multilateral Trade Negotiations: Legal and Economic Problems*, Studies in Transnational Economic Law, Vol. 5, 1988, pp. 219-235 at 231.
857. GATT document LT/TR/A/3, pp. 51-80 at 51.
858. SCM Code Note 3 clarified that only one remedy was available, a countervailing duty or a countermeasure.
859. GATT Article XVI.1 required serious prejudice for the subsidizing country to, upon request, discuss with concerned Contracting Parties, or with the CONTRACTING PARTIES, the possibility of limiting subsidization.
860. J.H. Jackson, W. Davey, *Legal Problems of International Economic Relations, Cases, Materials and Text*, 2nd ed., 1986, p. 730.

link between the subsidization and material injury to the domestic industry.[861] The term 'injury' also covered threat thereof and material retardation of the establishment of an industry. The determination of injury required evidence of an absolute or relative increase in subsidized imports vis-à-vis production or consumption, and an impact on the domestic industry (SCM Code Article 6).

The first four paragraphs of SCM Code Article 6 were practically identical to 1979 AD Code Article 3, which had lowered the bar of the injury requirement from the 1967 AD Code. Instead of the 'principal cause' of injury, imports were merely required to cause material injury. It has been observed that incorporating the injury requirement to both anti-dumping and countervailing duty proceedings '*may have been an unfortunate step, since the two subjects, although seemingly parallel, differ substantially in their underlying policy foundations*', albeit the weaker injury requirement was included for cases of subsidization[862] and the '*trade-offs between producers and consumers in the importing country (...), reflected in the automaticity and soft injury test of the 1979 countervailing duty law, seems weighted toward protectionism*'.[863]

In several GATT disputes concerning countervailing duties, the determination of injury, under SCM Code Article 3, was invoked. These disputes show how some Contracting Parties tried to broaden the scope of the provision in order to impose countervailing duties. In some cases, the term 'domestic industry' was flexibly interpreted to include input suppliers as producers, e.g., in *Canada – Manufacturing Beef CVD*.[864] In other cases, the national legislation was amended in order to broaden the scope of the provision, as shown in the *US – Wine and Grape Products* dispute, in which the Panel held that 'domestic industry' should be interpreted narrowly, due to the fact that countervailing duties permitted action against the MFN principle under GATT Article I.[865]

With respect to the causal link between the subsidized imports from the US and material injury, the Panel in the *Canada – Grain Corn* case found that Canada had failed to provide evidence of a causal link. It recognized, however, that domestic producers in Canada may have encountered serious problems due to foreign subsidization and recalled that there was an alternative: a multilateral procedure to resolve this matter,

861. The US acceptance and implementation of the requirement of material injury '*was the crux of the negotiations*' since the US had not previously incorporated the injury requirement in its domestic legislation. J.H. Jackson, W. Davey, *Legal Problems of International Economic Relations, Cases, Materials and Text*, 2nd ed., 1986, p. 730.
862. J.H. Jackson, J-V. Louis, M. Matsushita, Implementing the Tokyo Round: Legal Aspects of Changing International Economic Rules, *Michigan Law Review*, Vol. 81, No. 2, 1982, pp. 267-397 at 273, 274 https://doi.org/10.2307/1288518.
863. J.J. Barceló III, Subsidies, Countervailing Duties and Antidumping After the Tokyo Round, *Cornell International Law Journal*, Vol. 13, No. 2, 1980, pp. 257-290 at 288.
864. *Canada – Imposition of Countervailing Duties on Imports of Manufacturing Beef from the EEC* (GD/160). Complainant: EEC 10. The Panel considered that adopting a flexible interpretation would have required amending the SCM Code. GATT document SCM/85, 13 October 1987, para. 5.13.
865. *United States – Definition of Industry Concerning Wine and Grape Products* (GD/153). Complainant: EEC-10. GATT document SCM/71, 24 March 1986, para. 4.5.

provided under SCM Code Article 13.4 in case of '*injury, nullification or impairment, or serious prejudice*'.[866]

Regarding the impact on the domestic industry, the Panel in the dispute *US – Canadian Pork*[867] found that the '*evaluation of all relevant economic factors*' was absent. In this dispute, the reimbursement of countervailing duties was recommended for the first time.[868] The provision requiring the evaluation of all relevant economic factors was further developed under ASCM Article 15.5 (which mirrors ADA Article 3.5). Under the ASCM, the demonstration of the causal link (between subsidized imports and injury) also requires the examination of any other factors causing injury, i.e., the non-attribution analysis.[869] Compared to the SCM Code, the ASCM emphasized the obligation to examine all relevant economic factors to determine the causal link.[870]

One of the main objectives during the Uruguay Round negotiations of the ASCM was to contain the proliferation of countervailing duties, in order not to undermine the liberal trading system.[871] To this end, subsidies were classified based on the specificity test. For a subsidy to be countervailable, it must be 'specific', i.e., granted to an enterprise or industry or group of enterprises or industries within the jurisdiction of the subsidizing country. Permitted or non-actionable subsidies (green) are non-specific,[872] thereby exempted from countervailing action. Actionable subsidies (yellow) are specific and may be subject to countervailing duties in case they cause adverse effects (serious prejudice, injury or threat thereof). Prohibited subsidies (red) are considered

866. *Canada – Injury Determination on Grain Corn from the United States* (GD/179) Complainant: US. GATT documents SCM/140, 21 February 1992, para. 5.2.10.
867. *United States – Countervailing Duties on Fresh, Chilled and Frozen Pork from Canada* (GD/220). Complainant: Canada. GATT document L/6721, 18 September 1990.
868. As it first occurred in the anti-dumping case *New Zealand – Finnish Transformers*.
869. The provision established a non-exhaustive list, which includes '*the volumes and prices of non-subsidized imports of the product in question, contraction in demand or changes in the patterns of consumption, trade restrictive practices of and competition between the foreign and domestic producers, developments in technology and the export performance and productivity of the domestic industry*'.
870. Horlick considered that this main change was introduced as a consequence of the *US – Norwegian Salmon* in which the US countervailing duties were found consistent with GATT Article VI and the SCM Code. The requirement under SCM Code Article 2.1 of '*on behalf of the industry affected*' was fulfilled since the majority of domestic producers of Atlantic salmon had approved the petition as of the date of the initiation of the countervailing duty investigation. *United States – Imposition of Countervailing Duties on Imports of Fresh and Chilled Atlantic Salmon from Norway* (GD/249). Complainant: Norway. GATT document SCM/153, 4 December 1992, paras 232, 233, 350.
871. A major difficulty in this matter seems to have been bringing the US and EU positions together, with Canada aiming to protect itself from US countervailing duties. G. Depayre, Subsidies and Countervailing Measures after the Uruguay Round: An Overview, in J. Bourgeois, F. Berrod, E. Gippini Fournier (eds), *The Uruguay Round Results, A European Lawyers' Perspective: Proceedings of an International Conference Held at the College of Europe, Bruges*, 1999, pp. 247-254 at 255.
872. Until the end of 1999, certain specific subsidies for research and development, environmental, and regional programmes that met the conditions listed under ASCM Article 8.2 were considered non-actionable. ASCM Articles 8 and 9 expired five years after the entry into force of the ASCM, pursuant to ASCM Article 31.

to be specific per se (ASCM Article 2.3); therefore, they may also be subject to countervailing duties.[873]

The scope of countervailing measures has one more time been enlarged by the ASCM since only non-actionable subsidies (green)[874] are exempted from unilateral countervailing action, while most subsidies fall under the actionable (yellow) or prohibited (red) categories, and thus are countervailable. Furthermore, as far as the quantification of subsidization is concerned, the ASCM established the benefit to the recipient approach (as opposed to the cost to the government approach long advocated by the EU). In other words, the unilateral response to counteract foreign subsidization has been strengthened by the ASCM, undermining the envisaged liberalization of world trade. In fact, since the entry into force of the ASCM, the use of countervailing duties has increased and expanded.[875] Previously, mostly a US phenomenon,[876] the use of this unilateral remedy against foreign subsidization has become a global phenomenon.

B Ex Officio Initiation of Investigation and Undertakings

The option of an ex officio initiation of a countervailing duty investigation '*in special circumstances*' was expressly provided for in SCM Code Article 2.1. This implies that the authorities had the discretion to initiate an investigation without the request for protection by domestic industries. In the *US – Softwood Lumber II* case,[877] Canada's termination of an undertaking[878] was found by the Panel to be sufficient evidence of a threat of material injury to the US industry, justifying the initiation of an ex officio countervailing duty investigation.[879]

The SCM Code (Article 4) introduced the possibility of reaching undertakings to offset the effect of subsidies in the importing country.[880] Undertakings may be reached between governments of the importing and exporting countries, or between the importing country and exporters in the foreign country. In the first case, the exporting country would accept to limit or cease subsidization (or take other measures to offset its effects). In the second case, the importing country would set a minimum import price, which foreign exporters may accept or face the imposition of countervailing

873. To offset the effect of a prohibited or an actionable subsidy in the importing country, ASCM Note 35 provides for the imposition of either a countermeasure authorized through the dispute settlement proceeding (ASCM Article 4 or 7) or a countervailing duty (ASCM Articles 10-23). *See* Ch. 7, Section III.C.
874. Since 2000, only non-specific subsidies.
875. WTO website information, viewed at: https://www.wto.org/English/tratop_e/scm_e/CV_InitiationsByRepMem.pdf; https://www.wto.org/English/tratop_e/scm_e/CV_InitiationsRepMemVsExp. pdf.
876. J.H. Jackson, W. Davey, *Legal Problems of International Economic Relations, Cases, Materials and Text*, 2nd ed., 1986, p. 727.
877. *United States – Measures Affecting Imports of Softwood Lumber from Canada* (GD/258). Complainant: Canada. GATT document SCM/162, 19 February 1993.
878. It was reached on 30 December 1986 and terminated on 4 October 1991. GATT document SCM/162, 19 February 1993, para. 7.
879. GATT document SCM/162, 19 February 1993, paras 326-410.
880. Paragraphs 5 and 6 of the SCM Code Article 4.

duties on their products.[881] Moreover, the importing country was permitted to request information concerning the fulfilment of the undertaking by the exporting country or firm. In case of violation of the undertaking, the importing country could impose provisional countervailing duties (SCM Code Article 4.6).[882]

This possibility to reach undertakings has been maintained under ASCM Article 18. The only difference incorporated by the ASCM concerning the undertakings is the sunset clause under ASCM Article 21, which establishes that undertakings, as well as countervailing duties,[883] can only be in force for five years. Nevertheless, following a sunset review by the importing country, the undertaking (or the countervailing duties) can be extended for a new period (ASCM Article 21.3). With such undertakings in place in the importing country, prices of the protected product tend to be distorted and competition eliminated, eventually resulting in a 'cartelization' of the market.[884]

C Calculation of the Subsidy by Comparison or Construction of the Value

The SCM Code permitted to calculate the subsidy by comparison or construction of the value in special situations. Part IV of the SCM Code consists of Article 15: '*Special situations*', which established the provision under Note 2 *Ad* GATT Article VI.1. Notably, this interpretative note deals with determining the margin of dumping (price comparability) in cases where the exporting country has a complete (or substantially complete) monopoly of its trade and fixes prices.[885] SCM Code Article 15 established that, in such cases, either the SCM Code or the AD Code could be alternatively invoked (SCM Code Article 15.1). This means that the SCM Code made a GATT anti-dumping provision also applicable to countervailing actions.

The SCM permitted the calculation of '*the amount of the estimated subsidy*' by comparison of a like product in another than the subsidizing country, or construction of the value of the product. SCM Code Article 15 (Note 33) defined '*constructed value*' as the '*cost of production plus a reasonable amount for administration, selling and any*

881. In case of acceptance of an undertaking, the investigation could still be conducted at the request of any (importing or exporting) party. Even in the absence of threat of injury, the importing country was allowed to require the continuation of the undertaking [for '*a reasonable period*'] in cases where the absence of threat of injury was due to the existence of the undertaking (SCM Code Article 4.5.b). The importing country was '*free to determine that a threat of injury* [was] *more likely to be realized if the subsidized imports continue*'.
882. This provision was invoked by the US in the *US – Softwood Lumber II*, but the Panel rejected the claim since Canada had not violated the undertaking but terminated it. *United States – Measures Affecting Imports of Softwood Lumber from Canada* (GD/258). Complainant: Canada. GATT document SCM/162, 19 February 1993, paras 303-325.
883. ASCM Article 21.5 reads: '*The provisions of this Article shall apply mutatis mutandis to undertakings accepted under Article 18.*'
884. J. Tumlir, *Protectionism: Trade Policies in Democratic Societies*, 1985, p. 8.
885. Note 2 *Ad* GATT Article VI. 1 reads: '*It is recognized that, in the case of imports from a country which has a complete or substantially complete monopoly of its trade and where all domestic prices are fixed by the State, special difficulties may exist in determining price comparability for the purposes of paragraph 1, and in such cases importing contracting parties may find it necessary to take into account the possibility that a strict comparison with domestic prices in such a country may not always be appropriate.*'

other costs and for profits' (SCM Code Article 15.2). If none of these methods provided an adequate basis for determining the subsidy, the importing country was allowed to use its own prices '*if necessary, duly adjusted to reflect reasonable profits*'.[886]

While this provision was not incorporated into the ASCM, it was later used in the Protocol of Accession of the so-called *non-market economies*, such as China and Vietnam. Pursuant to these Protocols, when calculating the subsidy's benefit, WTO Members are allowed, under certain conditions, to disregard Chinese[887] and Vietnamese[888] benchmarks, and instead '*use alternative methodologies*'.[889] Unlike anti-dumping measures against imports from the countries concerned, there is no expiration date for the application of the countervailing duty provision.

These provisions are absent in the ASCM, but its Article 14 delegates the method to calculate the benefit (a requirement for a subsidy to be deemed to exist under ASCM Article 1.1.b) to WTO Members (i.e., '*in national legislations or implementing regulations of the Member concerned*'). Therefore, it leaves WTO Members with the discretion to adopt their own methodology to calculate the benefit conferred by another WTO Member to the recipient. ASCM Article 14 only requires the methodology to be subject to four guidelines, of which one requires determining the '*adequate remuneration*' by taking into account the market conditions of the product/service in the exporting country, '*including price, quality, availability, marketability, transportation and other conditions of purchase or sale*'.[890]

886. SCM Code Article 15.4 requires due allowance '*for the difference in conditions and terms of sale or in taxation and for the other differences affecting price comparability, so that the method of comparison applied is appropriate and not unreasonable*' as if calculating the amount of the subsidy by comparing prices or constructing the value were at all reasonable.
887. Section 15(b): '*In proceedings under Parts II, III and V of the SCM Agreement, when addressing subsidies described in Articles 14(a), 14(b), 14(c) and 14(d), relevant provisions of the SCM Agreement shall apply; however, if there are special difficulties in that application, the importing WTO Member may then use methodologies for identifying and measuring the subsidy benefit which take into account the possibility that prevailing terms and conditions in China may not always be available as appropriate benchmarks. In applying such methodologies, where practicable, the importing WTO Member should adjust such prevailing terms and conditions before considering the use of terms and conditions prevailing outside China.*' WTO document L/432, 23 November 2001, p. 9.
888. Paragraph 255(b) of the Working Party Report incorporated to the Protocol of Accession of Vietnam to the WTO: '*In proceedings under Parts II, III and V of the SCM Agreement, when addressing subsidies, the relevant provisions of the SCM Agreement shall apply; however, if there are special difficulties in that application, the importing WTO Member may then use alternative methodologies for identifying and measuring the subsidy benefit which take into account the possibility that prevailing terms and conditions in Viet Nam may not be available as appropriate benchmarks.*' WTO document ACC/VNM/48, 27 October 2006, p. 66.
889. In the particular case of China, the provision adds the obligation for the importing Member to, '*where practicable*', adjust the prevailing terms and conditions in China previous to their disregard.
890. ASCM Article 14.d. '*The provision of goods or services or purchase of goods by a government shall not be considered as conferring a benefit unless the provision is made for less than adequate remuneration, or the purchase is made for more than adequate remuneration. The adequacy of remuneration shall be determined in relation to prevailing market conditions for the good or service in question in the country of provision or purchase (including price, quality, availability, marketability, transportation and other conditions of purchase or sale).*'

This provision has been interpreted by the WTO Appellate Body in the *US – Softwood Lumber IV* case in a manner that investigating authorities can disregard market prices in the exporting country as the benchmark when prices are distorted '*because of the predominant role of the government in the market as a provider of the same or similar goods*', although they must still ensure that the '*alternative benchmark relates or refers to, or is connected* with, *prevailing market conditions in the country of provision*'.[891] This interpretation was confirmed by the Appellate Body in the *US – Carbon Steel (India)* case, which concluded that investigating authorities are allowed '*to construct a price based on any fees and royalties paid for the mining rights, plus the cost, plus profit of the extraction process*'.[892]

The prima facie burden or challenge for the investigating authorities to determine the existence of foreign subsidies and injury to the domestic industry has been made easier over time, which results in the facilitation of imposing countervailing duties. Through multilateral trade negotiations under the GATT and the WTO, the disciplines on countervailing duties have been tilted towards protectionist interests, even permitting undertakings with the exporting country or foreign exporters, thereby eliminating import competition and potentially cartelizing the market of the protected product.

Welfare economics and legal principles, as well as the history of countervailing duty provisions, call for the elimination of countervailing duty actions. In case other WTO Members do not comply with multilateral rules on subsidies, the only available option for complainants should be resorting to the multilateral proceeding, whereby countermeasures may be authorized to offset subsidies. The elimination of unilateral countervailing duties should be complemented by the amendment of the current rules on subsidies. Furthermore, it requires the abolition of the other two trade remedies (namely, anti-dumping duties and safeguard measures), as well as the incorporation of a multilateral agreement on competition and trade-restrictive practices. These matters will be explored in the following chapters.

891. *United States – Final Countervailing Duty Determination with respect to certain Softwood Lumber from Canada* (DS257). WTO document DS257/AB/R 19 January 2004, para. 167.B.

892. *United States – Countervailing Measures on Certain Hot-Rolled Carbon Steel Flat Products from India* (DS436). WTO document DS436/AB/R, 8 December 2014, para. 4.332.

CHAPTER 9
Anti-dumping

This chapter questions the need for anti-dumping laws, exploring their lack of economic and legal rationale, and the evolution of the main substantive issues through the history of multilateral provisions, i.e., dumping and injury determinations. Anti-dumping rules have been broadened and weakened to facilitate the imposition of duties, often by legitimizing anti-dumping practices in multilateral trade negotiations, thereby creating some of the most controversial issues in nowadays international trade relations.

I ECONOMIC AND LEGAL RATIONALE

The absence of an economic rationale for anti-dumping laws has been well established.[893] Anti-dumping aims at protecting the interests of certain domestic industries by restraining dumped imports. As a result, import-competing industries can maintain or increase their prices at the expense of importers, other industries and consumers. Import restrictions may increase, under certain circumstances, the wealth of the protected industries. Nonetheless, justifying anti-dumping laws merely due to the effect that the alleged dumped imports cause on import-competing industries reflects '*the crudest of protectionist reasoning*'.[894]

The protection of certain domestic industries is not based on economic principles, but on both the misconception of the effect of trade in the creation of national welfare and the political interest in supporting certain industries. First, the mercantilist's conception of wealth is represented by the balance of trade, i.e., excess of exports over imports, where the value of importation and its capacity to create national welfare is ignored. Second, certain domestic industries exert higher political pressure since

893. R. Dale, *Anti-dumping Law in a Liberal Trade Order*, 1980. M. Finger, *Antidumping: How It Works and Who Gets Hurt*, Ann Arbor, 1993.
894. J. Viner, *Dumping: A Problem in International Trade*, 1923, p. 138.

governments need their political and economic support. As a discriminatory instrument, anti-dumping permits governments to select which domestic industries they protect. '*More and more, antidumping policy is trade policy. But as a matter of policy the Antidumping Emperor, in fact, has no clothes.*'[895]

The welfare rationale of anti-dumping laws has been as widely studied as neglected. From the first study on dumping (by Viner), it has been recognized that if the economic welfare of the country as a whole were considered, the gains for consumers and non-competing producers would outweigh any eventual injury to the import-competing industries. In such a case, it would be '*unwise to restrain the importation of dumped commodities, and it might even reasonably be maintained that such importation should be encouraged*'.[896] The same would be true if global welfare were considered.

The interest of consumers is sacrificed for the benefit of producers, as Adam Smith already observed.[897] Consumers, as well as producers in the importing country, are deprived of the benefits of lower prices.[898] Indeed, anti-dumping restrains the freedom of consumers and producers in the importing country, as well as of the exporters abroad whose prices may reflect a comparative advantage. Unlike subsidization, selling abroad at lower prices on private initiative is at the expense of the exporting enterprise itself rather than taxpayers in the exporting country. Whether a private entity decides to sell below the cost of production should remain at its own risk. When entering the market of the importing country, exporters are threatened by the eventual imposition of anti-dumping duties, unless they voluntarily increase their price to a fixed minimum import price and/or reduce exports to a fixed quota, i.e., reach an undertaking. Therefore, exporters are also deprived of the freedom to sell abroad at lower prices. In other words, the freedom of private enterprises is at stake. All that is done in order to protect companies, established in the importing country, from the injury caused by the alleged dumped imports (or threat thereof).

Injury can more easily be shown as local companies are less efficient or greater their monopoly; it is precisely then when '*the local consumer's need for the low-priced imports is comparatively greater*', when more effective competition is needed. Yet, import competition is the greatest threat to an oligopoly price structure. With anti-dumping duties or undertakings in force, domestic sellers can maintain or increase their prices, permitting them to restore the oligopoly.[899] Anti-dumping is, therefore, the remedy par excellence to solve the '*problem of stiff competition from imports*'.[900]

Competitive export prices are perceived as a threat (or cause) of injury to the domestic industry. Nevertheless, competitive export prices may result from the

895. D. Palmeter, The Antidumping Emperor, *Journal of World Trade*, Vol. 22. No. 4, 1988, pp. 5-7 at 7.
896. J. Viner, *Dumping: A Problem in International Trade*, 1923, pp. 137, 138.
897. A. Smith, *The Wealth of Nations*, [1776], 2000, p. 877.
898. The benefit of consumers is not only viewed as '*ephemeral but also destructive insofar as it weakens or eliminates domestic firms*'. K.W. Dam, *The GATT: Law and International Economic Organization*, 1970, pp. 169-170.
899. K.W. Dam, *The GATT: Law and International Economic Organization*, 1970, pp. 170.
900. D. Palmeter, Competition Policy and Unfair Trade: First Do No Harm, *Aussenwirtschaft Zeitschrift für internationale Wirtschaftsbeziehungen*, Vol. 49, 1994, pp. 417-422, at 419.

comparative advantage of the exporter, regardless of the existence of dumping.[901] *'The one essential characteristic of dumping (...) is price-discrimination between purchasers in different national markets.'*[902] Dumping is determined when the export price is lower than the normal value in the domestic market of the exporting country. Price discrimination has been considered pro-competitive, except in the case of predatory discrimination; however, it has been well established, both in theory and practice, that predatory dumping is rare and less likely than predatory pricing in domestic markets.[903] Furthermore, competition/anti-trust laws *'give ample protection against predatory practices'*.[904] But anti-dumping has *'nothing to do with unfairness or predation'*.[905]

Since the first anti-dumping provision, the artificial creation of price discrimination has been permitted; hence, imports have been subject to anti-dumping duties, even in the absence of dumping. Costs are deducted from the export price (transport costs, administrative costs, duties in the importing country, etc.) while added to the normal value (selling, administrative, profits, etc.). The entire construction of the anti-dumping system lacks economic rationale. Prices have always been manipulated, so the export price is lower than it actually is, and the normal value is higher than its real value. Thus, this price discrimination between the export price and the normal value has never constituted a 'fair comparison'.

Experts in the field have observed that the anti-dumping system is inefficient.[906] In order to grant protection to a particular domestic industry, under certain circumstances, producer subsidies could be more efficient. With a subsidy, there would neither be a distortion of prices for consumers nor a substitution of socially costlier products for the alleged dumped products (by importers and consumers).[907] Notwithstanding that it would be to the detriment of taxpayers, the overall costs to society would be lower with subsidies; hence, from an economic perspective, anti-dumping is not the best instrument to grant protection.[908]

---

901. K.W. Dam, *The GATT: Law and International Economic Organization*, 1970, pp. 168-170.
902. J. Viner, *Dumping: A Problem in International Trade*, 1923, p. 4.
903. R. Dale, *Anti-dumping Law in a Liberal Trade Order*, 1980, pp. 32, 191. M.J. Marks, United States Antidumping Laws: A Government Overview, *Antitrust Law Journal*, Vol. 43, No. 3, 1974, pp. 580-589, at 581.
904. J.J. Barceló III, Antidumping Laws as Barriers to Trade the United States and the International Antidumping Code, *Cornell Law Review*, Vol. 57, No. 4, 1971-1972, pp. 491-560, at 559.
905. D. Palmeter, Competition Policy and Unfair Trade: First Do No Harm, *Aussenwirtschaft Zeitschrift für internationale Wirtschaftsbeziehungen*, Vol. 49, 1994, pp. 417-422, at 418.
906. Due to the fact that *'there may well be alternative less costly ways of providing the protection though necessary; producer subsidies are most often mentioned, with another possibility being temporary increases in conventional duty'*, G.N. Horlick, The United States Antidumping System, in J.H. Jackson, E.A. Vermulst (eds), *Antidumping Law and Practice: A Comparative Study*, 1989, pp. 99-166 at 166.
907. J. Tumlir, *Protectionism: Trade Policies in Democratic Societies*, 1985, p. 7.
908. Assuming that certain domestic industries may require some social protection, an ideal instrument would grant them protection while preventing harming the rest of the community. In other words, this analysis should be based on Pareto's optimum. The effect of anti-dumping is similar to the effect of a tariff, but raised to a higher power. While tariffs are bound, there is no limit to the (amount of) anti-dumping duties other than the margin of dumping. The protectionist effect is exacerbated in the case of reaching a price undertaking, whereby a quota or tariff quota is imposed. As protection increases, through a higher restrain of competition, the harm on the rest of the society increases.

From a legal point of view, anti-dumping laws are the perfect example of antonymy in the multilateral trading system, whose most fundamental economic principle is non-discrimination. Anti-dumping is a discriminatory instrument inconsistent with the most-favoured-nation and national treatment principles, established under GATT Articles I and III. Moreover, by permitting the imposition of anti-dumping duties over the bound tariffs, an inconsistency with GATT Article II is also created. In addition, anti-dumping laws conflict with competition laws. While countries enact legislation to prohibit competition restraints in the domestic markets, anti-dumping duties restrain import competition.

Anti-dumping was included in the GATT as an exception, on the grounds that it grants protection to the domestic industry. Therefore, the question is whether this exception is reasonably justified. A legal system may consider the incorporation of exceptional rules to protect the general interest. This is the case of some general exceptions established under GATT Article XX, such as the protection of public morals; human, animal or plant health; or conservation of natural resources. Nevertheless, the protection of selected domestic industries does not constitute a subject of general interest or supreme good, but constitutes a particular interest. On the contrary, free trade and the freedom of the rest of the community would have to be preserved over the particular interest of certain domestic industries.[909]

II 'DUMPING: A PROBLEM IN INTERNATIONAL TRADE'[910]

For centuries, allegations of dumping have been made against more competitive foreign exporters whose products represented a threat to import-competing industries. British manufacturers were first charged with this practice during the Industrial Revolution.[911] The practice of 'dumping', i.e., exporting at a lower price than the domestic price on private initiative, already existed in the XVIII century.[912] This initiative was based on the mercantilist conception of wealth, which focuses on a positive balance of trade, i.e., excess of exports over imports. Means to achieve this included export bounties granted either by governments (direct or indirect official export bounties) or on private initiative (unofficial export bounties). In the absence of, or in addition to, official bounties, unofficial export bounties were granted by industries to increase exportation.

909. '*Liberal international trade is-from the perspective of consumer welfare, economic efficiency and individual liberty-a mutually beneficial "international public good" that is no less important than other international public goods (such as internationally agreed minimum standards for animal and plant protection (…), international minimum standards for environmental, labour, and investment protection)*.' E.U. Petersmann, International Competition Rules for Private Business: A Trade Law Approach for Linking Trade and Competition Rules in the WTO, *Chicago-Kent Law Review*, Vol. 72, No. 2, 1996, pp. 445-582, at 582.

910. J. Viner, *Dumping: A Problem in International Trade*, 1923.

911. According to J. Viner, dumping on private initiative could not have existed until the Industrial Revolution, '*upon the development of large-scale production under monopolistic or quasi-monopolistic control*'. J. Viner, *Dumping: A Problem in International Trade*, 1923, pp. 36, 163.

912. Adam Smith observed that undertakers privately agreed to grant (unofficial) bounties '*out of their own pockets*' upon exportation. A. Smith, *The Wealth of Nations*, [1776], 2000, p. 678.

Nevertheless, the term 'dumping' appeared in the literature of economics only at the beginning of the XX century, when it was seen as *'a problem in international trade'*. Initially, 'dumping' covered a variety of practices, whether governmental or on private initiative, which resulted in an *'export price lower than the domestic price'*.[913] As a matter of fact, charges of 'dumping' were made against both the Russian system, consisting of official export bounties, and German cartels and US trusts, organized by private enterprises. Indeed, allegations of dumping against the US Steel Corporation prompted Canada to enact the world's first anti-dumping legislation in 1904. Notably, many of the current issues regarding anti-dumping were already present in that legislation, as follows.

First, anti-dumping laws are often a political recourse to disguise an import duty increase on specific products while avoiding a general increase in tariffs, and its eventual spillover effect on other imported products.[914] Canadian steel manufacturers at the time requested import protection from the Canadian government, which generally opposed tariff protection.

Second, unlike tariffs, which are a subject of debate at the legislative, anti-dumping is an instrument at the discretion of the government. Moreover, anti-dumping duties are imposed above tariff bindings. The Canadian 'special duty' was left at the discretion of the Minister of Customs, while tariffs had to be passed in Parliament, approved by the Senate and required royal assent. The 'special duty' was imposed above the general customs duty, constituting a flexible mechanism to increase revenue.

Third, anti-dumping has always been difficult to understand by outsiders, which increases the difficulty of finding public opposition. The Canadian 'dumping clause' dissipated opposition in the House of Commons since the methodology used was considered impossible to understand. The mere proposition of imposing a tariff on steel would likely have been rejected by the House of Commons.

Fourth, anti-dumping has consisted of a certain manipulation of numbers, aimed at obtaining dumping otherwise inexistent. The normal value has tended to be higher than it really is, while the export price has been forced to be lower than it is; hence, dumping has inevitably been found even where there is no price discrimination between the normal value and the export price. The Canadian 'dumping clause' provided for, on the one hand, the exclusion of all charges after the shipment from the selling price (i.e., export price), and, on the other hand, the addition of a 'reasonable profit' to the actual cost of production to determine the 'fair market value' (i.e., normal value). Even in the absence of dumping, imported products below the cost of production were subject to anti-dumping duties.

Fifth, anti-dumping has always been the instrument of discrimination 'par excellence'. Left at the discretion of the government, it has often been abused. Authorities have always found a way to leverage a loophole or legitimize an illegal practice. Complaints against determinations of dumping and injury have existed since

913. J. Viner, *Dumping: A Problem in International Trade*, 1923, p. 270.
914. As it occurred in the US with the Smoot Hawley in 1930. C. VanGrasstek, *The History and Future of the World Trade Organization*, 2013, p. 42.

the first anti-dumping provision. The Canadian 'dumping clause' permitted discrimination among imports of the same kind, and thus favouring only selected domestic industries or companies through governmental discretion. The Minister of Customs was entrusted with the valuation of products, the 'reasonable' profit and the amount of the duty. Customs officials were charged for often imposing too high anti-dumping duties by using inaccurate or obsolete foreign market value price lists as well as for occasionally imposing anti-dumping duties on Canadian importers, although they demonstrated that the invoice price corresponded to the fair market value in the exporting country.

Sixth, the 'raison d'être' of anti-dumping laws is to protect certain domestic industries without regard to the economic effects on other actors in the global value chains and consumers. While anti-dumping has merely benefitted protected industries, it has resulted in harmful effects on national and global welfare. Industries that exert more political pressure, which may already be protected by an import tariff, receive subsidies, or both, benefit from anti-dumping duties; whereas complaints from, *inter alia*, affected industries, importers, and consumers are ignored. Steel-using industries and consumers complained against the Canadian 'dumping clause' for depriving them of the benefit of low-price US steel. The Board of Trade, representing the interest of importers, requested the repeal of the 'dumping clause', alleging unwarranted restriction of free competition, impossibility of equitable administration, encouragement for fraud, and injustice to honest importers.

Seventh, while countries have enacted legislation to prevent restraints on domestic competition, they have supported the restraint of import competition through the enactment of anti-dumping laws. Canada, as well as other countries, enacted anti-dumping laws. Concern over dumping at the national level was soon brought to the League of Nations Economic Conferences, where dumping was considered a problem in international trade. Exceptional measures to offset dumping were suggested to be included in a multilateral trade agreement. As a result, an anti-dumping provision, similar to the Canadian 'dumping clause', was included under GATT Article VI.

III GATT ARTICLE VI

The anti-dumping provision under Article 11 of the US Suggested Charter was negotiated and redrafted during the preparatory work of the GATT and the ITO Charter to become the anti-dumping provision of GATT Article VI, albeit the UK made a reservation claiming that '*all anti-dumping and countervailing duties should be prohibited*',[915] and the US considered the provision non-essential to the GATT, suggesting its deletion one month before the signature of the GATT.[916]

During the discussions of the Preparatory Committee (held in London, New York, Geneva and Havana between 1946 and 1948), some amendments were suggested, but

915. UN document E/PC/CII/54, 16 November 1946, p. 16.
916. UN document E/PC/T/TAC/PV/10, 4 September 1947, p. 45.

not included in GATT Article VI.[917] Charges of dumping were presented against Japan, alleging low-price exports were due to practices such as *'low labour standards, exchange manipulation, and the use of subsidies'*.[918] Accordingly, some delegations suggested extending anti-dumping duties to other forms of dumping, i.e., social, exchange and service; notwithstanding, the Committee rejected it.[919]

At the time of the signature of the GATT in 1947, the last and 7th paragraph of GATT Article VI prohibited the imposition of measures other than anti-dumping duties to offset dumping. An interpretative note to this paragraph clarified that this obligation was subject to the provisions of GATT Article XIX, i.e., safeguard measures.[920] In other words, safeguards could not be used to offset dumping. Even though this paragraph was removed at the Havana Conference,[921] the Working Party on the modification of the GATT agreed with such an interpretation of GATT Article VI, i.e., *'measures other than compensatory anti-dumping and countervailing duties may not be applied to counteract dumping or subsidization except in so far as such other measures are permitted under other provisions of the General Agreement'*.[922]

More importantly, some amendments were incorporated into the anti-dumping provision, rendering GATT Article VI more protectionist than Article 11 of the US Suggested Charter.[923] These modifications were introduced by the Preparatory Committee in the GATT and the ITO Charter (in New York, Geneva and Havana), and by CONTRACTING PARTIES at the GATT Review Session of 1954-1955, the last time that GATT Article VI was amended. The evolution of the anti-dumping provision has resulted in the facilitation of both dumping and injury determinations and, thus, the imposition of anti-dumping duties. The main changes concerning the determination of dumping and injury are presented as follows.

A Determination of Dumping

A definition of dumping was introduced (at Havana) to clarify that it exists when the export price is lower than the 'normal value' (first sentence of paragraph 1).[924] Since

917. With respect to the determination of the margin of dumping, inserting *'is less by more than five per cent'* was proposed. The role of the Organization in evaluating the injury or authorizing the measure was suggested by some delegations. The Preparatory Committee considered the incorporation of a new paragraph to permit not to impose anti-dumping duties in a commodity agreement. UN document E/PC/T/34, 5 March 1947, p. 13.
918. UN document E/PC/CII/54, 16 November 1946, p. 3.
919. Complaints against Japanese practices gave rise to discussions on other forms of dumping other than price dumping. However, the US clarified that US Suggested Charter Article 11 only permitted measures to counteract price dumping and *'would obligate members not to impose anti-dumping duties with respect to the other three types'*. Belgium claimed that there was a *'tendency to describe any unfair practice as dumping'*. UN documents E/PC/T/C.II/48, 11 November 1946, p. 1; E/PC/CII/54, 16 November 1946, pp. 1-3; E/PC/T/C.6/55, 5 February 1947, p. 22; E/PC/T/34, 5 March 1947, p. 13.
920. UNTS, Vol. 55, pp. 187-316 at 216, 296.
921. This paragraph was absent in both the ITO Charter and the consolidated version of the GATT after the GATT Review Session of 1954-1955.
922. GATT/CP.2/22/Rev.1, 30 August 1948, p. 1, para. 12.
923. UNTS, Vol. 55, pp. 187-316 at 212-217.
924. Pending the ratification of the ITO Charter, the Working Party on the Modification of the GATT recommended the replacement, *'mutatis mutandis'*, of GATT Article VI by the corresponding

then, the benchmark price in the market of the exporting country has been termed normal value. The methodologies to determine dumping have evolved in a way that the normal value can be adjusted upwards and the export price downwards, so that the margin of dumping increases. Accordingly, dumping is deemed to exist where it would otherwise be absent.

1 Normal Value

The normal value depends on the selected terms of sale and the product's stage in the supply chain. The normal value determined at the consumption level will be higher than at the (retail/wholesale) buyers' level. As the normal value increases, the existence and margin of dumping increase as well, provided the export price is maintained. Under the original anti-dumping provision in Article 11 of the US Suggested Charter, the export price was compared to the price of '*the like or similar product charged to buyers in the domestic market of the exporting country*'. However, under GATT Article VI, the export price is compared to the price, '*in the ordinary course of trade*',[925] for the like (no similar) product when destined for consumption in the exporting country (paragraph 1(a), which was introduced at Geneva).

GATT Article VI provides for two alternative methods to determine the normal value. Initially, the alternative methods were ranked. In the absence of information to use the first alternative method, i.e., '*the highest comparable price* (...) *for export to any third country*', the use of the second alternative method was permitted, i.e., '*the cost of production* (...) *in the country of origin*'. After Geneva, both alternative methods are equally available (non-ranked options) to be selected by the investigating authorities of the importing country. Consequently, in the absence of the domestic price, determining the normal value as the cost of production is directly available. Remarkably, this method includes (since New York) the addition of selling cost and profit. Therefore, in the absence of a domestic price, the normal value can be constructed, which greatly increases the range of values available to investigating authorities.

The possibility to disregard domestic prices to determine the normal value was also introduced in cases where the country of origin has a '*complete or substantially complete*' monopoly of its trade and all domestic prices are fixed by the State (Note 2 *Ad* paragraph 1, incorporated at the GATT Review Session of 1954-1955). In such cases, investigating authorities are permitted to consider that a '*strict comparison with domestic prices*' is not appropriate,[926] '*which then and now continues to make no sense in the context of a non-market economy*'.[927] The options to construct the normal value by disregarding domestic prices were broadened by this provision.

provision of the Charter (i.e., Article 34) since it contained '*a useful indication of the principle governing the operation of that Article and constitute*[*d*] *a clearer formulation of the rules laid down in that Article*'. GATT document CP.2/22/Rev.1, 30 August 1948, pp. 1 (para. 4), 11-13. UN document E.CONF.2/78, 24 March 1948, p. 27 (Article 34).

925. UNTS, Vol. 55, pp. 187-316 at 212.
926. Basis of ADA Article 2.2 and Section 15 of the Protocol of Accession of China to the WTO.
927. G.N. Horlick, Jackson as a Resource for Scholars and Others, *Journal of International Economic Law*, Vol. 19, 2016, pp. 401-402 at 401 https://doi.org/10.1093/jiel/jgw040.

Through the multilateral negotiations of GATT Article VI, the anti-dumping provision evolved in a manner that the determination of the normal value could be adjusted upwards, and thus facilitating the existence of (a higher) dumping. Moreover, this was accompanied by the incorporation of circumstances in which the export price may be disregarded.

2 *Export Price*

Converse to the normal value, a decrease in the export price may also facilitate a determination of dumping. Adjustments of the relevant export price may also facilitate a determination of dumping. Compared with Article 11 of the US Suggested Charter, GATT Article VI includes two scenarios that may be considered dumping due to the selection of a lower export price. One is the devaluation of the currency in the exporting country (i.e., '*exchange dumping*'). In this case, dumping can be determined where '*multiple currency practices*' (governmental practices) result in a partial depreciation of the exporting country's currency (Note 2 *Ad* paragraphs 2 and 3, introduced at Geneva).[928] In this case, even if there is no price discrimination between the export price and the normal value, dumping is found due to an exchange value. The other may occur when the exporter and importer are related ('*associated*'). In both cases, the real export price can be disregarded to construct a lower export price, and thus facilitating the determination of dumping.

In the second scenario, GATT Article VI considers 'dumping' a situation in which the exporter and importer are associated, and the importer sells the product (in the destination country) at a lower price than, on the one hand, the price in the exporting country (domestic price) and, on the other hand, the price invoiced by the associated exporter (Note 1 *Ad* paragraph 1, incorporated at Geneva).[929] In such '*hidden dumping by associated houses*', the export price will be the price at which the importer resells the product, after deducting tariffs and supply chain costs as well as a reasonable profit, i.e., disregarding the price invoiced by the exporter (added at Havana to Note 1 *Ad* paragraph 1).[930]

In summary, multilateral negotiations of GATT Article VI have facilitated the determination of dumping by incorporating methods that permit selecting (or disregarding) the prices that will be considered in the price comparison, i.e., the normal value and the export price. On the one hand, this provides more flexibility to disregard prices in the exporting country to determine a higher normal value. On the other hand, it provides for situations in which dumping is found without real price discrimination between the normal value and the export price, by permitting to disregard the real export price and adjusting it to a lower export price. This results in an increase in the margin of dumping, and thus, in the anti-dumping duties. Moreover, under Note 1 *Ad* to paragraph 2, GATT Contracting Parties introduced (at Havana) the possibility to impose, '*in any case of suspected dumping*', anti-dumping duties before a final

928. UNTS, Vol. 55, pp. 187-316 at 296.
929. *Ibid.*
930. UN document E.CONF.2/78, 24 March 1948, p. 111.

determination, through the collection of bond or cash deposits for the payment of anti-dumping duties.[931]

3 *Disputes on the Determination of Dumping under GATT Article VI*

GATT disputes illustrate how, from the beginning of the history of the application of GATT Article VI, the normal value was constructed when determining dumping. *Sweden – AD Duties* (1955) and *Canada – Potatoes* (1962) are the sole two GATT dispute settlement reports in which GATT Article VI was invoked before the 1979 AD Code entered into force, i.e., from 1948 to 1980. In both cases, the normal value was constructed (hence, prices in the exporting country were disregarded) to find 'dumping'.

In the *Sweden – AD Duties* case, Sweden fixed a minimum export price, ignoring prices in Italy. Swedish customs authorities were exempted from demonstrating the existence of dumping '*or even to establish a prima facie case of dumping*'; hence, the burden of proof was reversed.[932] In the *Canada – Potatoes* dispute, Canada used an averaging mechanism to construct the normal value and disregarded prices in the US.[933] Consequently, dumping was found where there was no price discrimination between the export price and the normal value, i.e., in the absence of dumping.

B Determination of Injury

In order to ensure that dumping can only be condemned if it causes injury to a domestic industry or retards its establishment, the injury requirement, already established under paragraph 6 of GATT Article VI, was reiterated under the first paragraph of GATT Article VI, where the definition of dumping was also included at Havana. Nevertheless, GATT Article VI provides for exceptions to the injury requirement that were absent under Article 11 of the US Suggested Charter.

More specifically, its current paragraph 7 (incorporated at Geneva) consists of a presumption of non-determination of material injury in cases where dumping is the result of a '*stabilization of domestic prices or of the return to domestic producers of a primary commodity*'. In such cases, material injury is presumed not to exist if countries substantially interested agree, by consultation, on the application of one of the following circumstances: (a) the commodity has been exported at higher prices than sold in the domestic market, or (b) the operation of the system does not result in the 'unduly' stimulation of exports or seriously prejudice other countries (e.g., cause material injury).

More importantly, under paragraph 6(b), GATT Contracting Parties introduced (also at Geneva) an exception to the injury requirement in the importing country in

931. *Ibid.*, p. 112 (Annex P, Interpretative Note *Ad* Article 34).
932. *Swedish Anti-dumping Duties* (GD/23). GATT documents L/328, 23 February 1955, paras. 2, 15.
933. *Exports of Potatoes to Canada* (GD/67). Complainant: US. GATT document L/1927, 16 November 1962, para. 3.

cases where material injury (or threat thereof) has been caused to the industry of a third country that '*exported the product to importing contracting party*'.[934] In such cases, CONTRACTING PARTIES may waive the injury requirement to permit the imposition of anti-dumping duties.[935] Since this provision requires consensus, it is unlikely that a member would accept the imposition of anti-dumping duties on its products.[936]

These exceptions to the injury requirement were introduced to facilitate the imposition of anti-dumping duties. Therefore, multilateral negotiations of GATT Article VI tilted the anti-dumping provision towards protectionist interests through the facilitation of dumping and injury determinations, and thus of the imposition of anti-dumping duties. This became a tendency reinforced by GATT Anti-dumping Codes and the WTO Anti-dumping Agreement, which have legitimized protectionist practices by incorporating them into the legal framework of the international trading system.

IV GATT ANTI-DUMPING CODES AND WTO ANTI-DUMPING AGREEMENT

A Determination of Dumping

1 Determination of Dumping under the Anti-dumping Codes

The provision on the determination of dumping under Article 2 of the 1967 Code (maintained in the 1979 AD Code) introduced the requirement of establishing '*a fair comparison*' between the export price and the normal value. It established that both prices shall be '*compared at the same level of trade, normally at the ex-factory level*'.[937] Nevertheless, it increased the options to construct the normal value and the export price.

a Construction of Normal Value

Along with the situation established under GATT Article VI.1(b), i.e., in the absence of the domestic price, the construction of the normal value has also been allowed, since the 1967 AD Code, in cases where a proper comparison is not permitted due to the existence of a '*particular market situation*' in the exporting country.[938] This provision introduced a limit on the added profit to be the 'profit normally realized' in the country of origin. Nonetheless, it permitted adding more costs (administrative and other, not

934. UNTS, Vol. 55, pp. 187-316 at 214.
935. The requirement of been granted a waiver by the CONTRACTING PARTIES prior to the imposition of the duties was maintained under Article 12 of the 1967 and 1979 AD Codes, and it is currently established under ADA Article 14, which entrusts the WTO Council for Trade in Goods with the decision of granting the waiver.
936. Under the ITO Charter, 'the Organization' was entrusted to grant the waiver.
937. 1967 Code Article 2.f. and 1979 Code Article 2.6.
938. 1967 AD Code Article 2.d and 1979 AD Code Article 2.4.

only selling costs), which would result in a higher normal value and margin of dumping.[939]

Due to the absence of a definition of '*particular market situation*' in both AD Codes and the ADA, its interpretation has been left to the discretion of importing countries. The incorporation of this new provision under Article 2(d) of the 1967 AD Code facilitated the construction of the normal value, hence, the determination of dumping. The provision shifted the determination of the normal value '*from a general legal concept that was presumed to be universal to a specific, localised administrative task*', and it would be (one of the) basis of the third-country methodology used to determine the normal value.[940]

Furthermore, another possibility to construct the normal value was included, under the 1979 AD Code, in cases of sales below costs. In the 1970s,[941] the US innovated the practice of finding dumping when sales were below costs,[942] even when there was no price difference between export price and normal value, i.e., no dumping. During the Tokyo Round, this practice was legitimized through '*an informal agreement among the four big users (Australia, Canada, EC, US)*'[943] and incorporated into the 1979 AD Code,[944] by broadening the interpretation of '*when there are no sales of the like product in the ordinary course of trade in the domestic market of the exporting country*'.[945]

939. At first glance, the construction of the normal value in a '*particular market situation*' seems to mirror the Interpretative Note 2 *Ad* paragraph 1 of GATT Article VI (introduced at the GATT Review Session of 1954-1955), which refers to cases in which the exporting country has a monopoly of its trade and where all domestic prices are fixed by the State. Nevertheless, unlike the Note, the provision on the particular market situation does not require the mentioned conditions (namely, monopoly and fixed prices). Furthermore, an explicit reference to this note is established under the last paragraph of Article 2 of both Codes and the ADA, which provides that Article 2 '*is without prejudice to the second Supplementary Provision to paragraph 1 of Article VI in Annex I of the General Agreement*'.
940. F. Snyder, The Origins of the Nonmarket Economy: Ideas, Pluralism and Power in EC Anti-dumping Law about China, *European Law Journal*, Vol. 7, No. 4, 2001, pp. 369-424 at 388, 389 https://doi.org/10.1111/1468-0386.00135.
941. GATT document COM.AD/W/51, 29 December 1975, pp. 7-8.
942. In 1974, the US included *a 'below-cost criterion'*, requiring the recovery of full cost to foreign products while the US anti-trust laws only required the recovery of variable costs to the US products, '*a significant difference for capital-intensive industries such as steel, chemicals, and electronics*'. G.N. Horlick, Proposals for Reform of the GATT Antidumping Code, *Brooklyn Journal of International Law*, Vol. 18, No. 1, 1992, pp. 181-188 at 184.
943. G.N. Horlick, How Did Antidumping Get So Bad? in G.N. Horlick (ed.), *World Trade Organization and International Trade Law. Antidumping, Subsidies and Trade Agreements*, 2014, pp. 3-10 at 7.
944. '*The general practice is to regard all sales at a loss not in the ordinary course of trade and to disregard them in making price comparisons if they are substantial in number, occur over an extended period of time and are at prices which would not permit the recovery of all costs within a reasonable period of time. If the remaining sales provide an adequate basis for comparison, then only these sales (at or above cost) are used to determine normal value. If they do not, a constructed value may be used.*' GATT document COM. AD/W/83, 17 November 1978, p. 8.
945. 1967 AD Code Article 2.d and 1979 AD Code Article 2.4.

b Construction of Export Price

Both AD Codes permitted the construction of the export price in cases where there is no export price or when the investigating authorities consider it unreliable due to the association or an arrangement between the exporter and the importer or a third party. In these cases where the export price was constructed, the Codes required that allowance should be made for '*costs, including duties and taxes, incurred between importation and resale*'. The situation of '*hidden dumping by associated houses*' (introduced under Note 1 *Ad* paragraph 1, at Geneva) was elaborated by requiring that the construction of the export price shall be based on the first resale to an independent buyer. Nevertheless, in cases where the product was not resold to an independent buyer or not in the condition as imported, the investigating authorities were granted the discretion to determine the '*reasonable basis*' whereby the export price would be constructed.[946]

Concisely, during the Kennedy and Tokyo Rounds, the provisions on dumping determination under the 1967 and 1979 Anti-dumping Codes were again tilted towards protectionist interests by widening the possibilities for investigating authorities to construct both the normal value and export price, thus permitting to determine a higher margin of dumping and, as a result, to impose higher anti-dumping duties. Hence, anti-dumping began to be the protectionist device of preference, whereas tariffs were reduced at these multilateral rounds of trade negotiations, especially after the Tokyo Round.[947]

The highly technical character of anti-dumping laws was used by their administrators (particularly, the US, the EEC, Canada and Australia)[948] to implement unilateral changes, which resulted in an increased likelihood of imposition of anti-dumping duties.[949] Nevertheless, anti-dumping duties were not always imposed, since the 1967 AD Code (under Article 8) introduced the possibility of reaching price undertakings, whereby exporters agree to a (minimum) price and/or export quota as a way of avoiding anti-dumping duties. Price undertakings have been used since then, particularly by the EU,[950] as the preferred system to protect its '*oligopolistic*' industries (including steel and chemical) from import competitors due to their cartelizing effect on the market.[951]

946. 1967 AD Code Article 2.e, 2.f, and 1979 AD Code Article 2.5, 2.6.
947. G.N. Horlick, Proposals for Reform of the GATT Antidumping Code, *Brooklyn Journal of International Law*, Vol. 18, No. 1, 1992, pp. 181-188 at 184.
948. J.H. Jackson, W. Davey, *Legal Problems of International Economic Relations, Cases, Materials and Text*, 2nd ed., 1986, p. 663. GATT document BISD, 31st Supp., 1985, pp. 289, 290.
949. E.A. Vermulst, The Antidumping Systems of Australia, Canada, the EEC and the USA: Have Antidumping Laws Become a Problem in International Trade?, in J.H. Jackson, E.A. Vermulst (eds), *Antidumping Law and Practice: A Comparative Study*, 1989, pp. 425-466.
950. From 1980 to 1984, the EC initiated 120 anti-dumping actions, of which 63 terminated in price undertakings. J.H. Jackson, W. Davey, *Legal Problems of International Economic Relations, Cases, Materials and Text*, 2nd ed., 1986, p. 663. GATT documents BISD, 30th Supp., 1984, pp. 70, 71; BISD, 31st Supp., 1985, pp. 289, 290.
951. R. Denton, Overview of the Discussion During the Comparative Antidumping Law Mini-Conference, November 6 and 7, 1988, in J.H. Jackson, E.A. Vermulst (eds), *Antidumping Law and Practice: A Comparative Study*, 1989, pp. 467-476 at 469-470.

c GATT Disputes on the Determination of Dumping under the AD Code 1979

The determination of dumping under the 1979 AD Code Article 2 was interpreted in two GATT dispute settlement reports.[952] In the *US – Norwegian Salmon AD* case,[953] the normal value was constructed by using a sample, whereby the '*highest cost of production figure*' was imputed to one of the exporters.[954] Although the 1979 AD Code was silent on the use of sampling, the US measure was found inconsistent with 1979 AD Code Article 2.4 for failing to ensure the representativeness of the samples. As a result of this case's finding, current ADA Articles 5.4 and 6.10 require samples to be '*statistically valid*' or cover the highest volume of exports that can reasonably be investigated. Furthermore, the US failed to effect a '*fair comparison*', under 1979 AD Code Article 2.6. since export prices varied by weight category while the constructed normal value did not.[955]

The Panel in the *EC – Audio Cassettes* dispute[956] found that the EEC acted inconsistently with the '*fair comparison*' requirement under 1979 AD Code Article 2.6. since all advertising expenses related to sales in the EEC were deducted to construct an export price, while selling, marketing and promotion expenses were included to construct the normal value, resulting in an increased margin of dumping.[957]

2 Determination of Dumping under the Anti-dumping Agreement

Most of the paragraphs under the 1979 AD Code Article 2 have been maintained under ADA Article 2.[958] Nevertheless, ADA Article 2 introduced detailed rules for constructing the normal value and for establishing a fair comparison.[959] ADA Article 2 has introduced conditions under which domestic prices '*may be treated as not being in the ordinary course of trade*', thereby disregarding them to determine the normal value. It also provides methods to determine the normal value while establishing more specific rules on how to ensure a fair comparison. Although these rules provide for specific proceedings to be followed by investigating authorities, they facilitate the determination of dumping. ADA Article 2.2 has increased the possibility of constructing the normal value by incorporating the case of '*low volume of sales*' in the exporting country. ADA Article 2.4 provides for exceptions to establish a fair comparison, by

952. While the 1967 AD Code was in place, no disputes on anti-dumping were brought to the GATT.
953. *United States – Imposition of Anti-dumping Duties on Imports of Fresh and Chilled Atlantic Salmon from Norway* (GD/251). Complainant: Norway. GATT document ADP/87, 30 November 1992.
954. When enjoying its right to choose 'the facts available', pursuant to 1979 AD Code Article 6.8.
955. GATT document ADP/87, 30 November 1992, paras 426, 450, 471, 472.
956. *EEC – Imposition of Anti-dumping Duties on Imports of Audio Cassettes from Japan* (GD/253). Complainant: Japan. GATT documents ADP/136, 28 April 1995, ADP/136/Corr.1, 8 June 1995.
957. GATT documents ADP/136, 28 April 1995, paras 384, 465.
958. ADA 2.1 mirrors 1979 AD Code 2.1; ADA 2.6 corresponds to 1979 AD Code 2.2; ADA 2.5 is the equivalent of 1979 AD Code 2.3; ADA 2.3 is the former 1979 AD Code 2.5; and ADA 2.7 is equal to 1979 AD Code 2.7.
959. ADA Article 2.2 (former 1979 AD Code 2.4) and 2.4 (former 1979 AD Code 2.6).

permitting to compare a weighted-average normal value with individual export transactions.

a Construction of Normal Value (ADA 2.2) and Third-Country Methodology

ADA Article 2.2 introduces a third possibility to construct the normal value. Along with the other two situations in which it is permitted to construct the normal value, i.e., in the absence of sales in the exporting country, and when a particular market situation exists in the exporting country, this provision permits the construction of the normal value or the use of a comparable price of the like product when exported to '*an appropriate third country*'[960] in cases where there is a '*low volume of the sales in the domestic market of the exporting country*'.

As a general rule, ADA Article 2.2 requires a calculation of the costs based on records by the investigated exporters or producers (ADA Article 2.2.1.1), as well as a determination of the administrative, selling and general costs and profits based on '*actual data*' regarding the '*production and sales in the ordinary course of trade*' of the like products by the investigated exporters or producers (ADA Article 2.2.2).[961] Nonetheless, it permits disregarding actual data of sales in the exporting country (by considering them '*as not being in the ordinary course of trade*'), in cases where prices are '*below per unit (fixed and variable) costs of production, plus administrative, selling and general costs*'. Investigating authorities are required to determine that (actual) sales are '*made within an extended period of time in substantial quantities and are at prices which do not provide for the recovery of all costs within a reasonable period of time*' (ADA Article 2.2.1).

In cases in which actual sales prices are disregarded, three alternative methods[962] are provided under ADA Article 2.2.2 to determine the amounts of overhead costs and profits:[963] (1) the actual amounts of production and sales of the same general category of products in the country of origin by the exporter or producer in question; (2) the weighted average of the actual amounts of production and sales of the like product by

960. This requirement of using a comparable price when exported to '*an appropriate third country*' replaces '*any third country which may be the highest such export price*' under the 1979 AD Code Article 2.4.

961. The Appellate Body in *Ukraine – Ammonium Nitrate (Russia)* case stated that investigating authorities must ensure that the collected information is used to arrive at the cost of production in the exporting country. *Ukraine – Anti-dumping Measures on Ammonium Nitrate* (DS493). WTO document DS493/AB/R, 12 September 2019, para. 6.83.

962. The Panel in the *US – OCTG (Korea)* case established that Members may decide the criteria to select among the alternative methods. *United States – Anti-dumping Measures on Certain Oil Country Tubular Goods from Korea* (DS488). WTO document DS488/R, 14 November 2017, para. 7.20.

963. The Panel and the Appellate Body in *EC – Tube or Pipe Fittings* case interpreted this provision as allowing the exclusion of data from production and sales only when they '*were not made in the ordinary course of trade*'. *European Union (formerly EC) – Anti-dumping Duties on Malleable Cast Iron Tube or Pipe Fittings from Brazil* (DS219). WTO document DS219/AB/R, 22 July 2003, paras 89, 102.

other exporters or producers subject to investigation in the country of origin;[964] (3) '*any other reasonable method*', provided that the profit does not exceed the profit for products of the same general category when sold by other exporters or producers in the country of origin.

In summary, the exceptions whereby the normal value can be constructed have been increased under ADA Article 2.2. Furthermore, when constructing the normal value, actual costs of production, selling, administrative, etc., in the exporting country can also be disregarded for not to be considered '*in the ordinary course of trade*'. Alternative methods are permitted to construct a higher normal value, which will result in a higher margin of dumping and ultimately higher anti-dumping duties.

Members' increasing recourse to the construction of the normal value has been highlighted as the most serious substantive issue concerning the determination of dumping. The construction of normal value by investigating authorities tends to be '*too artificial and discretionary*'.[965] Particularly relevant is the construction of the normal value of imports from the so-called *non-market economies.*[966]

The first case in which dumping was found on imports from a 'non-market economy' was Bicycles from Czechoslovakia in 1960.[967] The US 'determined that the proper fair value comparison is between purchase price and either home market price or constructed value'.[968] Since this case, prices in the exporting country have been disregarded, i.e., the third-country methodology, when importing from countries referred to as 'non-market economies' (as well as non-GATT Contracting Parties/WTO Members), based on Note 2 *Ad* GATT Article VI.1, whereby importing countries are permitted not to establish 'a strict comparison with domestic prices' in the exporting

964. The Appellate Body in *EC – Bed Linen* case clarified the alternative calculation method that '*can only be used if data relating to more than one other exporter or producer is available*' and that a Member may not '*exclude sales by other exporters or producers that are not made in the ordinary course of trade*'. *European Communities – Anti-dumping Duties on Imports of Cotton-type Bed Linen from India* (DS141).WTO document DS141/AB/R, 1 March 2001, paras 76, 77, 82, 84.
965. Following ten years of the enactment of the ADA, a project with ten trade experts from ten different anti-dumping-using countries was undertaken by G.N. Horlick and E.A. Vermulst to underlie ten problems with anti-dumping, particularly those arising from national practice. According to trade experts in China, the EU, South Africa, Thailand and the US, the construction of the normal value is among the ten major problems with anti-dumping and the most relevant substantive issue concerning the determination of dumping. G.N. Horlick, E.A. Vermulst, The 10 Major Problems with the Anti-dumping Instrument: An Attempt at Synthesis, *Journal of World Trade*, Vol. 39, No. 1, 2005, pp. 67-73 at 70 https://doi.org/10.54648/trad2005007.
966. For a detailed analysis of the concept of a non-market economy, *see* F. Snyder, The Origins of the Nonmarket Economy: Ideas, Pluralism and Power in EC Anti-dumping Law about China, *European Law Journal*, Vol. 7, No. 4, 2001, pp. 369-424 https://doi.org/10.1111/1468-0386.00135.
967. Bicycles from Czechoslovakia. Determination of Sales at Less Than Fair Value. US Federal Register, Vol. 25, 14 July 1960, p. 6657. G.N. Horlick, S.S. Shuman, Nonmarket Economy Trade and US Antidumping/Countervailing Duty Laws, *International Lawyer*, Vol. 18, No. 4, 1984, pp. 807-840 at 808. F. Snyder, The Origins of the Nonmarket Economy: Ideas, Pluralism and Power in EC Anti-dumping Law about China, *European Law Journal*, Vol. 7, No. 4, 2001, pp. 369-424 at 384 https://doi.org/10.1111/1468-0386.00135.
968. '*In computing purchase price, deductions we made for ocean fright, insurance, and inland freight.*' US Federal Register, Vol. 25, 14 July 1960, p. 6657.

country when it has a monopoly of its trade and all prices are fixed by the State. This provision 'took an "administrative turn" that shifted the frame of reference for dealing with state-trading country dumping'.[969]

This possibility has been established under some of the Protocols of Accession to the GATT/WTO of some 'non-market economies'. The first case was the Protocol of Poland[970] (followed by Romania[971] and Hungary)[972,973] whereby importing countries were permitted to either use prices that prevailed in the Polish market or construct the normal value with prices from '*another country*', using a methodology '*appropriate and not unreasonable*'.[974] The Protocols of Poland and Romania explicitly provided that the Note 2 *Ad* GATT Article VI.1 applied, i.e., that a monopoly of its trade existed and all domestic prices were fixed by the State.[975] Henceforth, this reference to the Note 2 *Ad* GATT Article VI.1 has been absent in the rest of the Protocols of Accession.[976]

After the Uruguay Round, some Protocols of Accession to the WTO have included a specific provision that permits, under certain circumstances, the use of the third-country methodology. Since these Protocols constitute '*an integral part of the WTO Agreement*',[977] they have been the basis for the use of the third-country methodology.[978] This is the case of the Accession Protocols of China,[979] Vietnam,[980] and

969. F. Snyder, The Origins of the Nonmarket Economy: Ideas, Pluralism and Power in EC Anti-dumping Law about China, *European Law Journal*, Vol. 7, No. 4, 2001, pp. 369-424 at 388 https://doi.org/10.1111/1468-0386.00135.
970. Poland joined the GATT on 18 October 1967. GATT document L/2851, 19 September 1967.
971. GATT document L/3557, 5 August 1971, para. 13. Romania became a GATT Contracting Party on 14 November 1971. GATT document L/3601, 21 October 1971.
972. GATT document L/3889 20 July 1973, para. 18. Hungary became a GATT Contracting Party on 9 September 1973. GATT document L/3908, 14 August 1973.
973. G.N. Horlick, S.S. Shuman, Nonmarket Economy Trade and US Antidumping/Countervailing Duty Laws, *International Lawyer*, Vol. 18, No. 4, 1984, pp. 807-840 at 838. F. Snyder, The Origins of the Nonmarket Economy: Ideas, Pluralism and Power in EC Anti-dumping Law about China, *European Law Journal*, Vol. 7, No. 4, 2001, pp. 369-424 at 393-394 https://doi.org/10.1111/1468-0386.00135.
974. Furthermore, the Protocol of Poland established that '*the foreign trade of Poland was conducted mainly by State enterprises and that the Foreign Trade Plan rather than the customs tariff was the effective instrument of Poland's commercial policy*'. GATT document L/2806, 23 June 1967, paras 7, 13.
975. The Working Party, as an independent and multilateral body, had established that this situation applied. Nevertheless, trade experts doubted that Poland [and Romania] met these tests. G.N. Horlick, S.S. Shuman, Nonmarket Economy Trade and US Antidumping/Countervailing Duty Laws, *International Lawyer*, Vol. 18, No. 4, 1984, pp. 807-840 at 834. F. Snyder, The Origins of the Nonmarket Economy: Ideas, Pluralism and Power in EC Anti-dumping Law about China, *European Law Journal*, Vol. 7, No. 4, 2001, pp. 369-424 at 392 https://doi.org/10.1111/1468-0386.00135.
976. Interestingly, a few days after the adoption of the Protocol of Accession, on 30 June 1967, the Kennedy Round concluded with the enactment of the 1967 AD Code, whose Article 2(d) incorporated the possibility to construct the normal value in case of a particular market situation in the exporting country.
977. Second paragraph of each of these Protocol. WTO documents L/432, 23 November 2001; L/662, 15 November 2006; L/872, 11 December 2012.
978. Nonetheless, importing WTO Members, such as the US and the EU, have also applied the third-country methodology to other WTO Members without specific provisions under their Protocols of Accession (and to non-WTO members). In these cases, the only available legal basis for using the third-country methodology is the Interpretative Note 2 *Ad* to GATT Article VI.1. Arguably, the conditions under it do not apply in most of these countries, treated as

Tajikistan,[981] whereby the use of the third-country methodology has been conditioned on the 'non-market economy' status of these countries. Nevertheless, these Protocols lack a definition of market economy and leave the establishment of *market economy criteria'* to importing WTO Members, hence, increasing their margin of discretion. The use of the third-country methodology was permitted in cases where producers could not demonstrate that market economy conditions prevailed in their industries. This provision constituted a shift in the burden of proof, i.e., a *probation diabolica*, since it is assumed that non-market conditions prevail in the exporting country unless otherwise proven. This provision was deemed to expire after twelve years in the case of Vietnam, and fifteen years for China and Tajikistan,[982] after their dates of accession to the WTO.

Several WTO Members have continued using the third-country methodology on import from China and Vietnam, albeit the provisions under their protocols expired in 2016 and 2018, respectively. Some WTO Members have incorporated new provisions in their trade remedy laws to justify the construction of the normal value, on the basis of, *inter alia*, labour and environmental standards, or market distortions.[983] Nevertheless, the burden of proof shall now rest with the importing Member, which must demonstrate that in the exporting country exists either a particular market situation (ADA Article 2.2), or a monopoly of its trade and prices fixed by the State (Note 2 *Ad* GATT Article VI.1).

b *Fair Comparison (ADA 2.4) and Zeroing*

The '*fair comparison*' requirement to determine the margin of dumping has been further developed under ADA Article 2.4, which replaces the term '*domestic price in the exporting country*' with '*normal value*'. This provision mandates the investigating authorities to indicate to the parties involved the necessary information required to ensure a fair comparison (between the export price and normal value), as well as not imposing an '*unreasonable burden of proof*' on them. Moreover, it provides for the use

'non-market economies'. As a result, the methodology of the third country has been applied to all so considered 'non-market economies', irrespective of whether there was a specific provision under their Protocols of Accession or not. Countries treated as 'non-market economies' by the US are Armenia, Azerbaijan, Belarus, Georgia, the Kyrgyz Republic, Moldova, the Russian Federation, Turkmenistan and Uzbekistan. USITA, Non-Market Economy Countries List, viewed at: https://www.trade.gov/nme-countries-list. Countries treated as 'non-market economies' by the EU are Albania, Armenia, Azerbaijan, Belarus, Georgia, the Kyrgyz Republic, Moldova, Mongolia, North Korea, Turkmenistan and Uzbekistan. OJEU, L.176, 30.6.2016, p. 26.

979. Section 15 of the Protocol of Accession of China. WTO document L/432, 23 November 2001.
980. Paragraph 255 of the Report of the Working Party on the Accession of Viet Nam is part of its Accession Protocol. WTO documents L/662, 15 November 2006; ACC/VNM/48, 27 October 2006.
981. Paragraph 164 of the Working Party's Report on the Accession of Tajikistan constitutes an integral part of its Protocol of Accession. WTO documents L/872, 11 December 2012; ACC/TJK/30, 6 November 2012.
982. In the case of Tajikistan, this provision will expire in 2028.
983. *See* the Introduction to Part I and Ch. 12.

of equivalent levels of trade in cases where the export price is constructed (pursuant to ADA Article 2.3). Two new paragraphs have been added concerning the proceedings to establish a fair comparison.

The first new paragraph (ADA Article 2.4.1) concerns cases where a conversion of currencies is required to establish a '*fair comparison*', providing for the use of '*the rate of exchange on the date of sale*', and establishing a period (at least sixty days) that exporters shall be granted during the investigation to adjust their export prices to '*sustained movements in exchange rates*'.

More importantly, the second new paragraph (ADA Article 2.4.2) provides, subject to the '*fair comparison*' requirement, a determination of dumping margins (i.e., exceed of normal value over export price) based on two alternative methodologies, or under certain circumstances, a third exceptional methodology. This has been known as the '*the chapeau of ADA 2.4.2*'. The two methodologies consist of either comparing a weighted average of the normal value of all sales to a weighted average of the export price of all sales (W-W),[984] or comparing the normal value to the export price of individual sales, i.e., a transaction-to-transaction basis (T-T). The exceptional methodology permits comparing a weighted-average normal value to individual export transactions (W-T), in cases where investigating authorities '*find a pattern of export prices which differ significantly among different purchasers, regions or time periods*', and provide an explanation as to why using the other two methodologies '*cannot be taken into account appropriately*'.

In theory, if ADA Article 2.4.2 is strictly interpreted, the margin of dumping obtained through the indistinctive (and 'fairly') use of any of the three methodologies would be identical, assuming the same amounts of normal values and export prices are compared when using each of the methodologies.[985] Nevertheless, in practice, the exceptional methodology, W-T, has permitted to determine dumping otherwise inexistent under the other two methodologies. When using this exceptional methodology, sales comparisons in which export prices exceeded normal values are not taken into account by artificially reducing the export prices used in the comparison, hence, increasing margins of dumping.

The exceptional methodology, W-T, was already used by some countries, even before the enactment of the 1967 AD Code. During the Uruguay Round, this practice '*was the impetus for the compromise language of Article 2.4.2*',[986] despite the fact that experts in the field (and private parties) recommended prohibiting '*the use of averaging*' and requiring a fair comparison (as ADA 2.4 establishes). Comparing weighted-average normal values to individual export transactions '*was so demonstrably tilted that it became an easy example of the tilts in the antidumping calculation*'. Consequently, before the Uruguay Round, '*no differentiation was made between averaging*

984. This method was used by Mexico. G.N. Horlick, How the GATT Became Protectionist: An Analysis of the Uruguay Round Draft Final Antidumping Code, *Journal of World Trade*, Vol. 27, No. 5, 1993, pp. 5-17 at 13 https://doi.org/10.54648/trad1993027.
985. As shown in Chart 2 in E.A. Vermulst, D. Ikenson, Zeroing under the WTO Anti-dumping Agreement: Where Do We Stand?, *Global Trade and Customs Journal*, Vol. 2, No. 6, 2007, pp. 231-242 at 232 https://doi.org/10.54648/gtcj2007029.
986. *Ibid.*, at 233, 235.

and zeroing – they were viewed as the same phenomenon'. Since the Uruguay Round, the three methodologies under ADA 2.4.2 have been considered to be different from zeroing.[987]

Zeroing consists of reducing to zero sales comparisons in which export prices exceed normal values, i.e., non-dumped sales comparisons. As an illustration, if the normal value is 100 and the export price is 50, dumping is 50; however, if the normal value is 50 and the export price is 100, dumping is –50. Through zeroing, –50 becomes 0. Therefore, when averaging sales, if non-dumped sales comparisons are reduced to zero, dumping is found where it would otherwise be absent, and the margin of dumping increases. In other words, when comparing normal values to export prices '*through the magic of zeroing*', otherwise non-existent dumping is determined.

Accordingly, if zeroing is combined when determining dumping through each of the three different methodologies under the '*chapeau of ADA Article 2.4.2*', results often vary.[988] Under the W-W, positive and negative dumping amounts are automatically offset, whereas this does not occur when combining zeroing with the exceptional methodology, W-T, which '*virtually always yields higher dumping margins*' than the former. Nevertheless, results under the W-T methodology will not always be higher than under the T-T methodology, since the latter '*is subject to greater discretion in determining which sales to compare and it can produce arbitrary results*'.[989]

GATT Contracting Parties used (simple) zeroing before the enactment of the ADA. After the Uruguay Round, some WTO Members began to use model zeroing, whereby non-dumped comparisons from different models of products were reduced to zero to find dumping among models (i.e., inter-model zeroing). Under model zeroing, the dumping found on a specific model of a product is extended to other models of the same product in which there is no dumping. In other words, dumping on one model of a product suffices to determine dumping on other models of the same product.

987. In the US, it was used even before the 1967 AD Code. '*The goal was not just to ban zeroing or all averaging but rather to ban all tilts. The danger of listing each individual tilt, such as zeroing, was that national authorities might find new ones*'. G.N. Horlick, A Personal History of Zeroing, *Global Trade and Customs Journal*, Vol. 4, No. 5, 2009, pp. 161-163 https://doi.org/10.54648/gtcj2009019.

988. As an illustration of how the same result would be found under each of the three methodologies (W-W, T-T and W-T), if there were four sales where the normal values are: 100, 50, 150 and 100; and the export prices are 50, 100, 100 and 150; the dumping found would be zero, i.e., absent. Under the W-W methodology, 100–100 = 0. On a T-T basis, the results would be 50, –50, 50 and –50, which results in no dumping. Under the exceptional methodology, W-T, comparing the average (100) with each export price of each transaction, would result in 50, 0, 0,–50, resulting in no dumping. Nevertheless, if zeroing were combined with each of the three methodologies, results would vary. Under the W-W, dumping would still be absent since normal values would offset export values. Under the T-T methodology, through zeroing, negative results would be excluded (50, –50, 50, –50), resulting in dumping of 100. Lastly, combining zeroing with the exceptional methodology (W-T) would result in comparing an average of the normal value (100) with each export price, and counting as 0 the negative result (50, 0, 0, –50), thus finding a dumping of 50.

989. E.A. Vermulst, D. Ikenson, Zeroing under the WTO Anti-dumping Agreement: Where Do We Stand?, *Global Trade and Customs Journal*, Vol. 2, No. 6, 2007, pp. 231-242 at 234 https://doi.org/10.54648/gtcj2007029.

Therefore, under model zeroing, the scope of the anti-dumping duty is broadened by determining dumping on non-dumped imports.[990]

The consistency of zeroing with the '*fair comparison*' requirement under ADA 2.4 has been challenged at the WTO. The first time that the use of 'zeroing' was found inconsistent with the '*fair comparison*' requirement was in the *EC – Bed Linen* case, following the EC application of model zeroing when using the W-T methodology. It was found that through zeroing, export prices were treated '*as if they were less than what they were*', which resulted in a higher margin of dumping. While some have interpreted this case as '*prohibiting zeroing altogether*', others like Vermulst consider that simple zeroing under the W-T methodology remained allowed if the conditions are fulfilled. Consequently, since this dispute, the EU has applied simple zeroing rather than model zeroing, but only exceptionally.[991] The WTO DSB case law has provided contrary interpretations regarding the US use of zeroing under the three different methodologies.[992] Indeed, it has constituted one of the reasons why the US blocked the nomination of the members of the WTO Appellate Body (in 2017).[993]

---

990. The margin of dumping is the percentage resulting from diving the amount of dumping by the total export sales. Under simple zeroing, non-dumped export sales are disregarded to determine the amount of dumping, but taken into account to calculate the margin of dumping. Under model zeroing, non-dumped export sales are not included when determining the amount of dumping or when calculating (the percentage of) the margin of dumping. The non-inclusion of the non-dumped export sales increases the margin of dumping (e.g., a margin of dumping of one-sixth under simple zeroing and one-third under model zeroing). *Ibid.*, at 233.
991. *European Union (formerly EC) – Anti-dumping Duties on Imports of Cotton-type Bed Linen from India* (DS141) WTO document DS141/AB/R, 1 March 2001, para. 55. E.A. Vermulst, The 10 Major Problems with the Anti-dumping Instrument in the European Community, *Journal of World Trade*, Vol. 39, No. 1, 2005, pp. 105-113 at 107-108 https://doi.org/10.54648/trad2005011.
992. The Appellate Body in *US – Corrosion-Resistant Steel Sunset Review* case found that zeroing not only inflates margins of dumping, but may also distort the '*very existence of dumping*' by turning a negative margin of dumping into a positive one. Confirming this finding, the Appellate Body in the *US – Softwood Lumber V* case concluded that zeroing is prohibited when using both the W-W and T-T methodologies, that applying zeroing to the T-T is inconsistent with both ADA 2.4 and 2.4.2, and that investigating authorities are required to aggregate all the results and not disregarding results where export prices are higher than normal values (non-dumped). The DSB in the *US – Zeroing (EC)* case considered that while '*zeroing is not an impermissible allowance or adjustment*' under ADA Article 2.4, applying zeroing to the W-W methodology '*is inconsistent, as such, with Article 2.4.2*'. The Appellate Body in the *US – Zeroing (Japan)* case found that zeroing was inconsistent with ADA Article 2.4.2 and that its application on a T-T basis '*would inflate the margin of dumping to an even greater extent*' than in the case zeroing is used on a W-W basis. Applying zeroing under the W-T was found inconsistent with ADA Article 2.4.2 by the Appellate Body in the *US – Washing Machine* case. In line with this interpretation, the Appellate Body in the *US – Anti-dumping Methodologies (China)* case concluded that combining methodologies is not permitted and that the application of the W-T methodology is only allowed to '*pattern transactions*'. The Panel gave a contrary interpretation in the *US – Differential Pricing Methodology*, allowing an investigating authority '*to use zeroing while applying the W-T methodology to the pattern transactions*'. The Panel considered that '*the raison d'être of the W-T methodology is to unmask targeted dumping*', and its '*inability (...) will render this methodology inutile*'. WTO documents DS244/AB/R 15 December 2003, para. 135; DS264/AB/R, 11 August 2004, paras 101, 108, 113; DS264/AB/RW 15 August 2006, paras 122, 124, 139, 140-142; DS294/AB/R 18 April 2006, para. 122, 159; DS294/AB/R 18 April 2006, para. 222; DS322/AB/R 9 January 2007, paras 123, 125; DS464/AB/R 7 September 2016, para. 6.10; DS471/AB/R 11 May 2017, para. 5.107; DS534/R 9 April 2019, paras 7.106, 7.107.
993. '*One way in which the Appellate Body has undermined the right of WTO Members to address injurious dumping is through the creation and expansion of a prohibition on the use of "zeroing"*'

B Determination of Injury

1 Determination of Injury under the Anti-dumping Codes

Compared to GATT Article VI, the AD Codes established proceedings concerning the injury determination. Nevertheless, provisions to determine injury in the 1967 and 1979 AD Codes differed in some respects. Most notably, 1967 AD Code Article 3 provided that dumped imports were '*demonstrably the principal cause*' of injury.[994] The valuation of injury required the examination (based on positive evidence) of all factors affecting the industry in order to weigh the injury attributable to the alleged dumped imports against all other factors (first three paragraphs of 1967 AD Code Article 3). This (high) standard to determine injury caused controversy, particularly due to the US decision to ignore it and adopt '*a new minimis standard, under which positive findings increased dramatically*'.[995]

Consequently, the first four paragraphs of the 1979 Code Article 3 facilitated the determination of injury,[996] merely requiring to demonstrate that dumped imports were '*through the effects of dumping, causing injury*' rather than being the '*principal cause*' of injury.[997] It also incorporated two criteria for the injury determination: (1) the volume of dumped imports and their effect on prices and (2) the impact on domestic producers. Importantly, the established procedures softened compliance with these criteria. First, the increase in imports was calculated in absolute or relative terms, concerning either production or consumption in the importing country. Second, the effect on prices included price undercutting, depression of prices, or prevention of price increases in the importing country. Third, the examination of all other factors that may have also caused injury was no longer required, but a mere non-attribution of that injury to the dumped imports.

The development of the provision on the determination of injury became a technical and sophisticated system, but it resulted in a low threshold of injury determination, as reflected in disputes brought to the GATT. As a factual matter, in

---

in determining whether and to what extent dumping has occurred. The Appellate Body's approach is deeply flawed, as such a prohibition has no basis in the text of the GATT 1994 or the Antidumping Agreement.' USTR, Report on the Appellate Body of the World Trade Organization, 2020, p. 96.

994. Under the 1967 and 1979 AD Codes, as well as the ADA, a footnote provides that 'injury' shall, '*unless otherwise specified, be interpreted as covering cause of material injury to a domestic industry, threat of material injury to a domestic industry or material retardation of the establishment of such an industry*'.

995. '*Between 1964 and 1967, only 28% of the Tariff Commission decisions found injury; from 1968 to 1970, injury was found in nearly 86% of the cases decided*', J.W. Evans, Subsidies and Countervailing Duties in the GATT, *Maryland Journal of International Law*, Vol. 3, No. 1, 1977, pp. 211-245 at 228, 229.

996. The first four paragraphs of 1979 AD Code Article 3 were practically identical to those under SCM Code Article 6.

997. It was considered the '*saving grace of the 1967 Code*'. G.N. Horlick, How Did Antidumping Get So Bad? in G.N. Horlick (ed.), *World Trade Organization and International Trade Law. Antidumping, Subsidies and Trade Agreements*, 2014, pp. 3-10 at 6.

most (all except one)[998] GATT dispute settlement reports in which 1979 AD Code Article 3 was interpreted, the injury determinations were found to be consistent with it, i.e., in the *US – Norwegian Salmon AD*,[999] *EC – Audio Cassettes*,[1000] and *EEC – Cotton Yarn*.[1001] Interestingly, since New Zealand had not signed the 1979 AD Code,[1002] the Panel in the *New Zealand – Finnish Transformers* case[1003] interpreted the injury determination provision under GATT Article VI.6. In this case, injury was found to be caused by other factors, and not by the alleged dumped imports of Finish transformers, which constituted an almost insignificant part of the increase in imports.[1004] It remains uncertain whether the injury determination by New Zealand would have been found consistent with the 1979 AD Code if it had been applicable, due to the fact that its Article 3 permitted the increase in imports to be relative to domestic production.[1005]

In practice, the main users of anti-dumping (the US, EU, Canada and Australia) ensured that no injury was caused to their domestic industries through a variety of procedures. The US and Canada followed a mechanical procedure to impose duties equal to the margin of dumping, whereas the EEC and Australia established the '*lesser duty rule*', by which the duty could be lower than the margin of dumping if it offset the injury. Australia determined the minimum level for export prices at the FOB level, thereby ensuring that no injury was caused. The EEC normally calculated '*injury margins, i.e., margins by which prices of the foreign producers should be raised to allow the Community producer to cover their cost of production and earn a "reasonable" profit*'.[1006]

998. The only GATT report in which the determination of injury was found inconsistently with the 1979 AD Code was in *Korea – Resins* case, in which the Panel considered that Korean authorities had not provided sufficient reasoning in the determinations of injury, acting inconsistently with 1979 AD Code Article 3 (paras 1-4 and 6). *Korea – Anti-dumping Duties on Imports of Polyacetal Resins from the United States* (GD/254). Complainant: US. GATT documents ADP/92, 2 April 1993, para. 300; ADP/92/Corr.1, 6 April 1993.
999. GATT document ADP/87, 30 November 1992, para. 580.
1000. *EEC – Imposition of Anti-dumping Duties on Imports of Audio Cassettes from Japan* (GD/253). Complainant: Japan. GATT documents ADP/136, 28 April 1995, ADP/136/Corr.1, 8 June 1995.
1001. *EEC – Anti-dumping Actions on Cotton Yarn Originating from Brazil* (GD/255). Complainant: Brazil. GATT document ADP/137, 4 July 1995.
1002. Since New Zealand was not a signatory of the 1979 Anti-dumping Code, the Panel based its considerations on GATT Article VI, paras 1, 2 and 6(a). GATT document L/5814, 19 June 1985, paras 3.9, 4.1.
1003. *New Zealand – Imports of Electrical Transformers from Finland* (GD/150). Complainant: Finland. GATT document L/5814, 19 June 1985.
1004. Injury was found to be caused by the '*lack of new orders, diminishing orders on hand in certain product categories, declining profitability, a large increase in imports and considerable uncertainty as to new orders*'. GATT document L/5814, 19 June 1985, paras 4.7, 4.9.
1005. For the first time (in the history of GATT jurisprudence), the Panel recommended reimbursing the previously collected duties. GATT document L/5814, 19 June 1985, para. 4.14.
1006. E.A. Vermulst, The Antidumping Systems of Australia, Canada, the EEC and the USA: Have Antidumping Laws Become a Problem in International Trade?, in J.H. Jackson, E.A. Vermulst (eds), *Antidumping Law and Practice: A Comparative Study*, 1989, pp. 425-466.

2 Determination of Injury under the Anti-dumping Agreement

ADA Article 3 maintained practically verbatim the first three paragraphs of 1979 AD Code Article 3.[1007] It introduced the requirement to demonstrate a '*causal relationship*' between the alleged dumping and the injury, '*based on an examination of all relevant evidence before the authorities*'.[1008] The non-attribution of injury caused by other factors shall now be based on an examination of '*any known factors*' (ADA Article 3.5).[1009]

Moreover, the possibility of cumulating injury has been introduced under ADA Article 3.3. This provision permits cumulatively assessing the injury caused by products imported from different countries. This practice was already applied by the '*United States, Mexico, the EC, Canada, Australia and other countries*'.[1010] The cumulative assessment requires a *de minimis* margin of dumping, significant volume, as well as being '*appropriate in light of the condition of competition*'. Nevertheless, when the injury cannot be linked to the dumped imports from a certain country, then the scope of imports is broadened with products from other countries to establish the required causal relationship. In other words, through cumulation, the causal relationship between the alleged dumped imports and the injury (ADA Article 3.5) becomes a lower threshold.

Furthermore, ADA Article 5.8 introduced *de minimis* percentages of volume (imports share) below which no injury would be found. The *de minimis* threshold is 3% for imports from a single country unless injury of imports from different countries

1007. Paragraphs 1-3 of 1979 AD Code Article 3 correspond to paras 1, 2 and 4 of ADA Article 3. The only difference is that para. 4 under ADA Article 3 includes '*output*' and '*the magnitude of the margin of dumping*' among the listed economic factors to examine the impact of the dumped imports in the domestic industry. The three last paragraphs of the 1967 AD Code Article 3 have been maintained under the 1979 AD Code and the ADA. These paragraphs provide that the effect of the dumped imports shall be based on the examination of production of the '*like product*' or '*the narrowest group or range of products*' (1967 AD Code Article 3.d, 1979 AD Code Article 3.5, ADA Article 3.6); the threat of material injury shall be based on facts and '*studied and decided with special care*' (1967 AD Code Article 3.e and 3.f, 1979 AD Code Article 3.6 and 3.7, ADA Article 3.7 and 3.8). ADA Article 3.7 adds a list of cumulative factors to consider in the conclusion that '*further dumped exports are imminent and that, unless protective action is taken, the material injury would occur*'.

1008. As established under ASCM Article 15.5 and resembling ASG Article 4.2 (b).

1009. The Appellate Body in the *US – Hot-Rolled Steel* reversed the Panel's finding and concluded that investigating authorities are required to '*separate and distinguish the injurious effects of dumped imports from those of other known causal factors*'. This interpretation of the non-attribution language was based on the Appellate Body's reports in the *US – Wheat Gluten* (DS166) and *US – Lamb* (DS177), in which ASG Article 4.2(b) was interpreted since the Appellate Body found that although it is not identical, it can provide for guidance when interpreting the non-attribution language under ADA Article 3.5. *United States – Anti-dumping Measures on Certain Hot-Rolled Steel Products from Japan* (DS184). WTO document DS184/AB/R, 24 July 2001, paras 228-233.

1010. G.N. Horlick, How the GATT Became Protectionist: An Analysis of the Uruguay Round Draft Final Antidumping Code, *Journal of World Trade*, Vol. 27, No. 5, 1993, pp. 5-17 at 14 https://doi.org/10.54648/trad1993027.

collectively accounts (through cumulation) for more than 7% of imports. This inclusion of a 'negligibility provision' recognized the practice of the then major anti-dumping users (the US, EU, Canada and Australia) to use a *de minimis* percentage of market share. Remarkably, as a result of introducing a percentage of import share, rather than market share, injury is more easily determined.[1011]

In the US, injury is determined by 'an independent body',[1012] whereas in many countries '*there is too much administrative discretion in determining injury, causation or injury margins*', constituting the most relevant issue concerning the determination of injury, according to trade experts, who consider that the WTO DSB's interpretations with respect to injury and causation '*offer sufficient guarantees against abuse by administering authorities*'. Nevertheless, since the ADA is silent on the calculation of injury margins, it is left at the discretion of investigating authorities, which enjoy the non-disclosure of confidential information. Injury margins are calculated by comparing the '*prices of foreign exporters and the domestic producers in the importing country market*'.[1013]

An illustration of how the calculation of injury margins increases the possibility to determine injury is provided by the case of the EU, which uses two methods, price undercutting and price underselling. The price undercutting method compares prices of EU and foreign producers in the EU market, and the margin is '*expressed as a percentage of the exporters' CIF export price*'. Under the price underselling method, the EU Commission constructs prices for EU producers '*based on the full cost of production plus a "reasonable" profit margin*', after accepting the EU producers' demonstration that '*the dumped imports forced them to lower their prices in the* [EU] *market to such an extent that they either sold below cost or at less than reasonable profit*'.[1014]

The evolution of the determination of injury shows that it has become a low threshold through multilateral negotiations, especially since the enactment of the 1979 AD Code. Since the provision under the 1967 AD Code was ignored or not implemented by the main GATT Contracting Parties anti-dumping users, the 1979 AD Code eliminated the requirement that imports were the '*principal cause*' of injury. In the ADA, provisions to determine injury became more detailed and specific as well as more protectionist.

Through multilateral negotiations, determinations of dumping and injury have been facilitated, often by legitimizing the abusing practices already used by investigating authorities, through averaging, sampling or cumulation. While averaging and

1011. G.N. Horlick, E.C. Shea, The World Trade Organization Antidumping Agreement, *Journal of World Trade*, Vol. 29, No. 1, 1995, pp. 5-31 at 27 https://doi.org/10.54648/trad1995001.
1012. The USITC. G.N. Horlick, The 10 Major Problems with the Anti-dumping Instrument in the United States, *Journal of World Trade*, Vol. 39, No. 1, 2005, pp. 169-179 at 172 https://doi.org/10.54648/trad2005017.
1013. According to trade experts in Brazil, the EU, Indonesia, South Africa and Thailand, it is the main complaint regarding injury. G.N. Horlick, E.A. Vermulst, The 10 Major Problems with the Anti-dumping Instrument: An Attempt at Synthesis, *Journal of World Trade*, Vol. 39, No. 1, 2005, pp. 67-73 at 70, 71 https://doi.org/10.54648/trad2005007.
1014. E.A. Vermulst, The 10 Major Problems with the Anti-dumping Instrument in the European Community, *Journal of World Trade*, Vol. 39, No. 1, 2005, pp. 105-113 at 111-112 https://doi.org/10.54648/trad2005011.

sampling are used to increase the determination of dumping, cumulation permits to increase the determination of injury. The procedures to impose anti-dumping duties have increased in technicalities that have softened multilateral anti-dumping rules.

In precis, throughout the historical overview of multilateral rules on anti-dumping, it has been observed that the anti-dumping problem lies not only in multilateral provisions, but also in the practice at the national level, sometimes by abusing existing rules, other times by creating new methods to impose higher anti-dumping duties. Far from restraining their use, multilateral trade negotiations have resulted in the legalization of these discriminatory trade-restrictive measures, thereby making multilateral anti-dumping laws more protectionist. Consequently, after having analysed the evolution of multilateral anti-dumping provisions, and in the absence of their legal and economic sense, the only sensible conclusion is to suggest the complete abolition of anti-dumping laws.

CHAPTER 10

Safeguards

The evolution of the multilateral rules on safeguard measures has shown that their raîson d'être is the protection of domestic industries. This chapter, first, explores the rationale for safeguards from an economic, legal and political point of view; and second, by examining the history of safeguard provisions under GATT Article XIX and the WTO Agreement on Safeguards, it demonstrates that the safeguard rules have been broadened and weakened through multilateral trade negotiations, in order to facilitate the imposition of safeguards. As a result, this book argues that rules on safeguards risk undermining the multilateral trading system by, *inter alia*, diverging from the non-discrimination principle.

I THE RATIONALE OF SAFEGUARDS

Safeguard measures have been justified with a variety of political, economic and legal arguments. The political and economic rationales have been thoroughly analysed by Sykes;[1015] therefore, they are merely summarized in subsection A. The legal arguments offered by some legal scholars are questioned in subsection B. This section argues that the economic and legal arguments conferred to safeguard measures are unconvincing while history shows that the political rationale is the only one that justifies the existence of provision on safeguards.

A The Economic Rationale

The main arguments of an economic nature to justify safeguard measures are restoring competitiveness, compensation and adjustment costs. Proponents of safeguards have claimed that temporary import protection will permit the protected industries to

1015. A.O. Sykes, The Safeguards Mess: Critique of WTO Jurisprudence, *World Trade Review*, Vol. 2, No. 3, 2003, pp. 261-296 https://doi.org/10.1017/s1474745604001478.

survive and invest in new technology, which will allow them to compete with foreign firms without needing further protection at a later stage. Another argument points out that safeguard measures compensate those who suffer from trade liberalization, i.e., import-competing industries. More often, the justification for safeguards is their contribution to bear declining industries' adjustment costs,[1016] following the entry into force of a trade liberalization agreement, which benefits the country as a whole.[1017] Nevertheless, Sykes has explained that these economic explanations for safeguards (restoring competitiveness, compensation and adjustment costs) are unconvincing.[1018]

More efficient and less costly means of protection are available to address the issue of adjustment costs for declining industries. For instance, by granting a subsidy to an import-competing industry, the economic cost to society would be reduced. The subsidized industries would be larger, while the productive ones smaller, as Tumlir has pointed out. Unlike safeguard measures, a subsidy would not create '*distortion of the prices faced by consumers in the importing country and no substitution of socially costlier for the protected product*'.[1019]

Furthermore, protection attains two conflicting objectives: On the one hand, it avoids injury to domestic industries. On the other hand, it permits them to adjust in order to reestablish competitiveness. More specifically, a successful adjustment may require dislocation, which may create (rather than reduce) injury to the industry. Preventing dislocation, on the contrary, will eliminate competitiveness. Therefore, import protection '*not only constitutes an extremely imprecise method for limiting dislocation and for including modernization, but its two objectives are inherently contradictory*'.[1020]

B The Legal Rationale

From a legal point of view, the safeguard provision has been regarded by some legal scholars as a contractual *rebus sic stantibus* (i.e., hardship) clause.[1021] In principle, by

1016. With respect to the adjustment cost argument, Mavroidis and Horn have focused on the possibility to use safeguard measures to slow the pace of industry contraction, which may, under certain conditions, reduce costs of unemployment. H. Horn, P.C. Mavroidis, Review of the WTO *US – Lamb* Dispute, prepared for an American Law Institute conference on Principles of Trade Law, World Trade Organization, 2003.
1017. J.H. Jackson, W.J. Davey, A.O. Sykes, *Legal Problems of International Economic Relations: Cases, Materials and Text on the National and International Regulation of Transnational Economic Relations*, 5th ed., 2008, p. 694.
1018. A.O. Sykes, The Safeguards Mess: Critique of WTO Jurisprudence, *World Trade Review*, Vol. 2, No. 3, 2003, pp. 261-296 at 286-288 https://doi.org/10.1017/s1474745604001478.
1019. '*A subsidy granted to the import competing industry minimizes the overall cost. The favored industry will be larger than it would be without the subsidy and other, more productive industries, smaller. It is the relative virtue of the subsidy, though, that it leaves relative prices unchanged. There will thus be no distortion of the prices faced by consumers in the importing country and no substitution of socially costlier for the protected product*', J. Tumlir, GATT Rules and the Community of Law: A Comparison of Economic and Legal Functions, in M. Hilf, F.G. Jacobs, E.U. Petersmann (eds), *The European Community and GATT*, Studies in Transnational Economic Law, Vol. 4, 1986, pp. 1-22 at 4.
1020. R.Z. Lawrence, R.E. Litan, *Saving Free Trade: A Pragmatic Approach*, 1986, p. 77.
1021. The legal doctrine of International Law has widely interpreted this clause. It has also been established under Article 62 of the 1969 Vienna Convention on the Law of Treaties, according

requiring the existence of '*unforeseen developments*', GATT Article XIX seems to present the characteristic of a hardship clause (i.e., the unpredictability of a fundamental change of circumstances).[1022] Nevertheless, certain elements of the GATT provision on safeguards seem to deviate from the elements required in a *rebus sic stantibus* clause.[1023]

The safeguard provision under GATT Article XIX sets out the specific circumstances to be invoked, such as an increase in imports, which can be foreseen by the parties at the time of reaching a trade agreement. In order to increase their bilateral trade, parties commit to reduce trade barriers, thereby increasing imports. Therefore, an increase in imports cannot only be expected, but it is part of the object of the agreement. Furthermore, while *rebus sic stantibus* clauses normally allow for the renegotiation of the parties' obligations, the safeguard provision establishes a unilateral modification (or withdrawal) of the agreed obligations.

The study of hardship clauses, as employed in practice, shows that some present certain elements that seem to deviate from the doctrine of the *rebus sic stantibus* clause. Indeed, some hardship clauses present circumstances that are foreseen;[1024] others include a unilateral response or application in case renegotiation failed.[1025] Accordingly, some legal scholars have claimed that the GATT safeguard provision can be considered a hardship clause, whereby contracting parties are permitted to comply with GATT obligations as long as circumstances are maintained (*rebus sic stantibus*).

Nonetheless, the GATT safeguard provision provides for an essential requirement, which renders it discernible from a hardship clause: serious injury (or threat thereof) to domestic producers. A hardship clause confers protection to the contracting party whose performance of obligations has become unusually onerous or devoid of purpose by the change of circumstances. The safeguard provision merely confers protection to domestic producers of the contracting parties to the agreement. Therefore, under the safeguard provision, the subject granted protection is not a contracting party, as is the case under a hardship clause. Considering the safeguard provision as a *rebus sic stantibus* clause would require equating domestic producers with contracting parties to the trade agreement (i.e., states/countries). The safeguard provision under GATT Article XIX may seem to present the characteristics of a *rebus sic stantibus* clause, notwithstanding it lacks the elements to be of such a legal nature.

---

to which a party is allowed to terminate or withdraw from the treaty in case of fundamental change of circumstances, which were not foreseen by parties, if: (a) those circumstances were essential for the parties to grant their consent to be bound by the treaty and (b) the change has the effect to transform the obligations.

1022. M. Fontaine, F. De Ly, Hardship Clauses, in *Drafting International Contracts: An Analysis of Contract Clauses*, 2009, pp. 453-492 at 456, 486.

1023. D. Philippe, Pacta Sunt Servanda et Rebus Sic Stantibus, in Chambre de Commerce Internationale (ed.), *L'apport de la Jurisprudence Arbitrale*, 1986, pp. 181-259.

1024. A.H. Puelinckx, Frustration, Hardship, Force Majeure, Imprévision, Wegfall der Geschäftsgrundlage, Unmöglichkeit, Changed Circumstances: A Comparative Study in English, French, German and Japanese Law, *Journal of International Arbitration*, Vol. 3, No. 2, 1986, pp. 47-86 at 58 https://doi.org/10.54648/joia1986014.

1025. M. Fontaine, F. De Ly, Hardship Clauses, in *Drafting International Contracts: An Analysis of Contract Clauses*, 2009, pp. 453-492 at 458.

Moreover, the GATT includes special provisions that may be invoked in the circumstances described above. One is the provision on nullification or impairment, enshrined under GATT Article XXIII, whereby countries can resort to multilateral procedures in cases where their rights have been nullified or impaired.[1026] It can be a useful alternative to GATT Article XIX, especially if the intention is to withdraw concessions in a discriminatory manner, i.e., inconsistent with the most-favoured-nation clause under GATT Article I. The other provision, established under GATT Article XXVIII, provides for the possibility of renegotiating concessions, including permanently withdrawing concessions.[1027] A common characteristic of these two provisions is that they provide for multilateral procedures by which prior authorization is required for contracting parties to take measures.

Since the GATT already provides for the possibility to invoke the nullification or impairment clause under GATT Article XXIII, it can arguably be discussed whether the safeguard provision was essential to the GATT. As a matter of fact, in the first dispute in the history of the GATT, Cuba invoked GATT Article XXIII to request CONTRACTING PARTIES' authorization to take an emergency action under GATT Article XIX, i.e., the imposition of safeguard measures, against the US.[1028] The invocation of multilateral procedures under GATT Article XXIII permitted the parties to reach a mutually agreed

1026. Under the US Suggested Charter, it was established under the same section than the safeguard provision. GAT Article XXIII reads as follows:

> '1. *If any contracting party should consider that any benefit accruing to it directly or indirectly under this Agreement is being nullified or impaired or that the attainment of any objective of the Agreement is being impeded as the result of (a) the failure of another contracting party to carry out its obligations under this Agreement, or (b) the application by another contracting party of any measure, whether or not it conflicts with the provisions of this Agreement, or (c) the existence of any other situation, the contracting party may, with a view to the satisfactory adjustment of the matter, make written representations or proposals to the other contracting party or parties which it considers to be concerned. Any contracting party thus approached shall give sympathetic consideration to the representations or proposals made to it.*
>
> 2. *If no satisfactory adjustment is effected between the contracting parties concerned within a reasonable time, or if the difficulty is of the type described in paragraph 1 (c) of this Article, the matter may be referred to the CONTRACTING PARTIES. The CONTRACTING PARTIES shall promptly investigate any matter so referred to them and shall make appropriate recommendations to the contracting parties which they consider to be concerned, or give a ruling on the matter, as appropriate. The CONTRACTING PARTIES may consult with contracting parties, with the Economic and Social Council of the United Nations and with any appropriate inter-governmental organization in cases where they consider such consultation necessary. If the CONTRACTING PARTIES consider that the circumstances are serious enough to justify such action, they may authorize a contracting party or parties to suspend the application to any other contracting party or parties of such concessions or other obligations under this Agreement as they determine to be appropriate in the circumstances. If the application to any contracting party of any concession or other obligation is in fact suspended, that contracting party shall then be free, not later than sixty days after such action is taken, to give written notice to the Executive Secretary to the CONTRACTING PARTIES of its intention to withdraw from this Agreement and such withdrawal shall take effect upon the sixtieth day following the day on which such notice is received by him.*'

1027. J.H. Jackson, *World Trade and the Law of GATT (A Legal Analysis of the General Agreement on Tariffs and Trade)*, 1969, p. 556.

1028. GATT document CP.2/W12, 8 September 1948.

solution, which did not impair their GATT rights or obligations,[1029] instead of unilaterally imposing safeguard measures.

C The Political Rationale

By reducing import barriers, trade agreements tend to benefit exporters, importers and consumers. Nevertheless, import-competing industries, which can exert political pressure, often show opposition to trade agreements. With the safeguard provision, governments can compensate import-competing industries for the cost of reducing import barriers by granting them the possibility to request governmental protection.[1030] Once safeguard measures are imposed, the government of the exporting country may expect less political resistance from prosperous exporters, who accept temporary restrictions.[1031] Therefore, the inclusion of safeguard provisions allows governments to reach their '*ideal trade agreement*', maximizing the net political gains compared to the political costs (i.e., obtaining their Pareto frontier).[1032] This political rationale seems to coincide with the lessons taught by history.

Indeed, when the first 'safeguarding provision' was suggested in 1933, Cordell Hull already argued that the inclusion of exceptions in a trade agreement, such as the safeguard provision, facilitated political officials' task to reach trade agreements. Since its origins, the provision on safeguards has been aimed at protecting domestic industries that serve political interests. The 'escape clause', the basis for the current GATT Article XIX, was included in the US–Mexican agreement of 1942 at the request of domestic industries exerting political pressure. In 1945, during the US Congressional debate to grant the US President authority to negotiate trade agreements, domestic industries bargained to obtain something in return, which resulted in the decision to include a safeguard provision in every trade agreement. This tilt towards domestic industries is the raîson d'être of safeguard measures.

Through the years, this practice has been maintained, as the *US – Steel Safeguards* dispute reflects.[1033] In 2001, the US steel industry and US Congressional delegations stated that granting '*negotiating authority to the president would be directly related to action on steel imports*'. Unlike anti-dumping or countervailing duty proceedings, the US safeguard provision grants, following an affirmative determination by the USITC, the US President the discretion to take action and the authority to modify import restrictions.[1034]

1029. *Report of Working Party on the Cuban Schedule* (GD/1). Complainant: US. GATT document CP.2/43, 13 September 1948.
1030. A.O. Sykes, The Safeguards Mess: Critique of WTO Jurisprudence, *World Trade Review*, Vol. 2, No. 3, 2003, pp. 261-296 at 288 https://doi.org/10.1017/s1474745604001478.
1031. J.H. Jackson, W.J. Davey, A.O. Sykes, *Legal Problems of International Economic Relations: Cases, Materials and Text on the National and International Regulation of Transnational Economic Relations*, 5th ed., 2008, p. 694.
1032. A.O. Sykes, The Safeguards Mess: Critique of WTO Jurisprudence, *World Trade Review*, Vol. 2, No. 3, 2003, pp. 261-296 at 288, 291 https://doi.org/10.1017/s1474745604001478.
1033. *United States – Definitive Safeguard Measures on Imports of Certain Steel Products* (DS252).
1034. J.M. Finger, Flexibilities, Rules, and Trade Remedies in the GATT/WTO System, in M. Daunton, A. Narlikar, R.M. Stern (eds), *The Oxford Handbook on the World Trade Organization*, 2012, pp. 418-440 at 430, 431. These managerial skills are common to all jurisdictions of

II GATT ARTICLE XIX

A Origins

As illustrated in Part II, the first 'safeguarding provision' was suggested at the League of Nations Monetary and Economic Conference in 1933, when countries intended to abandon economic conflict and work towards economic recovery following the Great Depression. Through a multilateral trade agreement, they would commit to cease imposing new barriers as well as progressively reducing existing ones. The US suggested certain principles and exceptions to be incorporated in the multilateral agreement, which was aimed at attacking '*upon existing trade obstacles*'. The 'safeguarding provision' was listed among the possible exceptions to the most-favoured-nation principle, together with anti-dumping and countervailing duties. The political argument given for the inclusion of these exceptions, which has persisted since then,[1035] is that they would '*facilitate agreements for the lowering of trade barriers*'.[1036]

This 'safeguarding provision' was intended to protect domestic industries against '*a drastic*' ('*excessive*') increase of imports when the importing country had taken emergency measures that '*by raising wages, shortening hours and improving conditions of labour*' had caused a loss in competitiveness. The provision required that the measure would neither be '*more than sufficient to meet the emergency*' nor '*reduce foreign trade in the commodities affected below the level of a pre-determined period*'. The '*new or additional duties or restrictions*' would merely be imposed during the period of '*emergency*', and in a non-discriminatory manner.[1037]

Based on this 'safeguarding provision', the US included an 'escape clause' in its bilateral agreement with Mexico in 1942, and then in every trade agreement since 1945.[1038] Accordingly, in cases where an increase in imports caused injury (or threat thereof) to a domestic industry, as a result of unforeseen developments and the

WTO Members, where most commonly the Minister of Finance makes the final decision to impose or not safeguard measures. Therefore, this discretion has always been a high-level political decision, rather than '*a "technical track" or low level, rule-bound decision*'. R.C. de Grey, *Trade Policy and the System of Contingency Protection in the Perspective of Competition Policy*, 1986, p. 3. R. Grey, The Conflict Between Trade Policy and Competition Policy: A Comment, in E.U. Petersmann, M. Hilf, *The New GATT Round of Multilateral Trade Negotiations: Legal and Economic Problems*, Vol. 5, 1988, pp. 447-453, at 449.

1035. K.W. Dam, *The GATT: Law and International Economic Organization*, 1970, p. 99. M.A. Crowley, Why Are Safeguards Needed in a Trade Agreement?, in K. Bagwell, G. Bermann, P.C. Mavroidis, *Law and Economics of Contingent Protection in International Trade*, 2009, pp. 379-400.

1036. Section 1 of the Appendix 6 of the League of Nations document C. 435. M. 220. 1933. II. [Conf.M.E.22(l).], 27 July 1933, p. 42.

1037. *Ibid.*, p. 41.

1038. '*91 Cong. Rec. 4872 (1945) (remarks of Congressman Doughton); Hearings on the Extension of the Reciprocal Trade Agreements Act Before the Senate Finance Comm., 79th Cong., 1st Sess. 84, 86, 90, 179-80, 459 (1945); Hearings on the Extension of the Reciprocal Trade Agreements Act Before the House Comm. On Ways and Means, 79th Cong., 1st Sess. 273 (1945)*'. J.H. Jackson, *World Trade and the Law of GATT (A Legal Analysis of the General Agreement on Tariffs and Trade)*, 1969, p. 553.

concessions granted, the importing country was free to modify or withdraw the concession.

A provision similar to the escape clause was included under the first paragraph of Article 29 of the US Suggested Charter for an ITO, which later became the first paragraph of GATT Article XIX.[1039] Unlike the 'escape clause', Article 29 of the US Suggested Charter included a second paragraph permitting the affected exporting country to retaliate against the initial safeguard measure. According to the US, retaliation was included due to the concern about the eventual danger of abusing safeguards.[1040] Since then, the GATT provision on safeguards ('emergency action') has included the possibility of retaliation.[1041]

Throughout the history of multilateral trade negotiations, safeguard provisions have been drawn up at the behest of GATT Contracting Parties, making rules lean towards protectionism. Each time the provision has been further developed during multilateral negotiations, the imposition of safeguard measures has been facilitated. This has occurred from the first negotiations during the preparatory work of the GATT and the ITO Charter until the Uruguay Round negotiations for the WTO Agreement on Safeguards.

During the First Session of the Preparatory Committee, held in London in 1946, the provision on safeguards was further elaborated in order to permit, on the one hand, the imposition of provisional measures without previous consultation, under GATT Article XIX.2; and, on the other hand, emergency retaliation by the exporting country following the original measure without consultation, under GATT Article XIX.3(b). This emergency retaliatory measure could exceed the original measure, but required prior authorization by the Organization (under the ITO Charter), which became the Committee (under the first GATT draft Article XIX.3). The requirement of prior authorization to retaliate was eliminated at the Second Session of the Preparatory Committee, held in Geneva in 1947; hence, it was absent in the final version of the GATT as of its signature.

Despite the warning by some countries that the scope of the safeguard provision was too broad since it covered any concession or obligation of the ITO Charter, i.e., that safeguards could take the form of (additional) tariffs, quotas or even subsidies, the GATT provision maintained the broad possibility to modify or withdraw '*concessions or other obligations*'. At the Havana Conference, a fourth paragraph was incorporated into the safeguard provision of the ITO Charter, in order to restrict the scope of safeguards to tariff concessions granted under the GATT. Following the failure of the ITO, neither this paragraph nor other changes incorporated into the ITO Charter were included under GATT Article XIX. For instance, the adverb '*relatively*' was inserted to qualify the '*increased quantities*'.[1042] Although this adverb was not included under GATT Article

1039. J.H. Jackson, *World Trade and the Law of GATT (A Legal Analysis of the General Agreement on Tariffs and Trade)*, 1969, p. 553.
1040. UN document E/PG/T/C.II/PV/7, 11 November 1946, p. 15.
1041. Retaliation was first incorporated under the provision on safeguard of the US Suggested Charter (Article 29.2).
1042. Article 40 1(a) of the ITO Charter reads as follows: '*If, as a result of unforeseen developments and of the effect of the obligations incurred by a Member under or pursuant to this Chapter,*

XIX.1(a), the Working Party understood that it was *'intended to cover cases where imports may have increased relatively, as made clear in paragraph 1(a) of Article 40 of the Havana Charter'*.[1043] The relative increase in imports covers cases where domestic consumption declines, but imports remain stable. *'It seems that the "relative" increase concept is a protective device.'*[1044] Following the Uruguay Round, the Agreement on Safeguards included *'absolute or relative to domestic production'*.

B Non-discriminatory Interpretation of GATT Article XIX

At the Havana Conference, an interpretative note was added to Article 40 of the ITO Charter, the provision on safeguards providing for a non-discriminatory (MFN) application of safeguards pursuant to paragraph 1, i.e., original safeguard measure,[1045] and paragraph 3(b), i.e., emergency retaliation.[1046] The note also established *'that such action should avoid, to the fullest extent possible, injury to other supplying Member countries'*.[1047] Accordingly, the imposition of safeguard measures on a discriminatory basis was only permitted in case of retaliation with prior consultation under paragraph 3(a). The imposition of safeguard measures in other scenarios, including emergency

including tariff concessions, any product is being imported into the territory of that Member in such relatively increased quantities and under such conditions as to cause or threaten serious injury to domestic producers in that territory of like or directly competitive products, the Member shall be free, in respect of such product, and to the extent and for such time as may be necessary to prevent or remedy such injury, to suspend the obligation in whole or in part or to withdraw or modify the concession.'

1043. GATT/CP.2/22/Rev.1, 30 August 1948, p. 7, para. 30.

1044. J.H. Jackson, *World Trade and the Law of GATT (A Legal Analysis of the General Agreement on Tariffs and Trade)*, 1969, p. 558.

1045. *'1. (a) If, as a result of unforeseen developments and of the effect of the obligations incurred by a contracting party under this Agreement, including tariff concessions, any product is being imported into the territory of that contracting party in such increased quantities and under such conditions as to cause or threaten serious injury to domestic producers in that territory of like or directly competitive products, the contracting party shall be free, in respect of such product, and to the extent and for such time as may be necessary to prevent or remedy such injury, to suspend the obligation in whole or in part or to withdraw or modify the concession. (b) If any product, which is the subject of a concession with respect to a preference, is being imported into the territory of a contracting party in the circumstances set forth in subparagraph (a) of this paragraph, so as to cause or threaten serious injury to domestic producers of like or directly competitive products in the territory of a contracting party which receives or received such preference, the importing contracting party shall be free, if that other contracting party so requests, to suspend the relevant obligation in whole or in part or to withdraw or modify the concession in respect of the product, to the extent and for such time as may be necessary to prevent or remedy such injury.'*

1046. *'(b) Notwithstanding the provisions of subparagraph (a) of this paragraph, where action is taken under paragraph 2 of this Article without prior consultation and causes or threatens serious injury in the territory of a contracting party to the domestic producers of products affected by the action, that contracting party shall, where delay would cause damage difficult to repair, be free to suspend, upon the taking of the action and throughout the period of consultation, such concessions or other obligations as may be necessary to prevent or remedy the injury.'*

1047. UN document E.CONF.2/78, 24 March 1948, p. 113 (Annex P, Interpretative Note *Ad* Article 40): *'It is understood that any suspension, withdrawal or modification under paragraphs 1 (a), 1 (b) and 3 (b) must not discriminate against imports from any Member country, and that such action should avoid, to the fullest extent possible, injury to other supplying Member countries.'*

retaliation, i.e., following the imposition of a safeguard measure without prior consultation (paragraph 3.b.), had to be applied in a non-discriminatory manner, i.e., consistent with the most-favoured-nation principle under GATT Article I. This interpretative note is in line with the original 'safeguarding provision' suggested in 1933, which was conceived to be applied in a non-discriminatory manner.

This interpretative note on the non-discriminatory application of safeguards (except in cases where retaliation is preceded by consultations) was not incorporated into the GATT, and prompted interpretative issues. Following the Havana Conference, the ITO Charter would repeal GATT Articles I and III-XXIII.[1048] Pending the entry into force of the ITO Charter, CONTRACTING PARTIES adopted a Working Party report on the modification of the GATT, thereby merely amending provisions that would create '*serious difficulties for Contracting Parties*' if left unchanged. In order to solve difficulties with the application of provisions, Contracting Parties could resort to the procedures of joint action (GATT Article XXV) and '*observe to the fullest extent the Havana Charter*' (GATT Article XXIX.1).[1049]

Nonetheless, the non-inclusion of the interpretative note in the GATT has given rise to a legal debate among scholars concerning the non-discriminatory application of safeguards. Bronckers has claimed that the impact of the note on the application of GATT Article XIX '*can only be very limited*'.[1050] On the contrary, Koulen has argued that the interpretative note of the ITO Charter could be used as a source of interpretation of the non-discriminatory nature of GATT Article XIX,[1051] pursuant to Article 31.3.a. of the Vienna Convention on the Law of Treaties, whereby '*any subsequent agreement between the parties regarding the interpretation of the treaty or the application of its provisions*' shall be taken into account.[1052] Similarly, Jackson pointed out that the preparatory work as well as subsequent GATT practice clearly implies the non-discriminatory application of safeguard measures.[1053]

Indeed, the non-discriminatory nature of the safeguard provision (except in cases of retaliation with prior consultation) was recognized and generally applied in such a manner by GATT CONTRACTING PARTIES, as well as the GATT Secretariat, until the Uruguay Round, although some safeguard measures were imposed in a discriminatory

1048. UNTS, Vol. 62, No. 814, p. 26.
1049. Report of Working Party No. 3 on Modifications to the General Agreement. GATT/CP.2/22/Rev.1, 30 August 1948, pp. 1, 2.
1050. M. Bronckers, The Non-discriminatory Application of Article XIX GATT: Tradition or Fiction?, *Legal Issues of European Integration*, Vol. 8, No. 2, 1981, pp. 35-76 at 42 https://doi.org/10.54648/leie1981006. M. Bronckers, Reconsidering the Non-Discrimination Principle as Applied to GATT Safeguards Measures, A Rejoinder, *Legal Issues of European Integration*, Vol. 10. No. 2. 1983, pp. 113-137 at 114 https://doi.org/10.54648/leie1983016.
1051. M. Koulen, The Non-discriminatory Interpretation of GATT Article XIX.1. A Reply, *Legal Issues of Economic Integration*, Vol. 10. No. 2, 1983, pp. 87-111 at 93 https://doi.org/10.54648/leie1983015.
1052. Article 31.3.a of the Vienna Convention on the Law of Treaties, 1969.
1053. J.H. Jackson, *World Trade and the Law of GATT (A Legal Analysis of the General Agreement on Tariffs and Trade)*, 1969, p. 564.

way.[1054] However, during the Tokyo Round, several Contracting Parties insisted on the discriminatory interpretation of safeguard measures under GATT Article XIX.1.

1 *GATT Disputes*

During the GATT, a number of disputes addressed the matter of the non-discriminatory application of safeguard measures. Before the Tokyo Round, GATT Article XIX.1 was interpreted in a non-discriminatory manner by the GATT Contracting Parties. In 1953, in the context of an examination of the conditions of accession of Japan to the GATT, some Contracting Parties expressed concern that a '*violent disruption of trading conditions*' might be caused by the '*sudden flooding of certain markets with Japanese manufactures*'. Some suggested that safeguard measures be used to deal with such a situation. The Accession Committee examined GATT Article XIX, noting that an action consistent with GATT Article XIX '*would have to be non-discriminatory*'; and concluded that, since GATT Article XXIII provides for discriminatory action with the prior approval of CONTRACTING PARTIES, there was '*no justification for so drastic an amendment as to introduce discrimination into the application of Article XIX*'.[1055]

In this line, the non-discriminatory application of safeguard measures was confirmed in the dispute *German Import Restrictions*.[1056] Complaining against the German discriminatory application of import restrictions, some Contracting Parties argued that, provided the alleged circumstances existed, Germany could resort to the imposition of safeguard measures, which would be applied in a non-discriminatory fashion. Notably, they clarified that GATT Article XIX did not permit the imposition of quantitative restrictions '*to combat low-priced imports or to protect expanding industries*'.[1057]

In 1973, following the EEC's imposition of safeguards on magnetophones imported into Italy, Japan claimed that the measure was inconsistent with GATT Article XIX since it was applied neither to other EEC members nor to '*the associated countries*'.[1058] At the 29th Session of the CONTRACTING PARTIES, the EEC argued that notwithstanding that the application of safeguard measures was '*erga omnes*', parties to an agreement with the EEC could be exempted from these measures pursuant to GATT Article XXIV. Canada and Japan disagreed with the EEC interpretation that '*the*

1054. M. Koulen, The Non-discriminatory Interpretation of GATT Article XIX.1. A Reply, *Legal Issues of Economic Integration*, Vol. 10. No. 2, 1983, pp. 87-111 at 104 https://doi.org/10.54648/leie1983015. M. Bronckers, The Non-discriminatory Application of Article XIX GATT: Tradition or Fiction? *Legal Issues of European Integration*, Vol. 8, No. 2, 1981, pp. 35-76 at 53 https://doi.org/10.54648/leie1981006.
1055. GATT document L/76, 13 February 1953, paras 3-7.
1056. *German Import Restrictions* (GD/55). Complainants: Australia, Austria, Canada, Denmark, Greece, India, New Zealand, Norway, Pakistan Sweden, the UK, the US, Czechoslovakia, Japan. GATT document L/966, 10 April 1959. Consultations: GATT document L/949, 21 November 1958.
1057. Australia, Austria, Canada, Czechoslovakia, Denmark, India, Japan, New Zealand, Sweden, Norway, the UK and the US. GATT document L/966, 10 April 1959, paras 2, 21, 37.
1058. GATT document L/3847, 25 April 1973.

invocation of Article XXIV permitted the discriminatory application of Article XIX'.[1059] Moreover, some Contracting Parties expressed their concerns with respect to the interpretation that GATT Article XXIV.8(b) allowed a discriminatory imposition of safeguards; hence, the Working Parties reports on the agreements between the EEC and Austria, Iceland, Portugal, Sweden and Switzerland, adopted in 1973, clarified that '*safeguard action would be taken on a strictly most-favoured-nation basis*'.[1060]

Last, but not least, the non-discriminatory nature of GATT Article XIX was reaffirmed in *Norway – Textiles*,[1061] following the Norwegian imposition of a quota system among textile-supplying countries without allocating a share for imports from Hong Kong. The Panel found the action inconsistent with GATT Article XIII, which requires the non-discriminatory administration of quantitative restrictions,[1062] and concluded that '*the quantitative import restrictions (...), as the form of emergency action under Article XIX, were subject to the provisions of Article XIII, which governed the administration of such restrictions*'.[1063] The report of the Panel was endorsed in 1980; none of the Contracting Parties questioned that quantitative restrictions imposed under GATT Article XIX were governed by GATT Article XIII, i.e., the non-discrimination principle.[1064]

2 GATT Secretariat

During the Tokyo Round, the European Communities and the Nordic Countries attempted to reach an agreement allowing the discriminatory interpretation of GATT Article XIX.1. Nevertheless, a large number of Contracting Parties maintained the non-discriminatory interpretation of the provision,[1065] and requested the GATT Secretariat to prepare a study on the origin and practice of GATT Article XIX,[1066] which highlighted that '*the clear intent of the drafters of Article XIX was that it should be non-discriminatory in its application*'.[1067] It was discussed by the Council,[1068] yet some Contracting Parties refused to adopt it.[1069]

1059. GATT document SR.29/1 22, November 1973, pp. 5, 6. Cited in GATT document L/4679, 5 July 1978, paras 24, 25.
1060. GATT documents L/4679, 5 July 1978, para. 24; BISD, 20th Supp., 1972, pp. 156, 169, 181, 194, 207.
1061. *Norway – Restrictions on Imports of Certain Textile Products* (GD/100) Complainant: Hong Kong. GATT document L/4959, 24 March 1980.
1062. GATT documents L/4671, 1 March 1978, paras 15, 16.
1063. GATT document C/M/141, 18 July 1980, para. 4.
1064. M. Koulen, The Non-discriminatory Interpretation of GATT Article XIX.1. A Reply, *Legal Issues of Economic Integration*, Vol. 10. No. 2, 1983, pp. 87-111 at 110 https://doi.org/10.54648/leie1983015.
1065. Following the EEC imposition of safeguard measures (quotas) on portable TV sets from the Republic of Korea imported into the UK. GATT documents C/M/112, 5 March 1976; L/4613, 15 December 1977; C/M/124, 5 April 1978, p. 119.
1066. GATT document, C/M/126, 22 June 1978, p. 7 para. 5.
1067. The US memorandum on the historical background of the provisions included in the US Suggested Charter for an ITO in 1946 stated: '*These relevant provisions (of Article XIX) follow closely in substance those in the first detailed escape clause, contained in Article XI of the 1942 trade agreement with Mexico ... At the time the United States was putting escape clauses comparable to Article XIX into bilateral trade agreements and was proposing the multilateral*

The lack of agreement on a Code on Safeguards at the end of the Tokyo Round was mainly due to the disagreement regarding the inclusion of a provision that allowed the discriminatory imposition of safeguard measures.[1070] For this reason, the GATT Director General submitted a text for a formal decision by the CONTRACTING PARTIES to respect GATT Article XIX and the GATT Secretariat study until a Code on Safeguards was reached.[1071] Nevertheless, the final decision omitted the reference to the study, prepared by the GATT Secretariat, supporting the non-discriminatory interpretation.[1072]

III THE AGREEMENT ON SAFEGUARDS

Since a Code on Safeguards could not be reached at the Tokyo Round, the Agreement on Safeguards at the end of the Uruguay Round was hailed as a historical achievement.[1073] Following the proliferation of voluntary export restraints (VERs) during the 1980s, the Agreement on Safeguards was recognized for incorporating the prohibition of VERs (Article 11), as well as the limitation on the duration of safeguards (Article 7) and the reimbursement of provisional tariffs in case final measures are found unjustified (Article 6).[1074] The Agreement on Safeguards arguably contains

---

negotiation of comparable language it had no authority to take action under such a clause in other than a non-discriminatory manner and therefore must have contemplated its non-discriminatory use.' The Secretariat study did not include an interpretation of the relationship between the application of GATT Articles XIX and XXIV.8. GATT document L/4679, 5 July 1978, paras 1, 2, 23-26, 48.

1068. '*The representative of India, speaking under Other Business, said that his delegation was among those that had requested the secretariat study on modalities of application of Article XIX. He expressed his appreciation for the study, which had been circulated in document L4679. This study would be helpful in the understanding of the development of the application and interpretation of this Article. The representative of Pakistan also expressed his appreciation for the study. He hoped that this study would put an end to attempts to introduce fundamental changes in these provisions in the form of interpretations. If changes were made, they could only be introduced by consensus of the CONTRACTING PARTIES.*' GATT document C/M/127, 4 August 1978, para. 13.

1069. M. Koulen, The Non-discriminatory Interpretation of GATT Article XIX.1. A Reply, *Legal Issues of Economic Integration*, Vol. 10. No. 2, 1983, pp. 87-111 at 108 https://doi.org/10.54648/leie1983015.

1070. GATT document, The Tokyo Round of Multilateral Trade Negotiations, Vol. II. Supplementary Report, January 1980, pp. 14-17.

1071. '*CONTRACTING PARTIES would reaffirm their intention to continue to abide by the disciplines and obligations of Article XIX of the General Agreement. It would be expected that the existing rules and practices relating to the modalities of application of Article XIX, summarized in document L/4679 of 5 July 1978, would be adhered to by contracting parties when taking any future action under that provision.*' GATT document L/4884/Add. 1, 26 November 1979, para. 1.

1072. M. Koulen, The Non-discriminatory Interpretation of GATT Article XIX.1. A Reply, *Legal Issues of Economic Integration*, Vol. 10. No. 2, 1983, pp. 87-111 at 109 https://doi.org/10.54648/leie1983015.

1073. M. Bronckers, Voluntary Export Restraints and the GATT 1994 Agreement on Safeguards, in J. Bourgeois, F. Berrod, E. Gippini Fournier (eds), *The Uruguay Round Results: A European Lawyers' Perspective*, 1995, pp. 273-279 at 273.

1074. M. Bronckers, WTO Implementation in the European Community: Antidumping, Safeguards and Intellectual Property, *Journal of World Trade*, Vol. 29, No. 5, 1995, pp. 73-95

another improvement, whereby retaliation is prohibited during the first three years, '*provided that the safeguard measure has been taken as a result of an absolute increase in imports*' (Article 8.3); yet this was considered a loss for exporters.[1075]

Nonetheless, the Agreement on Safeguards has also been criticized for maintaining or incorporating certain inadequacies, such as the lack of a definition of authorized measures, differentiation with respect to the categories of developing countries, and the lack of direct rights for complaint procedures (unlike anti-dumping and countervailing duty proceedings).[1076] More importantly, the Agreement on Safeguards creates certain issues that undermine the multilateral trading system. It permits customs unions to apply safeguards inconsistently with the non-discriminatory principle, including in the form of country-specific allocated quotas, which restrict competition even more than a global quota (Article 5.2), and it has omitted the condition of '*unforeseen developments*', required by GATT Article XIX to impose safeguard measures. Moreover, while the prohibition of VERs was an advancement for the multilateral trading system (Article 11.3), it has proven not to be sufficient to correct the governmental practice of reaching agreements with exporters abroad, thereby restricting competition.

A Non-discriminatory Application and Relationship with GATT Article XXIV

The non-discriminatory application of safeguard measures is enshrined under ASG Article 2.2, whereby safeguards must be imposed irrespectively of the source or origin of imported products. The Agreement on Safeguards was finally agreed, mainly due to the introduction of a provision (footnote 1) permitting the imposition of safeguards by a customs union.[1077] This possibility brings into question the consistency of the non-discriminatory application of safeguards with Article XXIV.

1 Safeguards and Customs Unions (ASG Footnote 1)

The Agreement on Safeguards provides for the imposition of safeguards by a customs union as a single unit or on behalf of a member (footnote 1), and adds '*Nothing in this Agreement prejudges the interpretation of the relationship between Article XIX and*

https://doi.org/10.54648/trad1995031. T. Flory, The Agreement on Safeguards, in J. Bourgeois, F. Berrod, E. Gippini Fournier (eds), *The Uruguay Round Results, A European Lawyers' Perspective: Proceedings of an International Conference Held at the College of Europe, Bruges*, 1999, pp. 265-271.

1075. M. Bronckers, WTO Implementation in the European Community - Antidumping, Safeguards and Intellectual Property, *Journal of World Trade*, Vol. 29, No. 5, 1995, pp. 73-95 at 85 https://doi.org/10.54648/trad1995031.

1076. M. Bronckers, WTO Implementation in the European Community - Antidumping, Safeguards and Intellectual Property, *Journal of World Trade*, Vol. 29, No. 5, 1995, pp. 73-95 https://doi.org/10.54648/trad1995031. T. Flory, The Agreement on Safeguards, in J. Bourgeois, F. Berrod, E. Gippini Fournier (eds), *The Uruguay Round Results, A European Lawyers' Perspective: Proceedings of an International Conference Held at the College of Europe, Bruges*, 1999, pp. 265-271. E.U. Petersmann, Conclusions, in J. Bourgeois, F. Berrod, E. Gippini Fournier (eds), *The Uruguay Round Results: A European Lawyers' Perspective*, 1995, pp. 485-491 at 488.

1077. This (non-negotiable) request was apparently made by the European Union at the end of the Uruguay Round.

paragraph 8 of Article XXIV of GATT 1994.' This is arguably a *contradictio in terminis*. As noted in the introduction to Part III, GATT Article XXIV.8 provides definitions for a customs union, under subparagraph (a), and a free trade area, under subparagraph (b). In both cases, it requires the elimination of '*the duties and other restrictive regulations of commerce (...) on substantially all the trade between the constituent territories in products originating in such territories*', '*except, where necessary*', those restrictive measures under GATT Articles XI, XII, XIII, XIV, XV and XX.[1078] Hence, safeguard measures, under GATT Article XIX, are not among the listed measures that are permissible within a customs union or a free trade area.

ASG footnote 1 provides for the imposition of safeguards by a customs union in two scenarios, as a single unit or on behalf of a member. In the first scenario, i.e., as a single unit, as long as the action is exclusively applied to members outside the customs union and in a non-discriminatory manner, the interpretation of the relationship between GATT Articles XIX and XXIV.8(a) will not be prejudiced. In this case, the measure would arguably be consistent with GATT Article XIX and ASG Article 2.2, if applied in a non-discriminatory manner among members outside the customs union, and GATT Article XXIV.8(a), since the safeguard measure would be eliminated within the customs union.

Nevertheless, the imposition of safeguards by a customs union that is part of a free trade area may be inconsistent with either GATT Article XIX and ASG Article 2.2 (if applied discriminatorily), or with GATT Article XXIV.8(b) as the latter requires the elimination of safeguard measures within a free trade area. If the customs union excludes members of the free trade area from the safeguards, it would apply safeguards in a discriminatory manner, and thus inconsistently with the interpretation of GATT Article XIX and ASG Article 2.2. Furthermore, a safeguard measure imposed by the customs union on the rest of the members of the free trade area would be inconsistent with GATT Article XXIV.8.(b); it would undermine the meaning and purpose of a free trade area.

A similar inconsistency occurs in the second scenario, where a customs union imposes safeguards on behalf of a Member State, '*the measure shall be limited to that member State*'. This scenario would eliminate the free movement of goods within the customs union by reinstating border controls between members of the customs union, defeating the purpose of a customs union, hence being inconsistent with GATT Article XXIV.8(a)(ii), whereby '*substantially the same duties and other regulations of commerce are applied by each of the members of the union to the trade of territories not included in the union*' (subject to the preferences under GATT Article I.2.).

ASG footnote 1 claims not to prejudice the interpretation of GATT Article XIX in relation to GATT Article XXIV.8. Nevertheless, provided that safeguards were applied

1078. This provision was included under the Havana Charter, 1948, under Article 44.4. The exempted measures cited under that provision were those under Articles 20-24 (quantitative restrictions related to agricultural stabilization programmes and balance of payments), which correspond to GATT Articles XI-XV; as well as those under Article 45 (restrictions based on protection of public moral; animal, human or plant life, etc.), which correspond to GATT Article XX.

in a non-discriminatory manner, ASG footnote 1 permits a customs union to apply safeguards, either as a single unit, thus imposing them onto other members of a free trade area, inconsistently with GATT Article XXIV.8(b), or on behalf of member, undermining the meaning and purpose of a customs union, inconsistently with GATT Article XXIV.8(a). Consequently, ASG footnote 1 prejudges the interpretation of the relationship between GATT Articles XIX and XXIV.8.

2 *Safeguards and Free Trade Areas (ASG Article 2.2)*

Due to the proliferation of free trade agreements, the question of the non-discriminatory application of safeguards in relation to GATT Article XXIV.8(b), which does not list safeguards as permitted measures to be imposed within free trade areas, has gained importance. When WTO Members that are parties to free trade agreements impose safeguards, they violate either GATT Article XXIV.8(b) or both GATT Article XIX.1 and ASG Article 2.2. On the one hand, as the history of the GATT teaches, if other parties to the free trade agreement are exempted from the measures, safeguards are applied in a discriminatory manner, and thus inconsistently with GATT Article XIX.1 and ASG Article 2.2. On the other hand, if the safeguard measure is applied on a non-discriminatory (MFN) basis, i.e., also on the other parties to the free trade area, the WTO Member acts inconsistently with GATT Article XXIV.8(b).

Since the establishment of the WTO, the practice of WTO Members with respect to these provisions has worsened. Some WTO Members exempt free trade partners from safeguard measures, inconsistently with GATT Article XIX.1 and ASG Article 2.2, even after having taken into account imports from partners to determine the injury to the domestic industry (e.g., the US);[1079] or impose safeguard measures on free trade area partners, even though their FTA provides otherwise or remains silent (e.g., the EU). Furthermore, it has become a common practice among WTO Members to include safeguard provisions in their free trade agreements, a flagrant violation of GATT Article XXIV.8(b) that has not been challenged by any WTO Member. '*The increasing importance of non-tariff barriers and of administered protection, however, argues for a more rigorous application of the requirements of GATT Article XXIV.*'[1080]

Far from providing legal certainty and coherence within the multilateral trading framework, the Agreement on Safeguards creates an antinomy. A non-discriminatory interpretation of GATT Article XIX consistent with GATT Article XXIV.8 would disallow parties to free trade agreements to impose safeguard measures, i.e., invoke GATT Article XIX.1. The non-discriminatory interpretation of GATT Article XIX.1 by CONTRACTING PARTIES (confirmed by WTO Members under ASG Article 2.2) in relation to GATT Article XXIV.8(b) implies the prohibition to impose safeguard

1079. The US was found to violate the ASG for exempting Mexico and Canada from safeguards measures in spite of having taken into account their imports to determine serious injury to the domestic industry (in cases *US – Wheat Gluten, US – Lamb, US – Line Pipe* and *US – Steel).*

1080. M. Hart, Dumping and Free Trade Areas, in J.H. Jackson, E.A. Vermulst (eds), *Antidumping Law and Practice: A Comparative Study*, 1990, pp. 326-342 at 333.

measures for WTO Members that are parties to free trade areas, including customs unions, such as the EU.

The WTO DSB has neither reached consensus nor provided for clarification on the application of safeguards within free trade areas or customs unions. The WTO DSB in the *Argentina-Footwear (EC)*,[1081] *US – Wheat Gluten*,[1082] *US – Lamb*,[1083] *US – Line Pipe*[1084] and *US – Steel Safeguards* disputes[1085] had supported that a party to a free trade agreement '*may impose safeguards against other parties*' to the free trade agreement.[1086] In these cases, the Appellate Body did not address the issue of whether GATT Article XXIV served as an exception to justify the discriminatory application of safeguards,[1087] but only analysed the lack of '*parallelism*', i.e., imports from other parties to free trade agreements were considered to determine serious injury (or threat thereof) in the safeguard investigation, while exempted from the application of the safeguard measure.[1088] The Appellate Body in the *US – Line Pipe* case[1089] established two circumstances during the safeguard investigation under which it is relevant to question whether GATT Article XXIV '*serves as an exception*' to ASG Article 2.2: when imports from free trade area partners are not considered in the determination of serious injury (or threat thereof) as well as where, although taken into account in such determination, authorities justify that imports from outside the free trade area, alone, satisfy the conditions to impose safeguards.[1090]

1081. *Argentina – Safeguard Measures on Imports of Footwear* (DS121).
1082. *United States – Definitive Safeguard Measures on Imports of Wheat Gluten from the European Communities* (DS166).
1083. *United States – Safeguard Measure on Imports of Fresh, Chilled or Frozen Lamb from New Zealand* (DS177).
1084. *United States – Definitive Safeguard Measures on Imports of Circular Welded Carbon Quality Line Pipe from Korea* (DS202).
1085. *United States – Definitive Safeguard Measures on Imports of Certain Steel Products* (DS252).
1086. M. Matsushita, T.J. Schoenbaum, P.C. Mavroidis, *The World Trade Organization: Law, Practice and Policy*, 2003, p. 363.
1087. WTO documents DS121/AB/R, 14 December 1999, paras 110-114; DS166/AB/R, 22 December 2000, paras 93-100; DS202/AB/R, 15 February 2002, paras 178-199; DS252/AB/R, 10 November 2003, paras 433-474.
1088. The Panel and Appellate Body in *Argentina-Footwear (EC)* required (for the first time) 'parallelism' between imports considered in the investigation to determine injury and those on which the safeguard measure is finally applied, i.e., determination of serious injury (or threaten thereof) based on '*imports from all sources*' necessarily leads to the application of safeguards on '*imports from all sources*'. The Appellate Body in *US – Gluten* confirmed the parallelism requirement. WTO documents DS121/R, 25 June 1999, para. 8.91; DS121/AB/R, 14 December 1999, para. 113. WTO document DS166/AB/R, 22 December 2000, para. 96.
1089. *United States – Definitive Safeguard Measures on Imports of Circular Welded Carbon Quality Line Pipe from Korea* (DS202).
1090. '*One is when, in the investigation by the competent authorities of a WTO Member, the imports that are exempted from the safeguard measure are not considered in the determination of serious injury. The other is when, in such an investigation, the imports that are exempted from the safeguard measure are considered in the determination of serious injury, and the competent authorities have also established explicitly, through a reasoned and adequate explanation, that imports from sources outside the free-trade area, alone, satisfied the conditions for the application of a safeguard measure, as set out in Article 2.1 and elaborated in Article 4.2.*' WTO document DS202/AB/R, 15 February 2002, para. 198.

Nonetheless, previously, the Appellate Body in the *Turkey-Textiles* case,[1091] without discussing the issue in detail, '*endorsed the first interpretation*' on whether restrictions other than those permitted under GATT Article XXIV.8 (i.e., Articles XI-XV and XX) could be imposed within members of a customs union or free trade agreement.[1092] According to Gobbi Estrella and Horlick, the Appellate Body reports in *Turkey-Textiles* lead to an interpretation of GATT Article XXIV.8 as '*mandating abolition of trade remedies*' within customs unions and free trade agreements.[1093]

The options that would permit WTO Members that are parties to customs unions and free trade agreements to impose safeguard measures have been analysed by Pauwelyn, who considers that the preferable option is '*to exclude regional imports from the actual safeguard*'.[1094] Such procedure, based on GATT Article XXIV.8, entails a discriminatory interpretation of GATT Article XIX.1, something which CONTRACTING PARTIES and the GATT Secretariat sought to discourage. Pauwelyn concludes that a '*safeguard exclusively imposed on regional imports may, however, be possible under the regional trade deal itself*',[1095] a flagrant violation of GATT Article XXIV.8 (b) and a contradiction with the purpose of a free trade area. Notably, GATT Article XXIV.4. states that the purpose of a customs union or free trade area should be '*to facilitate trade between the constituent territories and not to raise barriers to the trade of other contracting parties with such territories*', as well as recalls the desirability to increase freedom of trade by developing economic integration.[1096]

Finally, China's Protocol of Accession to the WTO includes a provision permitting the imposition of selective safeguard measures on imports from China to prevent or remedy '*market disruption*'. This provision under Section 16 of the Protocol, *Transitional Product-Specific Safeguard Mechanism,* was only in force for twelve years.[1097] WTO Members were thus allowed to apply discriminatory safeguard measures on imports from China until December 2013.

1091. *Turkey – Restrictions on Imports of Textile and Clothing Products* (DS34).
1092. A.T. Gobbi Estrella, G.N. Horlick, Mandatory Abolition of Anti-dumping, Countervailing Duties and Safeguards in Customs Unions and Free-Trade Areas Constituted Between World Trade Organization Members: Revisiting a Long-Standing Discussion in Light of the Appellate Body's Turkey-Textiles Ruling, *Journal of World Trade*, Vol. 40, No. 5, 2006, pp. 909-944 at 910-913 https://doi.org/10.1093/acprof:oso/9780199206995.003.0006.
1093. *Ibid.*, pp. 909-944 at 913-933. WTO document DS34/AB/R, 22 October 1999, paras 48-63.
1094. J. Pauwelyn, J., The Puzzle of WTO Safeguards and Regional Trade Agreements, *Journal of International Economic Law*, Vol. 7, No. 1, 2004, pp. 109-142 at 142 https://doi.org/10.1093/jiel/7.1.109.
1095. *Ibid.*
1096. GATT Article XXIV.4 first appeared under the Havana ITO Charter Article 44.1, which stated: '*Members recognize the desirability of increasing freedom of trade by the development, through voluntary agreements, of closer integration between the economies of the countries parties to such agreements. They also recognize that the purpose of a customs union or free-trade area should be to facilitate trade between the parties and not to raise barriers to the trade of other Member countries with such parties.*'
1097. WTO document L/432, 23 November 2001, pp. 9, 10.

B Discriminatory Application of Safeguards Through Allocated Quotas

The Agreement on Safeguards explicitly permits, under its Article 5.2, the imposition of safeguard measures in the form of quotas allocated to individual countries. Subparagraph (a) of ASG Article 5.2 requires seeking an agreement with other Members having an interest in supplying the product; in the absence of which, the allocation will be based on previous representative periods. While this arguably seems to provide for similar requirements established under GATT Article XIII, which requires the imposition of quantitative restrictions in a non-discriminatory manner, subparagraph (b) of ASG Article 5.2 allows departing from the previous provision under certain circumstances in case of serious injury, but not threat thereof.

This provision could arguably be interpreted to imply that the Agreement on Safeguards grants the possibility to impose quotas in a discriminatory manner. Contrary to the interpretative note of the safeguard provision under the ITO Charter and CONTRACTING PARTIES' interpretation of GATT Article XIX.1 (reaffirmed in *Norway – Textiles*),[1098] the discriminatory imposition of safeguard measures (in the form of allocated quotas) may be permissible by the Agreement on Safeguards, provided consultations are conducted under the Committee on Safeguards and justification of the measure is demonstrated to it.

It is worth remembering that at the Havana Conference, Contracting Parties decided to restrict the scope of safeguard measures to concessions granted under the GATT, meaning that safeguards would only be applied in the form of (additional) tariffs. This restriction was included under a new (fourth) paragraph of the safeguard provision of the ITO Charter, but it was never transposed to GATT Article XIX. By permitting allocated quotas, the Agreement on Safeguards broadens the scope of safeguard measures. Although its preamble recognizes the '*need to enhance rather than limit competition in international markets*', the Agreement on Safeguards permits the allocation of quotas among supplying countries (ASG Article 5.2), thereby restraining competition. Allocated quotas restrain competition even more than a global quota.

As Tumlir explained, a quota is intended '*to isolate the protected industry from price changes abroad*'; therefore, it is more restrictive than a tariff.[1099] If the quota is applied on a non-discriminatory basis (i.e., a global quota), while competition is reduced domestically, it is preserved among supplying members. Importers will tend to buy from the most efficient (cheapest) exporter. Hence, competition will be maintained among supplying countries, which will also tend to enhance competition in the quota-protected domestic market. In the case of allocated quotas, this freezing of the market shares or cartelization of the market is a '*virtual denial of the very purpose of foreign trade*'.[1100] By permitting the allocation of quotas under its Article 5.2, the

1098. *Norway – Restrictions on Imports of Certain Textile Products* (GD/100) Complainant: Hong Kong. GATT document L/4959, 24 March 1980.
1099. J. Tumlir, GATT Rules and the Community of Law- A Comparison of Economic and Legal Functions, in M. Hilf, F.G. Jacobs, E.U. Petersmann (eds), *The European Community and GATT*, Studies in Transnational Economic Law, Vol. 4, 1986, pp. 1-22 at 4.
1100. With a quota imposed on a non-discriminatory basis, the domestic price of the protected product will be increased, while the price of the imported product will not deviate with respect

Agreement on Safeguards is not enhancing competition in international trade, but rather restricting it.

C Unforeseen Developments

One of the three conditions to impose safeguards under GATT Article XIX, namely '*unforeseen developments*', has been omitted in the Agreement on Safeguards. Since GATT Article XIX has neither been amended nor repealed, the omission in the Agreement on Safeguards has given rise to some controversy with respect to the conditions required to impose safeguards. While some WTO Members have rejected the need to require '*unforeseen developments*' in order to impose safeguards, the Appellate Body has maintained the requirements under GATT Article XIX including '*unforeseen developments*', together with the Agreement on Safeguards, as a condition to impose safeguard measures.

The omission of this requirement in the Agreement on Safeguards has given rise to different interpretations in WTO dispute settlement reports. In the *Argentina – Footwear (EC)* dispute,[1101] the Panel found, first, that negotiators of the Agreement on Safeguards at the Uruguay Round had expressly omitted the requirement to demonstrate the existence of '*unforeseen developments*'; and second, that safeguard investigations and measures that met the requirements of the Agreement on Safeguards satisfied the requirements of GATT Article XIX.[1102] The Appellate Body reversed the Panel's findings.

In this line, the Appellate Body in the *Korea – Dairy* case[1103] concluded that the developments that led to the increase of imports must have been '*unexpected*'[1104] and that they '*must be demonstrated as a matter of fact in order for a safeguard measure to be applied consistently with the provisions of Article XIX*'.[1105] This was confirmed by the Panel in the *Argentina – Preserved Peaches* dispute,[1106] which concluded that two requirements of GATT Article XIX.1(a) must be fulfilled before the imposition of a safeguard measure, i.e., the demonstration of increased imports, and unforeseen developments.[1107] Furthermore, the Appellate Body in the *US – Lamb* case[1108]

to world-market price. In the case of allocated quotas, the price of the imported product also deviates from the world-market price. Since a quota is guaranteed, there is not an incentive for other supplying firms to maintain a competitive price. The price of the imports can be increased up to the domestic price of the importing country, whose firms can, in turn, continue to increase domestic prices. J. Tumlir, GATT Rules and the Community of Law- A Comparison of Economic and Legal Functions, in M. Hilf, F.G. Jacobs, E.U. Petersmann (eds), *The European Community and GATT*, Studies in Transnational Economic Law, Vol. 4, 1986, pp. 1-22 at 4.

1101. *Argentina – Safeguard Measures on Imports of Footwear* (DS121).
1102. WTO document DS121/AB/R, 14 December 1999, para. 97.
1103. *Korea, Republic of – Definitive Safeguard Measure on Imports of Certain Dairy Products* (DS98).
1104. WTO document DS98/AB/R 14 December 1999, para. 84.
1105. *Ibid.*, paras 84, 85.
1106. *Argentina – Definitive Safeguard Measure on Imports of Preserved Peaches* (DS238).
1107. WTO document DS238/R, 14 February 2003, para. 8.
1108. *United States – Safeguard Measure on Imports of Fresh, Chilled or Frozen Lamb from New Zealand* (DS177) [and] *from Australia* (DS178).

considered that the demonstration of the '*conditions*' *and* '*circumstances*' under GATT Article XIX '*must also feature in the same report of the competent authorities*'.[1109]

Certain WTO Members have criticized the Appellate Body for interpreting GATT Article XIX together with the Agreement on Safeguards, thus requiring compliance with the existence of '*unforeseen developments*'. According to the US, by creating the requirement to demonstrate the existence of unforeseen developments to impose safeguard measures, the Appellate Body has established '*a high threshold for serious injury determinations*', rendering the imposition of safeguard measures more difficult.[1110] Moreover, the US claimed that a WTO Member is not required to demonstrate the existence of the requirements before the imposition of the measure, but only once it has been challenged; and that the Appellate Body's interpretation results in the shift of the burden of proof since the complaining party must demonstrate the absence of compliance with the requirements in the safeguard provisions. For this reason, the USTR qualifies as '*erroneous*' the Appellate Body's interpretations, in the disputes mentioned above, of requiring investigating authorities to demonstrate the existence of '*unforeseen developments*'.

Since the establishment of the WTO in 1994, until the obstruction of the appointments to the Appellate Body in 2017, the US had imposed five safeguard measures. Among the three disputes on manufactured (non-agricultural) goods, two concluded in DSB reports, *US – Line Pipe*[1111] and *US – Steel Safeguards*.[1112] In both disputes, the Panel found that the US had failed to demonstrate the existence of unforeseen developments prior to the imposition of the safeguard measures, thus acting inconsistently with its obligations under GATT Article XIX. Notwithstanding the Appellate Body in the *US – Line Pipe* case did not address the issue of unforeseen developments (for not being challenged by the parties), it referred to the Appellate Body's interpretation in *Argentina – Footwear (EC)*, which requires the existence of developments not been 'foreseen' or 'expected' by a Member in order to impose safeguards.[1113] The Appellate Body in the *US – Steel Safeguards* dispute upheld the Panel's finding that the US had failed to demonstrate that the existence of unforeseen developments had resulted in the increase in imports of the concerned products,[1114] hence found US safeguards to be inconsistent with GATT Article XIX and the Agreement on Safeguards.

The 'unforeseen developments' requirement under GATT Article XIX was first interpreted in the *US – Fur Felt Hats* case[1115] to mean 'developments occurring after the

1109. WTO document DS177/AB/R, DS178/AB/R 1 May 2001, para. 72.
1110. USTR, Report on the Appellate Body of the World Trade Organization, pp. 110-114.
1111. *United States – Definitive Safeguard Measures on Imports of Circular Welded Carbon Quality Line Pipe from Korea* (DS202).
1112. *United States – Definitive Safeguard Measures on Imports of Certain Steel Products* (DS252).
1113. WTO document DS202/AB/R, paras 79, 81.
1114. WTO document DS248/AB/R, DS249/AB/R, DS251/AB/R, DS252/AB/R, DS253/AB/R, DS254/AB/R, DS258/AB/R, DS259/AB/R, 10 November 2003, p. 166, paras 330, 509.
1115. *Assured Life of Tariff Concessions with regard to Article XIX/US – Fur Felt Hats* (GD/9). Complainant: Czechoslovakia. Respondent: US. GATT document CP/106, 27 March 1951. Other relevant GATT documents: CP.5/22, CP.5/SR.14, 10 November 1950; CP.6/SR.19, CP.6/SR.19/Corr.1, 22 October 1951 (adoption of the report).

negotiation of the relevant tariff concession which it would not be reasonable to expect that the negotiators of the country making the concession could and should have foreseen at the time when the concession was negotiated'.[1116] Due to this requirement under GATT Article XIX, the provision has been considered a *rebus sic stantibus* clause by some jurists, as explained above. This consideration cannot take place if unforeseen developments, an essential element of the *rebus sic stantibus* clause, is no longer required. In other words, without the requirement of unforeseen developments, the safeguard provision could not be considered a *rebus sic stantibus* clause.

D Causal Link

The Agreement on Safeguards specifies the procedures to impose safeguards. Particularly, its Article 4 provides for the determination of injury based on objective evidence of the existence of a causal link between the increase of imports and the serious injury (or threat thereof). This incorporation seems a legal improvement since in the first GATT safeguard dispute, the *US – Fur Felt Hats* case,[1117] the burden of proof was shifted by the Working Party, concluding that the complainant (exporting country) had not proved the absence of injury in the importing country.[1118] Nevertheless, the need for a causal link between the increase in imports and the injury has been criticized. From an economic perspective, as Sykes has explained, an increase in imports cannot cause injury, due to the fact that any increase in imports is the result of domestic supply and demand, and world-market prices. Economic shocks in the importing country or abroad can result in both an increase in imports and conditions of injury, such as '*decreased price and production, reduced employment*'. According to Sykes, it would be impossible to prove this causal link in practice; hence, it is incoherent to treat the increased imports as a potential cause of injury to import-competing industries.[1119]

The issue of the causal link is made even more complex by the non-attribution requirement, established under ASG Article 4.2, whereby investigating authorities shall exclude other factors that concurrently (with the increase in imports) cause injury (or threat thereof) to the domestic industry (as in anti-dumping and countervailing duty proceedings).[1120] The problem stems from the fact that such other factors are the economic shocks that result in an increase in imports.[1121] Therefore, in practice, it is impossible to show the existence of an absent causal link and the non-attribution of the

1116. GATT document CP/106, 27 March 1951, paras 9, 11.
1117. *Assured Life of Tariff Concessions with regard to Article XIX/US – Fur Felt Hats* (GD/9). Complainant: Czechoslovakia. Respondent: US. GATT document CP/106, 27 March 1951.
1118. GATT document CP/106, 27 March 1951, para. 30.
1119. A.O. Sykes, The Safeguards Mess: Critique of WTO Jurisprudence, *World Trade Review*, Vol. 2, No. 3, 2003, pp. 261-296 at 266, 267 https://doi.org/10.1017/s1474745604001478. A.O. Sykes, The Fundamental Deficiencies of the Agreement on Safeguards: A Reply to Professor Lee, *Journal of World Trade*, Vol. 40, No. 5, 2006, pp. 979-996 at 979, 980 https://doi.org/10.54648/trad2006048.
1120. ADA Article 3.5 and ASCM Article 15.5.
1121. A.O. Sykes, The Fundamental Deficiencies of the Agreement on Safeguards: A Reply to Professor Lee, *Journal of World Trade*, Vol. 40, No. 5, 2006, pp. 979-996 at 980 https://doi.org/10.54648/trad2006048.

injury to the factors that cause the increase in imports. Yet, since investigating authorities are required by the Agreement on Safeguards to demonstrate the causal link and the non-attribution analysis, the WTO DSB has interpreted the Agreement on Safeguards in such a manner, e.g., in *Argentina – Footwear (EC),*[1122] *US – Wheat Gluten,*[1123] and *US – Lamb.*[1124] An exception to this occurred in the *US – Tyres (China)* dispute,[1125] where the WTO DSB interpreted Section 16.4 of the Protocol of Accession of China to the WTO, concerning the product-specific safeguard mechanism, whereby investigating authorities are required to show evidence of a causal link and the non-attribution analysis, as required by the Agreement on Safeguards. Nevertheless, both the Panel and the Appellate Body in that case found that China had '*failed to establish that the USITC improperly attributed injury caused by other factors to subject imports*' from China,[1126] thus shifting the burden of proof to the complainant, as in the *US – Fur Felt Hats* case.[1127]

E Prohibition of VERs

One of the main improvements introduced by the Agreement on Safeguards is arguably the elimination of VERs and similar import or export measures (ASG Article 11). Examples of similar measures are provided under footnote 4, namely '*export moderation, export-price or import-price monitoring systems, export or import surveillance, compulsory import cartels and discretionary export or import licensing schemes, any of which afford protection*'. The ban on VERs constitutes an improvement in the sense that it prohibited Members from negotiating competition restrains (export or import barriers) bilaterally or with companies in a foreign country. It is the only new provision in the Agreement on Safeguards that goes in the direction of enhancing competition.

Nonetheless, ASG Article 11.c clarifies that this prohibition merely affects safeguard measures, i.e., pursuant to GATT Article XIX, while similar import and export restrictions (e.g., price undertakings) are permitted in anti-dumping and countervailing duty proceedings (under ADA Article 8 and ASCM Article 18). Therefore, the Agreement on Safeguards prohibition of VERs has merely resulted in the imposition of similar measures by invoking other WTO Agreements, such as the ADA or ASCM. The enhancement of competition, under ASG Article 11, is necessary; however, it cannot solely cover safeguard measures under GATT Article XIX, but should be extended to all measures, including anti-dumping and countervailing duties under GATT Article VI. For this reason, it is considered essential the enactment of a

1122. *Argentina – Safeguard Measures on Imports of Footwear* (DS121).
1123. *United States – Definitive Safeguard Measures on Imports of Wheat Gluten from the European Communities* (DS166).
1124. *United States – Safeguard Measure on Imports of Fresh, Chilled or Frozen Lamb from New Zealand* (DS177) [and] *from Australia* (DS178).
1125. *United States – Measures Affecting Imports of Certain Passenger Vehicle and Light Truck Tyres from China* (DS399).
1126. WTO document DS399/AB/R 5 September 2011, para. 319.
1127. *Assured Life of Tariff Concessions with regard to Article XIX/US – Fur Felt Hats* (GD/9). Complainant: Czechoslovakia. Respondent: US. GATT document CP/106, 27 March 1951.

multilateral agreement on competition and trade-restrictive practices, in line with the chapter on restrictive business practices of the ITO Charter.

Through the years, multilateral provisions on safeguards have been broadened and weakened, thus facilitating import restraints to the detriment of importers, consumers, and even the environment. The Agreement on Safeguards, far from being an achievement for the multilateral trading system, weakens the criteria to impose safeguards and creates more controversy rather than clarifying the ambiguities of GATT Article XIX. Since only a relative increase in domestic production is required, no actual increase in imports is needed. The existence of a causal link between the increase in imports and serious injury (or threat thereof) is inviable since both are concurrent causes of economic shocks. The '*unforeseen developments*' requirement under GATT Article XIX has been omitted in the Agreement on Safeguards, resulting in controversies with respect to the application of safeguards. The discriminatory application of safeguards has undermined the economic integration provided by free trade areas and customs unions pursuant to GATT Article XXIV.8, and through the allocation of quotas, competition is restrained even among supplying exporters. The prohibition of VERs is the only improvement towards the enhancement of the multilateral trading system and competition, albeit insufficient.

Notwithstanding it has been argued that safeguard measures can be extremely useful to '*relieve protectionist pressure*', thus facilitating tariff reduction and allowing governments to bear protectionist demands;[1128] history shows that safeguards have been at the service of governments with the mere objective of leaning towards protectionist pressures, without contributing to the liberalization of trade. Far from enhancing competition, safeguards restrain imports by cartelizing the market. Either in the form of tariffs, quotas, or tariff quotas, safeguards undermine the core principles of the multilateral trading system. Without another aim than protecting certain industries at the discretion of political interests, there is no supreme good to protect which justifies the non-compliance with the non-discrimination principle. The lack of economic and legal sense of safeguards suggests the elimination of this trade remedy, whose mere objective is the political discretion of protecting certain domestic industries to the detriment of the multilateral trading system.

1128. R.Z. Lawrence, R.E. Litan, *Saving Free Trade: A Pragmatic Approach*, 1986, pp. 23-24.

CHAPTER 11

Agreement on Competition and Trade-Restrictive Practices

This chapter explores the need to create coherence between trade and competition rules, as well as the attempt to incorporate rules on trade-restrictive practices or competition in the multilateral trading system, first in the International Trade Organization Charter, then in the GATT/WTO Agreement.

I COHERENCE BETWEEN TRADE AND COMPETITION RULES

As has been stated throughout this book, the main commonality between the three trade remedies is their aim to protect domestic industries from import competition. Safeguard measures have often been distinguished from anti-dumping and countervailing duties on the grounds that they target fair rather than unfair trade.[1129] Nevertheless, the distinction between fair and unfair has been considered to be '*in large part coincidence*'. More importantly, the three trade remedies focus on the impact of products in the importing country instead of the exporting country, i.e., (serious) injury or threat thereof.[1130]

While a system of tariff protection transparently offers benefits to producers and generally requires approval by the legislative authority, the administration of trade

1129. Allegations of unfair trade have existed in the multilateral trading system since the first discussions of the GATT Preparatory Committee at London in 1946, when competition from imports from Japan was considered a threat to domestic industries. *See* generally, G. Saxonhouse, A Short Summary of the Long History of Unfair Trade Allegations Against Japan, in J. Bhagwati, R.E. Hudec (eds), *Fair Trade and Harmonization. Prerequisite for Free Trade?*, Vol. I: Economic Analysis, 1996, pp. 472-513.

1130. '*So long as we are not willing to legislate world-wide uniformity in wage scales, exchange rates, environmental controls, debt/equity ratios, depreciation, interest rates, and accounting techniques, and indeed comparable relations between government and industry, what is fair and what is unfair is in large part coincidence.*' A. Lowenfeld, Fair or Unfair Trade: Does it Matter, *Cornell International Law Journal*, Vol. 13, No. 2, 1981, pp. 205-219 at 218.

remedy laws is left to the discretion of governments. Certain import-competing industries exercise more political pressure on governments than, *inter alia*, consumers. As a result, governments often protect these import-competing industries from import competition, rather than aiming at the welfare of the economy as a whole.

The system of contingency protection,[1131] like the mercantilist system described by Adam Smith, seems to consider '*production, and not consumption, as the ultimate end and object of all industry and commerce. In the restraints upon the importation of all foreign commodities which can come into competition with those of our own growth or manufacture, the interest of the home consumer is evidently sacrificed to that of the producer. It is altogether for the benefit of the latter that the former is obliged to pay that enhancement of price which this monopoly almost always occasions*'.[1132]

The administration of trade remedies is skewed towards anti-competitive interests. The government is the intermediary between the complaining domestic producer and the more competitive foreign exporter, in the agreement undertaken to restrain the import competition of products alleged to be dumped or subsidized.[1133] In the case of subsidized imports, government-led undertakings can also be reached with foreign governments. While trade remedy laws permit cartelization of the market by governments, competition laws aim at preventing private companies from reaching undertakings that cartelize the market.[1134] In other words, what is prohibited under competition rules is '*profitable and politically marketable*' under trade-restrictive laws.[1135]

Therefore, trade remedy laws represent the greatest contradiction to an effective competition regime. This inconsistency between domestic competition laws and trade remedy laws is illustrated in the case of the EU. On the one hand, internal barriers, including trade remedies, were eliminated within the customs union while common competition rules were set.[1136] On the other hand, common trade remedy laws were established to restrain import competition.[1137]

1131. Trade policy system centred on trade remedy laws. R.C. de Grey, *Trade Policy and the System of Contingency Protection in the Perspective of Competition Policy*, 1986, p. 1.
1132. A. Smith, *The Wealth of Nations*, [1776], 2000, p. 877.
1133. Subject to trade remedy laws proceedings, import-competing industries bring about the imposition of duties and/or quotas on competing imports. Particularly, through the imposition of safeguard measures or (the acceptance of) anti-dumping and countervailing undertakings, imports are subject to tariff quotas. In the case of undertakings, as it occurred with voluntary export restraints, governments agree to limit competition with foreign exporters, often in the form of tariff quotas.
1134. Cartelization is considered the last stage of protectionism. J. Tumlir, Protectionist Threat to International Order, *International Journal*, Vol. 34, No. 1, 1978, pp. 53-63, at 57 https://doi.org/10.2307/40201719.
1135. R. Grey, The Conflict Between Trade Policy and Competition Policy: A Comment in E.U. Petersmann, M. Hilf, *The New GATT Round of Multilateral Trade Negotiations – Legal and Economic Problems*, Vol. 5, 1988, pp. 447-453, at 448.
1136. As '*tariffs barriers were reduced within the Common Market, anti-dumping mechanisms were phased out, beginning in 1970. But to ensure that trade among Common Market member nations was not distorted, an active competition policy was considered necessary*'. F. Scherer, International Trade and Competition Policy, in E. Hope, P. Maeleng, *Competition and Trade Policies, Coherence or Conflict?*, 1998, pp. 13-30 at 15. '*Provisions on antidumping were included in the European Free Trade Association (EFTA), established by the Treaty of Stockholm in 1960; the EC-Sweden Agreement of 1972; and the between Australia-New Zealand*

Interestingly, the first worldwide trade remedy laws were coeval with the first worldwide competition laws. The first worldwide countervailing duty law, the US countervailing duty law on imports of sugar, was enacted in 1890, the same year in which the first anti-trust law, the US Sherman Antitrust Act, entered into force. Both US legislations were mainly the government's response to the petitions from farmers, who in those days accounted for 40% of the US force.[1138] Allegations of dumping against US steel trusts were the subject of an antitrust investigation in the US as well as the origin of the first worldwide anti-dumping law, the Canadian 'dumping clause' of 1904 against low-priced imports of steel. Canada passed its first anti-trust law in 1899. Similarly, Australia enacted its first competition and anti-dumping laws in 1906.[1139]

Trade remedy laws create conflict between international trade and competition. By restraining trade and competition, trade remedies are inconsistent with the core principles of the multilateral trading system and competition laws. Several factors seem to have maintained this legal incongruence between international trade and competition laws through the years. First, trade remedy laws constitute legally permitted exceptions to the non-discrimination principle (GATT Articles I and III), aimed at protecting 'domestic' industries by restraining import competition. Second, while trade remedy laws have been developed during the main GATT negotiations rounds (i.e., Kennedy, Tokyo and Uruguay Round), multilateral provisions on competition were never incorporated in the GATT or the WTO. Consequently, while the multilateral trading system has permitted restraining competition through trade remedy laws, it does not include competition rules within its framework.

Coherence between trade and competition policy would be welfare-enhancing, including for developing countries.[1140] Attaining this congruence at the multilateral

---

Closer Economic Relations Agreement of 1983.' In all these cases, anti-dumping provisions were later replaced by competition laws. M. Hart, Dumping and Free Trade Areas, in J.H. Jackson, E.A. Vermulst (eds), *Antidumping Law and Practice: A Comparative Study*, 1990, pp. 326-342 at 329.

1137. As the EU has been enlarging, trade barriers have been eliminated internally, while common competition and trade remedy laws have been enforced. *See* J.A. García López, M.I. García Catalán, La Expansión del Derecho Comunitario Europeolos Acuerdos Preferenciales y las Reglas de Origen en las Relaciones Comerciales Exteriores de la Unión Europea, *Revista de la Facultad de Derecho de la Universidad Complutense*, No. 89, 1998, pp. 87-104.

1138. F.M. Scherer, *Competition Policies for an Integrated World Economy*, 1994, p. 18.

1139. Out of the mercantilists' doctrine that one '*country's loss was another country's gain (...) evolved the doctrines of the essential rivalry, instead of harmony, between the economic interests of nations, and the belief that the use of power to gain wealth, including its use to impoverish rival countries, was a rational and often more effective program for the promotion of a country's economic welfare than the pursuit of efficiency in production and the sharing between countries through peaceful competition of the mutual benefits of friendly trade. There was here, of course, the sharpest of conflicts between the doctrine of the universal economy and mercantilist doctrine*'. J. Viner, Five Lectures on Economics and Freedom. Delivered At Wabash College, Crawfordsville, Indiana, June 1959. Lecture I. Early Attitudes Toward Trade And The Merchant, in D.A. Irwin, *Essays on the Intellectual History of Economics*, 1991, p. 44.

1140. B. Hoekman, Competition Policy and the Global Trading System A Developing-Country Perspective, Policy Research Working Paper 1735, The World Bank International Economics Department International Trade Division, 1997, pp. 13, 14.

level requires, first, the elimination of contingency trade remedies and,[1141] second, the adoption of multilateral rules to enhance competition and prevent trade-restrictive practices. Indeed, the elimination of trade remedy laws would be a first step towards the harmonization of trade and competition,[1142] before embarking on a process towards the creation of international competition laws.[1143] Hence, as this book has suggested, the elimination of trade remedy laws is fundamental to enhance trade and competition, and thus, global welfare.[1144]

Second, the incorporation of multilateral rules to prevent trade-restrictive practices would apply to commercial enterprises (both public and private), as well as to governments. Unilateral protection of 'domestic' industries attained by trade remedy laws should instead consist of judicial protection, whereby multilateral trade rules are interpreted and enforced by an independent body. This entails the incorporation of multilateral rules on competition/trade-restrictive practices, based on rules with economic and legal rationale, into the multilateral trading system. It would reinforce the multilateral trading system by enhancing trade, providing legal certainty, and granting judicial protection, to companies as well as to consumers, from anti-competitive practices undertaken by both private and public companies.

II MULTILATERAL AGREEMENTS ON TRADE-RESTRICTIVE PRACTICES AND COMPETITION

As seen in Part II, the first multilateral rules on competition were included in the US Proposals for Expansion of World Trade and Employment of 1945. Restrictions

1141. '*Beyond those competition-policy innovation, we should return to the historical origins of the tension between competition law and international trade policy in North America, and attend to the remaining protectionist elements in international trade policy- particularly trade remedy regimes such as anti-dumping and countervailing duty regimes- as well as setting seriously about the task of exorcising the residual elements of mercantilism that constrain the operation of international competitive forces far more than do any aspect of current domestic competition policy regimes.*' M.J. Trebilcock, Competition Policy and Trade Policy: Mediating the Interface, *Journal of World Trade*, Vol. 30, No. 4, 1996, pp. 71-106 at 106 https://doi.org/10.54648/trad1996030.

1142. '*Those who would include competition rules in GATT, therefore, would be wise to heed the oath of Hippocrates: primum non nocere, first, do no harm.*' D. Palmeter, Competition Policy and Unfair Trade: First Do No Harm, *Aussenwirtschaft Zeitschrift für internationale Wirtschaftsbeziehungen*, Vol. 49, 1994, pp. 417-422, at 422.

1143. M. Koulen, Potential Anti-Trust Liability of Exporters Participating in Various Forms of Exports Restraint Arrangements, in E.U. Petersmann, M. Hilf, *The New GATT Round of Multilateral Trade Negotiations: Legal and Economic Problems*, Vol. 5, 1988, pp. 437-446 at 446. D. Palmeter, Competition Policy and Unfair Trade: First Do No Harm, *Aussenwirtschaft Zeitschrift für internationale Wirtschaftsbeziehungen*, Vol. 49, 1994, pp. 417-422, at 420.

1144. '*It is the interest of* ["*those companies, considered as the sovereigns of the countries which they have conquered*",] *to open the most extensive market for the produce of his country, to allow the most perfect freedom of commerce, in order to increase as much as possible the number and the competition of buyers; and upon this account to abolish, not only all monopolies, but all restraints upon the transportation of the home produce (...) upon its exportation to foreign countries, or upon the importation of goods of any kind for which it can be exchanged. It is in this manner most likely to increase both the quantity and value of that produce, and consequently of his own share of it, or of his own revenue.*' A. Smith. *The Wealth of Nations*, [1776], 2000, pp. 845, 846.

imposed by companies '*to obtain the unfair advantage of monopoly*' were listed among the problems that prevented the expansion of trade.[1145] Therefore, a chapter on '*Restrictive business practices*' was included in the US Proposals of 1945 and maintained in the US Suggested Charter of 1946 (Articles 34-40). The importance of regulating these restrictive practices to safeguard the objectives of the organization was also recognized by the Preparatory Committee of the GATT and ITO Charter during the discussions in London, New York, Geneva and Havana.[1146] The chapter on '*Restrictive Business Practices*' was maintained in the ITO Charter (Articles 46-54), which was signed by fifty-three countries at the conclusion of the Conference on Trade and Employment in Havana, in 1948.[1147] Nevertheless, the ITO never came into being; consequently, the chapter on restrictive business practices did not enter into force, while the chapter on commercial policy, enshrined in the GATT, became the legal framework of the international trading system.

Importantly, these provisions were aimed at impeding commercial enterprises, whether private or public, from frustrating the objectives of the ITO through practices that restricted market access, restrained competition or fostered monopolistic control in international trade.[1148] Anti-competitive practices within the services sector were also covered.[1149] A multilateral proceeding was provided to deal with such practices. The ITO was entrusted with conducting investigations and hearings, requesting information, making recommendations, and requesting Members to provide reports on the enforcement. Members were mandated to cooperate with the organization with the aim to ensure that commercial enterprises within their jurisdiction (whether private or public) would not engage in trade-restrictive practices.

In precise, these provisions on restrictive business practices had the objective of guaranteeing that the trade liberalization commitments undertaken by governments would not be frustrated by commercial enterprises. If the ITO Charter had entered into force, its provisions on restrictive business practices (Chapter V) would have clearly conflicted with its trade remedy provisions under the chapter on commercial policy (Chapter IV), which became part of the GATT. Following the ITO failure, multilateral rules on restrictive business practices have been absent, while trade remedy laws have

1145. US Department of State, Proposals for Expansion of World Trade and Employment, 1945, p. 2.
1146. UN document EPCT/33. 31 October 1946, pp. 18, 19.
1147. Chapter V of the ITO Charter (Articles 46-54). UN document E/CONF.2/78, 24 March 1948.
1148. Article 34 of the US Suggested Charter clarified that 'commercial enterprises' referred to '*all persons and entities conducting business, including such entities in which there is a government interest as well as agencies of government conducting trade*'. US State Department, Suggested Charter for an International Trade Organization of the United Nations, September 1946, p. 26. Article 34 of the US Suggested Charter would become Article 46 of the Havana Charter. UN document E/CONF.2/78, 24 March 1948.
1149. Article 53.1 read as follows: '*The Members recognize that certain services, such as transportation, telecommunications, insurance and the commercial services of banks, are substantial elements of international trade and that any restrictive business practices by enterprises engaged in these activities in international trade may have harmful effects similar to those indicated in paragraph 1 of Article 46.*' UN document E/CONF.2/78, 24 March 1948.

been developed in multilateral negotiating rounds. Nevertheless, efforts have been made to find coherence between multilateral rules on trade and competition and restrictive business practices/competition.

Following the GATT Review Session of 1954-1955, CONTRACTING PARTIES established a Committee on Restrictive Business Practices, which set up a commission of experts for the elaboration of a report.[1150] A further group of experts reported to the GATT in 1960, concluding that a multilateral competition agreement was unrealistic due to a lack of consensus among countries. Nonetheless, GATT Contracting Parties followed its recommendation of adopting a decision by which consultations could be held in case of harm produced by '*restrictive business practices of firms from other parties*'. According to some of the experts, competition matters could be dealt with by invoking the provisions on nullification or impairment, under GATT Article XXIII, or joint action by Contracting Parties, under GATT Article XXV. Nevertheless, the majority of the experts recommended that, regardless of the legality of applying GATT Article XXIII, no action should be taken under this article since it would involve '*the grave risk*' of retaliation under its paragraph 2, '*which would be taken on the basis of judgments which would have to be made without factual information about the restrictive practice in question, with consequent counter-productive effects on trade*'.[1151]

A multilateral agreement on competition was suggested in 1986 by Grey, who studied the contingency protection system from the perspective of competition policy and considered the obligations on restrictive business practices contained in the ITO Charter (Chapter V) '*considerably more precise*'[1152] than the United Nations Conference on Trade and Development (UNCTAD) Set of Mutually Agreed Equitable Principles and Rules for the Control of Restrictive Business Practices.[1153]

During the Tokyo Round and thereafter, some trade experts suggested replacing anti-dumping, which discourages '*healthy price competition from imports*', with competition/anti-trust laws, for considering them '*entirely adequate to protect against the threat of predation from foreign dumpers*',[1154] as the Zenith case showed.[1155] This replacement was encouraged on the grounds that it would respect the spirit of the

1150. GATT documents L/384, 5 August 1955; L/907, 7 November 1958; L/988, 25 May 1959; L/1015, 30 June 1959.
1151. J.H. Jackson, Alternatives Approaches for Implementing Competition Rules in International Economic Relations, *Aussenwirtschaft Zeitschrift für internationale Wirtschaftsbeziehungen*, Vol. 49, 1994, pp. 177-200 at 192.
1152. R.C. de Grey, *Trade Policy and the System of Contingency Protection in the Perspective of Competition Policy*, 1986, p. 5.
1153. UN document TD/RBP/CONF/10/Rev.1, 1980.
1154. J.J. Barceló III, The Antidumping Law: Repeal It or Revise It, *Michigan Journal of International Law*, Vol. 1, No. 1, 1979, pp. 53-93 at 66, 78. *See also, inter alia*, R.W. Bierwagen, *GATT Article VI and the Protectionist Bias in Anti-dumping Laws*, 1990; B. Hoekman, P.C. Mavroidis, Dumping, Antidumping and Antitrust, *Journal of World Trade*, Vol. 30, No. 1, 1996, pp. 27-52 https://doi.org/10.54648/trad1996003.
1155. '*In a separate opinion involving the facts of Zenith, (...) the court held there was good venue, personal jurisdiction, and service of process in an antitrust action against an alleged foreign dumper (...) that the Sherman Act would be adequate protection against predatory price discrimination in the wholly domestic context.*' J.J. Barceló III, The Antidumping Law: Repeal It or Revise It, *Michigan Journal of International Law*, Vol. 1, No. 1, 1979, pp. 53-93 at 86 footnotes 72-75.

non-discrimination principle, in particular, national treatment under GATT Article III.[1156] The result of the Tokyo Round was, however, very different, with the further development of anti-dumping rules, enshrined in the 1979 Anti-dumping Code.

During the Uruguay Round, trade experts demanded the incorporation of competition rules within the framework of the WTO in order to prevent the undermining of the world trading system.[1157] For instance, Jackson, recognizing that the lack of competition rules concerning international trade was '*one of the most important gaps in the structure of international economic relations*',[1158] argued in favour of a '*competition policy code*' based on the model contemplated in the ITO Charter, i.e., with binding effect on governments and private enterprises, and applicability of the WTO dispute settlement.

Both academics and practitioners[1159] worked together on proposals to reach an agreement on competition. A European Commission Expert Group published a report on competition, which served as the basis for a proposal for a Plurilateral Agreement on Competition and Trade.[1160] Moreover, a group of academics and practitioners[1161] prepared an International Anti-trust Code (the 1993 'Munich Draft'),[1162] which was also intended to be part of the WTO Agreement, following the Uruguay Round.[1163] Nevertheless, the agreement on competition rules was not reached at the Uruguay Round.

1156. M.J. Trebilcock, Competition Policy and Trade Policy: Mediating the Interface, *Journal of World Trade*, Vol. 30. No. 4, 1996, pp. 71-106 at 80 https://doi.org/10.54648/trad1996030.
1157. J.H. Jackson, Alternatives Approaches for Implementing Competition Rules in International Economic Relations, *Aussenwirtschaft Zeitschrift für internationale Wirtschaftsbeziehungen*, Vol. 49, 1994, pp. 177-200 at 193.
1158. J.H. Jackson, Statement on Competition and Trade Policy Before the US Senate Committee on Judiciary, 18 June 1992, *Journal of World Trade*, Vol. 26, No. 5, 1992, pp. 111-116 at 111 https://doi.org/10.54648/trad1992037.
1159. *Ibid.*, p. 116.
1160. Commission of the European Communities, Competition Policy in the New Trade Order: Strengthening International Cooperation and Rules. Report of the Group Expert. EC COM (95) 359 final, 12 July 1995. The Expert Group members were U. Immenga, F. Jenny, E.U. Petersmann (external experts) and C.D. Ehlermann, J.F. Pons, R. Abbott, F. Lamoureux, J.F. Marchipont, A. Jacquemin (EC Commission officials).
1161. The Working Group was formed by J. Drexl, et al., International Competition Rules for Private Business: A Trade Law Approach for Linking Trade and Competition Rules in the WTO, *Chicago-Kent Law Review*, Vol. 72, No. 2, 1996, pp. 445-582 at 572.
1162. A detailed explanation of the Draft Anti-trust Code in W. Fikentscher, U. Immenga, *Draft International Antitrust Code*, 1995; D.J. Gifford, The Draft International Antitrust Code Proposed at Munich: Good Intentions Gone Awry, *Minnesota Journal of International Law*, 1997, Vol. 6, No. 1, pp. 1-66.
1163. EC Commissioner Sir Leon Brittan applied the EU experience by analogy, and in a speech at Davos in 1992 recognized competition policy as '*a necessary complement to the elimination of trade barriers. If, for example, customs duties were replaced by export subsidies or a cartel between companies to divide markets, what would have been achieved? In economic terms, very little*'. L. Brittan, K. Van Miert. Towards an International Framework of Competition Rules, *International Business Lawyer*, Vol. 24, No. 10, 1996, pp. 454-457. L. Brittan, A Framework for International Competition, Address to World Economic Forum, Davos on 3 February 1992.

After the establishment of the WTO, attention was given to competition policy also by both academics and practitioners.[1164] While some thought the WTO lacked the necessary institutional infrastructure for an International Competition Law,[1165] others have supported the incorporation of WTO competition rules,[1166] even using as a model the WTO experience in the telecommunication sector.[1167] In light of the reticence to surrender sovereignty and the substantial differences between their national competition policies, Scherer proposed a transition to multilateral coordination under the WTO. '*Any multilateral accord will have to be on some limited subset of core principles governing only transactions with significant implications for international trade and/or investment. The most likely candidates are export and import cartels, serious abuses of dominant positions in the world market, and merger approval procedures.*'[1168]

In the WTO, a Working Group on the Interaction between Trade and Competition Policy was established in 1996 as an outcome of the WTO Ministerial Conference in Singapore,[1169] yet its work was suspended in 2004.[1170] Multilateral efforts have also been undertaken outside the GATT/WTO framework to reach harmonization with competition rules. Of particular relevance are voluntary codes of the Organization for Economic Cooperation and Development (OECD), namely the OECD *Guidelines for Multinational Enterprises* of 1976, last reviewed in 2023;[1171] and the UNCTAD *Set of Mutually Agreed Equitable Principles and Rules for the Control of Restrictive Business Practices* of 1980, last reviewed in 2020.[1172] Nevertheless, these codes are not binding.

1164. E.U. Petersmann, International Competition Rules for Governments and for Private Business, *Journal of World Trade*, Vol. 30, No. 3, 1996, pp. 5-35 https://doi.org/10.54648/trad1996017; M.J. Trebilcock, Competition Policy and Trade Policy: Mediating the Interface, *Journal of World Trade*, Vol. 30, No. 4, 1996, pp. 71-106 https://doi.org/10.54648/trad1996030. J. Bellis, Anti-competitive Practices and the WTO: The Elusive Search for New World Trade Rules, in M. Bronckers, R. Quick (eds), *New Directions in International Economic Law: Essays in Honour of John H. Jackson*, 2000, pp. 361-368.
1165. F. Weiss, From World Trade Law to World Competition Law, *Fordham International Law Journal*, Vol. 23, No. 6, pp. S250-S273, 1999.
1166. E.U. Petersmann, International Competition Rules for Private Business: A Trade Law Approach for Linking Trade and Competition Rules in the WTO, *Chicago-Kent Law Review*, Vol. 72, No. 2, 1996, pp. 445-582, at 582.
1167. B. Hoekman, P. Low, P.C. Mavroidis, Regulation, Competition Policy and Market Access Negotiations: Lessons From the Telecommunications Sector, in E. Hope, P. Maeleng, *Competition and Trade Policies, Coherence or Conflict?*, 1998, pp. 115-139; and M. Bronckers, The WTO Reference Paper on Telecommunications: A Model for WTO Competition Law?, in M. Bronckers, R. Quick (eds), *New Directions in International Economic Law: Essays in Honour of John H. Jackson*, 2000, pp. 371-389.
1168. F. Scherer, International trade and competition policy, ZEW Discussion Papers, No. 96-18, Zentrum für Europäische Wirtschaftsforschung (ZEW), 1996.
1169. WTO document MIN (96)/DEC, 18 December 1996, p. 7.
1170. Nonetheless, '*the WTO Secretariat continues to respond to national requests for technical assistance in this area for the benefit of interested WTO Members and countries seeking accession to the WTO*'. WTO website information: https://www.wto.org/english/tratop_e/comp_e/comp_e.htm.
1171. OECD Declaration and Decisions on International Investment and Multinational Enterprises, 2023.
1172. UN documents TD/RBP/CONF/1, 26 June 1979; TD/RBP/CONF/10, 1980; A/RES/35/63, 5 December 1980; TD/RBP/CONF.9/9, 21 December 2020.

In conclusion, coherence between trade and competition rules is required to safeguard the multilateral trading system. Along with the elimination of trade remedy laws, this book finds it necessary that multilateral rules on competition and trade-restrictive practices be incorporated within the WTO framework. Judicial rather than unilateral protection should better serve the multilateral trading system. The reduction of trade-restrictive and anti-competitive practices by WTO Members and enterprises would enhance global welfare.

CHAPTER 12

Environmental and Labour Standards

> There may be a law of constant protection: You stop protection in one form and it pops up in some other form elsewhere.[1173]

This book has recommended the abolition of trade remedies. Nevertheless, even in the absence of these instruments, protectionism may find other forms. Indeed, a recent trend in the trade policies of some WTO Members has been to enact trade-restrictive legislation based on environmental and labour protection criteria in the exporting country. An analysis of this matter is essential in order to complete the suggested multilateral solution to reinforce the multilateral trading system and prevent the use of unilateral measures. Together with the elimination of trade remedy laws, amendment of the ASCM, and an agreement on competition and trade-restrictive practices, the incorporation of multilateral labour and environmental standards into the WTO Agreement is hereby proposed. Therefore, this chapter, first, reviews the recent US and EU trade-restrictive legislation on the basis of environmental and labour protections; second, offers a brief historical overview of environmental and labour standards in multilateral trade agreements; and concludes with a solution to the apparent conflict between trade liberalization, on the one hand, and environmental and labour protection, on the other hand.

I RECENT TRADE-RESTRICTIVE MEASURES FOR ENVIRONMENTAL AND LABOUR PROTECTION

Throughout the history of international trade relations, labour and environmental standards have appeared in conflict with trade liberalization policies.[1174] For decades,

1173. J.N. Bhagwati, The Demand to Reduce Domestic Diversity Among Trading Nations, in J. Bhagwati, R.E. Hudec (eds), *Fair Trade and Harmonization. Prerequisite for Free Trade?*, Vol. I: Economic Analysis, 1996, pp. 9-40 at 32. J.N. Bhagwati, *Protectionism*, 1988, p. 53.
1174. J.H. Jackson, International Economic Law: Reflections on the 'Boilerroom' of International Relations, *American University International Law Review*, Vol. 10, No. 2, 1995, pp. 595-606, at 603.

labour and environmental standards have been included in free trade agreements, whereby the elimination of trade barriers has been supplemented '*with attempts at imposing a minimum set of common standards*'.[1175] The first case was the North American Free Trade Agreement (NAFTA), enacted in 1994 and replaced by the US–Mexico–Canada Agreement (USMCA) in 2020.[1176] Ever since, bilateral and regional trade agreements have included trade-related environmental and labour provisions, including FTAs concluded by the US[1177] and EU.[1178]

Environmental and labour standards began to generate heated trade debates in the 1990s. At that time, the calls for 'fair trade' worried trade scholars, both lawyers and economists, who considered it '*the most fundamental challenge or threat to the liberal trading order*' of the previous decades.[1179] More recently, the increasing concerns about environmental and labour standards have been reflected in the national legislation of countries, such as the US and the EU, which provide for the imposition of trade-restrictive measures on the basis of environmental and labour protection in exporting countries. These trade-restrictive measures include import prohibitions, as well as anti-dumping and countervailing duties.

1175. J. Bhagwati, The Demand to Reduce Domestic Diversity Among Trading Nations, in J. Bhagwati, R.E. Hudec (eds), *Fair Trade and Harmonization. Prerequisite for Free Trade?*, Vol. I: Economic Analysis, 1996, pp. 9-40 at 35.

1176. While the North American Free Trade Agreement (NAFTA) contained a side agreement on labour, the US, Mexico, and Canada (USMCA) contains labour provisions (Ch. 23), which constitute the strongest provisions on labour in a trade agreement. It mandates parties to prohibit the importation of goods produced under forced or compulsory labour. Labour requirements have also been included in the determination of the origin of products (e.g., to export vehicles under preferential treatment, a labour value content of 40% for passenger vehicles or 45% for light trucks must be met. This includes a minimum of USD 16/hour on the production wage rate). USMCA Chapter on Labour. USMCA Appendix to Annex 4-B, Provisions Related to the Product-Specific Rules of Origin for Automotive Goods.

1177. US Congressional Research Service documents, Environmental Provisions in Free Trade Agreements (FTAs), updated version of 1 September 2023; Worker Rights Provisions in Free Trade Agreements (FTAs), updated version of 25 October 2023.

1178. EU trade agreements with the following countries include Trade and Sustainable Development chapters: Canada; Central America; Colombia, Peru, and Ecuador; Georgia; Japan; Moldova; Singapore; South Korea; Ukraine; the United Kingdom; and Vietnam. It is also the case of agreements awaiting ratification (with Chile, China, Kenya, Mercosur, Mexico and New Zealand) and those currently under negotiation (with Australia, Eastern and Southern Africa, India, Indonesia, and Thailand). Also, the EU has adapted to the more restricted scope of the agreements with sustainable development commitments with other countries (Armenia, Angola, Kyrgyzstan, Uzbekistan, Tajikistan, and Azerbaijan). EU Commission website, viewed at: https://policy.trade.ec.europa.eu/development-and-sustainability/sustainable-development/sustainable-development-eu-trade-agreements_en.

1179. R. Howse, M.J. Trebilcock, The Fair Trade-Free Trade Debate: Trade, Labor, and the Environment, *International Review of Law and Economics*, Vol. 16, No. 1, 1996, pp. 61-79 at 61 https://doi.org/10.4324/9781315254166-14. '*See, for example, J. Bhagwati, The World Trading System at Risk, Aggressive Unilateralism, and Fair Trade, Reciprocity and Harmonization, in Analytical and Negotiating Issues in the Global Trading System eds. A. Deardorff and R. Stern (Ann Arbor: University of Michigan Press, 1993); R. Hudec, Mirror, Mirror on the Wall: The Concept of Fairness in the United States Foreign Trade Policy, Proceedings of the Canadian Council on International Law 88 (1990)*'.

A Import Prohibitions on the Basis of Labour and Environmental Standards

The US has enacted legislation to prohibit imports from China's Xinjiang region through the enactment of the Uyghur Forced Labor Prevention Act. Meanwhile, the EU has adopted the Corporate Due Diligence and Corporate Accountability Directive, which may restrict imports on the basis of forced environmental, labour or other human rights violations that occur in the global value chains.

1 US Uyghur Forced Labor Prevention Act

The US has enacted the Uyghur Forced Labor Prevention Act to prohibit imports from China's Xinjiang region produced with forced labour.[1180] The prohibition of imports '*mined, produced or manufactured wholly or in part*' with forced labour was already provided for in the US Tariff Act of 1930.[1181] The Uyghur Forced Labor Prevention Act seeks to ensure that China '*does not undermine the effective enforcement*' of this prohibition. The Act entrusts the Forced Labor Enforcement Task Force with the development of a strategy to enforce the prohibition, which includes the elaboration of lists of entities that '*mine, produce, or manufacture wholly or in part*' products with forced labour, as well as lists of such products.[1182] The USCBP, as the enforcement agency, uses a list of International Standards from the International Labour Organization (ILO)[1183] and other International Organizations.[1184]

1180. US Public Law 117 – 78 – An act to ensure that goods made with forced labour in the Xinjiang Uyghur Autonomous Region of the People's Republic of China do not enter the United States market, and for other purposes, 23 December 2021, 135 Stat. 1525-1532.
1181. Section 307 of the Tariff Act of 1930, under the rubric '*Convict-made goods; importation prohibited*', states: '*All goods, wares, articles, and merchandise mined, produced, or manufactured wholly or in part in any foreign country by convict labor or/and forced labor or/and indentured labor under penal sanctions shall not be entitled to entry at any of the ports of the United States, and the importation thereof is hereby prohibited, and the Secretary of the Treasury is authorized and directed to prescribe such regulations as may be necessary for the enforcement of this provision.*' It has been in force since 1932. 19 US Code 1307.
1182. The Uyghur Forced Labor Prevention Act Entity List is published in the US Department of Homeland Security website (https://www.dhs.gov/uflpa-entity-list). US Federal Register, Vol. 88, No. 236, 11 December 2023, pp. 85899-85901.
1183. The International Labour Organization standards include those under the Tripartite Declaration of Principles concerning Multinational Enterprises and Social Policy; the publication Combating Forced Labour: A Handbook for Employers and Business; Guidelines Concerning the Measurement of Forced Labor; and General Principles and Operational Guidelines for Fair Recruitment. USCBP website, viewed at: https://www.cbp.gov/node/375773/printable/print.
1184. The United Nations Guiding Principles on Business and Human Rights; The Organization for Economic Co-operation and Development Guidelines for Multinational Enterprises; International Organization for Migration's Ethical Recruitment Standards; The Office of the High Commissioner for Human Rights Guide on The Corporate Responsibility to Respect Human Rights. USCBP website, viewed at: https://www.cbp.gov/node/375773/printable/print.

2 *EU Directive on Corporate Due Diligence and Corporate Accountability*

Meanwhile, in May 2024, the EU Commission approved the Directive on Corporate Due Diligence and Corporate Accountability (hereinafter 'Due Diligence Directive'), to deliver UN Sustainable Development Goals, thereby preventing and mitigating human rights and environmental adverse impacts in the value chains of companies operating in the EU market.[1185] The Due Diligence Directive lists violations of rights, internationally recognized objectives and prohibitions included in international human rights agreements and environmental conventions, as well as human rights and fundamental freedoms conventions, including ILO Conventions.[1186]

Before the final text, the EU Parliament resolved that operators must provide evidence that products placed in the internal market are in conformity with the established environmental and human rights criteria, and called for '*complementary measures such as the prohibition of the importation of products related to severe human rights violations such as forced labour or child labour*'.[1187] Despite that the Due Diligence Directive does not include such measures, the EU Commission is complementing it with other instruments that permit restricting or prohibiting imports on the basis of environmental and labour standards, particularly on forced and child labour, deforestation and forest degradation, and the adverse environmental impact of batteries, and other products.[1188]

More specifically, in 2023, the EU adopted the Regulation on batteries to permit prohibiting, restricting or impeding the making available on the market or putting into service batteries that to not comply with the conditions set forth, including the due

1185. Directive 2024/1760 (EU) of the European Parliament and of the Council of 13 June 2024 on corporate sustainability due diligence and amending Directive 2019/1937 and Regulation 2023/2859. OJEU, L.1760, 5 July 2024. The concept of due diligence is based on the OECD Guidelines for Multinational Enterprises of 2011, replaced by the OECD Guidelines for Multinational Enterprises on Responsible Business Conduct, 8 June 2023. The due diligence concept has also been incorporated in the ILO Tripartite Declaration of Principles concerning Multinational Enterprises and Social Policy, adopted in 1977, amended several times, most recently in 2022, p. 10.

1186. The International Covenant on Civil and Political Rights; The International Covenant on Economic, Social and Cultural Rights; The Convention on the Rights of the Child; Freedom of Association and Protection of the Right to Organise Convention, 1948 (No. 87); Right to Organise and Collective Bargaining Convention, 1949 (No. 98); Forced Labour Convention, 1930 (No. 29) and its 2014 Protocol; Abolition of Forced Labour Convention, 1957 (No. 105); Minimum Age Convention, 1973 (No. 138); Worst Forms of Child Labour Convention, 1999 (No. 182); Equal Remuneration Convention, 1951 (No. 100); Discrimination (Employment and Occupation) Convention, 1958 (No. 111). Annex to the Due Diligence Directive. OJEU, L.1760, 5 July 2024, pp. 54-58.

1187. Section 10 of the EU Parliament Resolution with recommendations to the Commission on the Directive of the European Parliament and of the Council on Corporate Due Diligence and Corporate Accountability, 10 March 2021.

1188. Directive 2009/125 (EC) of the European Parliament and of the Council of 21 October 2009 establishing a framework for the setting of ecodesign requirements for energy-related products. OJEU, L.285, 31 October 2009, p. 10.

diligence obligations;[1189] and the Regulation on deforestation and forest degradation to permit the prohibition on importation and exportation of relevant commodities and relevant products, in cases where certain conditions are not fulfilled, including being covered by '*a due diligence statement*'.[1190] The proposed Regulation on forced labour, which has been adopted by the EU Parliament at first reading, would '*effectively prohibit the placing and making available on the EU market and the export from the EU of products made with forced labour, including forced child labour*'.[1191]

B Environment and Labour in Anti-dumping and Countervailing Duty Laws

Additionally, the EU and the US have included the possibility to take into account environmental and labour protections in their anti-dumping and countervailing duty regulations. Interestingly, the use of labour standards to justify the imposition of anti-dumping and countervailing duties was already used by some countries before the enactment of the GATT in 1947.

1 EU Anti-dumping and Anti-subsidy Regulations

The EU has included in its most recent Anti-dumping Regulation the possibility of taking into account environmental and labour protections in the dumping and injury determinations of imports from countries that the EU considers as '*non-market economies*',[1192] e.g., China and Vietnam.[1193] With respect to the determination of dumping, the EU Commission is permitted to construct the normal value, disregarding actual prices and costs of production in the exporting country, on the basis that 'significant distortions' exist in that country. In such a case, the normal value can be constructed with costs of production and sale in a third country with an '*adequate level*' of social and environmental protections.[1194] This results in the determination of

1189. Regulation (EU) of the European Parliament and of the Council concerning batteries and waste batteries, amending Directive 2008/98/EC and Regulation 2019/1020 and repealing Directive 2006/66/EC. OJEU, L.191, 28 July 2023, pp. 1-117.
1190. EU Regulation 2023/1115 of the European Parliament and of the Council of 31 May 2023 on the making available on the Union market and the export from the Union of certain commodities and products associated with deforestation and forest degradation and repealing Regulation No. 995/2010. OJEU, L.150, 9 June 2023.
1191. Proposal for a Regulation of the European Parliament and of the Council on prohibiting products made with forced labour on the Union market. COM (2022) 453 final, 14 September 2022. The EU Parliament adopted it at first reading on 23 April 2024.
1192. EU Regulation 2016/1036 on protection against dumped imports from countries not members of the European Union (codification). OJEU L.176, 30 June 2016, p. 26. EU Regulation 2017/2321 amending EU Regulations 2016/1036 and 2016/1037. OJEU, L.338, 19 December 2017, p. 2.
1193. As well as Albania, Armenia, Azerbaijan, Belarus, Georgia, the Kyrgyz Republic, Moldova, Mongolia, North Korea, Tajikistan, Turkmenistan and Uzbekistan. OJEU, L.176, 30 June 2016, p. 26.
1194. EU Regulation 2017/2321 amending EU Regulation 2016/1036 and 2016/1037. OJEU, L.338, 19 December 2017, p. 3.

dumping otherwise inexistent or higher margins of dumping, and thus, higher anti-dumping duties. The determination of injury to EU industries is based on its artificial creation by adding actual or future costs derived from compliance with ILO Conventions as well as multilateral environmental conventions. The same consideration of hypothetical costs of compliance with environmental and labour standards has also been included in anti-subsidy (countervailing) investigations.[1195]

The EU Commission is entrusted with the elaboration of reports whereby it assesses the existence of market distortions in a certain sector or country.[1196] The assessment includes environmental and labour standards, which are covered under multilateral environmental agreements to which the EU is a party, and ILO Conventions.[1197] Moreover, the EU Commission has been requested to initiate ex officio interim reviews in cases where the EU industry faces an increase in costs due to higher social and environmental standards. The interim review could result in the withdrawal of any undertaking in force in cases where the exporting country withdraws from those ILO Conventions.[1198]

2 US Anti-dumping and Countervailing Duty Regulations

Similarly, in 2024, the US Department of Commerce enacted 'Regulations Improving and Strengthening the Enforcement of Trade Remedies Through the Administration of the Antidumping and Countervailing Duty Laws',[1199] whereby environmental, labour and human rights protections in foreign countries are included in subsidy, countervailing and anti-dumping proceedings. Due to the impact of the lack of enforcement of environmental, labour and human rights standards in lower foreign prices, the final rule adds provisions on subsidization and particular market situation, as well as amends existent anti-dumping and countervailing duty provisions.

1195. EU Regulation 2018/825 amending EU Regulations 2016/1036 and 2016/1037. OJEU, L.143, 7 June 2018, pp. 6, 13.
1196. *Ibid.*, p. 10.
1197. The following ILO Conventions are listed in the Regulation: Convention concerning Forced or Compulsory Labour, No. 29 (1930); Convention concerning Freedom of Association and Protection of the Right to Organise, No. 87 (1948); Convention concerning the Application of the Principles of the Right to Organise and to Bargain Collectively, No. 98 (1949); Convention concerning Equal Remuneration of Men and Women Workers for Work of Equal Value, No. 100 (1951); Convention concerning the Abolition of Forced Labour, No. 105 (1957); Convention concerning Discrimination in Respect of Employment and Occupation, No. 111 (1958); Convention concerning Minimum Age for Admission to Employment, No. 138 (1973); Convention concerning the Prohibition and Immediate Action for the Elimination of the Worst Forms of Child Labour, No. 182 (1999). Annex Ia of EU Regulation 2018/825 amending EU Regulations 2016/1036 and 2016/1037. OJEU, L.143, 7 June 2018, p. 18.
1198. EU Regulation 2018/825 amending EU Regulations 2016/1036 and 2016/1037. OJEU, L.143, 7 June 2018, p. 2.
1199. US Regulations Improving and Strengthening the Enforcement of Trade Remedies Through the Administration of the Antidumping and Countervailing Duty Laws, US Federal Register, Vol. 89, No. 58, 25 March 2024, pp. 20766-20841; US Federal Register, Vol. 88, No. 89, 9 May 2023, pp. 29850-29878.

With respect to subsidies, a new provision considers the fact of not collecting or forgoing fees, fines or penalties, a '*financial contribution*'.[1200] This includes costs associated with the implementation or enforcement of, *inter alia*, environmental, labour and human rights protection laws.[1201] Such government inaction is considered a countervailable subsidy by the new regulation. When determining the amount of the subsidy in countervailing duty proceedings, prices derived from '*weak, ineffective, or nonexistent*' environmental, labour or human rights protections will be excluded, thereby resulting in a determination of a higher subsidy.[1202]

Concerning anti-dumping proceedings, environmental, labour and human rights protections are included in dumping determinations. Prices derived from '*weak, ineffective, or nonexistent*' protection of, *inter alia*, environmental, labour and human rights in '*non-market economies*' would be disregarded to determine the normal value, which would be constructed based on the prices of a third ('*surrogate*') country.[1203] The Secretary of Commerce will decide the surrogate country, which would be a market economy country that has a different level of economic development than the '*non-market economy*' or is not a significant producer of the merchandise. Moreover, a new provision covers the determination of a '*particular market situation*' in the

1200. Provision § 351.529(a) reads: '*Financial contribution. When determining if a fee, fine, or penalty that is otherwise due, has been forgone or not collected, within the meaning of section 771(5)(D)(ii) of the Act, the Secretary may conclude that a financial contribution exists if information on the record demonstrates that payment was otherwise required and was not made, in full or in part.*' US Federal Register, Vol. 89, No. 58, 25 March 2024, pp. 20766-20841 at 20841.

1201. The Proposed Rule states that the lack of enforcement of such protections, '*lowers the cost of production for firms in their jurisdiction*', e.g., by allowing them '*to avoid paying costs associated with preventing or mitigating such adverse labor and human rights impacts and thereby reduce their costs of production*', referring to '*United Nations Human Rights Office of the High Commissioner, The Corporate Responsibility to Respect Human Rights (2012), at 5 and 40; and International Labor Organization, The benefits of International Labour Standards*'. US Federal Register, Vol. 88, No. 89, 9 May 2023, pp. 29850-29878 at 29859; US Federal Register, Vol. 89, No. 58, 25 March 2024, pp. 20766-20841 at 20783.

1202. Provision § 351.511(a)(2)(v) states: '*Exclusion of certain prices. In measuring the adequacy of remuneration under this section, the Secretary may exclude certain prices from its analysis, if parties have demonstrated, with sufficient information, that certain prices are derived from countries with weak, ineffective, or nonexistent property (including intellectual property), human rights, labor, or environmental protections, and that the lack of such protections would likely impact such prices, the Secretary may exclude those prices from its analysis.*' US Federal Register, Vol. 89, No. 58, 25 March 2024, pp. 20766-20841 at 20841.

1203. Provision § 351.408(d)(3) and (4) state: '*(3) If the Secretary determines (…) after reviewing all proposed values on the record derived from market economy countries which are at a level of economic development comparable to the nonmarket economy, that no such proposed value is appropriate to value a specific factor of production, the Secretary may use a value on the record derived from a market economy country which is not at a level of economic development comparable to that of the nonmarket economy country as a surrogate to value that specific factor of production. (4) If the Secretary determines (…) after reviewing all proposed surrogate values on the record derived from market economy countries which are significant producers of merchandise comparable to the subject merchandise, that no such proposed value is appropriate to value a specific factor of production, the Secretary may use a value on the record derived from a market economy country which is not a significant producer of merchandise comparable to the subject merchandise as a surrogate to value that specific factor of production.*' *Ibid.*, p. 20837.

exporting country,[1204] permitting to construct the normal value, in cases where foreign governments fail to protect environmental, labour or human rights, alleging the ineffective enforcement or absence of such protections may contribute to distort prices or costs of production.[1205]

II ENVIRONMENTAL AND LABOUR PROTECTIONS IN MULTILATERAL TRADE AGREEMENTS

Environmental and labour protections have been included in multilateral trade agreements since the League of Nations conferences. Labour standards were included in the ITO Charter, but it never entered into force; and solely GATT Article XX(e) refers to labour, to permit the adoption of measures relating to products of prison labour. Meanwhile, GATT Article XX(b) and (g) permit WTO Members the adoption of trade-restrictive measures relating to the protection of life, health, and natural resources. Although these measures must be imposed on a non-discriminatory basis, this protection has created conflict between trade and environmental policies of GATT Contracting Parties and WTO Members. Since the environment is a global concern, the approach should shift from conflict to consistency between trade and environmental policies. This study proposes a multilateral solution to enforce labour and environmental standards.

A League of Nations Conferences and UN Charter for an ITO

Trade rules and labour rights have been the subject of international cooperation for more than one hundred years and have been considered in major multilateral agreements since the Treaty of Versailles (1919), which established the League of

1204. A definition of '*particular market situation*' is absent under both Article VI of the GATT and the WTO Anti-dumping Agreement. Provision § 351.416 (a) reads: '*A particular market situation is a distinct circumstance or set of circumstances that does the following as determined by the Secretary: (1) Prevents or does not permit a proper comparison of sales prices in the home market or third country market with export prices and constructed export prices; or (2) Contributes to the distortion of the cost of materials and fabrication or other processing of any kind, such that the cost of production of the merchandise subject to an investigation, suspension agreement, or an antidumping order does not reflect the cost of production in the ordinary course of trade.*' *Ibid.*, p. 20837.

1205. Provision § 351.416(d)(3)(v) '*A determination that a market situation existed during the period of investigation or review such that the cost of materials and fabrication or other processing of any kind does not accurately reflect the cost of production in the ordinary course of trade (...) In determining whether a market situation exists in the subject country such that the cost of materials and fabrication or other processing does not accurately reflect the cost of production in the ordinary course of trade during the period of investigation or review, the Secretary will consider all relevant information placed on the record by interested parties, including, but not limited to, the following (...) (v) Information that property (including intellectual property), human rights, labor, or environmental protections in the subject country are weak, ineffective, or nonexistent, those protections exist and are effectively enforced in other countries, and that the ineffective enforcement or lack of protections may contribute to distortions in cost of production of subject merchandise or prices or costs of a significant input into the production of subject merchandise in the subject country.*' *Ibid.*, p. 20838.

Nations and the International Labour Organization. Under its Article 23, Members of the League of Nations committed '*to secure and maintain fair and humane conditions of labour for men, women, and children, both in their own countries and in all countries to which their commercial and industrial relations extend, and for that purpose will establish and maintain the necessary international organisations*'.[1206]

The League of Nations World Economic Conference of 1927 concluded that the main obstacles to an economic revival following World War I had been '*the hindrances opposed to the free flow of labour, capital and goods*'.[1207] Therefore, it recommended the Economic Organisation of the League of Nations to extend international trade '*on an equitable basis*' while taking into consideration '*the just interests of producers and workers in obtaining a fair remuneration and of consumers in increasing their purchasing power*'.[1208] To undertake this enquiry, it was suggested to consult with, *inter alia*, the International Labour Organization.[1209] Notably, the first Director of the ILO, A. Thomas, declared in 1930: '*What a strange idea (...) to find a contradiction between the "labour protectionism" of the International Labour Office and the theory of free or freer trade for which the League stands. You talk of labour protectionism. Yet surely the attempt at nationalistic labour protectionism is in contradiction with the attempt to secure common labour standards which we are pursuing here.*'[1210]

As seen in Part II, at the League of Nations Monetary and Economic Conference, held in London in 1933, the US presented a proposal for substantially reducing trade-restrictive barriers.[1211] Nevertheless, some exceptional measures and reservations were also suggested,[1212] namely those '*generally admitted in existing treaties, for purposes of safety, sanitation, plant and animal protection, morals, etcetera (...), and that for the purpose of exclusion of products of convict or forced labour*',[1213] nowadays established under GATT Article XX(b), (e) and (g). Remarkably, the reports of the League of Nations World Economic Conference of 1927 had warned that the imposition of trade-restrictive measures, such as '*unjustified health regulations*', would render inoperative the convention on import and export prohibitions and restrictions.[1214]

1206. Treaty of Peace with Germany (Treaty of Versailles), 28 June 1919.
1207. League of Nations document C.E.I. 44 (1), 3 June 1927, p. 13.
1208. '*The Conference took as its central problem the question of how costs could be reduced without injury to the consumer or the worker.*' *Ibid.*, p. 11.
1209. '*The Economic Organisation of the League of Nations should endeavour to promote international agreements with regard to the terms, methods and scope of industrial statistics employed, and should collate the information provided as to raw materials, production, etc., the International Labour Office dealing with wages, hours, employment, etc.*' *Ibid.*, p. 30.
1210. A. Thomas, *International Social Policy*, 1948, p. 114.
1211. League of Nations document C. 435. M. 220. 1933. II. [Conf.M.E.22(l).], 27 July 1933, pp. 40-43.
1212. Section 1 of the Appendix 6. *Ibid.*, p. 42.
1213. One of the exceptions was aimed at preventing an excessive increase of imports of particular commodities. It was intended to offset a governmental emergency action to raise wages, shorten hours and improve labour conditions, resulting in costs and price increases. This exception would later be known as the safeguard measure, established under Article XIX of the GATT. Yet, it was initially aimed at protecting the improvement of labour conditions in the importing country. League of Nations document C.435. M.220.1933. II. [Conf.M.E.22(l).], 27 July 1933, p. 42.
1214. League of Nations document C.E.I. 44 (1), 3 June 1927, p. 21.

The outbreak of World War II frustrated the aims of the League of Nations Economic Committee. Nevertheless, during the interwar period, experts from the UK and the US sought to achieve economic cooperation between all nations with the objective of, *inter alia*, '*securing, for all, improved labor standards, economic advancement, and social security*'.[1215] Proposals were elaborated for the creation of economic institutions that would grant worldwide economic and financial stability and prosperity,[1216] including the expansion of '*production, employment, and the exchange and consumption of goods, which are the material foundations of the liberty and welfare of all peoples*'.[1217]

Of particular relevance are the US Proposals for Expansion of World Trade and Employment in 1945, aimed at harmonizing policies in order to achieve full employment and enhance world trade.[1218] They highlighted that cooperation between trade and employment was considered indispensable to create an economic environment propitious for the maintenance of peaceful international relations. '*Trade connects employment, production and consumption and facilitates all three. Its increase means more jobs, more wealth produced, more goods to be enjoyed.*' The US Proposals recognized that while measures aiming at expanding trade are essential to contribute '*to maximum levels of employment, production and consumption*'; '*high and stable levels of employment are a necessary condition for an enlarged volume of trade*'. Therefore, it proposed to prevent countries from taking measures '*likely to create unemployment in other countries*'. It was also recognized that seeking '*employment by prohibiting imports or by subsidizing exports would be harmful and self-defeating*'. Accordingly, it was proposed that domestic programmes aimed at expanding employment should be consistent with the realization of '*the purposes of liberal international agreements and compatible with the economic well-being of other nations*'.[1219]

Based on the US Proposals, the US Suggested Charter maintained, under Article 32, some general exceptions allowing members to adopt or enforce measures '*necessary to protect human, animal or plant life or health*', including measures '*relating to the conservation of exhaustible natural resources if such measures are taken pursuant to international agreements or are made effective in conjunction with restrictions on*

1215. In the Atlantic Charter in 1941, the US (President F.D. Roosevelt) and the UK (Prime Minister W. Churchill) pledged '*to further the enjoyment by all states* (...) *of access, on equal terms, to the trade and to the raw materials of the world which are needed for their economic prosperity*; [and] *bring about the fullest collaboration between all nations in the economic field with the object of securing, for all, improved labor standards, economic advancement, and social security*'. Fourth and Fifth clauses of the Atlantic Charter, Joint declaration by the President of the United States and the Prime Minister of the United Kingdom, 14 August 1941. US Library of Congress website, viewed at: https://www.loc.gov/law/help/us-treaties/bevans/m-ust00 0003-0686.pdf.
1216. US Department of State Office of the Historian, Bretton Woods-GATT, 1941-1947, viewed at: https://history.state.gov/milestones/1937-1945/bretton-woods.
1217. Article VII of the Anglo-American Mutual Aid Agreement, 28 February 1942, viewed at Yale Law School Lillian Goldman Library online: https://avalon.law.yale.edu/wwii/angam42.asp #art7.
1218. US Department of State, Proposals for Expansion of World Trade and Employment, 1945, p. 7.
1219. *Ibid.*, pp. 2, 8-10.

domestic production or consumption'.[1220] This article on general exceptions would be the basis of GATT Article XX, in particular, its paragraphs (b) and (g), invoked to protect the environment. Furthermore, the US Suggested Charter incorporated employment provisions under its Chapter III (Articles 3-7), namely, the relation of employment to purposes of the ITO; general undertakings to promote full employment; avoidance of certain employment measures; as well as consultations and exchange of information on matters relating to employment.

In March 1948, the International Conference on Trade and Employment culminated with the signature of the ITO Charter,[1221] which included these provisions under its Chapter II, on '*Employment and Economic Activity*' (Articles 2-7). Article 7, '*Fair Labour Standards*', mandated Member States to take into account '*the rights of workers under inter-governmental declarations, conventions and agreements*' as well as consulting and cooperating with the ILO. It also provided for the elimination of unfair labour conditions, which hinder international trade, and the '*achievement and maintenance of fair labour standards related to productivity*', hence improving wages and working conditions.[1222] Since the ITO never came into existence, the provisions on labour standards did not become part of the legal framework of the GATT, which merely consisted of provisions on commercial policy.

B Labour and Environmental Protections in the GATT/WTO

Provisions on '*worker rights*' were proposed to be included on the agenda for the Uruguay Round. The US reminded that the preamble of the GATT, which provides that '*trade and economic endeavour should be conducted with a view to raising standards of living, ensuring full employment*', evolves from the ITO Charter commitment to eliminating '*unfair labour conditions*'.[1223] Nevertheless, labour standards were not negotiated in the Uruguay Round.

Over the GATT and WTO era, the use of labour standards as a protectionist device has increased. Indeed, '*it is quite commonly feared that countries with below-average labor standards are gaining unfair advantage in trade*'.[1224] As a result, claims of unfair imports, due to competition from low-wage foreign producers, have prompted some importing countries to enact trade-restrictive legislation. The current trend to include labour standards in anti-dumping and countervailing duty proceedings has a precedent before the origins of the GATT.

Indeed, prior to the GATT, anti-dumping was used to offset '*social dumping*' by some countries. In 1924, Austria targeted imported goods that had been produced under excessive working hours. In 1931, Argentina imposed anti-dumping duties on

1220. US State Department, Suggested Charter for an International Trade Organization of the United Nations, September 1946.
1221. UN document E/CONF.2/78, 24 March 1948.
1222. *Ibid.*, pp. 15-17.
1223. GATT document PREP. COM (86)W/43, 25 June 1986.
1224. D.K. Brown, A.V. Deardorff, R.M. Stern, International Labor Standards and Trade: A Theoretical Analysis, in J. Bhagwati, R.E. Hudec, *Harmonization and Fair Trade: Prerequisites for Free Trade?*, Vol. 1, 1996., pp. 228-280 at 266.

forced labour and low-wage imports. In 1935, Cuba similarly penalized low-wage imports.[1225] In 1934, Spain imposed anti-dumping duties in cases where lower prices were caused by the breach of international labour regulations, particularly those concerning wages and working hours.[1226] Unfavourable labour conditions in the exporting country were also used in countervailing duty investigations by Czechoslovakia in 1926.[1227]

As referred to in Part II, during the discussions for the establishment of the ITO Charter, some countries suggested considering the imposition of anti-dumping duties to offset other forms of dumping other than price dumping (i.e., exchange, freight and social). This suggestion arose from complaints against alleged low prices in Japan due to '*low labour standards, exchange manipulation, and the use of subsidies*'.[1228] It was then agreed that GATT Article VI could not be invoked to offset exchange, freight or social dumping, but merely price dumping.[1229] Therefore, GATT Contracting Parties and WTO Members had not used labour standards in anti-dumping proceedings until recently.

Based on the preceding historical overview, this study suggests retrieving multilateral trade proposals to achieve consistency between labour protection and trade liberalization policies, in the spirit of Adam Smith, who had emphasized the benefits of trade on labour and global welfare.[1230] '*Wage differences, which generally reflect differences in workers' productivity, are an inevitable part of the diversity that leads to gains from trade.*'[1231] Rather than using labour protection to restrain trade, trade policies should be '*directed to maintain open markets and encouraging the economic growth* [of all countries] *to achieve higher labor standards (...) since there is pervasive historical evidence that standards are improved with higher levels of per capita incomes*'.[1232]

With respect to environmental protection, GATT Article XX permits the imposition of measures, '(b) necessary to protect human, animal or plant life or health', as

1225. S. Charnovitz, The Influence of International Labour Standards on the World Trading Regime. A Historical Overview, *International Labour Review*, Vol. 126, No. 5, 1987, pp. 565-584 at 576-577.
1226. '*Que en la producción de la mercancía no rijan las reglas internacionales en materia social y especialmente sobre salarios y jornada obrera de trabajo*'. Spanish Ministry of Industry and Commerce, Decree of 10 March 1934, *Gaceta de Madrid*, No. 72, 13 March 1934, pp. 1952-1953.
1227. S. Charnovitz, The Influence of International Labour Standards on the World Trading Regime. A Historical Overview, *International Labour Review*, Vol. 126, No. 5, 1987, pp. 565-584 at 576-577.
1228. UN document E/PC/CII/54, 16 November 1946, p. 3.
1229. UN documents E/PC/T/C.6/55, 5 February 1947, p. 22; E/PC/T/34, 5 March 1947, p. 13.
1230. As A. Smith explained in The Wealth of Nations, '*By opening a more extensive market for whatever part of the produce of their labour may exceed the home consumption, it encourages them to improve its productive powers, and to augment its annual produce to the utmost, and thereby to increase the real revenue and wealth of the society.*' A. Smith, *The Wealth of Nations*, [1776], 2000, p. 582.
1231. R.A. Cass, R.D. Boltuck, Antidumping and Countervailing-Duty Law: The Mirage of Equitable International Competition, in J.N. Bhagwati R.E. Hudec (eds), *Fair Trade and Harmonization. Prerequisite for Free Trade?* Vol. 2: *Legal Analysis*, 1996, pp. 351-414 at 399.
1232. R. Stern, Labor Standards and Trade, in M. Bronckers, R. Quick (eds), *New Directions in International Economic Law, Essays in Honour of J.H. Jackson*, 2000, pp. 425-437 at 437.

well as those '(g) relating to the conservation of exhaustible natural resources if such measures are made effective in conjunction with restrictions on domestic production or consumption'. Nevertheless, GATT Article XX requires that those measures do not constitute an 'arbitrary or unjustifiable discrimination (...) or a disguised restriction on international trade'. When GATT Article XX is invoked, it has proven difficult to distinguish whether the measure is aimed at protecting the environment or, while appearing non-discriminatory, is *de facto* restricting imports.

Once the trade-restrictive measure has been found to be in violation of GATT Articles I, III or XI, the difficulty rests in determining whether it is justified or not under GATT Article XX. The protection of a greater good, such as life, health or the environment, may justify the imposition of unilateral trade-restrictive measures. This has created conflicts between trade and environmental policies, which received the attention and analysis of academics and trade policy experts, both jurists and economists,[1233] such as Bhagwati and Hudec, who classified these conflicts between trade and environmental policies into three types:

(1) Environmental regulations in the importing country that discriminate against imports, e.g., EU ban on imports of seal products from Greenland,[1234] or US standards on gasoline.[1235]
(2) Trade restrictions on exporters or countries to force them not to cause harm to the environment, e.g., US import prohibition on imports of shrimps to protect turtles.[1236] The term '*eco-imperialism*' was coined for this conflict,[1237] which led to one of the greatest controversies regarding GATT Article XX, as reflected in the *Tuna/Dolphin* cases,[1238] following the US imposition of marketing and sale measures on imports of tuna to protect dolphins.[1239]

1233. J.H. Jackson, World Trade Rules and Environmental Policies: Congruence or Conflict?, *Washington and Lee Law Review*, Vol. 49, No. 4, 1992, pp. 1227-1278 at 1235. R. Howse, M.J. Trebilcock, The Fair Trade-Free Trade Debate: Trade, Labor, and the Environment, *International Review of Law and Economics*, Vol. 16, No. 1, 1996, pp. 61-79 at 61 https://doi.org/10.4324/9781315254166-14.
1234. *European Communities – Certain Measures Prohibiting the Importation and Marketing of Seal Products* (DS400 and DS401). Complainants: Canada and Norway. WTO documents DS400/R, 25 November 2013; DS400/AB/R, 22 May 2014.
1235. *United States – Standards for Reformulated and Conventional Gasoline* (DS2). Complainants: Venezuela and Bolivia. WTO documents DS2/R, 29 January 1996; DS2/AB/R, 29 April 1996.
1236. *United States – Import Prohibition of Certain Shrimp and Shrimp Products* (DS58). Complainants: India, Malaysia, Pakistan and Thailand. WTO documents DS58/R, 15 May 1998; DS58/AB/R, 12 October 1998; DS58/AB/RW, 22 October 2001.
1237. J.H. Jackson, World Trade Rules and Environmental Policies: Congruence or Conflict?, *Washington and Lee Law Review*, Vol. 49, No. 4, 1992, pp. 1227-1278 at 1241.
1238. *United States – Restrictions on Imports of Tuna* (GD239 and GD266). Complainants: Mexico, EEC12 and the Netherlands. GATT document DS21/R, 3 September 1991; DS29/R, 16 June 1994.
1239. The US imposed restrictions on imports of tuna from countries that had not met the US standards on dolphin-safe methods (i.e., tuna caught excluding nets encircling dolphins). In both GATT disputes, the US restrictions were found unjustified under provisions of GATT Article XX(b) or (g). In *Tuna/Dolphin I*, the panel found that a trade restriction falling outside the jurisdiction (understood as territory) failed to qualify for an exception under GATT Article XX. In *Tuna/Dolphin II*, the panel did allow trade restrictions falling outside the national

(3) Trade-restrictive measures, such as trade remedies, imposed on the grounds of environmental protection on imports from countries with less rigorous policies.[1240]

Another category of conflicts between trade and environmental policies could be added. This kind of conflict occurs when trade remedies, or other trade-restrictive measures, are imposed on products that can help to protect the environment. Products used in renewable energies, such as solar panels or wind turbines, as well as their inputs, are frequently subject to trade remedies. Nonetheless, targeted products do not necessarily originate in countries with less rigorous environmental policies. The difference between these conflicts with respect to the three described above is that the protection of the environment is not used as a justification to impose trade restrictions. On the contrary, the imposition of trade-restrictive measures conflicts with environmental policies. Neither the environment nor free trade is protected in this type of conflict. Hence, trade-restrictive measures, including trade remedies, on environmental goods should be eliminated.

Trade experts such as Jackson have asked for the accommodation of environmental policies within the GATT/WTO system.[1241] In debates and WTO negotiations, the relation between trade and the environment has been included as a major topic of concern.[1242] This has seemed to imply that trade and environment are opposed to each other, i.e., that free trade cannot be guaranteed when the environment needs to be protected or, vice versa, that the environment cannot be protected without undermining trade liberalization. However, if aimed at increasing world welfare, trade and environmental policies should complement each other rather than conflict. Indeed, evidence has shown that as world welfare increases, demands for protecting the environment increase.[1243]

When aiming for global welfare, trade and environmental policies should complement each other. Impediments to this objective are trade-restrictive measures, such as trade remedies, which ignore environmental policies (e.g., trade remedies imposed on solar products). Although supported by certain GATT/WTO provisions,

territory, but not those trade restrictions aimed at coercing other countries to adopt certain environmental policies. Following this decision, an accorded interpretation of GATT Article XX was understood as implying that a trade restriction would be permitted if it consisted of a requirement for certification (in this case, stating that the tuna was '*harvested by dolphin-safe fishing methods*') to all imports without regard of their origin. R.E. Hudec, GATT Legal Restraints on the Use of Trade Measures Against Foreign Environmental Practices in J.N. Bhagwati, R.E. Hudec (eds), *Fair Trade and Harmonization. Prerequisite for Free Trade?* Vol. 2: *Legal Analysis*, 1996, pp. 95-174 at 117-119.

1240. R.E. Hudec, GATT Legal Restraints on the Use of Trade Measures Against Foreign Environmental Practices, in J.N. Bhagwati, R.E. Hudec (eds), *Fair Trade and Harmonization. Prerequisite for Free Trade?* Vol. 2: *Legal Analysis*, 1996, pp. 95-174 at 95.

1241. J.H. Jackson, World Trade Rules and Environmental Policies: Congruence or Conflict? *Washington and Lee Law Review*, Vol. 49, No. 4, 1992, pp. 1227-1278 at 1235.

1242. R.E. Hudec, GATT Legal Restraints on the Use of Trade Measures against Foreign Environmental Practices, in J.N. Bhagwati, R.E. Hudec (eds), *Fair Trade and Harmonization. Prerequisite for Free Trade?* Vol. 2: *Legal Analysis*, 1996, pp. 95-174 at 119.

1243. J.H. Jackson, World Trade Rules and Environmental Policies: Congruence or Conflict?, *Washington and Lee Law Review*, Vol. 49, No. 4, 1992, pp. 1227-1278 at 1228.

such as GATT Articles VI and XIX, these trade-restrictive measures do not aim at global welfare and are inconsistent with both trade liberalization and environmental policies. Therefore, the invocation of trade-restrictive GATT/WTO provisions should not be allowed when they are harmful to the environment or target environmental goods. In other words, global welfare requires the liberalization of international trade in environmental products.

When designing trade liberalization policies, the environment should be taken into account. Nevertheless, the danger is using the excuse of the environment as a protectionist device, e.g., asbestos from Canada.[1244] This has been recognized as a '*slippery slope problem*':[1245] on the one hand, the need to protect the environment, which should be a global goal; and, on the other hand, the need to prevent trade-restrictive measures whereby environmental protection is invoked, while the real aim is the protection of the domestic industry.

In this line, GATT Article XX precisely permits to protect a greater good, such as life, health and natural resources, without thus creating discrimination. For instance, in the *US – Tuna II* case,[1246] the US measure was found inconsistent with GATT Articles I.1 and III.4, but justified under GATT Article XX(g) since it was not applied in a manner that constituted '*a means of arbitrary or unjustifiable discrimination*'.[1247] In the *US – Shrimp* case,[1248] the US had negotiated the exportation of shrimp with some but not other exporting WTO Members, and subsequently imposed an import restriction, which was found discriminatory and 'unjustifiable', and thus inconsistent with GATT Article XX.[1249]

As observed by trade experts, the challenge remains 'to prevent Article XX from becoming a large loop hole that governments can use to justify almost any measures that are motivated by protectionist considerations'.[1250] There is a need to develop an institutional and legal framework that distinguishes the protection of the environment from protectionist aims, and minimizes the use of unilateral measures while maximizing the role of multilateral rules.[1251] The goal is to guarantee the protection of the environment as a global concern while safeguarding the multilateral trading system. This requires the incorporation of multilateral environmental standards and the enforcement of multilateral environmental rules. The following is proposed to better harmonize trade and environmental policies.

1244. D. Palmeter, Environment and Trade: Who Will Be Heard? What Law Is Relevant?, *Journal of World Trade*, Vol. 26, No. 2, 1992, pp. 35-41 https://doi.org/10.54648/trad1992009.
1245. J.H. Jackson, World Trade Rules and Environmental Policies: Congruence or Conflict? *Washington and Lee Law Review*, Vol. 49, No. 4, 1992, pp. 1227-1278 at 1240.
1246. *United States – Measures Concerning the Importation, Marketing and Sale of Tuna and Tuna Products* (DS381).
1247. WT/DS381/AB/RW/USA, 14 December 2018, para. 7.14.
1248. *United States – Import Prohibition of Certain Shrimp and Shrimp Products* (DS58). Complainants: India, Malaysia, Pakistan and Thailand.
1249. WTO document DS58/AB/R, 12 October 1998, p. 70.
1250. J.H. Jackson, World Trade Rules and Environmental Policies: Congruence or Conflict? *Washington and Lee Law Review*, Vol. 49, No. 4, 1992, pp. 1227-1278 at 1240.
1251. R. Howse, M.J. Trebilcock, The Fair Trade-Free Trade Debate: Trade, Labor, and the Environment, *International Review of Law and Economics*, Vol. 16, No. 1, 1996, pp. 61-79 at 78 https://doi.org/10.4324/9781315254166-14.

III INCLUSION OF ENVIRONMENTAL AND LABOUR STANDARDS IN THE WTO AGREEMENT

A Incorporation of Multilateral Environmental and Labour Standards

The protection of the environment and labour rights cannot be achieved unilaterally. It requires cooperation and legal certainty. Therefore, establishing multilateral environmental and labour standards is hereby proposed either directly within the WTO Agreement, or via cross-reference to ILO Conventions and multilateral or international environmental agreements, such as the Convention on International Trade in Endangered Species of Wild Fauna and Flora (CITES). A similar approach has been taken, for example, in the WTO Sanitary and Phytosanitary Agreement, which requires, *inter alia*, that sanitary and phytosanitary measures be based on international standards (i.e., those developed by the UN Food and Agriculture Organization and World Health Organization Codex Alimentarius, the World Organization for Animal Health and the International Plant Protection Convention). Such standards should be enforceable not only on WTO Members, but also on public and private enterprises. Therefore, a desirable option may be to include these standards in the suggested agreement on trade-restrictive practices proposed above to make them directly applicable to companies.

The incorporation of environmental standards requires an expeditious and science-based rule-making process. These standards would be proposed and/or analysed by independent experts, including the WTO Secretariat, to prevent these environmental rules from becoming another loophole for protectionism. Since environmental protection issues evolve, a group of jurists and economists is needed to adapt multilateral trading rules to the international trade situation. The WTO Trade and Environment Division might be entrusted with the responsibility of foreseeing issues and preventing disputes, by proposing environmental rules aiming at global welfare. This task could be accomplished with external technical assistance/experts in the field in different areas when necessary. With respect to labour standards, since the International Labour Organization and its members are responsible for developing and enforcing international labour standards, the WTO Secretariat and WTO Members should cooperate with the ILO to guarantee better incorporation and enforcement of labour standards.

B Recourse to WTO Multilateral Dispute Settlement Body

The termination of unilateral measures, even when aimed at protecting the environment or labour rights, is hereby suggested, along with permitting recourse to a multilateral dispute settlement mechanism to enforce multilateral environmental and labour standards. A WTO panel of experts, such as the case of the Group of Experts under the ASCM, may increase the efficiency and effectiveness of the multilateral proceeding in enforcing environmental and labour standards. In the case where environmental standards are not established within the WTO Agreement or a multilateral environmental agreement, the group of experts/WTO Secretariat would have the capacity to propose the incorporation of a multilateral standard within the WTO Agreement, thus ensuring the protection of the environment while avoiding the imposition of unilateral trade-restrictive measures.

C Elimination of Trade Remedies and Other Trade-Restrictive Measures

As explained above, environmental goods are often subject to trade remedies and other trade-restrictive measures. This study has advocated the elimination of trade remedies, and no other provision should be invoked to restrain imports of environmental goods. Since these measures harm both trade and the environment, they should be prohibited. Moreover, the subsidization of environmental goods may permit a transition towards renewable energies. This study has suggested the possibility of allowing, under certain conditions, certain subsidies on environmental goods used in renewable energies, thus considering them as non-actionable (green) subsidies. Nevertheless, multilateral subsidy disciplines would be required to prevent these subsidies from resulting in *de facto* discrimination of imports. Furthermore, the objective is to discourage WTO Members from imposing unilateral measures by invoking environmental or labour protections. Consequently, no unilateral measures should be permitted even by invoking GATT Article XX(b), (e) or (g). Ideally, the invocation of GATT Article XX should trigger a multilateral proceeding by which only authorized measures are imposed by importing WTO Members.[1252]

Concisely, there is a trend in some WTO Members towards resorting to unilateral trade-restrictive legislation on the grounds of '*unfair*' or lack of environmental or labour protections in exporting countries. While this is not a new phenomenon, trade liberalizing policies may appear to conflict with environmental or labour policies. Coherence between such policies is needed. The core principle of the multilateral trading system, i.e., non-discrimination, should also apply to trade-related environmental and labour protection measures. To attain this, rather than resorting to restrictive measures, this book suggests the multilateral enforcement of environmental and labour standards, entailing their incorporation into the WTO Agreement and recourse to the multilateral dispute settlement proceeding.

1252. '*The positive experience of the Uruguay Round negotiations – as well as the negative experiences of, e.g., UNCTAD, WIPO, and the OECD with negotiations on enforceable international competition rules – suggest that such "package negotiations" on multilateral minimum standards for environmental, social and investment rules might be more successful if carried out in the framework of the WTO.*' E.U. Petersmann, International Competition Rules for Private Business: A Trade Law Approach for Linking Trade and Competition Rules in the WTO, *Chicago-Kent College Law Review*, Vol. 72, No. 2, 1996, pp. 445-582, at 582.

Conclusions

The objectives formulated in the introduction have been achieved, leading to the following inductions.

First, over the last decade, trade remedy laws and subsidies have been at the centre of trade disputes and controversies, including the non-market economy treatment to China, the obstruction of appointment of members of the WTO Appellate Body, the trade war between the US and China, the expansion of subsidies before and after the COVID-19 pandemic, and the environmental and labour protections in global value chains. The prominent role of trade remedy laws upon the outbreak of the US–China trade war, as well as in the rest of the controversies, has shown that, far from constituting the escape valve of protectionism, they have contributed to undermining the multilateral trading system. The imposition of anti-dumping and countervailing duties by the US has exponentially increased since 2017. Following allegations of circumvention of these duties by shifting production to other locations, the US broadened the scope of the measures to cover imports from those countries. Moreover, this restraint of import competition through anti-dumping and countervailing duties, inherently discriminatory, was enhanced with the implementation of safeguards, designed to restrain import competition on a non-discriminatory basis. Consequently, the US applied the three trade remedy laws in combination in order to protect selected industries. Furthermore, the US obstructed the appointment of WTO Appellate Body members on the basis of allegations of overreach and erroneous interpretations of WTO Agreements, particularly on Subsidies and Countervailing Measures, Anti-dumping, and Safeguards. The ultimate guarantor of the multilateral trading system ceased functioning while the US invocation of the national security clause prompted a spillover effect of trade-restrictive measures by other WTO Members, an increase in disputes brought to the WTO, and escalated in tit-for-tat tariff measures imposed between the US and China.

Second, this critical moment in the history of the multilateral trading system raises fundamental questions about the necessity of trade remedy laws in the multilateral trading system. In order to approach this matter systematically, historical research has been conducted on the origins of trade remedy laws and their normative evolution through multilateral trade negotiations, demonstrating that their raîson d'être has always been the protection of domestic industries. Administered at governmental discretion, trade remedy laws aim at serving the interests of selected industries, which often benefit from subsidies. These restraints on import competition favour the protected producers to the detriment of, *inter alia*, importers, consumers, and eventually the environment. This approach whereby the interest of producers is attained at the expense of consumers is reminiscent of the mercantile system, already criticized in *The Wealth of Nations* by Adam Smith, for centring the political economy on the balance of trade, i.e., exceed of exports over imports; and considering production, rather than consumption, the ultimate end of trade.

In this attempt to restrain imports and promote exports, countries expanded subsidies on exportation. Accordingly, some European countries incorporated an 'anti-bounty clause', a commitment not to grant subsidies, in the 1860s bilateral commercial treaties, and in the Sugar Convention of 1864, which lacked an enforcement mechanism. Its failure in 1875 prompted some European countries to include a retaliatory measure to offset bounties in the 'anti-bounty clause' of their commercial treaties. In this context, the US and Belgium enacted the first worldwide countervailing duty provisions in domestic legislation. Soon after, the Brussels Sugar Convention of 1902, the first multilateral trade agreement, incorporated a countervailing duty provision which required prior authorization and determination of the alleged subsidy by a supranational permanent commission. Meanwhile, in 1904, Canada enacted the first worldwide anti-dumping provision, in order to protect the (subsidized) steel industry from alleged dumped imports from the US, which rapidly spread to other countries. The surge in protectionism during World War I rendered the Brussels Sugar Convention ineffective and prompted a further expansion of anti-dumping and countervailing duty laws in domestic legislation, which served as a basis for GATT Article VI.

Being the subject of international trade controversies, subsidies and trade remedy laws were part of the discussions and proposals of multilateral trade agreements at the League of Nations Conferences during the 1920s and 1930s, where the first safeguard provision was suggested, and later incorporated in US trade agreements, inspiring GATT Article XIX. Countries' protectionist measures of the time, which choked international trade, and World War II were overcome by (the US and UK) endeavours to reach a multilateral trade agreement, endorsed by an organization. The suggested International Trade Organization aimed at reducing trade-restrictive measures by governments and companies (public and private). Accordingly, provisions on subsidies and restrictive business practices were developed to prevent restraints on trade and competition, while trade remedy laws, conflicting with trade and competition-enhancing policies, were incorporated as exceptions into the multilateral trading system. On the basis of the US Proposals for Expansion on Trade and Employment of 1945 and Suggested Charter for an International Trade Organization of 1946, the UN delegations discussed and redrafted the ITO Charter, which was signed in 1948 by fifty-three countries. Its provisions on commercial policy had been framed and signed aside in 1947 as the General Agreement on Tariffs and Trade, which was provisionally applied pending the entry into force of the ITO Charter. Nevertheless, on account of the US failure to ratify the ITO Charter, it never entered into force. Consequently, provisions on employment, export subsidies, restrictive business practices and dispute settlement were absent in 1948 in the multilateral trading system, governed by the GATT. While provisions on export subsidies from the ITO Charter were incorporated into GATT Article XVI in 1955 and the dispute settlement body was created with the establishment of the WTO in 1994, provisions concerning employment and restrictive business practices have remained outside the multilateral trading system.

Far from constituting legal exceptions to safeguard a broad public interest (or supreme good), trade remedy laws serve the particular interest of selected producers to the detriment of the rest of the society. Multilateral trade remedy laws have been endorsed by some governments to the extent of considering them essential in undertaking tariff reduction and trade liberalization efforts, while others opposed their integration into the multilateral trading system. Their normative evolution through multilateral trade negotiations rounds, including the 1946-1948 UN work redrafting the US Suggested Charter into the ITO Charter, shows that they have been tilted towards protectionist interests. Often through the legitimization of trade-restrictive practices already conducted by some countries, the scope of multilateral trade remedy laws has been broadened, thus facilitating their implementation. The discriminatory application of trade remedy laws (*de iure* or *de facto*) has undermined the multilateral trading system.

Third, the historical research of multilateral trade remedy laws and subsidies has permitted to induce the need to strengthen the multilateral trading rule-based system with laws that are based on welfare economics and legal principles, consistent with each other and utmost compliance with the non-discrimination principle; and multilaterally enforced, rather than permitting unilateral action. Accordingly, this book defends a multilateral solution aimed at preventing restraints on trade and competition, as well as enhancing global welfare. To this end, it is hereby proposed to eliminate trade remedy laws; amend multilateral rules on subsidies; incorporate a competition-enhancing multilateral agreement; and include multilateral environmental and labour standards in the multilateral trading system. More specifically, multilateral disciplines on subsidies are suggested to be amended through a welfare economic approach in order to take into account the effects of subsidies not only on production, but also on consumption and the environment, and to be enforced exclusively through multilateral procedures, i.e., without permitting recourse to unilateral action to counter subsidies. In this attempt to strengthen the multilateral trading system, unilateral protection should be replaced by judicial protection. Accordingly, based on their absence of legal and welfare economic rationale, as well as coherence with trade and competition enhancement, this book calls for the abolition of trade remedy laws along with the incorporation of multilateral rules on competition and trade-restrictive practices in their stead. As intended in the ITO Charter, such trade and competition-enhancing rules should apply to WTO Members and commercial enterprises (both public and private). Moreover, due to the current trend of some WTO Members towards resorting to trade-restrictive legislation on the grounds of environmental or labour protections in exporting countries, it is hereby proposed to incorporate environmental and labour standards into the multilateral trading system, to prevent WTO Members from using them as a protectionist device, as well as to guarantee their multilateral enforcement, with recourse to the WTO dispute settlement system.

Appendices

APPENDIX 1

GATT Disputes on Trade Remedies and Subsidies Before the Tokyo Codes, 1948-1980

GATT Doc	*Complainant*	*Respondent*	*Dispute*	*GATT Articles*	*Consultations*	*Outcome*
GD/1	US	Cuba	*Report of Working Party 7 on the Cuban Schedule*	GATT Arts. XVIII, XIX, XXIII:1(b), XXV; Havana Charter Schedule IX (Cuba) No finding in light of mutually agreed solution	GATT/CP.2/W.12 08/19/1948	Report adopted, mutually agreed solution. Adjudicator's report: GATT/CP.2/43, 13/09/1948 Adoption of report: GATT/CP.2/SR.25, 14/09/1948 Mutually agreed solution: GATT/CP.3/SR.29, 29/06/1949
GD/5	Chile	Australia	*Australia – Subsidy on Ammonium Sulphate*	GATT Arts. I:2, I:4, III, III:8(b), III:9, XI:1, XVI, XXII, XXIII:1(b), Finding nullification or impairment XXIII:1(b)	GATT/CP.3/61 27/07/1949	Report adopted 31/03/1950 GATT/CP.4/39; BISD II/188 Adoption of report: 03/04/1950 GATT/CP.4/SR21 Mutually agreed solution: 06/11/1950 GATT/CP.5/SR.6, GATT/CP.5/SR.6/Corr.1

GD/9	Czechoslovakia	US	*Assured Life of Tariff Concessions with regard to Article XIX / US – Fur Felt Hats*	GATT Arts. XIX:1, XIX:2 No inconsistency found	GATT/CP.5/22; GATT/CP.5/SR.14 10/11/1950	Report adopted. GATT/CP/106, 27/03/1951 Adoption of report: GATT/CP.6/SR.19, GATT/CP.6/SR.19/Corr.1, 22/10/1951
GD/17	Greece, Turkey	US	*United States Export Subsidy on Sultanas*	GATT Article XVI No conclusion reached	L/39 (Greece) 03/10/1952 L/45 (Turkey) 10/10/1952	Report issued, not considered for adoption. L/146, L/146/Add.1 (Greece) 30/09/1953. L/148 (Turkey) 30/09/1953
GD/23	Italy	Sweden	*Swedish Anti-Dumping Duties*	GATT Arts. I:1, VI:4 No inconsistency found	L/215, 29/07/1954	Report adopted. L/328,23/02/1955. SR.9/37, 26/02/1955
GD/24	Italy	Turkey	*Turkish Import Taxes and Export Bonuses*	GATT Art. XVI	L/214, 30/07/1954	Mutually agreed solution SR.9/40, SR.9/40/Corr1. 02/03/1955
GD/36	Australia	France	*French Assistance to Exports of Wheat and Wheat Flour*	GATT Art. XVI:3 Inconsistency found	IC/SR.38 01/04/1956	Report adopted, L/924, 20/11/1958 Adoption of report: SR.13/20, 21/11/1958 Mutually agreed solution: L/1323, L/1548, SCM/W/48, 24/10/1960

GATT Doc	*Complainant*	*Respondent*	*Dispute*	*GATT Articles*	*Consultations*	*Outcome*
GD/38	Germany	Greece	*Greek Increase of Bound Duty*	GATT Article XIX:2 Inconsistency found	L/575 10/10/1956	Report issued. L/580, 09/11/1956 Mutually agreed solution: L/765, 29/11/1957 Withdrawal of request: L/765, 29/11/1957
GD/40	Denmark	US	*Export Subsidy on Poultry*	GATT Art. XVI	L/586 12/11/1956	Consultations held
GD/42	Denmark	United Kingdom	*Export of Subsidized Eggs and Cattle from the United Kingdom*	GATT Article XVI	L/627 24/04/1957	Mutually agreed solution IC/SR.34,19-23/09/1957
GD/44	Germany	Greece	*Greek Discrimination in Credit Facilities for Imported Goods*	GATT Art. XVI	IC/SR.34, IC/SR.34/Corr.1 19-23/09/1957	Consultations held. Request withdrawn. L/740, 08/11/1957
GD/53	Australia	Italy	*Italian Assistance to Exports of Flour*	GATT Art. XVI	L/853 12/09/1958	Consultations held Mutually agreed solution. SCM/W/48
GD/55	Australia, Austria, Canada, Denmark, Greece, India, N.Z, Norway, Pakistan, Sweden, UK, US, Japan, Czechoslovakia	Germany	*German Import Restrictions*	GATT Arts. II:1(b), XIII, XIX	L/949 21/11/1958	Report issued, no record of submission for adoption. L/966, 10/04/1959

GD/67	US	Canada	*Exports of Potatoes to Canada*	GATT Arts. II, VI, VII:2(a), Schedule V Inconsistency found	-	Report adopted. L/1927, 16/11/1962; Adoption of report: SR.20/13,16/11/1962 Mutually agreed solution: L/1968,02/01/1963
GD/75	Malawi	US	*United States – Export Subsidy on Unmanufactured Tobacco*	GATT Arts. XVI, XXXVII:3(c) No conclusion reached	L/2715, 05/12/1966; L/2856, 23/10/1967	Report adopted 22/02/1967, 20/11/1967, 04/12/1967 INT (67)50, L/2925, L/2925/Add.1; BISD 15S/116 Adoption of report: 21/11/1967 SR.24/13
GD/78	Australia	EEC-6	*EEC – Emergency Action on Table Apples*	-	L/3385, 03/04/1970.	Consultations held; request withdrawn. Withdrawal of the request: C/M/63, L/3385/Add.1, 15/07/1970
GD/83	EEC6	US	*United States – Income Tax Legislation (DISC)*	GATT Arts. XVI:1, XVI:3, XVI:4, XXIII:2 Inconsistency found	L/3851 04/02/1972	Report adopted L/4422, 02/11/1976 Adoption of report: C/M/154, 08/12/1981

GATT Doc	*Complainant*	*Respondent*	*Dispute*	*GATT Articles*	*Consultations*	*Outcome*
GD/85	US	France	*Income Tax Practices Maintained by France*	GATT Arts. XVI:4, XXIII:2 Inconsistency found	L/3860 24/05/1972	Report adopted. L/4423, 02/11/1976 Adoption of report: C/M/154, 07-08/12/1981
GD/86	US	Belgium	*Income Tax Practices Maintained by Belgium*	GATT Article XVI:4 Inconsistency found	L/3860 24/05/1972	Report adopted. L/4424, 02/11/1976. Adoption of report: C/M/154, 07-08/12/1981
GD/87	US	Netherlands	*Income Tax Practices Maintained by the Netherlands*	GATT Article XVI:4 Inconsistency found	L/3860 24/05/1972	Report adopted. L/4425, 02/11/1976; Adoption of report: C/M/154, 07-08/12/1981
GD/98	Japan	US	*United States – Suspension of Customs Liquidation Regarding Certain Japanese Consumer Electronic Products*	GATT Arts. VI:4, XVI Ad Note Inconsistency found	-	Report issued. L/4508 06/06/1977
GD/99	Chile	EEC9	*EEC – Refunds on Exports of Malted Barley*	GATT Art. XVI	L/4588 26/10/1977	Consultations held
GD/100	Hong Kong	Norway	*Norway – Restrictions on Imports of Certain Textile Products*	GATT Article XIX Inconsistency found	L/4671 01/03/1978	Report adopted. L/4959,24/03/1980; Adoption of report: C/M/141,18/06/1980

GD/102	Australia	EEC9	*EEC – Refunds on Exports of Sugar – Complaint by Australia*	GATT Arts. XVI:1, XVI:3 Inconsistency found	C/M/128, C/M/128/Corr.1 18/10/1978	Report adopted. 25/10/1979 L/4833; BISD 26S/290 and 28S/80 Adoption of report: 06/11/1979 C/M/135
GD/103	Brazil	EEC9	*EEC – Refunds on Exports of Sugar – Complaint by Brazil*	GATT Arts. XVI:1, XVI:3, XXXVI, XXXVIII, Part IV Inconsistency found	-	Report adopted. L/5011, 07/10/1980; Adoption of report: C/M/144, C/M/144/Corr.1 10/11/1980
GD/104	EEC9	US	*United States – Application of Countervailing Duties*	GATT Article VI:6(a)	L/4745 07/12/1978	Consultations held
GD/117	Japan	Austria	*Austria – Restrictions on Imports of Video Tape Recorders*	GATT Article XIX	L/5119 25/02/1981	Consultations held
GD/136	EEC-10	Switzerland	*Switzerland – Imports of Table Grapes*	GATT Article XIX	L/5371 29/09/1982	Consultations held

APPENDIX 2

GATT Disputes on Subsidies and Countervailing Duties after the SCM Code, 1980-1994

GATT Doc	*Complainant*	*Respondent*	*Dispute*	*SCM Code GATT Articles*	*Consultations*	*Outcome*
GD/115	India	US	*United States – Imposition of Countervailing Duty without Injury Criterion/Industrial Fasteners Imported from India*	GATT Arts. I, VI Defences raised: SCM Article 19:9	L/5028 22/09/1980	Report adopted. C/M/152 03/11/1981 Mutually agreed solution: L/5062/Add.1 25/09/1981 Withdrawal of the request: L/5062/Add.1 25/09/1981
GD/116	US	EEC10	*Greece – Export Subsidies*	SCM (no specific provision)	SCM/Spec/2 09/01/1981	Consultations held
GD/119	Australia	EEC10	*European Economic Community – Production Subsidies on Canned Fruit*	GATT Arts. XVI:1 and XXIII:1(b)	C/M/148, 11/06/1981, L/5167 01/07/1981	Consultations held
GD/122	US	EEC10	*European Economic Community – Subsidies on Export of Wheat Flour*	GATT Arts. XVI:2, XVI:3; SCM Arts. 8, 8:3(c), 8:4 fn. 26, 10:1, 10:2(a), 10:3	SCM/10 29/09/1981	Report issued: SCM/42 21/03/1983
GD/123	US	EEC10	*EEC – Subsidies on the Export of Poultry and Poultry Parts*	-	SCM/Spec/9 13/11/1981	Consultations held

GD/126	US	EEC10	*European Communities – Export Subsidies on Sugar*	GATT Arts. XVI, XVI Ad Note; SCM Arts. 8, 10, 10:3	L/5294 07/02/1982	Consultations held
GD/127	US	Brazil and EEC10	*The United States Complaint against the European Community and Brazil, Concerning the Granting of Subsidies on the Export and Production of Poultry*	GATT Art. XVI; SCM Arts. 8, 9, 10 Defences raised: SCM Arts. 12:3, 14:4	SCM/Spec/19 16/02/1982	Consultations held
GD/128	US	EEC10	*EEC – Subsidies on Export of Pasta Products*	GATT Arts. XVI:1, XVI:4; SCM Arts. 9, 9 fn. 29, 10 SCM Article 9 Inconsistency found	SCM/Spec/8 18/02/1982	Report issued. SCM/43 19/05/1983
GD/129	US	EEC-10	*EEC – Production Aids Granted on Canned Peaches, Canned Pears, Canned Fruit Cocktail and Dried Grapes*	Article XXIII:1(b) Defences raised: SCM Article 8:4(b)	L/5306 25/02/1982	Report issued. L/5778 20/02/1985 Mutually agreed solution: C/M/195, C/M/195/Corr.1 12/02/1986

GATT Doc	*Complainant*	*Respondent*	*Dispute*	*SCM Code GATT Articles*	*Consultations*	*Outcome*
GD/131	Argentina Australia, Brazil, Colombia Cuba, Dominican Republic, India, Nicaragua, Peru, Philippines	EEC-10	*European Communities – Sugar Regime*	GATT Arts. XVI:2, XVI:3	L/5309, 02/04/1982, L/5309/Add.3 04/05/1982	Consultations held
GD/132	India	US	*Certain Domestic Procedures of the United States (CVD Procedures)*	SCM Arts. 4:2, 4:9, 5	-	Consultations held
GD/137	Canada	US	*United States – Initiation of a Countervailing Duty Investigation into Softwood Lumber Products from Canada*	SCM (no specific provision	See SCM/40 27/10/1982	Consultations held
GD/140	EEC10	US	*United States – Subsidies on Exports of Wheat Flour to Egypt*	SCM Arts. 10:1, 10:3	Letter. SCM/M/Spec/8 01/02/1983	Consultations held
GD/148	Canada	EEC-10	*Canada – EEC Consultations on Imports of Beef*	SCM Article 10:3	SCM/51 16/06/1984	Consultations held

GD/153	EEC-10	US	*United States – Definition of Industry Concerning Wine and Grape Products*	SCM Arts. 6:1 fn. 18, 6:5, 6:6, 9 fn. 29; 19:5(a) Inconsistency found	SCM/54 29/11/1984	Report adopted. SCM/71,24/03/1986; Adoption of report: SCM/M/59 28/04/1992
GD/160	EEC10	Canada	*Canada – Imposition of Countervailing Duties on Imports of Manufacturing Beef from the EEC*	SCM Arts. 2:1, 6:5 Inconsistency found (All Arts.)	See SCM/75 30/10/1985	Report issued SCM/85 13/10/1987
GD/164	Canada	US	*United States – Measures Affecting the Export of Softwood Lumber from Canada*	GATT Art. VI; SCM Art. 2 No finding in light of mutually agreed solution	SCM/73 04/06/1986	Report adopted SCM/83 25/05/1987. Adoption of report: SCM/M/34, SCM/M/34/Corr.1 03/06/1987 Mut. agreed solution: CM/83, 30/12/1986
GD/165	EEC12	Canada	*Countervailing Duty Imposed by Canada on Pasta Products from the EEC*	SCM Arts. 2:1(a), 2:1(b), 2:1(c), 5:1	SCM/78 26/06/1986	Consultations held

GATT Doc	*Complainant*	*Respondent*	*Dispute*	*SCM Code GATT Articles*	*Consultations*	*Outcome*
GD/179	US	Canada	*Canada – Injury Determination on Grain Corn from the United States*	SCM Article 6:1	30/04/1987 SCM/82	Report adopted. 21/02/1992, 26/02/1992 SCM/140, SCM/140/Corr.1; BISD 39S/411 Adoption of report: 26/03/1992 SCM/M/58
GD/187	Brazil	US	*United States – Collection of Countervailing Duties on Non-Rubber Footwear from Brazil*	GATT Arts. VI:6(a), X:2; SCM Arts. 1:1, 2:1, 4, 5:2, 5:3, 5:6 No Inconsistency found	SCM/M/35 27-28/10/1987	Report adopted. SCM/94, 04/10/1989 Adoption of report: SCM/M/73 13/06/1995
GD/191	US	EEC12	*European Economic Community – Payments and Subsidies Paid to Processors and Producers of Oilseeds and Related Animal-Feed Proteins*	Arts. II, III:4, XXIII:1(b) Inconsistency found. II, III:4 Finding of nullification or impairment XXIII:1(b)	L/6328 19/02/1988, 19/04/1988	Report adopted. L/6627 14/12/1989; Adoption of report: C/M/238, C/M/238/Corr.1 25/01/1990

GD/206	Brazil	US	*United States – EEP Subsidy (Soya bean)*	GATT Art. XVI:2; SCM Arts. 8:2, 8:3(c), 8:4(c)	SCM/89 15/08/1988	Consultations held
GD/213	US	EEC-12	*German Exchange Rate Scheme for Deutsche Airbus*	SCM Article 9 Inconsistency found	SCM/92 20/03/1989	Report issued. 04/03/1992 SCM/142
GD/216	EEC12	US	*United States – Determination under Sections 304 and 305 of the Trade Act of 1974 in Respect of the European Economic Community's Subsidies for Producers and Processors of Oilseeds and Animal-Feed Proteins*	GATT Article XXIII	DS2/1 07/07/1989	Consultations held
GD/217	Canada	EEC12	*EEC – Subsidies for Producers and Processors of Oilseeds*	GATT Article III	DS3/1 17/08/1989	Consultations held
GD/220	Canada	US	*United States – Countervailing Duties on Fresh, Chilled and Frozen Pork from Canada*	GATT Art. VI:3; SCM Arts. 2:1,4:2 GATT Article VI:3 Inconsistency found	DS7/1 19/09/1989	Report adopted. L/6721 18/09/1990 Adoption of report: C/M/251 11/07/1991
GD/230	EEC12	Australia	*Export Subsidies Granted by Australia*	SCM Article 9	SCM/101 22/03/1990	Consultations held
GD/233	Brazil	US	*United States – Denial of Most-Favoured Nation Treatment as to Non-Rubber Footwear from Brazil*	GATT Arts. I:1, VI:6(a), X, XXIII:1(b), XXIII:1(c) Inconsistency found	DS18/1 07/08/1990	Report adopted. DS18/R.10/01/1992; Adoption of report: C/M/257, C/M/257/Corr.1 19/06/1992

GATT Doc	*Complainant*	*Respondent*	*Dispute*	*SCM Code GATT Articles*	*Consultations*	*Outcome*
GD/243	Norway	US	*United States – Countervailing Duty and Anti-Dumping Actions on Salmon*	AD Art. 15:1, SCM Art. 3	DS24/1 05/03/1991	Consultations held
GD/248	US	EEC12	*EEC – Subsidies Provided to the Airbus Consortium*	SCM Arts. 7, 7:1, 7:2, 8, 11	SCM/114, 31/05/1991 SCM/120 02/07/1991	Consultations held
GD/249	Norway	US	*United States – Imposition of Countervailing Duties on Imports of Fresh and Chilled Atlantic Salmon from Norway*	Arts. I, II, VI; SCM Arts. 2:1, 4:2, 4:9, 6:4, 11, 11:2 Found to fall outside of terms of reference (4:9) No inconsistency found (Rest of Arts.)	SCM/115 10/06/1991	Report adopted SCM/153 04/12/1992 Adoption of report: SCM/M/69 28/04/1994
GD/256	Canada	US	*United States – Measures Affecting the Export of Pure and Alloy Magnesium from Canada*	SCM Article 2:1	Letter. SCM/M/56 05/09/1991	Report issued, SCM/174 09/08/1993 Withdrawal of request: SCM/174 07/07/1993

GD/258	Canada	US	*United States – Measures Affecting Imports of Softwood Lumber from Canada*	SCM Arts. 2:1, 5:1	SCM/W/251 16/10/1991	Report adopted SCM/162 19/02/1993 Adoption of report: SCM/M/67, SCM/M/67/Corr.1 27/10/1993
GD/262	US	EEC12	*Follow up on the Panel Report "European Economic Community – Payments and Subsidies Paid to Processors and Producers of Oilseeds and Related Animal-Feed Proteins"*	GATT Arts. II, III:4, XXIII:1(b)	DS28/1 12/1992	Report issued, two interpretations as to whether the report was adopted. DS28/R 31/03/1992. Adoption of report: C/M/257, C/M/257/Corr.1 19/06/1992
GD/265	EEC12	Australia	*Australian Customs Amendment Act 1991 and Countervailing Duty Proceeding Concerning Imports of Glacé Cherries from France and Italy*	SCM Arts. 1, 6:1 fn. 18, 6:5; 19:5(a)	SCM/145, 09/03/1992, SCM/147 10/04/1992	Report issued. SCM/178 28/10/1993 Adoption of report: -Mutually agreed solution Withdrawal of the request: SCM/178 18/10/1993

GATT Doc	*Complainant*	*Respondent*	*Dispute*	*SCM Code GATT Articles*	*Consultations*	*Outcome*
GD/271	EEC12	Brazil	*Brazil – Imposition of Provisional and Definitive Countervailing Duties on Milk Powder and Certain Types of Milk from the European Economic Community*	SCM Arts. 1, 5:1, 6:1, 6:2, 6:3, 6:4 Inconsistency found (All Arts.)	23/06/1992 SCM/149, 06/07/1992, SCM/151 01/10/1992	Report adopted. SCM/179, SCM/179/Corr.1 27/01/1994. Adoption of report: SCM/M/69 28/04/1994
GD/275	US	Brazil	*Brazil – Countervailing Duty Investigation on Imports of Wheat from the United States*	SCM Arts. 2,3:4, 5	13/10/1992 SCM/154 07/12/1992	Consultations held
GD/277	EEC12	Argentina	*Argentina – Countervailing Duties on Dairy Products from the European Community*	GATT Article VI:6(a)	DS35/1 16/11/1992	Consultations held
GD/278	EEC12	Argentina	*Argentina – Countervailing Duties on Canned Peaches from Greece*	GATT Article VI:6(a)	DS36/1 18/12/1992	Consultations held
GD/280	EEC-12	US	*United States – Definitive Affirmative Injury Determinations Concerning Certain Carbon Steel Flat Products from Several Member States of the EEC*	GATT (no specific provision); SCM Arts. 1, 4:2 Inconsistency found	SCM/159, 02/02/1993 SCM/159/ Add.1, 12/02/1993	Report issued. SCM/185 15/11/1994
GD/281	Brazil	US	*United States – Anti-Dumping and Countervailing Actions on Steel Products*	-	ADP/89, SCM/161, 10/02/1993. ADP/105, SCM/172 12/07/1993	Consultations held

GD/285	Sweden	US	*United States – Imposition of Provisional Countervailing Measures on Imports of Cut-to Length Steel Plate and Corrosion Resistant Steel Plate from Sweden*	SCM Article 2	SCM/165 02/04/1993	Consultations held
GD/286	Australia	EEC12	*EEC – Export Subsidies on Glacé Cherries*	SCM Article 9	SCM/166 07/04/1993	Consultations held
GD/287	US	EEC12	*European Communities – Subsidies Used in Connection with the Production of Thyristors*	GATT (no specific provision); AD Article 12:4	SCM/168 23/04/1993	Consultations held
GD/290	Argentina	US	*Subsidies on Wheat Exports*	-	C/M/264 01/06/1993	Consultations held
GD/294	EEC12	US	*United States – Definitive Affirmative Countervailing Duty Determinations Concerning Certain Carbon Steel Flat Products from Several Member States of the EEC*	GATT Arts. X:1, XI:1, XIII:1, XXIII:1(a)	DS45/1, 07/09/1993. DS45/2 20/06/1994	Consultations held
GD/300	Argentina	EEC12	*EEC – Countervailing Charges on Lemons*	GATT Arts. X:1, XI:1, XIII:1, XXIII:1(a)	DS45/1, 07/09/1993; DS45/2 20/06/1994	Consultations held
GD/301	US	Mexico	*Mexico – Initiation of Countervailing Duty Investigation on Certain Steel Products from the United States*	(Decision of 12 April 1989 L/6489) (BISD 36S/61-62)	DS46/1 08/09/1993	Consultations held
GD/302	EEC12	US	*United States – Countervailing Duties on Certain Carbon Steel Flat Products from Several Members States of the EEC*	SCM Arts. 1,4:2, 6	SCM/175 16/09/1993	Consultations held

APPENDIX 3

GATT Disputes on Anti-dumping after the 1979 AD Code, 1980-1994

GATT Doc	*Complainant*	*Respondent*	*Dispute*	*1979 AD Code GATT Articles*	*Consultations*	*Outcome*
GD/141	EEC10	Canada	*EEC Complaint Concerning Anti-Dumping Action by Canada on Electric Generators Imported from the Community*	Art. 2:1	ADP/M/10, ADP/M/10/Corr.1 26-27/04/1983	Consultations held
GD/150	Finland	New Zealand	*New Zealand – Imports of Electrical Transformers from Finland*	GATT Article VI:1(a) Inconsistency found	C/M/180 11/07/1984	Report adopted L/5814, 19/06/1985; Adoption of report: C/M/191, 17-19/07/1985
GD/170	EEC-12	Japan	*Japan – Trade in Semi-Conductors*	GATT Arts. I, VI, X, XI:1, XVII:1(c), XXIII:1(b)	L/6057 08/10/1986	Report adopted. L/6309,24/03/1988; Adoption of report: C/M/220 04/05/1988
GD/204	Sweden	US	*United States – Imposition of Anti-Dumping Duties on Imports of Seamless Stainless Steel Hollow Products from Sweden*	Arts. 1, 2:6, 3:2, 5:1 first sentence Inconsistency found: Arts. 1, 5:1 first sentence	ADP/38 14/07/1988	Report issued. ADP/47 20/08/1990

GD/205	Japan	EEC-12	*EEC – Regulation on Imports of Parts and Components*	GATT Arts. III:2 first sentence, III:4, SCM Article 13:10 Inconsistency found	L/6381 29/07/1988	Report adopted. L/6657 22/03/1990. Adoption of report: C/M/241, C/M/241/Corr.1 16/05/1990
GD/212	Finland	Australia	*Anti-Dumping Duties on Power Transformers from Finland*	Arts. 2:2, 2:6	Letter. ADP/42 16/01/1989	Consultations held
GD/215	Hong Kong	EEC12	*Definitive Anti-Dumping Duties on Video Cassettes originating in Hong Kong*	-	ADP/44 22/06/1989	Consultations held
GD/234	Mexico	US	*United States – Anti-Circumvention Inquiry with Respect to Colour Television Picture Tubes*	GATT (no specific provision); AD (no specific provision)	ADP/52 12/10/1990	Consultations held; request withdrawn
GD/235	Brazil	Mexico	*Mexico – Anti-Dumping Duties on Electric Power Transformers from Brazil*	Arts. 2:1, 2:6, 3:1, 3:2, 5:1, 5:3, 6:1, 6:2, 6:3, 6:7, 8:1, 10:1	ADP/91 04/08/1992	Consultations held
GD/236	Canada	US	*United States – Investigation of Circumvention of Anti-Dumping Order on Colour Television Picture Tubes*	GATT. AD No specific provision	DS19/1 16/10/1990	Consultations held
GD/237	Mexico	US	*United States – Anti-Dumping Duties on Grey Portland Cement and Cement Clinker from Mexico*	Art. 5:1 Inconsistency found	24/10/1990 ADP/51	Report issued. 07/09/1992 ADP/82

GATT Doc	*Complainant*	*Respondent*	*Dispute*	*1979 AD Code GATT Articles*	*Consultations*	*Outcome*
GD/238	Canada	US	*United States – Anti-circumvention Inquiry with Respect to Colour Television Picture Tubes*	GATT (no specific provision); AD (no specific provision)	ADP/50 26/10/1990	Consultations held; request withdrawn
GD/243	Norway	US	*United States – Countervailing Duty and Anti-Dumping Actions on Salmon*	Art. 15:1, SCM Art. 3	DS24/1 05/03/1991	Consultations held
GD/245	Hong Kong	US	*Anti-dumping duties in the United States against Imports of Man-Made Fibre Sweaters from Hong Kong*	Arts. 2, 2:4, 3:2, 3:4 fn. 5, 5:1, 6:1, 6:8	ADP/54 08/04/1991	Consultations held
GD/246	Hong Kong	US	*United States – Anti-Dumping Duties on Imports of Man-Made Fibre Sweaters from Hong Kong*	No specific provision	25/04/1994 ADP/119	Consultations held
GD/247	Sweden	US	*United States – Anti-Dumping Duties on Imports of Stainless-Steel Plate from Sweden*	Arts. 8:3, 9:1, 9:2 Inconsistency found. (9:2)	ADP/56 06/05/1991	Report issued. ADP/117,24/02/1994 ADP/117/Corr.1 30/03/1994
GD/251	Norway	US	*United States – Imposition of Anti-Dumping Duties on Imports of Fresh and Chilled Atlantic Salmon from Norway*	Arts. 2:4, 2:6, 5:1, 6:1, 6:8, 8:3, 9:1 Inconsistency found. (2:4, 2:6, 6:8)	ADP/57 17/06/1991	Report adopted. 30/11/1992 ADP/87. BISD 41S/229 Adoption of report: ADP/M/44 25-26/04/1994

GD/253	Japan	EEC12	*EEC – Imposition of Anti-Dumping Duties on Imports of Audio Cassettes from Japan*	Arts. 2:1, 2:4, 2:6, 3, 3:1, 3:2, 3:4, 4:1(ii), 5:1, 5:3, 8:3 Inconsistency found (2:6)	ADP/79 07/1991, 10/1991, 12/1991, 04/1992	Report issued. ADP/136,28/04/1995, ADP/136/Corr.1, 08/06/1995
GD/254	US	Korea	*Korea – Anti-dumping Duties on Imports of Polyacetal Resins from the United States*	Arts. 3:1, 3:2, 3:3, 3:4, 3:6, 8:5 Inconsistency found (all Arts.)	Letter. ADP/M/34 21/07/1991, 30/09/1991	Report adopted., ADP/92,02/04/1993 ADP/92/Corr.1. 06/04/1993 Adoption of report: ADP/M/40, ADP/M/40/Corr.1 27/04/1993
GD/255	Brazil	EEC12	*EEC – Anti-Dumping Actions on Cotton Yarn Originating from Brazil*	Arts. 13, 2:4, 2:6, 3:1, 3:2, 3:3, 3:4, 8:2 No inconsistency found	ADP/63 03/09/1991	Report adopted. ADP/137, 04/07/1995. Adoption of report: ADP/M/50, 30/10/1995
GD/261	US	Canada	*Canada – Anti-Dumping Duties on Imports of Beer from the United States*	Arts. 2:6, 4:1(ii)	Unknown 24/12/1991	Mutually agreed solution 28/07/1994 ADP/M/45
GD/267	Japan	EEC12	*EEC – Treatment of Anti-Dumping Duties as a Cost in Refund Procedures*	No specific provision	ADP/78 21/04/1992	Consultations held

GATT Doc	*Complainant*	*Respondent*	*Dispute*	*1979 AD Code GATT Articles*	*Consultations*	*Outcome*
GD/274	Pakistan	Turkey	*Turkey – Antidumping Measures on Imports of Cotton Yarn from Pakistan*	-	29/09/1992- C/M/259, C/M/259/Corr.1 01/10/1992	Mutually agreed solution C/M/264 16-17/06/1993
GD/276	Brazil	Mexico	*AD Proceeding on Brazilian Textiles*	AD Article 15:2	ADP/86 16/10/1992	Consultations held, mutually agreed solution. C/M/264, 17/06/1993
GD/281	Brazil	US	*United States – Anti-Dumping and Countervailing Actions on Steel Products*	AD Art. 15:2. SCM Art. 3:2	ADP/89, SCM/161, 10/02/1993. ADP/105, SCM/172 12/07/1993	Consultations held
GD/282	EEC12	US	*Certain Steel Products: Definitive and Provisional Anti-Dumping Measures*	AD Article 15	ADP/90, ADP/90/Corr.1 02/03/1993	Consultations held
GD/283	Mexico	US	*United States – Anti-Dumping Investigation of Imports of Steel Wire Rope from Mexico*	No specific provision	ADP/98 31/03/1993	Consultations held
GD/284	Sweden	US	*United States – Imposition of Provisional Anti-Dumping Measures on Imports of Cut-to-Length Steel Plate from Sweden*	Art. VI. Arts. 2:4, 2:6, 3, 5:3, 6:8	ADP/93 02/04/1993	Consultations held

GD/291	Japan	US	*United States – Provisional Anti-Dumping Measures against Imports of Certain Hot-Rolled Carbon Steel Flat Products, Certain Cold Rolled Carbon Steel Flat Products and Certain Corrosion-Resistant Carbon Steel Flat Products*	Arts. 3:1, 3:4, 6:8	ADP/100 09/06/1993	Consultations held
GD/292	Canada	US	*United States – Application of Section 781 of the US Tariff Act of 1930 as amended by the Omnibus. Trade and Competitiveness Act of 1988 (Anti-Circumvention Law) to Brass Plate from Canada*	AD Arts. 1, 10:1, 2, 3, 5, 8:3	ADP/101 11/06/1993	Consultations held
GD/295	EEC12	US	*United States – Anti-Dumping Duties on Certain Steel Products (Hot-Rolled, Cold Rolled, Corrosion Resistant and Cut-to-Length) from Various Member States of the European Economic Communities*	Arts. 3, 5, 5:1, 10, 10:1	ADP/103 02/07/1993	Consultations held
GD/297	Australia	US	*United States – Final Determination on Dumping and Provisional Anti-Dumping Measures against Imports of Certain Corrosion-Resistant Carbon Steel Flat Products from Australia*	Arts. 5:1 (a), 5:1 (b), 5:1 (c), 6:8	ADP/104 15/07/1993	Consultations held

GATT Doc	Complainant	Respondent	Dispute	1979 AD Code GATT Articles	Consultations	Outcome
GD/303	Finland	US	*United States – Anti-Dumping Measures against Imports of Cut-to-Length Carbon Steel Plate from Finland*	Art. VI. Arts. 2:4, 3, 5:3, 6:8	ADP/109 18/10/1993	Consultations held
GD/304	EEC12	Canada	*Canada – Anti-Dumping Duties on Certain Steel Products (Cold-Rolled Steel Sheet, Flat Hot-Rolled Carbon Steel Sheet and Hot-Rolled Carbon and Alloy Steel Plate) from Various Member States of the European Economic Communities*	No specific provision	ADP/110 22/10/1993	Consultations held
GD/305	EEC12	Canada	*Canada – Anti-Dumping Investigation of Certain Hot-Rolled Carbon Steel Plate and High Strength Low Alloy Plate, Heat Treated or Not, originating in or Exported from, inter-alia, Italy and Spain*	Art. 5	ADP/112 23/11/1993	Consultations held
GD/307	Singapore	EEC12	*EC – Refund of Anti-Dumping Duty*	Art. VI. Arts. 2:6, 8:3	ADP/115 20/01/1994	Consultations held
GD/310	EEC12	Brazil	*Brazil – Imposition of Provisional Anti-Dumping Duties on Imports of Certain Peaches Originating in Greece*	Arts. 6:2, 6:7, 8:5, 10:1	ADP/118 28/02/1994	Consultations held
GD/311	The Czech Republic	Argentina	*Argentina – Provisional Anti-Dumping Duties on Imports of Three-Phase Electric Motors*	Art. VI:6(a)	DS50/1 05/04/1994	Consultations held

GD/313	Hong Kong	US	*United States – Imports of Man-Made Fibre Sweaters Originating in Hong Kong*	GATT Art. VI; AD Arts. 2:4, 3, 3:2, 3:4, 3:4 fn. 5, 5:1	ADP/119 25/04/1994	Consultations held
GD/314	EEC12	US	*United States – Imposition of Provisional Anti-Dumping Duties on Photographic Paper from the Netherlands*	Art. 2:4	ADP/129 29/06/1994	Consultations held

Bibliography

Ahn, D., Why Reform Is Needed: WTO 'Public Body' Jurisprudence, *Global Policy*, Vol. 12, No. 3, 2021, pp. 61-70.

Aufricht, H., *Guide to League of Nations Publications. A Bibliographical Survey of the Work of the League*, 1920-1947, 1951.

Bagwell, K., Staiger, R.W., Will International Rules on Subsidies Disrupt the World Trading System?, *American Economic Review*, Vol. 96, No. 3. 2006, pp. 877-895.

Barceló III, J.J., A History of GATT Unfair Trade Remedy Law: Confusion of Purposes, Cornell Law Faculty Publications Paper 517, 1991, pp. 311-333.

Barceló III, J.J., Antidumping Laws as Barriers to Trade the United States and the International Antidumping Code, *Cornell Law Review*, Vol. 57, No. 4, 1971-1972, pp. 491-560.

Barceló III, J.J., Subsidies, Countervailing Duties and Antidumping after the Tokyo Round, *Cornell International Law Journal*, Vol. 13, No. 2, 1980, pp. 257-290.

Barceló III, J.J., The Antidumping Law: Repeal It or Revise It, *Michigan Journal of International Law*, Vol. 1, No. 1, 1979, pp. 53-93.

Barceló III, J.J., The Two-Track Subsidies Code: Countervailing Duties and Trade Retaliation, in Quinn, J., Slayton, P. (eds), *Non-tariff Barriers after the Tokyo Round*, 1982, pp. 121-152.

Bellis, J., Anti-competitive Practices and the WTO: The Elusive Search for New World Trade Rules, in Bronckers, M., Quick, R. (eds), New Directions in International Economic Law: Essays in Honour of John H. Jackson, 2000, pp. 361-368.

Bhagwati, J.N., *Protectionism*, 1988.

Bhagwati, J.N., Ramaswami, V.K., Domestic Distortions, Tariffs and the Theory of Optimum Subsidy, *Journal of Political Economy*, Vol. 71, No. 1, 1963, pp. 44-50.

Bhagwati, J.N., The Demand to Reduce Domestic Diversity among Trading Nations in Bhagwati, J.N., Hudec, R.E. (eds), *Fair Trade and Harmonization. Prerequisite for Free Trade?*, Vol. I: Economic analysis, 1996, pp. 9-40.

Bhagwati, J.N., The World Trading System at Risk, Aggressive Unilateralism, and Fair Trade, Reciprocity and Harmonization, in Deardorff, A., and Stern, R. (eds), *Analytical and Negotiating Issues in the Global Trading System*, 1993.

Bierwagen, R.W., *GATT Article VI and the Protectionist Bias in Anti-dumping Laws*, 1990.

Bourgeois, J., The GATT Rules for Industrial Subsidies and Countervailing Duties and the New GATT Round: The Weather and the Seeds, in Petersmann, E.U., Hilf, M. (eds), *The New GATT Round of Multilateral Trade Negotiations: Legal and Economic Problems*, Studies in Transnational Economic Law, Vol. 5, 1988, pp. 219-235.

Bronckers, M., Reconsidering the Non-discrimination Principle as Applied to GATT Safeguards Measures, A Rejoinder, *Legal Issues of European Integration*, Vol. 10, No. 2. 1983, pp. 113-137.

Bronckers, M., The Non-discriminatory Application of Article XIX GATT: Tradition or Fiction?, *Legal Issues of European Integration*, Vol. 8, No. 2, 1981, pp. 35-76.

Bronckers, M., The WTO Reference Paper on Telecommunications: A Model for WTO Competition Law?, in Bronckers, M., Quick, R. (eds), *New Directions in International Economic Law: Essays in Honour of John H. Jackson*, 2000, pp. 371-389.

Bronckers, M., Voluntary Export Restraints and the GATT 1994 Agreement on Safeguards, in Bourgeois, J., Berrod, F., Gippini Fournier, E. (eds), *The Uruguay Round Results: A European Lawyers' Perspective*, 1995, pp. 273-279.

Bronckers, M., WTO Implementation in the European Community: Antidumping, Safeguards and Intellectual Property, *Journal of World Trade*, Vol. 29, No. 5, 1995, pp. 73-95.

Brown, K., Deardorff, A.V., Stern, R.M., International Labor Standards and Trade: A Theoretical Analysis, in Bhagwati, J.N., Hudec, R.E. (eds), *Harmonization and Fair Trade: Prerequisites for Free Trade?*, Vol. 1, 1996, pp. 228-280.

Carr, J.C., Taplin, W., *History of the British Steel Industry*, 1962.

Cass, R.A., Boltuck, R.D., Antidumping and Countervailing-Duty Law: The Mirage of Equitable International Competition, in Bhagwati, J.N., Hudec, R.E. (eds), *Fair Trade and Harmonization. Prerequisite for Free Trade?*, Vol. 2: Legal Analysis, 1996, pp. 351-414.

Charnovitz, S., The Influence of International Labour Standards on the World Trading Regime: A Historical Overview, *International Labour Review*, Vol. 126, No. 5, 1987, pp. 565-584.

Crowley, M.A., Why Are Safeguards Needed in a Trade Agreement?, in Bagwell, K., Bermann, G., Mavroidis, P.C. (eds), *Law and Economics of Contingent Protection in International Trade*, 2009, pp. 379-400.

Dale, R., *Anti-dumping Law in a Liberal Trade Order*, 1980.

Dam, K.W., *The GATT: Law and International Economic Organization*, 1970.

Denton, R., Overview of the Discussion During the Comparative Antidumping Law Mini-Conference, November 6 and 7, 1988, in Jackson, J.H., Vermulst, E.A. (eds), *Antidumping Law and Practice: A Comparative Study*, 1989, pp. 467-476.

Depayre, G., Subsidies and Countervailing Measures after the Uruguay Round: An overview, in Bourgeois, J., Berrod, F., Gippini Fournier, E. (eds), *The Uruguay Round Results, A European Lawyers' Perspective: Proceedings of an International Conference Held at the College of Europe, Bruges*, 1999, pp. 247-254.

Donald, W.J.A., *The Canadian Iron and Steel Industry*, 1915.

Eskridge Jr., W.N., Dynamic Interpretation of Economic Regulatory Legislation (Countervailing Duty Law), Law and Policy in International Business, Vol. 21, No. 4, 1990, pp. 663-698.

Evans, J.W., Subsidies and Countervailing Duties in the GATT, *Maryland Journal of International Law*, Vol. 3, No. 1, 1977, pp. 211-245.

Evans, J.W., The General Agreement on Tariffs and Trade, *International Organization*, Vol. 22, No. 1, 1968, pp. 72-98.

Evenett, S.J., Sicken thy Neighbour: The Initial Trade Policy Response to COVID-19, *The World Economy*, Vol. 43, No. 4, 2020, pp. 828-839.

Fikentscher, W., Immenga, U., *Draft International Antitrust Code*, 1995.

Finger, J.M., *Antidumping: How It Works and Who Gets Hurt*, 1993.

Finger, J.M., Flexibilities, Rules, and Trade Remedies in the GATT/WTO System, in Daunton, M. Narlikar, A., Stern, R.M. (eds), *The Oxford Handbook on the World Trade Organization*, 2012, pp. 418-440.

Finger, J.M., The Origins and Evolution of Antidumping Regulation, Policy Research Working Paper Series 783, The World Bank, 1991.

Fiorito, L., Nerozzi, S., *Jacob Viner's Reminiscences from the New Deal (February 11, 1953)*, 2008.

Flory, T. The Agreement on Safeguards, in Bourgeois, J., Berrod, F., Gippini Fournier, E. (eds), *The Uruguay Round Results, A European Lawyers' Perspective: Proceedings of an International Conference Held at the College of Europe, Bruges*, 1999, pp. 265-271.

Fontaine, M., De Ly, F., Hardship Clauses, in *Drafting International Contracts: An Analysis of Contract Clauses*, 2009, pp. 453-492.

García López, J.A., García Catalán, M.I., La Expansión del Derecho Comunitario Europeolos Acuerdos Preferenciales y las Reglas de Origen en las Relaciones Comerciales Exteriores de la Unión Europea, *Revista de la Facultad de Derecho de la Universidad Complutense*, n. 89, 1998, pp. 87-104.

García López, J.A., Moreno Sancho, M., The US and EU Solar Trade Remedies Saga: The Globalization of Mercantilism, *Journal of World Trade*, Vol. 56, No. 4, 2022, pp. 615-632.

Gardner, R.N., *Sterling Dollar Diplomacy*, 1956.

Gass, P., et al., Raising Ambition Through Fossil Fuel Subsidy Reform: Greenhouse Gas Emissions Modelling Results from 26 Countries, The International Institute for Sustainable Development, 2019.

Gifford D.J., The Draft International Antitrust Code Proposed at Munich: Good Intentions Gone Awry, *Minnesota Journal of International Law*, 1997, Vol. 6, No. 1, pp. 1-66.

General Agreement on Tariffs and Trade documents

Grey, R. de C., The Decay of the Trade Relations System, in Snape, R.H. (ed.), *Issues in World Trade Policy: GATT at the Crossroads*, 1986, pp. 17-31.

Grey, R. de C., *Trade Policy and the System of Contingency Protection in the Perspective of Competition Policy*, 1986.

Grey, R. de C., The Conflict Between Trade Policy and Competition Policy: A Comment, in Petersmann, E.U., Hilf, M., *The New GATT Round of Multilateral Trade Negotiations: Legal and Economic Problems*, Vol. 5, 1988, pp. 447-453.

Hart, M., Dumping and Free Trade Areas, in Jackson, J.H., Vermulst, E.A. (eds), *Antidumping Law and Practice: A Comparative Study*, 1990, pp. 326-342.

Hirsh, B., *Resolving the WTO Appellate Body Crisis: Proposals on Overreach, Commissioned by the National Foreign Trade Council*, 2019.

Hoekman, B., Competition Policy and the Global Trading System A Developing-Country Perspective, The World Bank Policy Research Working Paper 1735, 1997.

Hoekman, B., Low, P., Mavroidis, P.C., Regulation, Competition Policy and Market Access Negotiations: Lessons from the Telecommunications Sector, in Hope, E., Maeleng, P., *Competition and Trade Policies, Coherence or Conflict?*, 1998, pp. 115-139.

Hoekman, B., Mavroidis, P.C., Dumping, Antidumping and Antitrust, *Journal of World Trade*, Vol. 30, No. 1, 1996, pp. 27-52.

Hoekman, B., Mavroidis, P.C., WTO Reform: Back to the Past to Build for the Future, *Global Policy*, Vol. 12, No. 3, 2021, pp. 5-12.

Hoekman, B., Subsidies and Spillovers in a Value Chain World: New Rules Required? *E15Initiative*, International Centre for Trade and Sustainable Development and World Economic Forum, 2015.

Horlick, G.N., Proposals for Reform of the GATT Antidumping Code, *Brooklyn Journal of International Law*, Vol. 18, No. 1, 1992, pp. 181-188.

Horlick, G.N., A Personal History of the WTO Subsidies Agreement, *Journal of World Trade*, Vol. 47, No. 2, 2013, pp. 447-452.

Horlick, G.N., A Personal History of Zeroing, *Global Trade and Customs Journal*, Vol. 4, No. 5, 2009, pp. 161-163.

Horlick, G.N., Clarke, P.A., Rethinking Subsidy Disciplines for the Future. E15 Task Force on Rethinking International Disciplines - Policy Options Paper, *E15Initiative*, Geneva, International Centre for Trade and Sustainable Development and World Economic Forum, 2016.

Horlick, G.N., Clarke, P.A., The 1994 WTO Subsidies Agreement, *World Competition*, Vol. 17, No. 4, 1994, pp. 41-54.

Horlick, G.N., Clarke, P.A., The Agreement on Subsidies and Countervailing Measures, in Horlick, G.N. (ed.), *World Trade Organization and International Trade Law: Antidumping, Subsidies and Trade Agreements*, 2014, pp. 217-272.

Horlick, G.N., Clarke, P.A., WTO Subsidies Discipline During and after the Crisis, *Journal of International Economic Law*, Vol. 13, No. 3, 2010, pp. 859-874.

Horlick, G.N., Gobbi Estrella, T., Mandatory Abolition of Anti-dumping, Countervailing Duties and Safeguards in Customs Unions and Free-Trade Areas Constituted Between World Trade Organization Members: Revisiting a Long-Standing Discussion in Light of the Appellate Body's Turkey-Textiles Ruling, *Journal of World Trade*, Vol. 40, No. 5, 2006, pp. 909-944.

Horlick, G.N., How Did Antidumping Get So Bad? in Horlick, G.N. (ed.), *World Trade Organization and International Trade Law. Antidumping, Subsidies and Trade Agreements*, 2014, pp. 3-10.

Horlick, G.N., How the GATT Became Protectionist: An Analysis of the Uruguay Round Draft Final Antidumping Code, *Journal of World Trade*, Vol. 27, No. 5, 1993, pp. 5-17.

Horlick, G.N., John Jackson and the Development of GATT/WTO Subsidies Rules, in Bronckers, M., Quick, R. (eds), *New Directions in International Economic Law, Essays in Honour of J.H. Jackson*, 2000, pp. 177-184.

Horlick, G.N., John Jackson as a Resource for Scholars and Others, *Journal of International Economic Law*, 2016, Vol. 19, No. 2, pp. 401-402.

Horlick, G.N., Shea, E.C., The World Trade Organization Antidumping Agreement, *Journal of World Trade*, Vol. 29, No. 1, 1995, pp. 5-32.

Horlick, G.N., Shuman, S.S., Nonmarket Economy Trade and US Antidumping/Countervailing Duty Laws, *International Lawyer*, Vol. 18, No. 4, 1984, pp. 807-840.

Horlick, G.N., The 10 Major Problems with the Anti-dumping Instrument in the United States, *Journal of World Trade*, Vol. 39, No. 1, 2005, pp. 169-179.

Horlick, G.N., The United States Antidumping System, in Jackson, J.H., Vermulst, E.A. (eds), *Antidumping Law and Practice: A Comparative Study*, 1989, pp. 99-166.

Horlick, G.N., Trade Remedies and Development of Renewable Energy, Clean Energy Technologies and the Trade System: Proposals and Analysis, *E15Initiative*, Geneva, International Centre for Trade and Sustainable Development and World Economic Forum, 2013, pp. 69-73.

Horlick, G.N., Vermulst, E.A., The 10 Major Problems with the Anti-dumping Instrument: An Attempt at Synthesis, *Journal of World Trade*, Vol. 39, No. 1, 2005, pp. 67-73.

Horn, H., Mavroidis, P.C., Review of the WTO US: Lamb Dispute, prepared for an American Law Institute Conference on Principles of Trade Law, World Trade Organization, 2003.

Howell, T., Ballantine, D., Dumping: Still a Problem in International Trade in National Research Council, in Wessner, C. (ed.), International Friction and Cooperation in High-Technology Development and Trade: Papers and Proceedings, 1997, pp. 325-377.

Howse, R., Trebilcock, M.J., The Fair Trade-Free Trade Debate: Trade, Labor, and the Environment, *International Review of Law and Economics*, Vol. 16, No. 1, 1996, pp. 61-79.

Hudec, R.E., GATT Legal Restraints on the Use of Trade Measures Against Foreign Environmental Practices, in Bhagwati, J.N., Hudec, R.E. (eds), *Fair Trade and Harmonization. Prerequisite for Free Trade?*, Vol. 2: *Legal Analysis*, 1996, pp. 95-174.

Hudec, R.E., Mirror, Mirror on the Wall: The Concept of Fairness in the United States Foreign Trade Policy, in Hudec, R.E., *Canada, Japan and International Law: Proceedings of the 1990 Canadian Council on International Law*, pp. 88-110.

Hudec, R.E., *The GATT Legal System and World Trade Diplomacy*, 1975.

Iliasu, A., The Cobden-Chevalier Commercial Treaty of 1860, *The Historical Journal*, Vol. 14, No. 1, 1971, pp. 67-98.

Irwin, D.A., Mavroidis, P.C., Sykes, A.O., *The Genesis of the GATT*, 2008.

Irwin, D.A., Multilateral and Bilateral Trade Policies in the World Trading System: An Historical Perspective, in De Melo, J., Panagariya, A., *New Dimensions in Regional Integration*, 1993, pp. 90-119.

Irwin, D.A., The GATT in Historical Perspective, *The American Economic Review*, Vol. 85, No. 2, 1995, pp. 323-328.

Jackson, J.H., Alternatives Approaches for Implementing Competition Rules in International Economic Relations, *Aussenwirtschaft Zeitschrift für internationale Wirtschaftsbeziehungen*, Vol. 49, 1994, pp. 177-200.

Jackson, J.H., Davey, W.J., *Legal problems of International Economic Relations, Cases, Materials and Text*, 2nd ed., 1986.

Jackson, J.H., Davey, W.J., Sykes, A.O., *Legal Problems of International Economic Relations: Cases, Materials and Text on the National and International Regulation of Transnational Economic Relations*, 5th ed., 2008.

Jackson, J.H., International Economic Law: Reflections on the 'Boilerroom' of International Relations, *American University International Law Review*, Vol. 10, No. 2, 1995, pp. 595-606.

Jackson, J.H., Louis, J-V., Matsushita, M., Implementing the Tokyo Round: Legal Aspects of Changing International Economic Rules, *Michigan Law Review*, Vol. 81, No. 2, 1982, pp. 267-397.

Jackson, J.H., Perspectives on Countervailing Duties, *Law and Policy in International Business*, Vol. 21, No. 4, 1990, pp. 739-762.

Jackson, J.H., *Restructuring the GATT System*, 1990.

Jackson, J.H., Statement on Competition and Trade Policy Before the US Senate Committee on Judiciary, 18 June 1992, *Journal of World Trade*, Vol. 26, No. 5, 1992, pp. 111-116.

Jackson, J.H., *The Jurisprudence of GATT & the WTO, Insights on Treaty Law and Economic Relations*, 2002.

Jackson, J.H., *The World Trade Organization, Constitution and Jurisprudence*, Chatham House Papers, 1998.

Jackson, J.H., *The World Trading System: Law and Policy of International Economic Relations*, 2nd ed., 2000.

Jackson, J.H., *World Trade and the Law of GATT (A Legal Analysis of the General Agreement on Tariffs and Trade)*, 1969.

Jackson, J.H., World Trade Rules and Environmental Policies: Congruence or Conflict?, *Washington and Lee Law Review*, Vol. 49, No. 4, 1992, pp. 1227-1278.

Johnson, H.G., Optimal Trade Intervention in the Presence of Domestic Distortions, in Baldwin R.E., et al. (eds), *Trade, Growth and the Balance of Payments, Trade, Growth, and the Balance of Payments: Essays in Honor of Gottfried Haberler*, pp. 3-34, 1965. Reprinted in Johnson, H.G., *Aspects of the Theory of Tariffs*, 1971.

Koulen, M., Potential Anti-Trust Liability of Exporters Participating in Various Forms of Exports Restraint Arrangements, in Petersmann, E.U., Hilf, M., *The New GATT*

Round of Multilateral Trade Negotiations: Legal and Economic Problems, Vol. 5, 1988, pp. 437-446.

Koulen, M., The New Anti-dumping Code Through Its Negotiating History, in Bourgeois, J., Berrod, F., Gippini Fournier, E. (eds), *The Uruguay Round Results, A European Lawyers' Perspective: Proceedings of an International Conference Held at the College of Europe, Bruges*, 1999, pp. 151-232.

Koulen, M., The Non-discriminatory Interpretation of GATT Article XIX.1. A Reply, *Legal Issues of Economic Integration*, Vol. 10. No. 2, 1983, pp. 87-111.

Lawrence, R.Z., Litan, R.E., *Saving Free Trade: A Pragmatic Approach*, 1986.

League of Nations Documents

Leflon, J., Uruguay Round Comments: A View from UNICE, in Bourgeois, J., Berrod, F., Gippini Fournier, E. (eds), *The Uruguay Round Results: A European Lawyers' Perspective*, 1995, pp. 59-65.

Lockhart, N.J.S., Mitchell, A.D., Regional Trade Agreements Under GATT 1994: An Exception and Its Limits, in Lockhart, N.J.S., Mitchell, A.D., *Challenges and Prospects for the WTO*, 2005, pp. 217-239.

Long, R. United States Law and the International Anti-dumping Code, *International Lawyer*, Vol. 3, No. 3, 1969, pp. 463-489.

Lowenfeld, F., Fair or Unfair Trade: Does It Matter, *Cornell International Law Journal*, Vol. 13, No. 2, 1981, pp. 205-219.

Mallet, S.L., Minutes of the International Sugar Conferences on Drawbacks of Refined Sugars Established by the Convention of 8 November 1864, Vol. 27, LXV, 1973, pp. 597.

Marks, M.J., United States Antidumping Laws: A Government Overview, *Antitrust Law Journal*, Vol. 43, No. 3, 1974, pp. 580-89.

Martineau, G., The Brussels Sugar Convention, *The Economic Journal*, Vol. 14, No. 53, 1904, pp. 34-46.

Maskus, K. Research and Development Subsidies: A Need for WTO Disciplines? *E15Initiative*, Geneva, International Centre for Trade and Sustainable Development (ICTSD) and World Economic Forum, 2015.

Matsushita, M., Schoenbaum, T.J., Mavroidis, P.C., *The World Trade Organization: Law, Practice and Policy*, 2003.

Miranda, J., Interpreting Paragraph 15 of China's Protocol of Accession, *Global Trade and Customs Journal*, Vol. 9, No. 3, 2014, pp. 94-103.

Miranda, J., More on Why Granting China Market Economy Status after December 2016 Is Contingent upon Whether China Has in Fact Transitioned into a Market Economy, *Global Trade and Customs Journal*, Vol. 11, No. 5, 2016, pp. 244-250.

O'Brien, K.A., The Applicability of the United States Countervailing Duty Law to Imports from Nonmarket Economy Countries, *Fordham International Law Journal*, Vol. 9, No. 3, 1985, pp. 596-633.

Palmeter, N.D., Competition Policy and Unfair Trade: First Do No Harm, *Aussenwirtschaft Zeitschrift für internationale Wirtschaftsbeziehungen*, Vol. 49, 1994, pp. 417-422.

Palmeter, N.D., Environment and Trade: Who Will Be Heard? What Law Is Relevant?, *Journal of World Trade*, Vol. 26, No. 2, 1992, pp. 35-41.

Palmeter, N.D., The Antidumping Emperor, *Journal of World Trade*, Vol. 22. No. 4, 1988, pp. 5-7.

Parsons, D.O., Edward, J.R., The United States Steel Consolidation: The Creation of Market Control, *Journal of Law and Economics*, Vol. 18, No. 1, 1975, pp. 181-220.

Parsons, D.O., Edward, J.R., The United States Steel Consolidation: The Creation of Market Control, *Journal of Law and Economics*, Vol. 18, No. 1, 1975, pp. 181-220.

Pauly, L.W., The League of Nations and the Foreshadowing of the International Monetary Fund, *Princetown Essays in International Finance*, No. 201, 1996.

Pauwelyn, J., The Puzzle of WTO Safeguards and Regional Trade Agreements, *Journal of International Economic Law*, Vol. 7, No. 1, 2004, pp. 109-142.

Petersmann, E.U., Conclusions, in Bourgeois, J., Berrod, F., Gippini Fournier, E. (eds), *The Uruguay Round Results: A European Lawyers' Perspective*, 1995, pp. 485-491.

Petersmann, E.U., International Competition Rules for Governments and for Private Business, *Journal of World Trade*, Vol. 30, No. 3, 1996, pp. 5-35.

Petersmann, E.U., International Competition Rules for Private Business: A Trade Law Approach for Linking Trade and Competition Rules in the WTO, *Chicago-Kent Law Review*, Vol. 72, No. 2, 1996, pp. 445-582.

Philippe, D., Pacta Sunt Servanda et Rebus Sic Stantibus, in Chambre de Commerce Internationale (ed.), *L'apport de la Jurisprudence Arbitrale*, 1986, pp. 181-259.

Pigman, G.A., Hegemony and Trade Liberalization Policy: Britain and the Brussels Sugar Convention of 1902, *Review of International Studies*, Vol. 23, No. 2, pp. 185-210.

Porritt, E., *Sixty Years of Protection in Canada, 1846-1907: Where Industry Leans on the Politician*, 1908.

Posner, T.R., A Comment on Interpreting Paragraph 15 of China's Protocol of Accession by Jorge Miranda, *Global Trade & Customs Journal*, Vol. 9, No. 4, 2014, pp. 146-153.

Prusa, T.J., Vermulst, E.A., United States: Certain Methodologies and Their Application to Anti-dumping Proceedings Involving China – Nails in the Coffin of Unfair Dumping Margin Calculation Methodologies, *World Trade Review*, Vol. 18, No. 2, 2019, pp. 287-307.

Puelinckx, H., Frustration, Hardship, Force Majeure, Imprévision, Wegfall der Geschäftsgrundlage, Unmöglichkeit, Changed Circumstances: A Comparative Study in English, French, German and Japanese Law, *Journal of International Arbitration*, Vol. 3, No. 2, 1986, pp. 47-86.

Reback, C., Merger for Monopoly: The Formation of US Steel, *Essays in Economic and Business History*, Vol. 25, 2007, pp. 105-117.

Rivers, R., Greenwald, J., The Negotiation of a Code on Subsidies and Countervailing Measures: Bridging Fundamental Policy Differences, *Law and Policy in International Business*, Vol. 11, No. 4, 1979, pp. 1447-1496.

Saxonhouse, G., A Short Summary of the Long History of Unfair Trade Allegations Against Japan, in Bhagwati, J.N., Hudec, R.E (eds), *Fair Trade and Harmonization. Prerequisite for Free Trade?*, Vol. I: Economic analysis, 1996, pp. 472-513.

Scherer, F.M., *Competition Policies for an Integrated World Economy*, 1994.

Scherer, F.M., International Trade and Competition Policy, in Hope, E. Maeleng, P., *Competition and Trade Policies, Coherence or Conflict?*, 1998, pp. 13-30.

Scherer, F.M., International Trade and Competition Policy, Zentrum für Europäische Wirtschaftsforschung (ZEW) Discussion Papers, No. 96-18, 1996.

Siepmann, H.A., The International Financial Conference at Brussels, *The Economic Journal*, Vol. 30, No. 120, 1920, pp. 436-459.

Smith, A., *The Wealth of Nations*, [1776], Electric Book Company, 2000.

Snyder, F., *The EU, the WTO and China: Legal Pluralism and International Trade Regulation*, 2010.

Snyder, F., The Origins of the Nonmarket Economy: Ideas, Pluralism and Power in EC Anti-dumping Law about China, *European Law Journal*, Vol. 7, No. 4, 2001, pp. 369-424.

Stern, R., Labor Standards and Trade, in Bronckers, M., Quick, R. (eds), *New Directions in International Economic Law, Essays in Honour of J.H. Jackson*, 2000, pp. 425-437.

Sykes, A.O., Countervailing Duty Law: An Economic Critique, *Columbia Law Review*, Vol. 89, No. 2, 1989, pp. 199-263.

Sykes, A.O., Second-Best Countervailing Duty Policy: A Critique of the Entitlement Approach, *Law and Policy in International Business*, Vol. 21, No. 4, 1990, pp. 699-722.

Sykes, A.O., The Economics of WTO Rules on Subsidies and Countervailing Measures, John M. Olin Program in Law and Economics Working Paper No. 186, 2003.

Sykes, A.O., The Fundamental Deficiencies of the Agreement on Safeguards: A Reply to Professor Lee, *Journal of World Trade*, Vol. 40, No. 5, 2006, pp. 979-996.

Sykes, A.O., The Questionable Case for Subsidies Regulation: A Comparative Perspective, Stanford University School of Law, Law & Economics Research Paper Series, Paper No. 380, 2009.

Sykes, A.O., The Safeguards Mess: Critique of WTO Jurisprudence, *World Trade Review*, Vol. 2, No. 3, 2003, pp. 261-296.

Taylor, B., The Brussels Sugar Convention, *The North American Review*, Vol. 190, No. 646, pp. 347-358, 1909.

The Solar Energy Industries Association, *The Section 201 Tariffs on Imported Solar Cells and Modules Have Caused Great Harm to the US Solar Industry and the Broader Economy*, 2019.

Thomas, A., *International Social Policy*, 1948.

Trebilcock, M.J., Competition Policy and Trade Policy-Mediating the Interface, *Journal of World Trade*, Vol. 30, No. 4, 1996, pp. 71-106.

Trebilcock, M.J., Is the Game Worth the Candle: Comments on a Search for Economic and Financial Principles in the Administration of US Countervailing Duty Law, *Law and Policy in International Business*, Vol. 21, No. 4, 1990, pp. 723-738.

Tumlir, J., GATT Rules and the Community of Law: A Comparison of Economic and Legal Functions, in Hilf, M., Jacobs, F.G., Petersmann, E.U. (eds), The European Community and GATT, *Studies in Transnational Economic Law*, Vol. 4, 1986, pp. 1-22.

Tumlir, J., *Protectionism: Trade Policies in Democratic Societies*, 1985.

Tumlir, J., Protectionist Threat to International Order, *International Journal*, Vol. 34, No. 1, 1978, pp. 53-63.

US Department of State, Proposals for Expansion of World Trade and Employment, 1945.

US Department of State, Suggested Charter for an International Trade Organization of the United Nations, 1946. US Publication 2598, Commercial Policy Series 93.

United Nations Document

United Nations Treaty Series Documents

VanGrasstek, C., *The History and Future of the World Trade Organization*, 2013.

Vermulst, E.A., Ikenson, D., Zeroing under the WTO Anti-dumping Agreement: Where Do We Stand?, *Global Trade and Customs Journal*, Vol. 2, No. 6, 2007, pp. 231-242.

Vermulst, E.A., Sud, J.D., Evenett, S.J., Normal Value in Anti-dumping Proceedings Against China Post-2016: Are Some Animals Less Equal Than Others?, *Global Trade and Customs Journal*, Vol. 11, No. 5, 2016, pp. 212-228.

Vermulst, E.A., The 10 Major Problems with the Anti-dumping Instrument in the European Community, *Journal of World Trade*, Vol. 39, No. 1, 2005, pp. 105-113.

Vermulst, E.A., The Antidumping Systems of Australia, Canada, the EEC and the USA: Have Antidumping Laws Become a Problem in International Trade?, in Jackson, J.H., Vermulst, E.A. (eds), *Antidumping Law and Practice: A Comparative Study*, 1989, pp. 425-466.

Viner, J., *Dumping: A Problem in International Trade*, 1923.

Viner, J., Five Lectures on Economics and Freedom. Delivered at Wabash College, Crawfordsville, Indiana, June 1959, in Irwin, D.A., *Essays on the Intellectual History of Economics*, 1991.

Viner, J., *Memorandum on Dumping*, League of Nations Document C.E.C.P. 36(1), 1926.

Weiss, F., From World Trade Law to World Competition Law, *Fordham International Law Journal*, Vol. 23, No. 6, pp. S250-S273, 1999.

World Trade Organization Documents

World Trade Organization, *GATT Disputes: 1948-1995, Vol. 1: Overview and One-Page Case Summaries*, 2020.

Wu, M., The China, Inc, Challenge to Global Trade Governance, *Harvard International Law Journal*, Vol. 57, 2016, pp. 1001-1063.

Official Websites

Canadian Parliamentary Historical Resources
Internet Archive
Ministry of Commerce of China
Ministry of Finance of China
Official Journal of the European Union

Organisation for Economic Cooperation and Development
United Kingdom Department for International Trade
United States Census Bureau
United States Congress
United States Congressional Research Service
United States Customs and Border Protection
United States Department of Commerce
United States Department of Commerce International Trade Administration
United States Department of State
United States Department of State Office of the Historian
United States Federal Register
United States Government Information
United States International Trade Commission
United States Library of Congress
United States National Archives
United States Senate
United States Tariff Commission
United States Trade Representative
United States White House
World Trade Organization

Press

Financial Times
Gaceta de Madrid
Reuters
The Iron Age
The New York Times

Index

GLOBAL TRADE LAW SERIES

1. Emmanuel T. Laryea, *Paperless Trade: Opportunities, Challenges and Solutions,* 2002 (ISBN 90-411-9897-0).
2. Xiang Gao, *The Fraud Rule in the Law of Letters of Credit: A Comparative Study,* 2002 (ISBN 90-411-9898-9).
3. Yuwa Wei, *Comparative Corporate Governance: A Chinese Perspective,* 2003 (ISBN 90-411-9908-X).
4. Ross P. Buckley (ed.), *The WTO and the Doha Round: The Changing Face of World Trade,* 2003 (ISBN 90-411-9947-0).
5. Bradley J. Condon, Joyce C. Sadka & Tapen Sinha (eds), *Insurance Regulation in North America: Integrating American, Canadian and Mexican Markets,* 2003 (ISBN 90-411-2301-6).
6. Jan Hoogmartens, *EC Trade Law Following China's Accession to the WTO,* 2004 (ISBN 90-411-2301-6).
7. Yang Guohua, Bryan Mercurio & Li Yongjie, *WTO Dispute Settlement Understanding: A Detailed Interpretation,* 2005 (ISBN 90-411-2361-X).
8. Jan Job de Vries Robbé, Paul U. Ali, *Securitisation of Derivatives and Alternative Asset Classes, Yearbook,* 2005 (ISBN 90-411-2375-X).
9. Markus W. Gehring, Marie-Claire Cordonier Segger, *Sustainable Development in World Trade Law,* 2005 (ISBN 90-411-2366-0).
10. Yann Aubin & Arnaud Idiart, *Export Control Law and Regulations Handbook: A Practical Guide to Military and Dual-Use Goods Trade Restrictions and Compliance,* 2007 (ISBN 90-411-2601-5).
11. Henry Kibet Mutai, *Compliance with International Trade Obligations: The Common Market for Eastern and Southern Africa,* 2007 (ISBN 978-90-411-2664-1).
12. Yong-Shik Lee, *Economic Development through World Trade: A Developing World Perspective,* 2007 (ISBN 978-90-411-2681-8).
13. Yanning Yu, *Circumvention and Anti-Circumvention Measures: The Impact on Anti-Dumping Practice in International Trade,* 2007 (ISBN 978-90-411-2686-3).
14. Ross Buckley, Vai Io Lo & Laurence Boulle, *Challenges to Multilateral Trade: The Impact of Bilateral, Preferential and Regional Agreements,* 2008 (ISBN 978-90-411-2711-2).
15. K.D. Raju, *World Trade Organization Agreement on Anti-dumping: A GATT/ WTO and Indian Jurisprudence,* 2008 (ISBN 978-90-411-2780-8).
16. Xiaochen Wu, *Anti-dumping Law and Practice in China,* 2008 (ISBN 978-90-411-2790-7).
17. Amin Alavi, *Legalization of Development in the WTO: Between Law and Politics,* 2008 (ISBN 978-90-411-2795-2).
18. Henrik Andersen, *EU Dumping Determinations and WTO Law,* 2009 (ISBN 978-90-411-2827-0).

19. Sherzod Shadikhodjaev, *Retaliation in the WTO Dispute Settlement System*, 2009 (ISBN 978-90-411-2811-9).
20. Yi Shin Tang, *The International Trade Policy for Technology Transfers: Legal and Economic Dilemmas on Multilateralism versus Bilateralism*, 2009 (ISBN 978-90-411-2825-6).
21. Reem Anwar Ahmed Raslan, *Antidumping: A Developing Country Perspective*, 2009 (ISBN 978-90-411-3128-7).
22. Pietro Poretti, *The Regulation of Subsidies within the General Agreement on Trade in Services of the WTO: Problems and Prospects*, 2009 (ISBN 978-90-411-3162-1).
23. Esther Lam, *China and the WTO: A Long March towards the Rule of Law*, 2009 (ISBN 978-90-411-3144-7).
24. Jorge Alberto Huerta-Goldman, *Mexico in the WTO and NAFTA: Litigating International Trade Disputes*, 2009 (ISBN 978-90-411-3169-0).
25. Laurence Boulle, *The Law of Globalization: An Introduction*, 2009 (ISBN 978-90-411-2828-7).
26. Daniel Lovric, *Deference to the Legislature in WTO Challenges to Legislation*, 2010 (ISBN 978-90-411-3145-4).
27. Gregory W. Bowman, Nick Covelli, David A. Gantz & Ihn Ho Uhm, *Trade Remedies in North America*, 2010 (ISBN 978-90-411-2840-9).
28. Madalina Diaconu, *International Trade in Gambling Services*, 2010 (ISBN 978-90-411-3248-2).
29. Mohamed Ramadan Hassanien, *United States Bilateral Free Trade Agreements: Consistencies or Conflicts with Norms in the Middle East?*, 2010 (ISBN 978-90-411-3281-9).
30. Marie-Claire Cordonier Segger, Markus W Gehring & Andrew Newcombe, *Sustainable Development in World Investment Law*, 2011 (ISBN 978-90-411-3166-9).
31. Nellie Munin, *Legal Guide to GATS*, 2010 (ISBN 978-90-411-2824-9).
32. Thomas G. Kelch, *Globalization and Animal Law: Comparative Law, International Law and International Trade*, 2011 (ISBN 978-90-411-3338-0).
33. Yann Aubin & Arnaud Idiart (eds), *Export Control Law and Regulations Handbook: A Practical Guide to Military and Dual-Use Goods Trade Restrictions and Compliance*, Third Edition, 2016 (ISBN 978-90-411-5443-9).
34. Yulia Selivanova (ed.), *Regulation of Energy in International Trade Law: WTO, NAFTA and Energy Charter*, 2011 (ISBN 978-90-411-3264-2).
35. Germano Franceschin & Francesco Misuraca, *India: Commercial Law, Customs and Taxation*, 2011 (ISBN 978-90-411-2836-2).
36. Humberto Zúñiga Schroder, *Harmonization, Equivalence and Mutual Recognition of Standards in WTO Law*, 2011 (ISBN 978-90-411-3657-2).
37. Kati Kulovesi, *The WTO Dispute Settlement System: Challenges of the Environment, Legitimacy and Fragmentation*, 2011 (ISBN 978-90-411-3406-6).
38. Martín Molinuevo, *Protecting Investment in Services: Investor-State Arbitration versus WTO Dispute Settlement*, 2012 (ISBN 978-90-411-3827-9).
39. Joachim Åhman, *Trade, Health, and the Burden of Proof in WTO Law*, 2012 (ISBN 978-90-411-3825-5).

40. Umair Hafeez Ghori, *Global Textiles and Clothing Trade: Trade Policy Perspectives*, 2012 (ISBN 978-90-411-3875-0).
41. Yenkong Ngangjoh Hodu, *Theories and Practices of Compliance with WTO Law*, 2012 (ISBN 978-90-411-3228-4).
42. Dan Wei & Fernando M. Furlan, *Brazil in World Trade: Contingent Protection Measures*, 2012 (ISBN 978-90-411-3335-9).
43. Jorge A. Huerta-Goldman, Antoine Romanetti & Franz X. Stirnimann (eds), *WTO Litigation, Investment Arbitration, and Commercial Arbitration*, 2013 (ISBN 978-90-411-4686-1).
44. Gilles Muller, *Liberalization of Trade in Legal Services*, 2013 (ISBN 978-90-411-4853-7).
45. Christian Struck, *Product Regulations and Standards in WTO Law*, 2014 (ISBN 978-90-411-4950-3).
46. Gonzalo Villalta Puig, *Economic Relations between Australia and the European Union: Law and Policy*, 2014 (ISBN 978-90-411-3405-9).
47. Maurizio Gambardella, Davide Rovetta & Simon van Cutsem, *Remission and Repayment of Customs Duties in the EU*, 2014 (ISBN 978-90-411-4764-6).
48. Lisa Spagnolo, *CISG Exclusion and Legal Efficiency*, 2014 (ISBN 978-90-411-5407-1).
49. Dennis Ndonga, *Single Windows and Trade Facilitation: A Tool for Development*, 2015 (ISBN 978-90-411-5834-5).
50. Malebakeng Agnes Forere, *The Relationship of WTO Law and Regional Trade Agreements in Dispute Settlement: From Fragmentation to Coherence*, 2015 (ISBN 978-90-411-6274-8).
51. Julien Chaisse & Jiaxiang Hu (eds), *International Economic Law and the Challenges of the Free Zones*, 2019 (ISBN 978-94-035-0893-1).
52. Boris Praštalo, *Uniformity in the Application of the CISG: Analysis of the Problem and Recommendations for the Future*, 2020 (ISBN 978-94-035-2072-8).
53. Manuel A.J. Teehankee, *Trade and Environment Governance at the World Trade Organization Committee on Trade and Environment*, 2020 (ISBN 978-94-035-2202-9).
54. Marco Tulio Molina Tejeda (ed.), *Practical Aspects of WTO Litigation*, 2020 (ISBN 978-90-411-8596-9).
55. James J. Nedumpara, Satwik Shekhar & Akshaya Venkataraman (eds), *Handbook on Product Standards and International Trade: Navigating the Regulatory Landscape in India*, 2021 (ISBN 978-94-035-3413-8).
56. José Rijo, *Customs Law in the European Union: Legal, Doctrinal and Jurisprudential Framework*, 2022 (ISBN 978-94-035-3811-2).
57. Lauri Railas, *Incoterms® 2020 Handbook: Effecting Deliveries in Challenging Times*, 2023 (ISBN 978-94-035-2076-6).
58. Mark K. Neville, Jr., *The Customs Valuation Agreement: Origin, Standards and Interpretations*, 2023 (ISBN 978-94-035-3096-3).
59. María Moreno Sancho, *Trade Remedy Laws: The Trojan Horse in the Multilateral Trading System*, 2025 (ISBN 978-94-035-3929-4).

www.ingramcontent.com/pod-product-compliance
Ingram Content Group UK Ltd.
Pitfield, Milton Keynes, MK11 3LW, UK
UKHW020235290926
15470UKWH00002B/560

9 789403 539294